WHITE
SAVAGE

WHITE SAVAGE

William Johnson
and the Invention of America

FINTAN O'TOOLE

excelsior editions

State University of New York Press
Albany, New York

Published by
State University of New York Press, Albany

First Excelsior Editions paperback printing: 2009
Excelsior Editions is an imprint of State University of New York Press, Albany
www.sunypress.edu

Illustration credits appear on page 354.

Library of Congress Cataloging-in-Publication Data

O'Toole, Fintan, 1958–
  White savage : William Johnson and the invention of America / Fintan
O'Toole.
    p. cm.
  Originally published: New York : Farrar, Straus and Giroux, ©2005.
  Includes bibliographical references and index.
  ISBN 978-1-4384-2758-4 (pbk. : alk. paper)
  1. Johnson, William, Sir, 1715–1774. 2. Pioneers—United States—
Biography. 3. Soldiers—United States—Biography. 4. Irish—United States—
Biography. 5. Colonial administrators—New York (State)—Biography.
6. Johnson, William, Sir, 1715–1774—Relations with Indians. 7. Iroquois
Indians—History—18th century. 8. Six Nations—History. 9. New York
(State)—History—Colonial period, ca. 1600–1775. 10. New York (State)—
History—French and Indian War,
1755–1763. I. Title.

E195.J63087 2009
973.2092—dc22
[B]   2009001396

10 9 8 7 6 5 4 3 2 1

To Clare Connell, as always

Contents

═══

CONTENTS

Preface

═══

This is the first of three loosely related books. Unfolding in three different centuries and telling the stories of people with no direct connection to each other, they are linked only by a set of shared concerns. Broadly speaking, those concerns are with the creation of a modern mythology. I want to explore some of the circumstances that gave rise to America's myth of itself, and the part played by one particular culture – that of Ireland – in its creation.

At the start of the twenty-first century, the big issue for people around the world is the process of globalisation. In cultural terms, globalisation is really a fancy name for Americanisation. When the marketing arms of great corporations dream of a world in which the same products and the same advertisements can carry the same freight of meaning and emotion across the globe, what they imagine is a universal America. Much of the power that America enjoys is based on the hard facts of economic and military might. But much of it, too, derives from the potency of the American epic: the conquest of a New World; the triumph of 'civilisation' over 'savagery'; the vestigial glamour of the defeated indigenous peoples; the invention of the 'white race'; the allure of heroic, individualist violence.

There are obvious ways to deal with the overwhelming force of these myths. One is to go with the flow, to accept that these American stories have simply replaced the older narratives that used to underlie other cultures. The other is to retreat into a defensive redoubt of atavism and nostalgia, or, in the extreme, to construct a counter-myth from the materials of an anti-modernist and anti-American backlash. Neither of these options seems to me a good one.

There is a third possibility, though: to remember that the American myth was created by people from a wide variety of other cultures. The vivid rainbow that now spans the globe is made up of colours borrowed from many different palettes. Almost every culture on earth can unweave the rainbow in its own way. The stories that formed the basis for American mythology can be retold from any number of perspectives and, in a sense, be reclaimed by many other countries. The most powerful retellings come from the points of view of Native Americans and of African Americans; but most Asian and European cultures – Chinese, Japanese, Vietnamese, Korean, Indian, Jewish, Polish, Italian, Spanish, Portuguese, Scandinavian, French, Dutch, Scottish, Welsh, English, German – can follow their own threads, too, and, in the process, help to unravel the myths.

I make no special claims for an Irish perspective, though it does have some advantages. The Irish involvement in the shaping of modern America goes back almost to the beginning of the story, making it possible to take a long view. And that involvement has often had to do with mediating between other cultures. The ambivalence of the Irish situation as colonised people who became colonisers, as 'savages' who came to see themselves as civilisers, and as white people who often appeared to official Anglo-American eyes as virtual blacks, has tended to place the Irish at some interesting crossroads. Remembering how some of them behaved at these intersections may help to unravel, not just some American myths, but some Irish ones too.

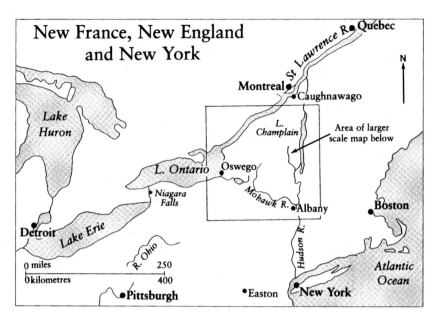

New France, New England
and New York

N

St Lawrence R. ●Quebec

Montreal●
●Caughnawago

Lake
Huron

L.
Champlain

Area of larger
scale map below

L. Ontario ●Oswego

● Niagara
Falls

Mohawk R. ●Albany

●Boston

Detroit Lake Erie

R. Ohio

0 miles   250
0 kilometres   400

Hudson R.

Atlantic
Ocean

●Pittsburgh   ●Easton   ●New York

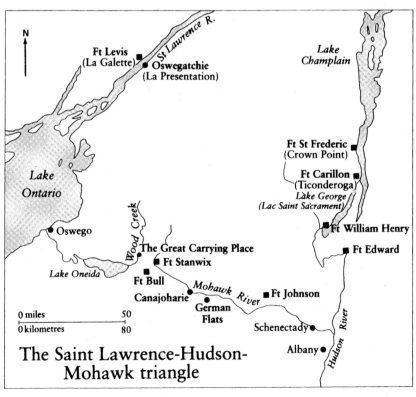

N

St Lawrence R.

Ft Levis
(La Galette)■ ● Oswegatchie
              (La Presentation)

Lake
Champlain

Lake
Ontario

Ft St Frederic ■
(Crown Point)

Ft Carillon ■
(Ticonderoga)
Lake George
(Lac Saint Sacrament)

●Oswego

Wood Creek

■Ft William Henry

The Great Carrying Place
■ Ft Stanwix

■ Ft Edward

Lake Oneida

Ft Bull ●
Canajoharie ●

Mohawk River

■ Ft Johnson

German
Flats

0 miles   50
0 kilometres   80

Schenectady●

Hudson River

Albany ●

The Saint Lawrence-Hudson-
Mohawk triangle

History is philosophy drawn from examples.

Dionysius of Halicarnassus

I

Tears, Throat, Heart

═════

One thing leads to another. Causes have their effects. But the wind blowing on one continent may ultimately be caused by a tiny shift in the air over another. The fall and rise of the wave may be influenced by the unperceived motion of a fish. Events may be connected by broken threads whose traces form strange, irrational patterns. Otherwise, the lives of an old Irishman and a young American Indian woman could not intersect in a way that would be, to both of them, inexplicable.

In January 1763 an obscure old Catholic man died on a quiet farm twenty miles west of Dublin and was buried amid the sonorous cadences of Latin prayers, the opulent aroma of incense and a haze of smoke from guttering candles wafting around his coffin. Christopher Johnson had lived for seventy-nine years in the lush pastures of County Meath, most of them as a tenant of his wife's family.[1] His public insignificance was not entirely a matter of choice. Throughout his adult life, people like him – idolaters and potential traitors who looked kindly on the claims of exiled pretenders to the throne of Britain and Ireland – were barred by law from public life, the professions and the armed forces. If he had ever aspired to glory, he had soon learned that such foolish dreams were incompatible with his place in history.

When he was still a child, his class of people – the respectable, well-to-do native Catholics of Ireland – had imagined for a while that their hour had come again, that the accession to the throne of Great Britain and Ireland of their co-religionist King James II heralded their resurrection. In what had seemed an almost miraculous deliverance, a Catholic king had been crowned and their hopes of being saved from oppression had been made flesh. They thought they would rise again

1

and reclaim the lands and status that had been taken from them by the Protestant British colonists who had come to power in Ireland over the course of the seventeenth century. And then James had been deposed in a British coup and replaced by his impeccably Protestant daughter Mary and her husband William of Orange. For the last time, two men who had been crowned King of Britain fought a civil war for the throne, and this time Ireland was the battlefield.

As a little boy, Christopher Johnson had watched his older kinsmen ride out in all their pride and hope to fight in grand battles for King James, one of them on the River Boyne near his home. He had watched them ride back again in tatters from bloody disasters or from captivity, and the Jacobite cause gradually subside into a broken dream. He had learned how to live with the slow death of a defeated culture, how to keep his head down, how to hold his tongue, how to move amid undercurrents, how to survive. That he died at such a late age, and in such comfortable obscurity, was a testament to his mastery of those lessons.

Christopher Johnson's death was of no concern to anyone in Ireland beyond his family and his neighbours; but 2,000 miles away, across the vast Atlantic and through the dense forests of upstate New York, the word spread and was heard with great solemnity. It eventually reached Lake Oneida, about twenty miles north of present-day Syracuse, and the Tuscarora village at Oquaga, which was off the usual track along which messages travelled through the territories of the Iroquois nations.

In early June 1763, after a journey eastwards of about 100 miles, six young warriors from the village arrived at the grand new house of Christopher Johnson's son William about halfway between Albany and Utica, in the present-day city of Johnstown. They were gauche and nervous, hoping that they could remember the proper ceremony that would convey their condolences on the death of Christopher Johnson. Having fortified themselves with a dram of rum and a pipe of tobacco, they formally addressed William Johnson and asked for his forgiveness, 'as we are but Youngsters', for 'any mistakes which for want of knowledge we may make'.[2]

They spoke the Three Bare Words which banished the pall of grief from the son's body: 'Tears, throat, heart.' In their foundation myth, these were the words first spoken by the legendary Mohawk chief Ayonhwathah (Hiawatha) when he was stricken with grief at the death of his three daughters. The waters of a lake had then magically risen up, revealing the sacred shell beads that the Indians would call 'wampum'. The prophet Deganawidah had taken the shells, strung them together and performed a ritual to clear Ayonhwathah's mind of grief.[3]

These stories and rituals recapitulated the process by which five Iroquoian-speaking nations – the Mohawks, the Oneidas, the Onondagas, the Cayugas and the Senecas – came together in the Great League of Peace. (In late 1722 or early 1723, the Five Nations became the Six Nations when the Tuscaroras of North Carolina, who had fled northward into New York under intolerable pressure from European settlement were formally adopted into the league.) The confederacy was founded some time between 1450 and 1500, when, according to the myth, Deganawidah ('the Peacemaker', in colloquial usage), disturbed by the internecine wars between the nations, set out to preach peace. He converted Ayonhwathah from cannibalism, and then together with him confronted the wicked Onondaga wizard Thadodaho and transformed him into a humane chief whose people would be the 'fire-keepers' of the new order. Having created rituals of condolence and gift-giving through which the dead could be appeased symbolically rather than through blood-feuds, Deganawidah instructed the Five Nations to form a grand council under the Tree of Great Peace at Onondaga, which thus became the symbolic centre of Iroquois life.

The confederacy itself was likened in the orally transmitted Great Law of Peace to a longhouse, the typical common dwelling house of the Iroquois peoples. The Mohawks guarded the eastern door, the Senecas the western, and the Onondagas the fireplace in the middle, with the Oneidas and Cayugas securely housed under the roof. The confederacy was also imagined as a tree, the Great White Pine, whose branches sheltered the Five Nations and whose roots spread out to all peoples, regardless of their origins.

The Tuscarora boys, struggling to remember the right formula, now re-enacted for Christopher Johnson's son the same rites of condolence that Deganawidah had taught to Ayonhwathah. They wiped a string of sacred wampum beads over his face to brush the tears from his eyes so that he might look cheerfully and with friendship on his brother Indians again. They placed another string of wampum on his throat to clear the obstructions which might otherwise prevent him from speaking freely and in the tones of a brother. A third string stripped Christopher Johnson's death bed and wiped the blood from the dead man's eyes so that his spirit would rest and cause them no harm. With a white belt, they covered his grave so that he would bring his son no more grief. With another they collected all the bones of William's dead relatives and buried them deep in the earth so that they would be out of his sight for ever. 'As you now sit in darkness,' they said, 'we remove all the heavy clouds which surround you that you may again behold the light and sunshine.' Then they poured the clearest water into his body to cleanse his breast and remove the disturbance from his mind.4

These anxious youngsters from the west were followed in late July by twenty of their chiefs, or sachems, who repeated the ritual. They were the last in a line of Indians that had come to Johnson's house through that summer of 1763 to perform the rites of condolence for his father. On 12 May two chief warriors of the Onondaga nation from near what is now Syracuse, two of the Cayugas, from the area roughly north and south of what is now Auburn, and two of the Mohawks, who lived near him in the area drained by the Mohawk and Hudson Rivers, came to Johnson's house. Representing the entire Six Nations of the Iroquois confederacy, they had wiped his tears, cleared his throat and heart, covered his father's grave and buried the bones of his ancestors. A week later, a larger body of Iroquois, including several representatives of the largest and most westerly nation, the Senecas, from the region east of Lake Erie and south of Lake Ontario, had repeated the ceremony.

The repercussions of Christopher Johnson's death continued to resonate in the forests, swamps and hills of north-eastern America into the spring of the following year. In early March 1764, a party of Iroquois and allied warriors surprised a group of forty-one Delaware Indians on the Northern branch of the Susquehanna River, far to the south-west of Johnson's home.5 Among the captives they took was a young Delaware woman. They brought her north to the Mohawk valley and gave her to William Johnson as a replacement for his dead father.

They did this to lay Christopher Johnson to rest once and for all by filling the hole in the fabric of tribal and family life that had been left by his demise. It was an old custom. As the Jesuit missionaries who were among the first Europeans to penetrate Iroquois society had written in 1647: 'These Barbarians are accustomed to give prisoners, whom they do not choose to put to death, to the families who have lost their relatives in war. These prisoners take the place of the deceased, and are incorporated into that family, which alone has the right to kill them or let them live.'[6] But, however venerable the custom, it would have been hard to explain to that young Delaware woman why she was now the spiritual substitute for an old Irish farmer who had died so far away and with such little fuss.

William Johnson, on the other hand, understood these rituals very well. He knew how to greet the Indians who came to condole his loss and how to respond to their performances. He was well aware of what an important compliment had been paid to him in the presentation to him of the young Delaware woman. He had acted out these rituals himself.

Eight years earlier, Johnson had led one of the most elaborate condolence ceremonies of the period. It was a time of death, when the British and French empires and their respective Indian allies were struggling for control of the porous frontiers between New York and Quebec and ultimately of the entire continent of North America. The leading Onondaga sachem, Kakhswenthioni, known to the British as 'Red Head', had died. William Johnson journeyed to the neighbouring nation of Oneida to join the side of the Clear-minded, those whose place it was to commiserate with the Mourners. In this case, tradition demanded that two of the confederated nations, the Oneidas and Cayugas, would play the part of the Clear-minded, while the Mohawks, Senecas and Onondagas would be the Mourners. At Oneida he and the sachems prepared their wampum belts and their speeches and reminded themselves of their parts.

Five miles from Onondaga, they were joined by the Cayugas. In accordance with custom, they stopped for two hours to settle the formalities. Then William Johnson led them along the road again, singing out the song that recalled the ancestors who had founded the Iroquois confederacy and laid down the Great Law that governed it:

> *Ha-i ha-i-i ha-i ha-i ha-i ha-i ha-i ha-i ha-i ha-i-i*
> *Ke ya da we des Ke na wero ne'I . . .*

[Now then hear us
You who established it
The Great Law

It has grown old
It is overgrown with brush
Hail, grandfather.]

When they came within sight of the Onondaga village, the Mourners came out and sat in a semi-circle 'in profound silence' at the edge of the woods.7 Johnson and the Clear-minded stopped their song, and the Mourners sang theirs:

Oneh weni serah deh
Waga dyene goh wa
desa mena wera de
nege deyo ho do

[Now today
I noticed your voice
Coming this way
Over the forest.]

For the next hour, the two sides exchanged the Three Bare Words, wiping each other's tears and clearing each other's throats and hearts. At the end of this ceremony, the Onondaga sachem Rozinoghyata and the other headmen stood and took Johnson by the hand to lead him into the village. As they followed, the Clear-minded again took up the song of the Great Law. Their hosts greeted them as they entered the village with a fusillade and they returned the salute by themselves firing into the air. They were conducted to a 'green bower' erected for the council beside Red Head's house. Johnson, as the head of the Clear-minded, waited outside while the others took up their places opposite each other on either side of the council fire. Then he was formally invited to enter the bower and greeted again with the Three Bare Words. This completed the day's ceremonies.

The next day, the Mohawk sachem Abraham acted as Johnson's spokesman, presenting in turn five belts of wampum to cover Red Head's grave, to comfort the Mourners, to admonish the survivors to stick to their old alliances, to dispel clouds and restore the sun, and, since it was now night, to restore the moon and stars. These words were reinforced with fourteen more strings or belts of wampum. The ceremony culminated in the presentation of an enemy scalp as a spiritual replacement for the dead man, and a glass of rum to wash down grief.

These fifteen concluding gestures – the presentation of the fourteen

6

strings or belts of wampum and the scalp – symbolised the fifteen stages of the full speech of condolence. To wipe away tears. To unplug the ears. To unblock the throat. To restore the disturbed organs of the body. To wipe the blood from the mat. To dispel the darkness and bring the light. To make the sky beautiful. To bring the sun back into the sky. To level the earth over the grave. To bind the bones together. To gather the scattered firebrands and rekindle the fire. To raise up the minds of women and warriors. To dispel the insanity of grief. To put back in its place the torch that had been carried through the longhouse to announce the death. To restore the chief by raising him up again in the form of another man.[8]

On the following day, the Mourners performed the ritual replies and Johnson then led the Clear-minded away the prescribed distance of five miles. Over the next week, various diplomatic negotiations were concluded, but the condolence ceremonies did not culminate until ten days after they had begun. The scalp had replaced Red Head as a man, but he still had to be replaced as a chief in the ranks of Onondaga sachems. To do so, Johnson hung a medal around the neck of the unnamed Onondaga speaker who had carried their part of the ceremony, symbolising his elevation as a new sachem and marking the end of mourning for Red Head, who now formally joined the ancestors.

Even when he had left Onondaga, Johnson's journey home retained its ritual significance. He called at a village of the Tuscarora nation, and presented the scalps of two Frenchmen to a warrior, who grabbed them and carried them round the longhouses, singing the war song.[9] That same evening, the Oneida sachems came out to meet Johnson to tell him that their chief had just lost his nephew. The condolence ceremony for the edge of the woods had to be performed again, and the appropriate songs exchanged. He then entered the Oneida village in the same way as before and took part in the same ceremonies to wipe away grief.

It was these ritual journeys and solemn performances that the Indians who came from near and far to mourn the death of Christopher Johnson in 1763 were reciprocating. In doing so, they were acknowledging that William Johnson had become a master of the living, the dead, and the dangerous borderlands that divided them. In the world of the Iroquois, grief was a terrible force that must be appeased. The dead wished to take the living with them, to keep them in the grip of pain and loss so that their derangement would threaten the order that was necessary for survival. Grief created paralysis, an inability to function. The bereaved covered their faces and clothes with ashes. They lay in the dark, unable to prepare food or hunt or tend children or go to war. Their senses became weak and their inner organs were poisoned and polluted. The rituals were necessary 'to dispel the insanity of grief'. Without them, in a culture that had known so much grief, it would be impossible to survive. Death would have its way.

William Johnson knew about grief and about the need to let it go. He owed his ability to understand and perform the Iroquois rituals of death to the fact that they were not entirely alien to the world of his youth. He, like the Iroquois, had grown up in a culture that felt itself in danger of extinction, and that responded with a system of ritual in which each individual death had to be treated as a moment of immense danger for the entire society. Just as the mourning half of an Iroquois village chanted death songs, the Irish Catholic culture of Johnson's childhood had a formal system of elaborate lamentation. The Iroquois had the all-female institution of O'gi'weoa'no' – the Chanters of the Dead – whose job it was to sing the songs that would release the earth-bound spirits of those who had died and allow them to depart from this world.[10] The Irish had the similar all-female institution of keening.

As late as the beginning of the twentieth century, the nearest large town to William Johnson's home, Navan in County Meath, still had professional keeners – women who performed a display of woeful desolation on behalf of the bereaved community:

The lamentation was weird and frightful. The keeners (all women) went ahead of the funeral – that is before the corpse which in those days was carried all the way. When the cortège came in sight of the churchyard the lament began, first in a low murmuring chant and then rising to a mournful piercing wail. On entering the churchyard, it rose to the highest pitch of wailing – the writhing bodies and waving arms of the keeners keeping time with the lament. Usually when the funeral rites were over, the keeners and the relatives of the departed were in a state of collapse and had to be revived with drinks of water or mouthfuls of whiskey.[11]

Coming from such a culture, William Johnson had been able to understand the Indian death ceremonies well enough to know that when they came to lift his grief at the death of his father in Ireland, the Iroquois leaders and warriors were acknowledging their fear that he would succumb to the terrible paralysis of sorrow. He had performed the ceremonies so well himself that it made sense to think that he would need them. Yet in that very assumption there was an acknowledgement too that this was a man with an extraordinary capacity to adapt and survive. They needed him to throw off the burden of grief because, in the way he had escaped the death of his own world, he had become necessary to their own survival.

2

Spectres and Apparitions

On the evening of 24 April 1710, at the Queen's Theatre in Haymarket, London, the Irish actor Richard Wilks appeared as Macbeth. The audience did not come, however, to see Wilks as the Scottish regicide. The advertisement in the *Daily Courant* had announced that this particular staging of Shakespeare's tragedy would be 'for the Entertainment of the Four INDIAN KINGS lately arrived'. Four sachems of the Mohawk people, one of the Iroquois nations whose favour was being courted by the British empire, had met five days earlier with Queen Anne in Buckingham Palace. Then, from their base at the Two Crowns and Cushions, an upholsterer's shop in King Street, they had journeyed out to see the exotic natives.

The four men were not in fact kings, for the Mohawks had no time for such a strange anachronism as monarchy. They were leading men – speakers, counsellors, rhetoricians, diplomats. Sa Ga Yean Qua Prah Ton, known to the English and Dutch as Brant, and Oh Nee Yeath Ton No Prow, whom they called John, were both members of the Wolf clan and signed themselves with a representation of that animal. Elow Oh Kaom, christened Nicholas, was a Mohican who had been adopted into the Mohawks, but was regarded by the English as 'King of the River Nation' – the remnants of the Algonquians of the Hudson River basin.

Yet the youngest of the four was also clearly the most influential. Tee Yee Neen Ha Ga Row, whom the English imagined as 'the Emperour of the Six Nations', was no older than thirty. He was also known as Tiyanoga, and by the name the Dutch had given him – Hendrick Peters, or simply Hendrick. It was he who had delivered the Mohawks' speech to Queen Anne, reminding her that the alliance which her government sought for a war against France had to serve the interests of the Mohawks by securing their 'Free hunting' and 'Great Trade with our Great Queen's Children'.

The English visit of these four Mohawks had been conceived from the start as a publicity stunt. Peter Schuyler, the Mayor of Albany, a frontier trading town 150 miles north of New York City on the Hudson River, was a successful merchant and one of the few diplomats then trusted by the Mohawks. He was concerned that the affairs of New York and the competition with the French for influence with the Iroquois had a low priority in overall imperial policy-making. He conceived the idea of an Indian delegation to London, chose its members and stage-managed its public and private appearances.[1] The delegation was in fact much less authoritative than Schuyler pretended: only the Mohawks and the River Indians were represented, and only Hendrick had any real internal standing. Even then, the name he assumed for the trip – Teyohninhohakara:wehn, which the English heard as Tee-Yih-Neen-Ho-Ga-Row – was a pretence. It was the hereditary title of one of the chiefs of the Iroquois league, and was reserved for a sachem of the Seneca nation.[2] It was, in Indian terms, just as much of an assumed identity as 'Emperour of the Six Nations'.

After their formal encounter with the Queen, Hendrick and his companions embarked on a grand tour. They dined with the Duke of Ormond at his estate near Richmond. They sailed on the royal barge up to the Royal Observatory in Greenwich. They reviewed the Life Guards in Hyde Park. They went to see the dockyards at Woolwich, and St Paul's cathedral. On one of their perambulations, one of the sachems allowed a poor woman to kiss his hand and gave her half a guinea to buy blankets.

And everywhere they went they were sights as well as sightseers. That night, at the performance of *Macbeth* at the Haymarket, after three of them took their seats in the front box, the audience expressed its anger. They had paid their money, not to see the play, but to see the Indian Kings. Now, only their backs were in view. Chants of 'The kings we will have!' drowned out the performance. Eventually Wilks asked the Mohawks to sit on the stage, and they graciously complied.

The audience could now see their majestic figures, clad in black waistcoats and breeches, scarlet blankets and yellow moccasins, 'well-formed, being of a stature neither too high nor too low, but all within an inch or two of six Foot. Their habits are robust, and their Limbs muscular and well-shap'd; they are of brown Complexions, their Hair black and long, their visages . . . very awful and majestick, and their features regular enough, though something of the austere and sullen.'3

The desire of audiences to see Hendrick and his fellow sachems was such that almost every showman in London began to advertise his performances as 'for the entertainment of the Four Indian Kings'. On a handbill advertising a puppet show at Punch's Theatre under this rubric, there is a rough portrait of them, with Hendrick described as 'The Emperor Tee Yee Neen Ho Ga Row', which suggests one aspect of their appeal. With their long cloaks, crowns and dark faces, they are made to look somewhat like the familiar images of the Three Kings of Orient who visit the infant Christ in the Christmas story. Their awful majesty is thus rendered benign and warm, unthreatening.

Hendrick could also be regarded virtually as a European of an older, more courtly time. A portrait of him which Queen Anne commissioned from John Verelst, shows him as something close to a medieval European gentleman in scarlet cloak and buckled shoes, brandishing nothing more warlike than a belt of wampum. His tomahawk lies quietly at his feet like a sleeping dog that will not bark at his British friends. Widely distributed in prints throughout England and the colonies, this is the most benevolent, and least menacing, image of the Noble Savage.

Hendrick created such an impression, indeed, that his imaginary voice could be used to mock English society. A year after his departure, the great essayist Joseph Addison, in *The Spectator*, claimed that he had obtained a 'little bundle of papers' Hendrick had accidentally left behind at the Two Crowns and Cushions. In these papers, which were serialised in *The Spectator*, 'Hendrick' comments on the supposed civility of England. 'Reasons', he notes, '. . . make us think that the natives of this country had formerly among them some sort of worship; for they set apart every seventh day as sacred; but upon my going into one of these Holy houses on that day, I could not observe any circumstance of devotion in their behaviour . . . They were most of them bowing and curtsying to one another, and a considerable number of them fast asleep.'

Hendrick is disgusted to see 'young lusty rawboned fellows carried up and down the streets in little covered rooms'. He finds English dress 'likewise very barbarous, for they almost strangle themselves about the neck' and instead of sporting 'Beautiful feathers' on their heads they buy 'a monstrous bush of hair . . . with which they walk up and down the streets, and are as proud of it as if it were their own growth'. As for the visit to *Macbeth*, it was a grave disappointment. When he and his fellow kings were invited to a public entertainment, he had hoped to see the great men chasing a stag or performing other feats that would reveal the true abilities of the natives. Instead, 'They conveyed us into a huge room lighted up with abundance of candles, where this lazy people sat still above three hours to see several feats of ingenuity performed by others, who it seems were paid for it.'

Addison used Hendrick's imaginary reflections on England to make a plea for tolerance. By showing that English normality might look strange and foolish to someone unaccustomed to its conventions, he suggested that the apparently universal truths of Christian civilisation were not absolute: 'We are all guilty of this narrow way of thinking, which we meet with in this abstract of the Indian journal, when we fancy the customs, dresses, and manners of other countries are ridiculous and extravagant, if they do not resemble those of our own.'4 Gentle and playful as it was, Addison's essay had important implications for British colonial policy in North America. It hinted at an alliance with the Mohawks based, not on their assimilation to a superior civilisation, but on a mediation between different, equally valid cultures.

Within a year, however, there was a sudden strange shift in the English meaning of the term 'Mohock' (Mohawk), as if somehow its benign associations could not easily inhabit the prevailing mindset in which 'Mohock' was more comfortably affiliated with savagery and paganism. A gang calling itself the Mohocks became the terror of London, and wild stories of its alleged depravities spread through fashionable society. Lady Wentworth, for example, wrote in March 1712: 'I am very much frighted with the fyer, but much more with a gang of Devils that call themselves Mohocks; they put an old woman into a hogshead, and rooled her down a hill, they cut soms nosis, others hands and several barbarass tricks, without any provocation.'5 Jonathan Swift complained of 'this race of rakes' that 'Play the devil about this town every night' and John Gay wrote about their attacks on innocent gentlefolk.

The significance of this terrible gang is that it did not exist. It was simply the shape assumed by a nameless anxiety. *The Spectator* noted in April 1712 that this alarm was similar in character to earlier fears that Irish Catholics were plotting to murder the denizens of Protestant England in their beds:

The Terror which spread itself over the whole Nation some Years since on account of the *Irish*, is still fresh in most People's Memories, tho' it afterwards appeared there was not the least ground for that general Consternation. The late Pannick Fear was, in the Opinion of many deep and penetrating Persons, of the same Nature. These will have it, that the *Mohocks* are like those Spectres and Apparitions which frighten several Towns and Villages in Her Majesty's Dominions, tho' they were never seen by any of the Inhabitants. Others are apt to think that these Mohocks are a kind of Bull-Beggars, first invented by prudent married Men, and Masters of families, in order to deter their Wives and Daughters from taking the Air at unseasonable Hours; and that they will tell them *the* Mohocks *will catch them*, it is a caution of the same Nature with that of our Fore-fathers, when they bid their Children have a care of *Raw-Head* and *Bloody-bones*.[6]

The Spectator went on, though, to publish another purported letter from Hendrick, in which he both condemned 'several Outrages committed on the Legs, Arms, Noses and other parts of the good People of *England* by such as have stiled themselves our Subjects' and claimed that the attacks were merely meant to punish 'Persons of loose and dissolute Lives'. Hendrick thus instructs his supposed followers that they should come out only at night and attack those who are in need of Mohawk-style correction in order to be reformed. He also warns husbands, fathers and 'Masters of Families' to 'repair themselves to their respective Habitations at early and seasonal Hours'; but also to 'keep their Wives and Daughters, Sons, Servants and Apprentices, from appearing in the Streets at those Times and Seasons which may expose them to Military Discipline, as it is practised by [my] good Subjects the *Mohocks*'.

In this way, Hendrick and his nation came to inspire at the heart of the empire feelings of wonder, admiration, excitement, dread, panic. They were noble and majestic, austere and sceptical – a moral rebuke to English dissolution. They were also savage creatures of the night, lurking in the dark with designs of irrational and unprovoked violence, bogeymen with which to frighten children and wives into good behaviour.

The real Hendrick probably knew nothing of what was being written in his name, but he did understand the complex, ambivalent and continually shifting nature of English attitudes to his people. He was a sophisticated man, an experienced go-between. Hendrick had been an active Iroquois diplomat since the late 1690s, when he was still in his late teens, and by the 1740s he was the most widely recognised Indian leader in the northern colonies. In a portrait made of him when he again visited London in 1740, he wears English court dress: a blue dress coat trimmed in lace, a ruffled shirt with florid cuffs, a cocked hat and a cravat. He also holds a tomahawk in one hand and a string of wampum in the other, so that his image combines English gentility with exotic barbarity.

His family was at least partly Christian. His brother Abraham was said in 1749 to 'have read Prayers for several Years past to the Indians in their several Castles'. His nephew Petrus Paulus 'has made it his Study to teach the Mohawk Children to read'.[7] Whereas other Iroquois sachems signed deeds and treaties with their clan marks, he used a stylised version of his initials: HP.[8] This cultural ambiguity was important to his diplomatic career. For the Mohawks, Hendrick's adoption of some English clothes established his status as a mediator between themselves and the colonisers. For the English, his retention of an Iroquois identity gave him the representative status that they needed in a diplomat.[9]

Successful go-betweens, however, need partners. They need to deal with people like themselves, people who are useful to their own side precisely because they have become a little like the other. Hendrick needed, from the British Empire, someone who would imagine him and his fellow-Indians, not as savage bogeymen, but merely as human beings with different notions. As an Indian who had become partly European, he required a European who could become partly Indian. He needed a counterpart who could match his own ability to be at home simultaneously in different cultures. In confident, expansionist, triumphal England it was hard to find such people. In Ireland, on the other hand, they were thick on the ground.

3

Amphibians

===

Charles Reilly's old school friend William Fitzsymons from the Irish village of the Athboy, in County Meath, Ireland, was married to William Johnson's sister Ellis. Charles Reilly's brother had been best man at Johnson's brother's wedding. He had heard the Johnsons boast of how well their son William was doing in the wilds of America, how the local boy had become a rich trader, a colonel in the New York militia and an intimate acquaintance of powerful men like the governor, Charles Clinton, and the colonial politician and administrator Cadwallader Colden.

So when Charles Reilly himself took the boat to America to work as a schoolmaster in the New York town of Goshen, he hoped to avail himself of the old ties of ethnic and local solidarity. By August 1749 his teaching contract was due to expire in two months and he had no immediate offers of more work. He had some indication through a third party that Johnson remembered him and might be willing to help. So he thought very carefully about the letter he sent in to 'Collonel William Johnston at his house at ye Mohawk Castle', on the ragged and contested borderlands between two Empires, the British and French, who disputed control of North America with sporadic but ferocious violence.

He needed to be at once ingratiating and impressive, intimate but respectful. He had to distinguish himself from the normal run of needy flatterers, the swarm of supplicants whose steady hum was the background music of societies that worked on patronage. He was trying to exert what the Irish called 'pull', to conjure up the spirit of mutual obligation through which a community under pressure reinforced and sustained itself. He needed to bring into play certain common but unspoken assumptions that would, in this strange world of exile, quietly remind the powerful man that he and the humble schoolmaster, for all their differences of station and fortune, belonged together.

So Charles Reilly dipped his pen in the inkwell and began to write:

Domine,
Adducar ut credam te interesse doctos, hac causa hoc more Scribo, nuncio tuo misso Carolo Clinto Armigero decorabar, Responsoque, notum facio atque tibi affirmo ut gratia amicitiae egregiae subsistitur inter nostros Parentes, atque respectus teneo ulli ducenti originem a Patre tuo Domino Christophero Johnston habitante propre Dunshaughlin, ut mangopere guaderem si capax essem benefacere aut utilem esse tibi qua in re.

[Sir,
Being led to believe that men of learning interest you, I write to you in this manner, having been honoured by your message sent to Charles Clinton Esquire; and in response I inform and assure you that the pleasure of a rare friendship exists between our parents, and I respect anyone who is descended from your father Mister Christopher Johnston from near Dunshaughlin, and that I should greatly rejoice if I had the capacity to serve you or to be useful to you in any way.]

His decision to write in Latin was in part a compliment to both himself and William Johnson. In the eighteenth century, classical allusions and quotations were a code that bound educated gentlemen together and excluded the vulgar masses. Reilly was indicating that he knew Johnson was a gentleman, while also implicitly claiming the same status for himself. But in the context of a compliment to Johnson's family origins, it also indicated something else. As the language of the Mass and the priesthood, Latin had deep importance to the Irish adherents of an outlawed church.

After the defeat of the Jacobites, the Catholics of Ireland had been made subject to a series of penal laws, banishing their bishops and regular clergy, severely restricting their rights to own or lease land, excluding them from parliament and the professions, depriving them of the right to vote. By 1703 Catholics, a substantial majority of the Irish population, owned just 14 per cent of the land; by the early 1750s, this would fall yet further to just five per cent.[1] Yet Catholic allegiance remained strong. As part of the resistance to the new order, Latin was kept alive by informal teachers. It expressed, not just a continuing link to the faith and learning of the past, but a high-flown pride, a defiance of the new social hierarchies in which dispossessed Catholics had lost their status.

Reilly's letter to Johnson continued in Latin, explaining his own situation and his accomplishments as a teacher, musician and carriage-maker, and politely wondering if he might visit Johnson. He then added two postscripts. The first, again in Latin, explained his connections to Johnson's family and sent his regards to four named men 'omnibusque alteris hibernicus in illo loco' ('and all the other Irishmen in that place'). The second, adding information on the mechanics of reaching him with a reply, was in polite and formal English. He signed off with a master-stroke, a finishing touch in which the artfulness of his begging letter was fully revealed: 'Banaght Lath gu veke, meh, hu'.

Here was a third language, neither Latin nor English, but a private signal whose apparently casual nature in fact drew attention to its profound undertones. The phrase is in Gaelic, the language of a defeated indigenous Ireland: 'beannacht leat go bhfeice me thu' – a blessing on you till I see you. Reilly wrote it, though, using a phonetic spelling that was peculiar to a small strand of the Irish population. This way of writing Gaelic, using English orthography to represent its particular sounds, belonged to Protestant missionaries who were trying to convert the Catholic population. It had been invented in the early eighteenth century for a Protestant Gaelic-language catechism, and was then used in the Protestant charter schools established to teach and convert Catholic children.[2]

With this final stitch in his trilingual tapestry, Reilly was hinting at something that he and William Johnson shared beyond the friendship of their parents and their mutual acquaintances. He understood, and wished Johnson to know that he understood, that they both belonged to the largely silent subculture of the convert. Reilly was a Protestant (otherwise he could not have been a schoolmaster in a colony where Catholicism was repressed by law). So was Johnson. But such a bald statement of identity came nowhere near the complex reality of men who had abandoned a very old allegiance and chosen to accommodate themselves to the demands of a new order. In that little blessing, Reilly was evoking for Johnson a shared memory of another culture and a common experience of the painful and never quite total adoption of a new personality. One man who lived between worlds was calling out to another.

Like all the most high-class performances of its time, Reilly's letter came with a musical accompaniment, an imaginary soundtrack that underlined its content. In his Latin postscript, he suddenly switched into a dreamy description of the added pleasure he could bring to

Johnson's wilderness home: 'Thank God, I can practice various arts . . . with which I amuse myself in solitude . . . at any time I am fatigued, with playing various musical instruments, now the bagpipes, now the German flute, then the hautboy, then the violin which with other things, when I engage in recreation, I relax my mind.' To emphasise the importance of this accomplishment, he appended to his letter a note in English: 'I'll also if you please bring with me all my musical instruments Fiddle German flute Hautboy & Bagpipes.'[3]

The repetition of this list of instruments was another statement of his mastery of different cultures. He was conjuring up for Johnson what he imagined would be a congenial range of forms. Johnson's hours of relaxation, too, could be filled with the sprightly civility and baroque refrains of polite European chamber music. But they could also be punctuated with the dark chant of the Irish uileann pipes, whose warped notes and swirling drones blared out the slow laments honed by repeated defeats and the fast jigs that induced a heady forgetfulness.

Charles Reilly's letter opens a small window into the mental world in which William Johnson had been formed. It was, of its nature, a murky and secretive place whose inhabitants had every reason not to advertise their inner thoughts; a world of fluidity and compromise, of abandoned loyalties and assumed allegiances, of swallowed pride and subtle strategies; a culture that had faced the truth that it is ruled by forces it cannot master; a world whose deepest currents would have been familiar to the Mohawk sachem Hendrick.

William Johnson was born in Smithstown, the name given to a group of fields in the rich pasture-lands of County Meath, about 20 miles north-west of Dublin, around 1715[4] – just a quarter of a century after the last of Catholic Ireland's last stands. It is a place where the vibrant green of the fields is broken by damp ditches and thick hedgerows and sheltered by rolling ridges and gentle folds topped by old ash, lime and oak trees. His family's farm was part of the small estate of Warrenstown,[5] whose lush fields and neat copses were drained by a stream, the Skane. It ran into the River Boyne on whose banks, in 1690, William of Orange had defeated the army of King James II in whose ranks Johnson's ancestors had fought.

The Johnsons were tied through marriage and a vestigial feudal hierarchy to some of the grand dignitaries of Irish Catholicism. They were tenants of the Warrens, who in turn were tenants of the Plunketts, Earls of Fingal, who held about 20,000 acres in 1727. William Johnson's maternal grandmother Catherine, before her marriage to Michael Warren, had been the wife of Sir Nicholas Plunkett. She herself was the daughter of Sir Christopher Aylmer, baronet of Balrath, a prominent member of the Catholic gentry, and the granddaughter of Lord Mathew Plunkett, fifth Earl of Louth.[6]

These men and women belonged to a caste that was known, rather misleadingly, as the 'Old English' – a wealthy elite whose origins in Ireland went back, in the case of the Warrens, to the Norman conquest of the twelfth century. Absorbed into the native gentry, they remained staunchly Catholic after the Reformation and tended to resent the newer Protestant English colonists. They saw themselves, and were largely accepted, as the natural leaders of the Catholic Gaelic-speaking majority.

Thus, even though the Warrens had come down in the world, young Johnson knew that through his grandmother – who was still alive during the first decade of his life – he was connected to what had until recently been one of the most powerful Catholic family networks in Ireland. The Plunkett name had a particular resonance: Archbishop Oliver Plunkett, Primate of All Ireland, had been beheaded in London in 1681 for high treason, becoming in the process a venerated martyr and later a saint.

Along with the Tyrrells, another related family[7] to whom young Johnson was particularly close, this web of Old English Catholic families in County Meath had been extraordinarily adept at holding on to its lands through the Reformation and the subsequent wars. In 1640, 85 per cent of the land in Meath was held by the Old English, the vast majority of them described as 'Papists'. Even after the upheavals and expropriations of the 1640s, when Oliver Cromwell's Puritan army defeated the Royalist and Catholic forces in Ireland, Oliver Plunkett himself had reported to the Vatican in 1675: 'The Catholics in this diocese [Meath] have more property than all the other dioceses' in Ireland.[8]

The Warrens, though, had a narrow escape. Their 320 acres of land had been forfeited in the Cromwellian settlement of the 1650s as belonging to traitors who had taken part in the bloody Catholic rebellion of 1641, a conflict that left deep but selective memories of atrocities against civilians on both sides. Johnson's great-grandfather Oliver

Warren got the land back in 1662 under the restored Stuart monarchy of Charles II. This experience of dispossession and repossession undoubtedly welded the Warrens and their wider family network to the Stuart cause, especially when the succession passed to the Catholic James II. In the civil war which followed the overthrow of James by the Protestant William of Orange, in 1688, the Warrens rallied to the Jacobite cause.

Johnson's maternal grandfather Michael Warren served as a captain in the King's Royal Regiment of Infantry in the army of James II. Michael's brothers James and Peter also served in the Jacobite forces, as did another brother or cousin Oliver Warren. John and Thomas Warren, also listed as 'of Warrenstowne' and presumably cousins, were outlawed as Jacobite traitors. Cousins of the Warrens, the Aylmers of Balrath, who served in James's forces, were placed in the same category.

On his father's side, William Johnson's ancestors had lived through a similar history of dispossession, repossession, and Jacobitism. The Johnsons had their own notions of a grand past, but it was somewhat different from the Warren family's self-image as the descendants of Norman knights. Their name sounds English, but Christopher Johnson seems to have been the first to style himself exclusively in this fashion. His father, William, seems originally to have called himself MacShane – a Gaelic name that translates simply as John's son – hence 'Johnson'. His father in turn was Thomas MacShane, whose father was Sean or John O'Neill (hence 'son of John') from Dungannon in County Tyrone – heartland of the greatest of all the Gaelic aristocratic families of Ireland.[9]

Johnson's ancestors were not from the main line of the O'Neill family, but from an intriguing branch.[10] The O'Neills of the Fews, from whom he was directly descended, were, as far back as the sixteenth century, a frontier tribe. They had broken away from the main O'Neill dynasty of Tyrone to further their own interests in the hills and valleys of the Fews area of South Armagh. Like most similar sub-chieftains, they saw some advantages in the new English system of land ownership and sought to balance the benefits of English recognition of their dubious titles against the threat of English domination. Their stronghold of Glassdrumman Castle, on the southern edge of County Armagh, marked the border between a semi-autonomous Gaelic lordship and the increasingly assertive influence of the English-ruled area of the east coast of Ireland known as the Pale. Literally and metaphorically, the O'Neills of the Fews were just a little beyond the pale.

As part of the English effort to colonise Ireland, the Fews area had been granted in 1571 to Captain Thomas Chatterton, a native of Wiltshire, in England, but his attempts at planting a British Protestant colony on his lands failed and his grant was revoked. An aggrieved Sir Turlough McHenry O'Neill took part in the great revolt of the Gaelic chiefs against Elizabeth I in the 1590s, but changed sides at an opportune time in the 1602, received a pardon, and was re-granted 9,900 acres of the Fews, the rest being allocated for colonisation by Scottish Protestants. Sir Turlough's accommodation with the new order was so thorough that he even settled some British tenants on his own lands.

Sir Turlough's son Sir Henry (Christopher Johnson's great-great-grandfather) cannily avoided involvement with the next great Catholic uprising in 1641. His caution did not save him, however. Since all of his children and most of his kin took part in the rising, and since the Catholic armies had been supplied from O'Neill lands, he lost all of his estates in Armagh. In Oliver Cromwell's infamous policy of sending the rebellious Irish 'to Hell or Connacht', he was promised land in County Mayo, but most of it was never delivered.[11]

This family history would undoubtedly have been well-known to the later generations of the O'Neills. The disruptions and dispossessions of the sixteenth century, far from breaking the continuity of family memory, made it, among the Gaelic upper classes, something of an obsession.

William Johnson's father Christopher was too young to fight in the Jacobite war, since he was around eight years old when James was finally defeated.[12] There is no doubt, though, that his wider family was heavily implicated. His maternal grandfather, James FitzSimons of Tullynally, County Westmeath, was outlawed for high treason, along with the latter's uncle Gerald FitzSimons. Kinsmen of his grandmother, Frances Fay of Derrynagarragh, also in County Westmeath, were also declared traitors.[13] The Dease family, with whom the Johnsons remained closely allied in the next generation, were themselves deeply embroiled.

From both sides of his family, therefore, William Johnson inherited defeat. The new order into which he had been born was one in which all civil and political power was reserved, under the Penal Laws, to members of the Protestant state religion, the Church of Ireland. Both

Catholics and dissenting Protestants were excluded from the armed forces and most professions. Catholics faced, in law at least, severe restrictions on the practice of their faith, their access to education and their property rights.

For the poor, who never enjoyed such rights anyway, the consequences of defeat were felt most sharply as an alienation from cultural and religious power. For the very rich, like the Plunketts, there were always ways and means of holding on to a position of privilege. Hardest hit, though, were those in the middle, like the Warrens and the Johnsons, with high notions of their own place in the world but without the means to sustain them. They needed to be able to pass their land on to their heirs. They needed enough money to allow their daughters to marry well. They needed to be able to turn the advantages of education and connections into military, ecclesiastical or professional careers for their younger sons.

All of these necessities were threatened by laws that barred Catholics from universities, the legal profession and military commissions, outlawed the old church institutions with their ranks of parish priests, abbots, bishops and provincials, and limited Catholic opportunities to buy or lease land. Yet all of these problems could be solved by the simple expedient of becoming Protestant. On one side there was a sense of ethnic and religious identity that had been forged over centuries and tempered in the violent struggles of the seventeenth century. On the other was a sense of pride in family status, and of horror at the thought of being pushed downwards into the undifferentiated mass of the Catholic poor.

Between these fierce imperatives, there was the tempting escape hatch of God's infinite mercy. Perhaps God, who could see into the darkest depths of the soul, didn't really care about how things looked on the outside. Did it really matter to the Almighty if one went through the necessary forms of Protestant faith while remaining true to Catholicism in private prayer? – especially if, in preserving oneself, one was also preserving the one true faith from destruction. Many Catholics with land managed to persuade themselves that God was more understanding than the British Crown. As one Irish 'convert', Ignatius Gahagan, put it in 1757, 'I would rather at any time entrust God with my soul than the laws of Ireland with my lands.'[14]

The lands of Warrenstown, where William Johnson grew up, were at risk, not just from the laws of Ireland, but from the effects of half a century of conflict in which, for those who were repeatedly involved on the losing side, the steady accumulation of wealth had been impossible. These lands were again declared forfeit in 1690 and again returned under the terms of the capitulation of the Jacobites at Limerick in 1691. Like the rest of the Jacobite officer corps, Johnson's grandfather Michael Warren was offered the choice of either surrendering his estates and going into exile in France, or submitting to King William and retaining them. He chose to stay and submit.

The seizures and disruptions had undermined the family's fortunes. In 1673 Oliver Warren had been forced to take out a mortgage of £500 on the estate. By the time Michael Warren died in 1712, the debt stood at £1,850. In 1723, when William Johnson was still a child, half of the Warrenstown lands were sold for £2,100, and there was still a mortgage of £400 on the remainder.[15] It was perhaps a mark of decline in itself that Michael Warren's daughter Anne had married Christopher Johnson.

Christopher Johnson was not, admittedly, poor. As well as renting land from the Warrens, he leased nearly 200 acres of adjoining land at Smithstown directly from the Earl of Fingal. It is not clear how long he had farmed this latter property: when the lease was renewed in 1736, it was described as 'then in the possession of the said Christopher Johnson', making it likely that there was a previous lease going back to the early years of the century.[16] Catholics were limited to short leases, however, and the Johnsons' longer-term security still depended on their relationship with the Warrens, for whom they acted as both tenants and agents, collecting their rents from others. The Warrenstown rent roll of 1735 shows the Johnsons as the second-largest tenants of the estate, with an annual rent of £30/12/-. The favourable position they enjoyed is clear, however, from the rent roll of 1741. In the intervening six years, the rent of the larger tenants, the Gaffneys, had risen from £60 to £70/10/-. That of the Johnsons remained unchanged.[17]

This privileged position also created a strong degree of dependency. While even the smaller tenants, James Brady and James Rooney, had leases, Christopher Johnson held his land 'at pleasure' – essentially for as long as the Warrens let them have it. While the ties of marriage and business may have made it extremely unlikely that the Johnsons would be evicted, their lack of legal security must also have been a constant reminder of their subordinate position. Gratitude was the intangible part of the Johnsons' rent.

These family histories and the high notions to which they gave rise ought to have made the rational choice of conformity to the new order and conversion to Protestantism relatively easy. The Warrens, Johnsons and their wider network of kith and kin could claim that they had done their best for the old cause in the 1640s and 1690s and been honourably defeated. The threat of ruin, moreover, was now an immediate pressure. By 1717, when William Johnson was two years old, the Warrenstown estate was mortgaged to the tune of £2,376. Michael Warren's wife had been left just £3 to buy a mourning ring in his will. Johnson's mother, and her brothers and sisters, got nothing. The decision was therefore made that her youngest brother Peter, now around thirteen, and with no money or prospects, should be raised as a Protestant so that he could join the Royal Navy.

This decision was not abstract. Matthew Aylmer, who was Anne Johnson and Peter Warren's uncle, had converted as far back as 1674 and joined the navy. The result had been a spectacular success. By 1716 he was Admiral of the Fleet and Governor of the Royal Hospital at Greenwich. Two years later he was raised to the Irish peerage as Lord Aylmer of Balrath. With such a powerful patron to look out for their interests and such a stellar example of the advantages of conformity, the idea of embarking on a naval career was both obvious and infinitely promising. Both the eldest and youngest of the Warren children, Oliver and Peter, set out on this hopeful voyage. Peter, when he joined the navy in Dublin as an ordinary seaman, in April 1716, was no more than thirteen years old. His career would profoundly affect the life of his infant nephew William Johnson.

The subsequent scale of Peter Warren's success, the world-shaping impact that would stamp his name on the streetscapes of New York, London, Charleston and Louisbourg and on an ugly monument in the east transept of Westminster Abbey, would make him an icon of Protestant Britain. His naval victories would be commemorated in the Warren Streets of London and Greenwich Village in New York and in the towns of Warren, Rhode Island and Warren, New Hampshire. His rise would make him fabulously wealthy, and in his genteel retirement on his Hampshire estate, he would play the role of Protestant philanthropist, making large donations to English hospitals and contributing to the building of Anglican churches in Boston and New York and, in Ireland, to the Society for Promoting Protestant Working Schools. Nothing would be more obvious than his firm and sincere devotion to the established Church. He seemed to epitomise a simple but complete transformation of the Warren and Johnson families from diehard Catholic rebels to loyal Protestant subjects. The reality, however, was much more ambiguous.

The Protestant establishment in Ireland in the early eighteenth century was well aware that Catholic landowners would be tempted to declare their allegiance to the established Church, gain access to the privileges of conformity and yet remain effectively Catholic. For this reason, an act of 1703 'to prevent the further growth of popery' made it obligatory on converts to provide public proof of their adherence to the new orthodoxy. Converts were required first to sign a form abjuring all allegiance to the Church of Rome and the Stuart pretenders to the British Crown. They then had to read this statement in public at a Protestant service, and be formally received into the Church. When the clergyman who officiated at this ceremony reported it to the ecclesiastical authorities, the local bishop then issued a certificate of conformity to the convert.[18]

There is no doubt that Peter Warren went through these prescribed forms. What is significant, though, is the date of his formal conversion. He was not certified as a convert until 9 July 1752, and enrolled on the convert list five days later.[19] He therefore completed the formalities of conversion thirty-six years after he joined the navy. He did so, moreover, at a time when he probably knew he was in danger of death. He died in Dublin after a short illness and just fifteen days after he was enrolled as a Protestant. This suggests that the reason for going through the formalities was primarily to ensure that there were no legal problems with the handing on of his substantial estate.

This is not to suggest that Peter Warren did not think of himself as a Protestant. He was, as an adolescent boy, thrown into the dangerous and demanding world of the naval service and, in the fierce struggle to survive and succeed, old religious loyalties were probably the least of his worries. The more prominent and powerful he became, and the longer he was away from Ireland, the easier it would have been to settle into the established Anglican order of things. The reluctance to make a public recantation of the Catholic and Jacobite heritage of his childhood is nevertheless a reminder that he and his younger protégé William Johnson had a silent hinterland beyond their public selves.

In Johnson's extended family, Protestantism was a means to an end, but the continuity of the old Catholic culture was an end in itself. For those who had to leave, Protestantism was a necessary passport for the journey into the power structures of the British Empire. For those who could stay, Catholicism still mapped the local world.

However many laws were passed to penalise papists and encourage the established church, there was little real change in the affiliations of those who lived in County Meath. In the 1732 census, the county had 1,448 Protestant and 13,180 Catholic families, and these figures understate the scale of the Catholic majority, who tended to have larger families.[20] Most Protestant parishes in the county remained small and isolated. Jonathan Swift, who was Church of Ireland vicar at Laracor, in Meath, in the early eighteenth century, was reputed to have so small a congregation that he began his sermons, 'Dearly beloved Roger', referring to the parish clerk, who was his only auditor. In Warrenstown, the local Protestant church of Knockmark was poor and neglected, even by Meath standards. A statement on the 'State of the Diocese of Meath' drawn up for Bishop Welbore Ellis around 1733, when Johnson was in his late teens, notes the sparse nature of the accoutrements: 'no Communion table, nor place railed in for it, nor raised, no linen or carpet, nor flagon; there is a chalice of pewter'.[21] Clearly, the surrounding Protestant population was small and the local landowners had little interest in subsidising the Church of Ireland.

It is likely that whatever limited generosity the Warrens had to bestow would have continued to go to the Catholic Church. When the eldest son Oliver Warren, who had converted on joining the navy, died unmarried in 1724, the Warrenstown lands passed to the next son Christopher, who was still Catholic. He sold them to Peter, who was now becoming wealthy on the spoils of licensed naval piracy, in 1730. Even if this made the lands officially Protestant again, most of the occupants, including the Johnsons, were still Catholic.

The Warrens, moreover, retained deep connections to the Roman church. Although Catholic clergy were effectively outlawed by the Banishment Act of 1697, many ignored or circumvented the law. In 1704, the Warrenstown area had as one of its registered inhabitants the Reverend Michael White, who had been ordained in Lisbon and was now 'Popish Priest of Dunshaughlin, Knockmark and Culmullen'.[22] He is almost certainly the Michael White who witnessed Michael Warren's will in 1712.[23] That he was also left £8 in that same will suggests that he was close to the Warren family and tended to their spiritual needs.

One of the most intriguing survivals of active Catholicism in this period of official suppression was the Franciscan community at Multyfarnham, which continued to function under a succession of annually appointed Guardians. In 1731, there were eight friars at Multyfarham.[24] The Guardian of this friary in 1703, 1705, 1717, 1720 and 1724 was the Reverend Peter Warren. He was a senior Franciscan, a former head of the order's Irish province, with the titles of Apostolic Notary, Lector Emeritus of Theology and Commissary Visitor of Leinster. He had previously been Guardian of the Franciscan convent at Louvain in Belgium in 1696, which suggests that he had been trained for the priesthood in that city, along with hundreds of other sons of Irish Catholic landowners who escaped to the continent for a theological education that was illegal in Ireland. The Reverend Peter Warren was almost certainly a brother of the Jacobite Captain Michael Warren, and thus an uncle of William Johnson's mother.[25]

Nor was this venerable old Franciscan simply an embarrassing vestige of past allegiances. Johnson's mother had three brothers, and within a year or two of Johnson's own birth, the oldest and the youngest of them were Protestants making their way as sailors in the service of the British crown. The third brother, Christopher, was also moving up into the officer class of a highly regimented institution. In 1729 the Very Reverend Christopher Warren was appointed Guardian of the Franciscan convent in Kildare.[26] There, presumably, he could pray to God and ask him to understand the shifts and subtleties to which the painful necessities of a fallen world had forced his brothers.

What makes sense of these apparent contradictions and places the uncertain structure of family loyalties on solid ground is the ground itself, the land that has always been the ultimate allegiance of Irish farmers. Peter Warren enjoyed an astonishing career as a naval commander, fighting pirates off West Africa, capturing off the West Indies Spanish ships weighed down with gold and silver, founding Greenwich Village and buying a large chunk of Manhattan, laying siege to a French fortress off Nova Scotia and becoming a Knight of the Bath and an admiral. He visited Ireland a few times, but never returned to live there. Yet through all his spectacular adventures, he held on to one imperative: get back the ancestral lands.

As soon as he could afford to do so, Peter Warren bought what remained of Warrenstown. He filed a lawsuit, claiming that half of the estate, which had been sold by his brother in 1723 to pay off debts, still belonged to the family. He spent twenty years, from February 1730 to March 1750, and far more money than the land was actually worth, getting title to the full estate.[27] He also went to the trouble of securing a royal patent for the holding of an annual fair in Warrenstown – the only such licence granted in Ireland in the 1730s.[28] It is almost as if Peter Warren's efforts to add continents to his royal master's empire were just a means to the greater end of securing Warrenstown for the Warrens. And having won back the land, he left it, in his will, in the hands of a Catholic, William Johnson's brother John.[29]

The world in which young William Johnson grew up therefore was one of hidden layers and quiet undercurrents. After the furious battles of the seventeenth century, this was a time for deft evasions. The courage and flamboyance of those who had declared their allegiances to the old faith in battle would now have to be supplemented by the equivocator's skill of telling people what they wanted to hear. William grew up knowing that, while his family contained both pious Irish friars and dashing British officers, the family itself was neither Catholic nor Protestant. It was amphibious, and those who emerged from it would learn to thrive simultaneously in very different elements.

4

'Most Onruly and Streperous'

===

In the late autumn of 1755 the French general Ludwig-August, Baron de Dieskau, spent a month in William Johnson's house in Albany.[1] He was not a guest but a prisoner, captured in battle by Johnson's forces, and suffering from wounds in his leg, his knee, his hip and his bladder. He and Johnson had spent a week and a half after the battle in each other's company and struck up a remarkably affectionate relationship for men who had been trying to kill each other. Johnson described the Baron as 'a Man of Quality, a Soldier & a Gentleman', and gave orders that he was to be protected, not just from harm, but from 'impertinent curiosity' of the Albanians and from anything that might 'retard his cure or offend him'.[2] The regard was mutual: Dieskau described Johnson as 'a brave man, full of honour and feeling',[3] for whom he felt a 'sincere attachment'.[4]

Outpourings of fellow-feeling in the aftermath of battle may not be rare, even among enemies, but the relationship between Johnson and Dieskau seems to have been warmer than any temporary emotional disturbance might explain. Johnson lent Dieskau money. Dieskau felt real grief that Johnson's brother-in-law had been killed by Dieskau's own men. Johnson, not a man given to effusive outbursts, even told Dieskau: 'It shall be the Ambition of my Life to manifest to the World in general that I am not unworthy of your Friendship.'[5]

The bond was formed in the nine days when Johnson and Dieskau, both wounded, lay in a military camp having their wounds dressed, recuperating, and talking. They talked, presumably, of the battle that had just been fought, of the wider war between France and Britain, and of the likely outcome of the conflict. But they probably talked about the past as well, wanting to know about each other and how two Europeans had ended up spilling their blood in the same patch of American forest. They were both well-known men: Dieskau a comrade of the great French commander the Marechal de Saxe, and a veteran of immense European battles; Johnson the colourful commander of Indians. And as they talked they would have discovered some sardonic truths about the strangeness of war and history, the paradox that Dieskau's conqueror could easily have been his protégé.

In the middle of the eighteenth century, when men of William Johnson's class in Ireland, the remnants of the defeated Catholic Jacobites, wanted some imaginary compensation for all their defeats, they drank to the Battle of Fontenoy. There, in May 1745, outside Tournai in Flanders, over 100,000 soldiers, the French under Saxe, the British and their allies under George II's son, the Duke of Cumberland, engaged in a ferocious clash. Dieskau had commanded Saxe's cavalry. The battle had been turned by a last-ditch charge by the Irish Brigade of the French army, its officers chanting in Gaelic 'Cuimhnigh ar Limneach agus feall na Sasanaigh' – 'Remember Limerick and the treachery of the English'. Their heroic role in the defeat of Cumberland was turned, in the imagination of the Irish Jacobite underground, into revenge for the Battle of the Boyne. Johnson had read about it: he ordered a copy of An Historical Review of the Transactions of Europe from the Commencement of the War with Spain from London in 1750. Now he had an important participant – Dieskau – to describe it to him.

Since Dieskau undoubtedly knew that Johnson was the nephew of the famed naval commander Sir Peter Warren, they probably talked of the other Warrens who had fought with the French at Fontenoy. Prominent in the Irish Brigade that day were two of Johnson's kinsmen, the brothers John and William Warren from Corduff, about ten miles from Warrenstown on the other side of the Dublin–Meath border. Dieskau would certainly have known their more famous brother Richard Warren, who was, like Dieskau himself, a protégé of the Marechal de Saxe. Richard had missed the Battle of Fontenoy because he was engaged in important negotiations in Paris, helping to plan the last Jacobite invasion of Britain under Charles Edward Stuart – Bonnie Prince Charlie.

These other Warrens provided William Johnson with the sense of an alternative life, in which many similarities were obliterated by one great difference. The Corduff Warrens had started out in the same place and in the same political and economic circumstances; they had been minor Catholic and Jacobite middlemen from the fertile plains west of Dublin; and they had ended up in the same nexus of violent imperial struggle, exile and self-advancement. Yet they had fought on opposite sides in world-shaping conflicts. While Peter Warren and William Johnson had chosen the British Empire as the arena in which they would win back their family's prestige and wealth, John, William and Richard Warren of Corduff had chosen the French.

John and William Warren were present on the Stuart side at the bloody extinction of the Jacobite cause in the Scottish glen of Culloden in April 1746. William Johnson would name his own summer house in America after their conqueror, the Duke of Cumberland, cursed by the Jacobites as 'Butcher' Cumberland. Richard Warren was made a baronet by the Pretender for his daring rescue of Bonnie Prince Charlie from Scotland after the defeat. William Johnson would be made a baronet by the king whom the Pretender had been trying to dethrone. In 1765, as Governor of Belleisle, Richard Warren, by then Marechal-de-Camp Baron de Warren of Corduff, would resettle French refugees driven from North America by a British campaign in which William Johnson was a key figure.[6] In his great kindness to Dieskau, Johnson was perhaps honouring a memory of these kinsmen and remembering how easily, in the amphibious culture that shaped him, he could have been their comrade rather than their enemy.

One of the reasons William Johnson took so well to the borderlands between the French and British Empires in North America was that he had grown up along just such a border. Spiritually and culturally, though not literally, the milieu of Johnson's youth was a Franco-British frontier. Richard Warren was just one of the so-called Wild Geese, sons of Irish Catholic landowners who continued to stream into the armies of the Catholic powers, especially Spain and France. Service in continental armies was, for them, the alternative to conversion.

These were young men who didn't want to be kept down on the farm. In the same year as Johnson's encounter with Dieskau, one of the largest remaining Catholic landowners in Ireland, Lord Kenmare, complained that the lack of improvements on his estate was the fault of the Catholic head tenants and middlemen, who disdained to raise their sons for agriculture. 'If they have sons, they are all to be priests, physicians, or French officers.'[7]

Even though Johnson never joined these French officers, he was certainly influenced by their style. In the 1730s, when he was on the brink of manhood, these glamorous figures who came and went, boasting of their exploits on European fields, had an insolent flamboyance that gave them the kind of allure that bandits could acquire for the oppressed in other times and places. Like those outlaws, however, their allure was tragic. The poems and songs in which they were remembered were all laments.

Insolence, objectively speaking, was foolish. Figures like the Irish Brigade veteran and French recruiting officer Morty Og O'Sullivan, murdered in Ireland in 1754, were commemorated in mournful poems that praised their defiant élan but reminded those who listened of what happened to defiance when it collided with power. This tradition culminated in 1773 with the greatest Irish poem of the century – perhaps the greatest poem of the century anywhere – 'Caoineadh Airt Ui Laoghaire' – 'The Lament for Art O'Leary'.

O'Leary, a twenty-six-year-old Catholic who had served as a cavalry officer on the continent, epitomises the dilemma of Johnson's class in the eighteenth century. The poem describes in loving detail his uppity array: a silver-hilted sword, five-ply stockings, riding boots to the knee, a black beaver hat in winter and in summer a gold-banded Caroline hat edged with lace, gloves, a brooch, a cambric shirt and an immaculate suit. His slim, high-strung horse has a menacing prance.[8] But his pride was the death of him. Under the penal laws, a Catholic was obliged to sell any horse to a Protestant who offered him five guineas. O'Leary was shot dead by a Protestant when he refused to sell his. The poem, written collectively by the keening women who helped to bury him, is narrated in the voice of his widow.

This kind of doomed glamour was an option for the young Johnson growing up around Warrenstown. He had the temperament for it. There is a glimpse of him aged eleven in Peter Warren's diary in May 1726: 'William is a Spritely Boy, well grown, of good parts, Keen Wit but most Onruly and Streperous.' He also had, or at least acquired, the taste for elegant display. Even if the tilt towards Protestant conformity that had been taken by his two Warren uncles made a career in the Wild Geese impossible, the cultural style of the class from which he came shaped his personality in crucial ways.

The depressed Catholic gentry had a curious relationship with their poor co-religionists. The general rule that the more minor the gentry, the greater its obsession with social distinctions did not really apply. People like the Warrens and the Johnsons needed their poor neighbours because they were the only ones who remembered, or recognised, their former status as important people. Those neighbours, in turn, needed their gentry to uphold the oppressed honour of the tribe in the face of ethnic and religious insult. They indulged them with a residual respect, provided they played their part as local champions.

A young man like William Johnson therefore had to learn a kind of balancing act if, though merely the son of a head tenant and middleman, he was to be regarded as a gentleman. He had to be proud and elegant, with some of the swagger of an Irish Brigade officer. He also had to be familiar and accessible, a good sport, willing to join in the games and preferably to win, to dance with the girls and, when he was old enough, to drink with the lads. In 1740, shortly after Johnson came to manhood, Laurence Whyte described these young Catholic gentlemen in his poem 'The Parting Cup':

> They seldom did refuse a summons
> to play at football or at commons,
> to vault or take a ditch or hedge
> at leisure hours to unfold a riddle,
> or play the bagpipes, harp or fiddle.[9]

Johnson learned to be a pre-eminent exponent of this style, an adaptable social creature who could mix familiarly with all sorts of people, drink with a peasant or amuse a lord, knock out a fiddle tune or play a game of football, and yet retain a commanding air of reserve. What was unusual about him was that instead of drifting away into a dreamy dilettantism or hardening into a doomed defiance, these qualities in him became, by an accident of circumstance, internationally significant.

This adaptability was fostered by a society that, for all its rural localism, was already multicultural. The old Gaelic culture was still alive, its artists dependent now on an impoverished gentry and forced to consort with the common people. About two-thirds of the Irish population still spoke Gaelic, and Johnson, dealing every day with the local community, would have needed at least a working knowledge of the language. In his youth, one of the last of the old Gaelic bards, Seamas Dall Mac Cuarta, was still active in the Boyne valley. The great blind harper and composer Turlough O'Carolan, a Meath man, was still moving around the country, playing in the bigger houses that welcomed him. Johnson's later intense interest in this Gaelic harp tradition suggests that he may have heard O'Carolan play, or at least encountered some of his less famous contemporaries.

As well as Gaelic, and the Latin that he also mastered, there was, of course, English. With very few Gaelic books available, English was the language of literacy and education. Long before Johnson's birth, the Warrens were fluently anglophone, and the shift in name from MacShane suggests that the Johnsons had been so for at least two generations as well. With the language went English notions of civility in manners, dress and social aspirations, and since even a restoration of the Stuart monarchy would leave intact Ireland's political ties to England, the fulfilment of those aspirations would always require an ease with English ways. Especially as Peter Warren's career in the Royal Navy began to flower, there would have been no doubt that young Johnson's future lay, in one form or another, within an essentially English culture.

The likelihood is that his early education took place at home. An Act of 1695 outlawed Catholics who taught at school, but prosecutions seem to have been rare, and many Catholics continued to work as informal schoolmasters. In the early 1690s Anthony Dopping, the Protestant Bishop of Meath, listed thirty-four 'Popish schoolmasters' in the diocese, including one in Navan called Warren, who may have been related to Johnson's family. A report in 1731 by his successor Ralph Lambert records that there were then forty-one Catholic schools in the diocese, as well as 'several Popish tutors whose numbers cannot be exactly returned'.[10]

It is probable that young William had the benefit of one of these private 'Popish tutors' and then went on to one of the higher-class schoolmasters whose curricula included Latin and philosophy. There were at least three such masters operating in Meath in the 1690s, and this informal educational network continued to operate during Johnson's youth. Since his uncle Peter Warren, rising all the time in the naval hierarchy, was watching out for his welfare from an early age, he may well have contributed to his schooling. By 1726, when Johnson was eleven, Warren was a senior lieutenant. The following year, he was given command of his own vessel, the seventy-gun *Grafton*. In 1730, Peter acquired what was left of the family's Warrenstown lands and was trying to recover the rest.

By the time William Johnson was fifteen, Peter Warren was obviously the great hope of the extended family. He was making himself a small fortune, both by illicit trade in wines, spirits and slaves, and by a very favourable marriage. He was posted to New York in 1730 as commander of the *Solebay*. The following year, he married Susannah De Lancey, daughter of a wealthy and well-connected New York fur trader. Stephen De Lancey had gone to America as a Huguenot (French Protestant) refugee, and himself married into the powerful Van Cortlandt family of Dutch merchants there. By marrying into the De Lanceys, Peter Warren acquired a network of connections with the powerful Dutch clans of New York. He also got some serious money. In his complex marriage settlement with Susannah, she got the title to the farm at Warrenstown and to a farm on Manhattan Island that Warren had purchased. He got £3,000 in New York currency, and joint ownership of a £6,000 trust.[11] By the age of twenty-six, therefore, Peter Warren had already made his fortune. He would massively add to it throughout the 1730s and 1740s by seizing Spanish and French vessels and claiming prize money. Between 1739 and 1748 alone, he took goods and precious metals worth at least £127,405 sterling from captured ships.[12]

His uncle's rise shaped William Johnson's destiny. His options, as the eldest son of a family of Catholic middlemen and tenants, had been limited. He could eventually succeed to his father's tenancy. He could go into the French army or the Catholic priesthood. There is some slight evidence that he may have considered studying for the law, which was a subject that interested him throughout his life, but Catholics were debarred from practising law in Ireland and Britain.[13]

Peter Warren's wealth and power, however, opened up a new horizon. Warren began to accumulate vast properties in New York. Between 1731 and 1741 he acquired a 300-acre estate in Greenwich Village on Manhattan Island. By 1746, he also owned an 11-acre plot bounded by what is now West 21st Street; parts of Pearl Street and Cortland Street; part of the Cortland Manor estate in Westchester, and perhaps the finest private house in New York City, with the resounding address of Number 1 Broadway. For his energetic young nephew, Peter Warren provided both an example of the fabulous possibilities of the New World and the means to make those possibilities his own.

By his early twenties, William Johnson was effectively working for Peter Warren. The captain visited Ireland in 1733, and presumably renewed his acquaintance with his nephew. He clearly liked the look of him. From then on, young Johnson assisted his father in collecting rents for Warren's Irish lands. There are references to him in Warren's accounts for 1734 and 1736.[14] By 1737, he had decided that it made sense to place his destiny in the hands of his brilliant uncle, who now thought of himself as Johnson's surrogate father. For his part, Warren was confident that Johnson's 'diligence and Application will put him Soon in a good way'.[15] The good way he had in mind was probably a vast new interest he had acquired in the wild frontier territory of northern New York, where the tenuous but increasingly insistent claims of the British and French Empires pushed up against each other.

Warren acquired from the widow of the corrupt New York governor William Cosby a huge tract of undeveloped land about 180 miles north of New York City, just south of the Mohawk River, and near its junction with the Schoharie. The purchase price – just £110 for 14,000 acres – was a mark of the difficulty of turning what was mostly primeval forest that had belonged to the Mohawk nation into a commercial land-holding. Warren, however, thought he had the man to do it. In now lost letters, probably written in 1736 or early 1737, he invited the nephew he affectionately called 'Billy' to gather a group of willing tenants and colonise the Mohawk lands. From Johnson's later recollections, it seems that Warren both exerted a persuasive pressure and held out great prospects. 'It was', he wrote of Warren, 'at his particular persuasion and even intreaty that I came to this Country, when he made me very large promises.'[16]

It seems highly unlikely that William Johnson's decision to accept the invitation and emigrate was forced on him by his family's financial circumstances. Christopher Johnson was clearly enjoying a reasonable level of prosperity. In January 1736 he renewed his lease on Smithstown from the Earl of Fingal with a down payment of £209 and at a rent of £70 a year.[17] A decade later, he was able to advance a loan of £200 to a local man.[18] These were substantial enough sums and do not indicate a family on its uppers. Pride was much more important than money alone, however. For an energetic and ambitious young man like William, a quiet, careful existence like his father's, staying loyal to the old faith but keeping out of trouble, was not a happy prospect. Peter Warren's example of daring adventure fabulously rewarded had an irresistible appeal.

Warren clearly offered him more than a job in his service. Though no formal agreement was drawn up, young Johnson was given strong hints that, if he made a success of the settlement, which his uncle was now calling Warrensburgh, most of it would be his. He had 'great Reason to believe as well by verbal as litteral Authorities from his Uncle' that the estate was 'if not entirely, at least a good part of it intended for him'.[19] From the prospect of eventually inheriting from his father an insecure short-term lease on a couple of hundred acres in Ireland he now had hopes of being lord of a great American estate.

There was, though, just one obstacle. Johnson's family was still devoutly Catholic. The pragmatic Peter Warren had no objection to Catholicism, but he was not about to risk his rising status in American colonial society by entrusting a large estate on the sensitive frontier between Catholic France and Protestant Britain to a Catholic. This sensitivity was probably all the greater because the Cosby patent under which Warren had acquired the Mohawk valley lands was both legally dubious and anathema to some Albany families, who claimed an earlier patent to the same lands.[20] He was certainly not going to place this potentially valuable property in the hands of a Catholic nephew and allow the disgruntled Albanians to denounce a Papist plot.

William Johnson's conversion is not recorded, and he did not go through the public process of renouncing his old faith. That he did convert, however, is clear from a later letter from Peter Warren to Johnson's younger brother John urging him to 'see the error of his way' like himself and William and 'join the Protestant church'.[21] With his eyes on such a prize as Warren was offering, young William Johnson, who never showed any signs of a great religious faith, did what was necessary. The price seems to have been a cooling of his relations with a father, who doted on him. The loss of his eldest boy to a distant continent was hard for Christopher Johnson to take. The possible loss of his soul may have been even harder. A decade later, William's brother John wrote to him from Dublin to tell him that their father, 'in all his discourses about you . . . usually end[s] in tears'.[22]

5

An Outlandish Man

That the summer days were two hours shorter than in Ireland and the winter days two hours longer. That turkeys abounded and that at times the sky was dark with the flocks of passenger pigeons, their wings slate-blue, their breasts wine-red, their eyes a bloody scarlet, their numbers so immense that you could shoot them for hours and still seem to make no difference. That trout rippled through the river in such abundance that the Indians caught them in baskets. That there were deadly snakes that went into holes in the rock at the onset of winter and came out in April, thin and weak. That 'The Panther is very Dangerous to be met with, it holloos like a human Creature & is soe Nimble as to leap on One, at above forty yards Distance, & immediately drives his Claws in you.'[1]

That the cold could be so intense when the wind blew from the north-west that strong hot punch would be covered in a scum of ice within twenty minutes. That 'Handling Brass or Iron leaves a Blister on the Fingers; & in Bed People are cold even with ten Blankets on.' That 'Ink on a table is frozen, before the fire.' Coming from the lush and temperate plains of County Meath, these were things that a young Irishman would notice amid the forests and rivers of the Mohawk valley – these, and of course the strange peoples and languages.

Above all, there was the scale of things. Johnson was nearly 160 miles north of New York City, and very far indeed from urban civilisation. The Mohawk valley is a huge glacial scar cut between a high plateau to the south and the higher Adirondack Mountains to the north. The broad river, flanked by rich alluvial flats, flowed over steep falls and around craggy islands, forming the only natural connection between the Atlantic seaboard and the vast, barely known continental interior. Before the Europeans arrived, the land in every direction had been covered with an almost continuous forest of beech, birch and maple, scattered with pine and hemlock and, towards the north, with aspen, fir, spruce and cedar. Even now, the cleared lands were patches of cultivation on a vast blanket of wilderness. The land was both forbidding and fruitful, blueberry and bilberry bushes springing from the crags, strawberries carpeting the alluvial flats after the snows thawed, the rapids teeming with pike, eels, perch, sturgeon and catfish. And all of it had, for Europeans, the thrilling and terrifying sense of being up for grabs.

Nature itself seemed to point out the distances that were there to be measured and conquered. Nearly 30,000 miles of streams and brooks emerged from the mountains and forests to feed a thousand miles of powerful Adirondack rivers. Water flowed east from the mountains to Lake Champlain, north-west to the St Lawrence River, west to Lake Ontario, and southward to the Mohawk and Hudson Rivers. The tight, bounded space of the island on which Johnson had lived all of his previous days was transformed here into a dizzying array of trajectories and perspectives.

It took him time to find his bearings. Unused to the extremes of cold, William Johnson nearly died in one of his first New York winters. As he later told his brother, he was 'very near being perished in a snow squall, coming from Schenectady to his Own House; his Strength was soe Exhausted, as to be obliged to take hold of a big Dog (he had with him) by the Tail, which helped him to a House, very near him; It was late in the Night, & the People could hardly hear him, it blew soe hard'.[2]

Making himself understood was a problem even in less dramatic circumstances. At first, William Johnson found it very difficult to talk to any of the inhabitants, 'he [being] an entire Stranger to both Whites and Indians and their Language, there being none but a few Dutch Settlers in his Neighbourhood . . .'[3] The Indians were Mohawks. On the south side of the river, west of Warrensburgh, was the Mohawk village of Canajoharie, home to about 300 people and usually referred to as 'the Upper Castle'. (Iroquois villages were called 'castles' by white settlers because they were usually surrounded by palisade walls.)

Near the mouth of the Schoharie Creek was the other Mohawk village, Tiononderoga, which had a small colonial garrison, Fort Hunter, and a tiny Anglican church attached to it and which was usually called the Lower Castle. To the east, containing about 300 houses, was the Dutch trading town of Schenectady, which Johnson's brother would later describe as 'a dirty little village'.4 Sixteen miles further to the south-east of Schenectady was Albany, the largest town of upstate New York, but, in the eyes of the same brother, 'A Nasty dirty town'. Both to the east and west of Canajoharie there were small, scattered settlements of German Protestants (often called 'Dutch' or 'High Dutch' by the English), who had fled the Rhenish Palatinate over a generation before and now lived in isolated farmhouses or in villages like Stone Arabia, Palatine and German Flats.

Johnson sailed from Ireland for Boston, probably in the spring of 1738, with his cousin Mick Tyrrell and twelve Irish Protestant families who were to be the initial tenants. The Fort Hunter minister, Henry Barclay, noted that his congregation had been increased by this influx of 'very honest, sober, industrious, and religious' people.5

Peter Warren's intention was that Johnson, as well as clearing the land and settling the tenants, would begin to trade 'a little' with the Indians. Warren sought advice from his father-in-law Stephen De Lancey and wrote to a contact in Schenectady, Major Jacob Glen. In September Warren thanked Glen for his 'great civility to My nephew Mr Johnson whose welfare I have much at heart'.6 Presumably, Johnson had gone first to Schenectady and consulted with Glen, then made his way twenty miles upriver to the grandly named Warrensburgh, in reality a huge tract of thick woodland with occasional clearings, bounded on the north by the wide, swiftly flowing Mohawk and on the east by the narrower Schoharie. Johnson set about turning this land into something like an Irish estate. He later claimed: 'Before I set the Examples, no farmer on the Mohock River ever raised so much as a single Load of Hay,' and 'The like was the case in regard to sheep, to which they were intire strangers until I introduced them.'7

His early days in Warrensburgh cannot have been easy. His nearest white neighbours were Dutch or Palatine Germans. The Mohawks were interested in trade, selling furs and buying clothes, iron implements, guns and gunpowder. Trading was important for Johnson, not just as a source of income, but as a way of forming relationships with the Mohawks, whose goodwill would be vital to the success or failure of Warren's estate. Unfortunately, however, Warren's plans in this regard were seriously askew.

Johnson quickly realised that Warren's land was on the wrong side of the river for trading. The trade routes for both the Dutch and German settlers and the Indians bringing furs to Schenectady and Albany were on the north side of the Mohawk, and Johnson was stuck on the south. The trade goods with which Warren supplied him, moreover, were either inadequate or laughably inappropriate. One lot of stockings that Warren arranged to have sent to him turned out to be 'Mostly Moth Eaten, and I fear the Rest will be so if not Already.' Warren ordered huge amounts of linen from Dublin and some from Scotland to be sent to Johnson, and debited from his account. Yet Indians had little use for linen, which was not suitable for forest life.[8]

These impositions and Warren's way of addressing him like a captain dealing with an inexperienced midshipman began to grate on Johnson. Warren sent him unsaleable goods and demanded animal skins, wheat, corn and peas to be sent downriver to New York in return. He gave detailed advice on the management of the estate, even though he knew nothing of the terrain and the conditions. Initially, Johnson thought of his benefactor Warren as 'the best of friends & only Father in this part of the world'.[9] Gradually, he felt the need to assert his independence.

In spite of the difficulties and frustrations, Johnson gradually increased the number of tenants and cleared enough forest that 'his Farm was the most considerable in the Mohawk country'. The overriding problem was that Warren showed no signs of firming up his promise to hand over much of the estate to Johnson. He seems to have enjoyed the power he got from keeping his nephew in a state of uncertainty. He sent Johnson about £4,000 worth of goods to help establish him as a trader. The arrangement, though, was that Johnson would pay back this money once the goods were sold. Warren made his nephew sign a bond for £5,398, incorporating these and other debts, 'Chiefly or with a View to make him frugal and Diligent in his Business', though he privately informed his agent that 'he did not know whether he would ever Demand the payment of it but chose to have it in his Power'.[10]

At the same time, however, he was continuing to intimate that 'William might reasonably Expect to be generously Considered and rewarded' for his work in developing Warren's properties. Johnson had from Warren, as he later wrote, 'constant assurances . . . ever since he persuaded me over to this country of sharing a part of his very large fortune'.[11] His assumption seems to have been that Warren would eventually sign over the Warrensburgh estate to him. On the strength of these promises, Johnson 'continued slaving himself in Settling of tenants and improving a Spot for his Domain with great Labour, Trouble & many Disappointments, no Undertaking being so difficult & discouraging as the making an Opening & Settlement into so very thick a Forrest or Wood as said estate was'.[12] Caught between the high hopes that Warren had encouraged and his desire to be his own man, Johnson tried to please both his uncle and himself.

Within a year of his arrival in the Mohawk valley, therefore, Johnson, while continuing to oversee the development of Warrensburgh, struck out on his own. He realised that with proper management, there was good money to be made in the Indian trade which was then 'very brisk and lucrative'. So Johnson purchased 'a House and Small Farm on the north side of the Mohawk River about two miles from his first Settlement', which he called, as a grandiloquent statement of intent, Mount Johnson. He established a store and a sawmill on the flatter, more open terrain there. He also hired an interpreter and went on a trading expedition to the new Indian town of Oquaqa, far to the west on the banks of Susquehanna River.[13]

This declaration of independence caused all kinds of trouble. Peter Warren was 'displeased'. So were the Dutch merchants of Albany. By establishing himself as a trader on the north bank of the Mohawk and by setting up connections with Indians as far west as Oquaga, Johnson was effectively intercepting some of Albany's Indian trade. On visits to the town, he was attacked more than once. He later told his brother that 'the Dutch hate both English and Irish' and that he was 'often waylayed by Numbers of them, & had at one Time, at Albany, 8 Lusty dogs of them upon them, of which he got the Better by the assistance only of one Irish man, & almost destroyed them . . .'[14]

The enmity was mutual. Johnson came to despise 'The Albany Grandees whose Soul and Blood are money'.[15] In 1743 those Albany grandees, who made up the Commissioners for Indian Affairs and were in charge of colonial relations with the Indians, sought to take some polite revenge on Johnson by having him summonsed for selling clothes and 'Rum or other distilled Liquors' illicitly to the Indians.[16] Yet even as he was making enemies, Johnson was also making friends. As early as May 1739, Johnson was able to report to Peter Warren that the Mohawk sachems were 'well pleased at my Settling here, and keeping what necessarys they wanted'.[17] By dealing fairly with the Indians, who had become used to merchants who plied them with rum and defrauded them of the value of their furs, he was gradually coming to the attention of Mohawk sachems like Hendrick. In this, he was making alliances far more important to him in the long term than the disgruntlement of Peter Warren or of the Albany merchants.

He was also making another sort of alliance that declared his independence in a different but no less emphatic way. If the Mohawk valley initially presented itself to him as a wild frontier full of outlandish people, strange weather and unfamiliar tongues, he began to see the advantages of being beyond the pale of his family and the intimate and watchful Irish community in which he had grown up. He was now cut off from many familiar comforts, but also free of established respectability.

Shortly after his arrival on the Mohawk, Johnson took a young German servant girl, Catharine Weisenberg, into his house as his sexual partner. Thirty-five years later, in his will, he would refer to her as 'my beloved wife Catharine Johnson'[18] and express his desire for her to be buried with him; but they would not in fact marry for many years, if at all. Their relationship, though clearly affectionate, was partly that of lovers but partly, too, that of older employer with younger servant. If she was his mistress, he was also her master.

Catharine, known to Johnson and his friends as 'Catty', has left behind only the faint traces that are the usual vestiges of the lives of the poor. They reveal her, though, as an attractive, high-spirited and tough-minded young woman. Her antecedents lay somewhere in the Rhenish Palatinate in Germany, an area whose mostly Protestant inhabitants had been driven into large-scale emigration by the ravages of war and famine earlier in the century. Thousands had fled to England and Ireland, and many were subsequently shipped off by the British government to New York, where they settled along the Hudson and Mohawk valleys.

Catharine may have been born in the Palatinate, but it seems more likely that she came from a Palatine community in England, since she arrived in New York from London and spoke good English. She got to America through the same device by which most of Johnson's more obscure compatriots paid for their passage: she bound herself to a ship's captain to be sold on arrival as an indentured servant for a fixed term in return for her board and transport. What can be said with certainty, however, is that she soon broke her bond and ran away from Richard Langden, the ship's captain who had brought her to America. Langden placed an ad in the *New York Weekly Journal* in January and February 1739:

RUN away from Capt. Langden of the City of New-York a Servant maid, named Catherine Weissenburg, about 17 years of Age, Middle stature, Slender, black-ey'd, brown complexion, speaks good English, tho' a Palatine born; had on when she went away, a homespun strip'd wa(i)stcoat and peticoat, blew-stockings and new Shoes, and with her a Calico Wraper, and a striped Calamanco Wraper, besides other Cloaths: Whoever take her up and brings her home, or secures her so that she may be had again, shall have *Twenty Shillings* reward, and all reasonable Charge; and all Person(s) are forewarned not to entertain the said Servant at their Peril.[19]

Her new shoes and manufactured clothes suggest that Catharine was neither destitute nor, in material terms at least, badly treated by Langden. The success of her escape to the Mohawk valley and her ability to take a significant amount of clothes with her suggest that her flight was well planned. All of this points to her joining Palatine relatives or friends already living in northern New York. She may even have run away to join her mother, who subsequently lived with her daughter and Johnson, to whom she was known simply as 'the Old Woman'. Their son, John Johnson, referred to 'Dear Grandmother' and 'Granny' living with them until her death in June 1766.[20]

One folkloric account suggests that she worked initially for two brothers, Alexander and Hamilton Philips, who had settled on the south side of the Mohawk River, a few miles from Warrensburgh. The most colourful account of the beginning of a relationship with Johnson has one of the Philips brothers explaining to a visitor who enquired about her absence: 'Johnson, that damned Irishman, came the other day and offered me five pounds for her, threatening to horse-whip me and steal her if I would not sell her. I thought five pounds better than a flogging, and took it, so he got the gal.' This has the feel of florid embroidery: it is hard to imagine Johnson, a young and still very recent immigrant, storming into a neighbour's home demanding that he hand over a woman. The truth is probably closer to another oral account: that Johnson saw her at the Philips's house, liked the look of the slender, black-eyed girl in her striped petticoat and blue stockings, and made the brothers an offer even more attractive than their young German servant.[21]

It is likely also that, initially at least, Catharine came to Johnson as a housekeeper. That she was young and vulnerable and that she was quickly seduced or cajoled into his bed is equally probable. Yet her well-executed flight from Langden shows an intrepid young woman with a will of her own and probably a supportive network of friends and relatives among the local Palatine community. She was certainly capable of running way if she was unhappy. The circumstances suggest therefore that she was a willing partner for Johnson.

An indication of the beginning of their sexual relationship may well be the engraving on a woman's plain gold ring found with Johnson's remains when they were disinterred in 1862: 'June 1739, 16.' That he took this ring with him to the grave suggests that it was meant to mark an event of great meaning. The odd sequence of the numbers suggests that the '16' is not the date, but her age, which would fit with the 'about 17' of Langden's ad. It may be that he regarded the arrival of her sixteenth birthday as an opportunity to present her with a token of their union that was not a marriage licence. The need for such a token probably came from the evidence that she was pregnant with his child.

Their sexual relationship was certainly well under way by the summer of 1739. Their daughter Ann was baptised by the Reverend Henry Barclay at Fort Hunter on 8 June 1740, and sponsored by Anna Clement, a Dutch neighbour of Johnson's on the north bank of the Mohawk.[22] Given that eighteenth-century baptisms usually followed two or three months after the birth, the likelihood is that Ann was conceived in the late spring of 1739, a fact that would have been obvious to her parents by June.

In November 1741 Johnson and Catharine had a son, John, who was baptised by Barclay in the following February. In 1744 they had their third child, Mary. It is certain that they were not married at the time of these births. In the baptismal records, Catharine is still referred to as 'Wysenberg', 'Wysen Bergh' and 'Wysenberk'.[23] That Barclay did nevertheless baptise the children without apparent demur suggests that this was not especially unusual or scandalous in the conditions of frontier society.

The establishment of this unorthodox family meant, however, that William Johnson had decided within two years of arriving on the Mohawk that he was going to stay in New York. His cousin Mick Tyrrell, who came over with him in 1738, didn't last long and had left by 1740. Johnson, though, was settling in. With his German lover and his American children, he was starting to belong to the polyglot and porous world beyond the boundaries of the old Europe from which he had come. He was on the verge of achieving a new identity and a new name.

6

How the White Man Came to America

═══

Near the end of the eighteenth century, Handsome Lake, a sick and alcoholic old Seneca sachem living on the Allegheny River but thinking himself close to death, was visited by three mystical beings wearing traditional Iroquois dress. They came to him while he was lying in a stupor in a small reservation that was one of the remaining shards of a shattered confederacy. Iroquois culture was itself near death, the great lands of the Six Nations now reduced to a scattering of reservations, the Great Law that encoded their union shredded by mutual suspicion and recrimination.[1] Handsome Lake's unearthly visitors came to help him understand what had happened, so that he could become a great prophet of revival. They told him the story of how the white man came to America.

A long time ago, they said, and across the great salt sea that stretches east, there was a world like ours, ruled by a great queen, where so many people swarmed that they had no place left for hunting.[2] Among the queen's servants was a young man who preached the native religion. One day, the queen told him to clean some old books that lay in a hidden chest. When he was cleaning the last volume, he looked around furtively and listened carefully to check that no one was coming. He opened the book and began to read.

Next morning the young man looked out at the river and saw an island he had never noticed before. On the island, among the trees, was a great golden house. He thought, 'So beautiful a house on so beautiful an island must indeed be the abode of him whom I seek.' He crossed the bridge to the island and walked boldly up to the house. He knocked and a handsome young man welcomed him in. The owner of the golden house spoke to him and said, 'You are wise and afraid of nobody. Listen to me and you will be rich.

'Across the ocean that lies towards the sunset there is another world and a great country and people you have never seen. These people are virtuous, they have no unnatural evil habits and they are honest. A great reward is yours if you will help me. Here are five things that men and women enjoy; take them to these people and make them as white men are. Then shall you be rich and powerful and you may become the chief of all the great preachers here.'

The young man took the bundle containing the five things that men and women enjoy and agreed to do as he was asked. He crossed back over the river and when he reached the bank, he looked behind him and saw that the bridge, the golden house and the island itself had all vanished. It struck him that he had forgotten to ask the handsome stranger if he was indeed the Lord, but it was now too late. He opened the bundle the stranger had given him and found a flask of rum, a pack of playing cards, a handful of coins, a violin and a decayed leg bone. He thought that these were strange things to give to the people beyond the great salt sea, but he remembered the promise of riches and power.

He looked for someone to tell his story to and eventually found a man called Columbus. Columbus got great canoes with wings and sailed to the new world. After he went back and told everyone what he had found, many great ships came bringing many people, each carrying the bundle of five things that men and women enjoy. They spread their gifts among all the people of our world.

Then the vanished man of the golden house that had disappeared laughed and said, 'These cards will make them gamble away their wealth and idle away their time. This money will make them dishonest and covetous and they will forget their old laws. This fiddle will make them dance with their arms about their wives and bring about a time of tattling and idle gossip. This rum will turn their minds to foolishness and they will barter their country for baubles. Then will this secret poison eat the life from their blood and crumble their bones.'

The man in the golden house was of course Hanisse'ono, the evil one; but in time, even his laugh turned to tears when he saw the havoc and misery his trick had effected. 'I think I have made a great mistake,' he said, 'for I did not dream that these people would suffer so much.'

In 1768 Eleazar Wheelock, who was trying to establish a Protestant school for Indian children, went looking among the eastern Iroquois for an exotic gift, suitably redolent of their authentic culture, to send to his patron the Earl of Dartmouth, in England. He wanted a genuine Iroquois artefact, a small token of the native genius, 'perfectly Simple and without the least Mixture of any foreign Merchandise'. To his dismay and embarrassment, he could find nothing except 'some articles which were defaced by Use'.³ As he discovered, almost every artefact the Iroquois owned was sold to them by European traders. The most authentic souvenirs he could have sent would have been English iron pots or blankets from the mills of Lancashire.

Or even, perhaps, a cup of tea. While tea-drinking was still a mark of gentility in Europe, it had already, in William Johnson's time, become a common habit among the Iroquois. Johnson told the Swedish naturalist Peter Kalm, who stayed with him in 1750, that 'several of the Indians who lived close to the European settlements had learned to drink tea'. They drank it, moreover, in the European manner.⁴ Johnson included tea, sugar and teapots for 'Chief Familys' among the presents he gave to Indians. He spent nearly £6 on tea, sugar and punch 'for the many meetings of the different Nations' in June 1755, £4 on twelve quart-sized teapots for similar purposes the following month, and thirteen shillings for a teapot and basin for a treaty conference at Onondaga the next year.⁵

The Indians also acquired a taste for another luxury item to which Europeans were becoming addicted. In Johnson's papers there is a note from a Tuscarora sachem: 'Sarah the wife of Isaac Gives her kind love to your honour. And Desires the favour of a little Chocolate if you please.'⁶

When Johnson came to America, the dominant view of sympathetic Europeans and colonists was that the Indians offered a window onto their own antiquity. They were mankind in its natural state, without the accretions and distortions of power and greed. They were living social fossils. Johnson's friend Cadwallader Colden wrote: 'We are fond of searching into remote Antiquity to know the manners of our earliest progenitors: if I be not mistaken, the Indians are living images of them.' To understand the ancient world, it was necessary simply to study the Indians: 'The present state of the Indian Nations exactly shows the most Ancient and Original Condition of almost every Nation.'⁷

In fact, the Iroquois, far from being a primitive and anachronistic survival of prehistoric man, were at the very cusp of global modernity.

At the root of the emergence of industrial society was the creation and satisfaction of new demands. Global trade and the expansion of European empires led to both an awareness of new products and the possibility of bringing them to western markets. A new kind of person – the consumer – was emerging in the late seventeenth and early eighteenth centuries. Tea and coffee, cotton and china, sugar and spices all became symbols of status and luxury whose value went far beyond their mere utility.

In Europe, consumerism remained, for a long time, the preserve of the elites. The Iroquois and other Indians of north-eastern America more accurately reflected Europe's future than its past because they were all consumers. Their entire societies came to depend on the purchase of manufactured goods. In their adaptation to European colonisation, they created a new kind of economy, and it could not survive without using commodities it did not make for itself. The basics of everyday living – growing crops, hunting game, cooking, fighting, wearing clothes, even conducting traditional ceremonies – all came to involve the use of European consumer goods. While, in Europe, exotic imports were desirable luxuries, for the Iroquois they became vital necessities.

This happened because, with the arrival of Europeans, the Indians discovered, not just new and fascinating objects, but a scale of trade unlike anything they had known before. Though at first trade was understood by them as a form of ritual exchange with a symbolic and diplomatic, rather than a purely economic, meaning, the demand for furs which for them had been of relatively little value, came as a delightful revelation. While Dutch, French and English traders congratulated themselves on getting valuable goods in exchange for useless trinkets, the Indians felt the same smug satisfaction. Europeans wanted beaver skin because its soft under-fur could be used to make felt hats for gentlemen. The natives seldom used beaver. The European fashion for using marten, otter, lynx and black fox skins to trim ladies' gowns created a similar demand for pelts that had not previously been important to the Indians. For many Indians it was almost unbelievable that relatively worthless furs could be traded for extraordinary metal goods. 'The English have no sense,' as one remarked, 'they give us twenty knives like this for one Beaver skin.'[8]

The Iroquois of New York were early and enthusiastic suppliers of this growing market. In 1626, they and the Mohicans brought about

8,000 beaver and otter skins to the Dutch settlements at Fort Orange (Albany) and New Amsterdam (New York). By the late 1650s, 46,000 pelts were traded at Fort Orange alone.9

This enthusiasm was fuelled by a growing taste for the things the Europeans could offer in exchange. Once the magical novelty of strange objects wore off, the Iroquois became choosy customers. One early missionary noted, '[They] are rather shrewd and let no one out-wit them easily. They examine everything carefully and train them-selves to know goods.'10 And the goods they wanted were convenient replacements for their own traditional artefacts that had to be labori-ously made of skin, bone, stone and wood.

The biggest sellers were the coarse woollen blankets called strouds, which the Iroquois found to be lighter than fur and skin, easier to dry and therefore more suitable for a mobile life in a terrain of forest and river. They also came in bright colours which natural berry and root dyes could not match. Indian women were liberated from the tedious work of curing, dressing and cutting skins to make clothes. The high quality and relatively low price of English cloth were so much appre-ciated by the Iroquois and other Indian nations that they represented perhaps the biggest single advantage the English enjoyed over the French colony in Canada in the competition for trade and allies.

When William Johnson began to trade in earnest from 1740 onwards, he provided woollens in shades of blue, red and black as well as flowery serge and striped calicoes in 'lively Colours'. His demands for Indian goods from London were very specific, suggesting that the Indians had expressed definite preferences. He wanted some cloth that was 'Aurora or Crimson', some 'common Red', some 'deep purple Ratteen', ribbons in 'deep red', 'deep blue', 'deep green' and deep yellow; scarlet, blue and green stockings for women; and coats of blue cloth with red cuffs.11

On ceremonial occasions, sachems and boys who were being pre-pared for the chieftaincy wore ruffled shirts without buttons and hats decorated with lace. In 1744, Dr Alexander Hamilton watched Hen-drick lead a procession of Iroquois leaders into Boston for a treaty conference and noted that they 'had all laced hats, and some of them laced matchcoats and ruffled shirts'.12 Gradually, Johnson came to realise that these costumes were not just fashion accessories but were becoming the symbols of chieftainship that even a traditional sachem needed as a visible expression of his status. Over time, he also came to understand the political leverage that could come from the supply of these goods.

Mostly, though, the Iroquois bought lengths of cloth. To shape this cloth into leggings, breechclouts, tie-on sleeves or mantles, however, the women needed scissors and metal knives. The Iroquois had never had a large supply of metal tools before the Europeans came. Great Lakes copper had been valued and traded for thousands of years, but copper is too soft and pliable for most mundane purposes, and in any case large-scale metallurgy was not available to the forest nations. European iron was brighter, more durable and more hard-edged and it saved hours of hard labour. The Indians quickly discovered the great utility of iron axes in cutting down trees. They used hatchets in chopping firewood, awls in punching holes in leather and shell, chisels in breaking open beaver lodges. Butchers' knives replaced brittle flint blades for cutting meat, fish-hooks of iron replaced barbed bone. Hoes broke ground more easily than the breast-bone of a deer, and iron pots and brass kettles were lighter and less fragile than clay pots. As early as 1634, Harmen Meyndertsz van der Bogaert, one of the first Europeans to explore Iroquois territory, noted that the interior doors of the traditional longhouse dwellings had iron hinges: 'In some houses we also saw ironwork: iron chains, bolts, harrow teeth, iron hoops, spikes . . .'[13]

If these products revolutionised the domestic and agricultural world that was largely the domain of women, the impact on the hunting, military and political culture of the men was no less profound. The overwhelming innovation, of course, was the gun. The Iroquois discovered its devastating force by being on the receiving end of the new firepower in their early wars with the French and their Indian allies. They made the acquisition of these weapons a priority in their dealings with the Dutch, and soon mastered this new technology with hard work and fierce discipline. Like other Indian buyers, they became discerning consumers of firearms, going to great lengths to 'set [a new musket] streight, sometimes shooting away above 100 Loads of Ammunition, before they bring the Gun to shoot according to their Mind'.[14] By 1643 the Jesuit Isaac Jogues, taken captive and held in an Iroquois village, noted in a letter to the Governor of New France: 'There are here nearly three hundred arquebuses, and seven hundred Iroquois; they are skilled in handling them.'[15]

Guns had profound social as well as military effects. They largely replaced arrows and spears for the hunting of game. More subtly, they led to an increased sense of individualism and a weakening in the authority of the sachems. Whereas previously Indians fought in tight-knit groups, now each warrior could shelter behind a tree and take pot-shots at his enemy. As Johnson noted: 'Since the Introduction of Fire Arms They no longer fight in close bodies but every Man is his own General. – I am inclined to think this circumstance has contrib-uted to lessen the power of a Chief.'[16] At the same time, however, the new world of trade created a whole new kind of chief: the mediator and diplomat who could secure for his people the material goods they wanted by maintaining alliances with the European traders.

The warrior's new sense of self was enhanced by another European object: the mirror. Looking glasses had reached even the remote Senecas on the western edge of Iroquoia by the 1620s, and by Johnson's time they had become an essential item for every warrior. The same rise in male vanity that created the eighteenth-century European fops and beaus was experienced by the Indians. Peter Kalm noted that, among the Iroquois, 'the men upon the whole are more fond of dressing than the women' and that they carried their mirrors with them all the time.[17] The mirror also to some degree separated women from the preparations for war. Previously, a wife or sister had applied the war-paint to the warrior's face. Now he could paint him-self, weakening the power of the women to veto or sanction war. The mirror also added to the terrible scourge of European diseases that devastated the Indian populations from the sixteenth century on-wards. It made smallpox even more deadly, since many of those who survived the disease could not bear to look at their faces disfigured by pock-marks and committed suicide.

Mirrors themselves generated a further consumer demand among the Iroquois: cosmetics. The Iroquois had long mixed their own dyes with bear grease to make cosmetic colours, but these too were replaced with imported products in which Johnson traded. Chinese vermilion, sold in small packets like tea-bags, gradually took the place of native red ochre for face and body-paints, and verdigris, a colour not previously used, was added to their palette.

The traditional meanings of face-colourings also began to lose their grip. Since it was more important to be painted than to stick with the proper significance of colours, it was possible for Indians who could not get their hands on the proper imported cosmetics even to paint themselves black, the colour of death. As the spokesman for a group of black-faced Mississauga Indians once explained apologetically to Johnson, 'I hope You Don't think that we have Anything bad in our hearts on account of our faces being Coloured black, we assure You we have not, & that they are as white as Snow, it is for want of paint that we have painted black.'[18]

The quantities of body-paint imported were significant. When Johnson was equipping the Iroquois for war against the French in the mid-1750s, he ordered from London twenty dozen looking glasses, five hundredweight of vermilion and two hundredweight of verdigris.[19] He had earlier told Governor Charles Clinton, 'You Cannot fitt out an Indian Warriour Compleatly' if you do not supply, not just guns, knives, powder and shot but also 'Virmillion' and 'Looking Glasses'.[20]

By the time Johnson was establishing himself as a trader, almost every aspect of Iroquois culture, from music to ceremonies to dancing, involved European manufactured goods. Hawk's bells, which were used in European falconry and were one of the first items brought to America for Indian trade by Columbus, were tied around the wrists and ankles for decoration and dancing and remained popular with the Iroquois. Johnson ordered thirty gross on one occasion in the mid-1750s. Brass mouth-harps (known as Jew's harps) were incorporated into Iroquois music-making and Johnson ordered fifty gross at the same time. Even the pipes which were so gravely smoked in the most solemn deliberations at the Iroquois ceremonial centre Onondaga were supplied from London.[21] The strings and belts of wampum, which carried ceremonial messages, and which were originally made from freshwater shells, were now made from imported beads. According to Johnson, a hundred good black wampum beads were worth a beaver skin, or three racoons or two minks.[22]

While most of the consumer goods they bought replaced, directly or indirectly, artefacts they had long made and used themselves, the Iroquois also came to depend on an import that had no equivalent in their previous culture: alcohol. The forest nations had no previous history of using hallucinogens or intoxicants, with the exception of tobacco, and even that was confined to sacred and ceremonial uses. They also had none of the conventions of social drinking which, to some extent, limited the abuse of alcohol among Europeans. Discovering the power of alcohol to create an altered state of consciousness, they drank solely for the purpose of attaining that state and therefore tended to see drink simply as a shortcut to oblivion. The stress of catastrophic epidemics, of aggressively encroaching Europeans and of sporadic wars made the promise of escape irresistible to some. The opportunity not only for profit but also for embezzlement which this presented to unscrupulous traders was just as irresistible. Even scrupulous traders like Johnson regarded rum and brandy as essential components of their stock.

Johnson ruefully informed his brother that the Mohawks 'were moderate untill we corrupted them, & now love Rum Excessively, & are very troublesome, when drunk, & mighty hard to be got Away'.[23] Yet his attitude to the Indian rum trade was revealingly ambivalent. In the role he began to play as a political mediator between the Empire and the Indians, he deplored the way that 'the Indians in general are so devoted to & so debauched by Rum that all Business with them is thrown into confusion by it & my transactions with them unspeakably impeded'. Yet, as a merchant and capitalist, he also saw rum not just as a profitable commodity in itself but as the fuel for the wider process of Indian commerce. Without the desire for rum, as he would admit in a moment of frankness, the Indians' needs could be met with a moderate amount of fur and skins. It was the necessity of paying for alcohol that forced the hunters to increase their productivity. Without alcohol, as Johnson confessed, 'the Indians can purchase their cloathing with half the quantity of Skins, which will make them indolent, and lessen the fur trade'.[24] In this rank hypocrisy, he epitomised the dilemma of the European traders and diplomats who saw rum as a terrible evil, but a necessary and delightfully profitable one.

Aside from alcohol, though, it was not European products themselves but the Indians' failure to learn the mysteries of their manufacture that revolutionised their cultures. At first many Indians were confident that the 'Quera or good Spirit' would teach them how to make these essential European commodities 'when that good Spirit sees fit'.[25] But the European industrial revolution had resulted from centuries of change, and could not be suddenly reproduced within Indian cultures. Not only did the Iroquois come to depend completely on colonial traders for the basic tools of their livelihood, from the hoes that helped to grow the corn and the guns that shot the game to the pots to cook it in, but they also lacked the ability to maintain and repair these goods. The guns were useless without gunpowder, which only the Europeans could supply and the repairs which only European smiths could effect. The history of Johnson's relations with the Iroquois is peppered with pleas for blacksmiths to be sent to their villages.

To see the Iroquois as a consumer society, however, is not to suggest that their attitudes to commodities were the same as those of Europeans. Their demands remained static and relatively simple – clothing, alcohol, tools, guns, gunpowder and personal ornaments – and they did not tend to accumulate goods they did not need. Generosity was, for them, both a mark of power and a means to achieve it. Older ideas of reciprocity retained their importance, so that the giving and receiving of presents still had a ritual and political, as well as a merely economic, function. No agreement was binding without the exchange of gifts, and the scale of the presents was a statement of the importance of the deal. Goods wisely and sensitively bestowed were a sign of leadership and a source of power. Goods received with dignity were also a source of power because they could be shared with the recipient's wider social network, creating and reinforcing other obligations.

What distinguished William Johnson from the run-of-the-mill European trader was that he understood this ritual dimension of exchange in Indian cultures and paid as much attention to it as he did to the accumulation of profits. There were aspects of his Irish background that made him peculiarly sensitive to the nature of Indian culture. Watching him closely and seeing his ability to operate in part on their terms, Hendrick and the other Mohawk sachems began to identify William Johnson as the man they needed.

7

The Holy Well

===

In 1748, when he had been in America for ten years, William Johnson led a group of Iroquois warriors northwards into the no man's land between the British and French Empires. They travelled sixty miles through the forest up to the long, narrow, serpentine lake that formed a watery highway to Lake Champlain and therefore a corridor between the French bastions on the St Lawrence River and the vulnerable frontier settlements of the northern colonies of New York and New England. The French Jesuits had given it a sacred name: Lac Saint Sacrement – the Lake of the Holy Sacrament. They had thus claimed as French and Catholic territory a region the Iroquois regarded as theirs and that the British therefore viewed as falling within their sphere of influence.

This journey had the symbolic purpose of marking and claiming territory. There was nothing to capture in this wilderness of spruce and sedge, of rock and river, and Johnson's party of Iroquois warriors was not equipped to build a fort. The usual way to assert sovereignty over disputed ground was to raise a flag or, as the French had done on the Ohio River, to bury inscribed metal plates in the ground. Johnson did neither of these things. Instead, he had the warriors of the Oneida nation choose a symbolic tree and carve into it the image of the phallic stone, the Onoyot, that represented them and gave them their name.[1] The carving of this emblem, which the warriors painted red, and the symbols of the other Iroquois nations, made the tree itself an image of the Tree of Great Peace, the allegorical cipher of the Iroquois confederacy, under which were 'deep under-earth currents of water flowing to unknown regions'.[2] These mythic images of stone, tree and spring, alien to most Europeans, were an inescapable part of the landscape of William Johnson's Irish childhood.

Even now, the gnarled hawthorn tree beside the holy well is decked out with fragments of pained lives. Colour photographs of children left by parents who want its magic to restore their health; keys driven into the bark by couples who need a house; coins pushed into the cracked branches in the hope that the tree's merciful spirits will return the offering in enough abundance to rescue a family from debt; strips of rags to appease the spirit of the tree; holy medals of the Blessed Virgin, driven into the bark to apply a Christian veneer to the act of supplication; a watch signifying some inscrutable supplication – the tree accepts them all in silence and keeps its ancient vigil by the sacred spring.

The sides of the well itself are lined with rippled concrete since an overenthusiastic restoration job in the 1940s. The spring flows now through a tap, making it easier to catch its potent waters in cupped hands before they disappear underground again and reappear a few yards away as a metallic brown stream that gushes between rocks and ducks into the earth again beneath a rich green field. In the grove that surrounds and shelters the well, the rush and burble of the water chimes with the soft sound of the breeze.

When William Johnson was young, the well, which was on the Warren land and just a few hundred yards from the Warrens' house, attracted huge crowds every year on St John's Eve, 23 June. They were drawn by the belief that water from the well was used by Saint Patrick, who brought Christianity to Ireland in the fifth century, to baptise his converts. In the first hour of St John's Day, the feast of the Baptist, between midnight and one in the morning, the waters would bubble and roil. Whoever drank them in that state would be blessed and healed. The well, back then, was covered with a stone arch and hidden from view by a front wall on which were carved images of Saint Mary and Saint John. The water flowed out through a stone conduit, and those seeking healing stood for a moment on a flagstone beneath it and let the water fall onto their heads and into their mouths.[3]

The ritual, for all the later accretion of saints and feast days, was a survival of the ancient animist religion that had been incorporated into early Irish Christianity. It marked the summer solstice with an interwoven homage to the sun and the dark, to the underworld from which the spring emerged and the bright water that flowed free for a moment before returning to its Stygian origins. It may also have been connected to the nearby hill of Tara, the holiest place of pagan Ireland, where one of the rituals of kingship was associated with the story of a shape-shifting goddess of sovereignty who guards a well and gives a drink to the king who sleeps with her, and where Saint Patrick was said to have converted the pagan kings of Ireland.[4]

Tara itself was an unavoidable part of the landscape of Johnson's childhood. About four miles north of Smithstown, it is only 500 feet high and just 300 feet above the surrounding plains. But the flatness of those midland counties is such that Tara commands an astonishing panorama of Ireland, from Slieve Gullion on the north-east coast to Mount Leinster far to the south, and from Howth Head and the Irish Sea to the east to the hill of Uisneach to the west. It was this 360-degree view of a wide stretch of inviting land that made Tara for thousands of years the symbolic centre of Irish power. Climbing up to play at the top, the young Johnson would have found himself among the ruins of ancient halls and tombs, one of them dating back to the third millennium BC, the vestigial contours of a lost culture's sacred places. Tara had once been a place where this world and the other world mingled and solemn rituals sanctioned power.

He would also have been drawn to the phallic stone that stands on top of one of the burial mounds as a statement of the continuity of life amid death: the Lia Fail. He would have heard the stories that listed the Lia Fail as one of the four great treasures brought to Ireland by the divine race, the Tuatha de Danaan, who subsequently became the inhabitants of a parallel reality. The stories would have appealed to him because he was an O'Neill and the Lia Fail was long associated with the O'Neill claim to kingship of Tara and thus pre-eminence over other Irish rulers.[5]

This sense of inhabiting a landscape that had a mythic layer just beneath the soil was very much alive in Johnson's youth. The holy well on the Warrens' land was not just a piece of local colour. Its annual ritual, to which people flocked from all over Meath and the surrounding counties, was a serious national concern. It horrified and disturbed the Protestant rulers of Ireland, probably because the night-time gathering in the wood at Warrenstown to enact a pagan ritual was a wild, unruly affair. With few priests around to enforce their authority, and men and women mingling after an evening's drinking, it was probably marked by both sexual and political licence.

Even beyond the febrile context of early eighteenth-century Ireland, holy wells were offensive to Protestant sensibilities. They were vestiges of a pagan past and therefore associated not just with Catholicism, but with Satanism. Even half a century after William Johnson's death, a Protestant polemicist was reminding his readers:

Holy wells throughout Ireland are remnants of Heathen superstition . . . conse-crated to . . . imaginary deities who were supposed particularly to delight in groves and fountains of water; and who, resorting thither to disport or enjoy themselves, rendered the locality sacred by their presence; and in these places such of the peo-ple as wished to ensure their favour or protection used to hang garlands upon trees and leave offerings of wine, milk and honey; fancying also that any sudden misfortunes or sickness, either to themselves, their families, or their cattle, was produced by the anger of those inferior deities, they hoped, by attendance at their favourite places of resort, and the offerings they made them, to appease their wrath . . . In those various particulars we find an exact counterpart of the pro-ceedings which take place at many of the holy wells of Ireland.[6]

To this general disdain was added, in Johnson's youth, the sharp scent of sedition. The political significance of the pilgrimage to St John's Well – 10,000 unsupervised Catholics gathered on the lands of known Jacobites on the outskirts of the capital city – was impossible to ig-nore. On St John's Day in 1710, just five years before Johnson was born, the (entirely Protestant) Irish parliament discussed an emergency motion tabled in alarm at the size and unruliness of the congregation. Its text evokes the anxiety stirred in the hearts of civil Protestant gen-tlemen by the strange rites that were enacted in Warrenstown:

The House being informed by several members that above 10,000 Papists are, at this Juncture, assembled from several parts of the Kingdom under pretence of Religious Worship, at a place called St John's Well, within fourteen Miles of this City, to the great Disturbance and Hazard of the public peace, and Safety of the Realm, Resolved, Nemine Contradicente, That an Address be forthwith made to his excellency the Lord Lieutenant, that he will be pleased immediately to give such necessary Directions as may effectually put a Stop to the said tumultuous, dangerous, and unlawful Assembly. *Ordered* that such Members of this House as are of Her Majesty's Most Honourable Privy Council, do attend his Excellency the Lord Lieutenant, and lay the Resolution of this House before his Excellency.[7]

Those who persisted in attending were threatened with being 'fined, imprisoned and Whipt'.[8] Enforcing such a prohibition, however, would have required a major military operation every year, and the pilgrimage continued as before.

Had he gone on to be a lawyer in Dublin or an army officer in France, these aspects of Johnson's childhood would probably have created nothing more than colourful memories or at most an element of antiquarian interest. In America, however, he found himself in a culture where belief was not a simple matter of accepting one true faith and discarding all others, but of laying one system of understanding on top of another so that they formed shifting strata of meaning. Just as the culture he grew up in encompassed Protestant rationalism, Catholic faith and an older layer of pre-Christian ritual and myth, the Indian culture he had entered did not see attendance at church, honouring the Great Spirit and appeasing the Manitous or spirits that pervaded the natural world, as mutually exclusive activities. The Iroquois view of the world as one in which parallel realities co-existed and sometimes met, in which the power of the dead must be taken seriously, and in which all things were alive with spirits, was not nearly as alien to this white European Christian as might be supposed.

In a sense, the Indians William Johnson was now moving among were just as much emigrants as he was. The ever-increasing presence of the French, the British and the other incomers from Ireland, Holland, Germany and elsewhere was gradually removing the indigenous population from the world it knew. Over the previous two centuries, much in their societies had quite literally disappeared, as new diseases wiped out vast numbers of Indians. Whole nations and entire languages were obliterated.

The Kiowa of the southern plains have a legend in which a Kiowa man meets Smallpox riding on a horse. 'Where do you come from and what do you do and why are you here?' he asks. 'I am one with the white men – they are my people as the Kiowa are yours. Sometimes I travel ahead of them and sometimes behind . . . I bring death. My breath causes children to wither like young plants in spring snow. I bring destruction. No matter how beautiful a woman is, once she has looked at me she becomes as ugly as death. And to men I bring not death alone, but the destruction of their children and the blighting of their wives. The strongest of warriors go down before me. No people who have looked on me will ever be the same.'[9]

The work of destruction begun by microbes was gradually pushed forward by human settlement. In 1753 the Onondaga sachem Red Head complained to William Johnson in tones that could have been uttered at any time from the early seventeenth century to the late nineteenth: 'We don't know what you Christians, French and English together, intend. We are so hemmed in by both, that we have hardly a Hunting place left, in a little while, if we find a Bear in a Tree, there will immediately Appear an Owner for the Land to Challenge the Property, and hinder us from killing it which is our livelyhood, we are so perplexed, between both, that we hardly know what to say or to think.'10

Knowing what to say and think was especially hard for the Iroquois, because the traumatic changes brought by European warfare and disease had gradually eroded their elaborate system for creating and sustaining a united policy. That system had evolved as a way of diffusing political power among the different nations of the confederacy. As the keepers of the two doors of the longhouse, the Mohawks and Senecas were the 'elder brothers' of the confederacy. At a council, they began the debate among themselves, then passed the question over to the 'younger brothers', the Cayugas and Oneidas. Their consensus was then passed back to the elder brothers for confirmation, before finally going to the Onondagas for decision. The Onondagas' role was to test the emerging consensus against the Great Law. If it passed the test, they handed the decision back to the elder brothers, who announced it to the council.

This system was still the political and religious context of Iroquois life when William Johnson became involved with it in the early 1740s. It had, however, come under catastrophic strain. In the seventeenth century, when France established its colony on the St Lawrence, its main aim was to maximise its profits from the fur trade with its Huron allies. The Iroquois, traditional enemies of the Huron, posed the major threat to that goal. They turned to the Dutch settlers of the New Netherlands, who had established a trading post at Albany in 1614, for guns and trade goods while raiding New France's Indian allies for the thicker northern furs that brought higher prices than their own rapidly diminishing supply of pelts. They also sought captives to replace their members lost to epidemics and conflict.

After the English supplanted the Dutch in New York in 1664, Iroquois diplomats established relations with the new power in a treaty known as the Covenant Chain. Whereas, in the metaphorical language they used for diplomacy, the Iroquois had referred to their treaty with the Dutch as an iron chain, the link to the English was imagined as a chain of silver, marking the transition from a largely material connection to a political and economic alliance. After 1677 the Covenant Chain was expanded to link them not just to New York but also to Massachusetts and Maryland. In return for protection from the French, the Iroquois helped the English colonies to suppress Indian rebellions within their territories and to push back colonial frontiers by removing weaker tribes.

English assistance against the French proved inadequate, however. In the 1690s French and Algonquian invaders burned villages and crops, killed warriors and threatened the delicate balance of subsistence, leaving the Iroquois depleted, poor and often hungry. These severe losses forced the Iroquois to make peace with the French and their Indian allies in the so-called Grand Settlement of 1701. Peace came at a price: the Iroquois had to abandon the hunting territories they claimed west of Detroit and allow Onontio (their name for whoever held the office of French colonial governor) to arbitrate their conflicts with his Indian allies. They also promised to remain neutral in any future Anglo-French wars. Partly to ensure the fulfilment of this promise, the French built Fort Detroit in the west and encouraged Alqonquian peoples to settle around it as a potential instrument to chastise the Iroquois in the event of any breach of faith. At the same time, the French actually discouraged Algonquian attacks on the Iroquois for fear of driving them into the arms of the English.

This left the Iroquois in a complex diplomatic situation, with treaty obligations to both the English and the French. But it also gave them – in the short term at least – peace, access to a competitive market in European trade goods, and a dominant role among the Indians of the North-East.

This whole process of engagement with Europeans had been demographically disastrous, however, and particularly so for the people that Johnson had settled among, the Mohawks. Disease, warfare and economic disruption thinned the Iroquois population in general. Not only, however, did the Mohawks, as the most easterly of the Iroquois nations, bear the brunt of the wars, but they also lost a significant part of their population to Canada and Catholicism. Successful Jesuit missions to the Mohawk villages from the late 1660s onwards had created a deep split in the nation. The many Mohawks converted to Catholicism were brought within the political ambit of New France. Amid rising tensions, these Catholic Indians were pushed out into Canada, where they settled almost 250 miles to the north of their homeland, at Caughnawaga, above the rapids of Sault St Louis, near Montreal. By the time of Johnson's arrival, two-thirds of all Mohawks were living in Canada. Whole lineages, including the holders of some of the traditional league titles, were thus missing from Mohawk society.

These repeated blows had taken a dreadful toll on the nation's power. In 1630 the Mohawks, as 'elder brothers' and the largest group in the confederacy, were a mighty and much-feared people, with an estimated population of 7,740 people. The other elder brothers, the Senecas, had about 4,000 people. By the time William Johnson arrived in America, the remaining Mohawk population had collapsed to just 580 men, women and children, while the Senecas still had about 2,000. By 1748 the French governor of Canada, the Marquis de la Galissonière, could refer to 'an Indian nation so insignificant as that of the Mohawks'.[11]

The Mohawks had been further diminished as economic actors in the late 1720s, when the British built a trading post at Oswego, a port on the eastern shore of Lake Ontario, 120 miles to the west of their territories. The establishment of Oswego meant that western Indian nations who wished to trade their furs with the British no longer had to send them all the way to Albany or Schenectady. The fur trade thus no longer passed through the Mohawk village of Canajoharie. At the same time, the Albany magnates who controlled New York's relations with the Indians had become more interested in the Canadian Indians who carried furs south from Montreal to their Hudson River depots than with their own immediate neighbours. Caught in this web of crises, the Mohawk leadership needed to find a way to restore their nation's prestige, wealth and influence, both within and beyond the Iroquois confederacy.

The way to do this was obvious enough. The visit of Hendrick and the other Mohawks to London in 1710 had been part of a strategy of identifying the nation as the strongest link in the Covenant Chain that bound the Iroquois to Britain. The one great asset the Mohawks still had was their ritual and diplomatic position as elder brothers of the confederacy. So long as the British saw them as the key to influencing the confederacy as a whole, they had serious standing in the imperial mind, and that standing in turn could renew and sustain their prestige within the confederacy. They could be at once the British door into the Iroquois confederacy and the Iroquois window onto the colonial world.

The whites who formed their link to British power, however, the Albany-based merchants on the Commission for Indian Affairs, were more interested in dealing with the Canadian Indians who supplied their fur trade. Their neglect of the Mohawks, and a series of attempted land frauds by Albany merchants, convinced Hendrick in particular that the Mohawks needed a new intermediary between themselves and the Empire. In 1745 Hendrick complained at a council in Albany that the Mohawks 'were become the property of Albany people, they were their dogs'.[12] He was willing to express these complaints so openly because he had by then found what he needed.

The New York colonial politician Cadwallader Colden noted of William Johnson that there was 'something in his natural temper suited to the humour of the Indians'.[13] That something was a fusion of the circumstances that created him and his own individual personality. As Johnson once explained of the Indians, 'Personal regard & attachment has vast influence over their actions.'[14] Johnson learned quickly that the Indians had little interest in abstract institutions of power and preferred to have them embodied in an individual. They used fixed names for the holders of important colonial offices with whom they interacted, so that these great powers could be imagined as if they were a person. The governor of New France was always Onontio, the head of the Jesuit order always Achiendase, the governor of Virginia Assaragoa, the governor of New York Corlear, and so on. Some time in the early 1740s, Johnson came to have a name of his own and to gain through personal regard and attachment a vast influence over the Mohawks.

Johnson was physically an imposing man. He was proud enough of his physique to add a note to a portrait of himself he sent home to Warrenstown in 1754, asking his father to have it touched up: 'The greatest fault in it is, the narrow hanging Shoulders, which I beg you may get altered as Mine are very broad and square.'[15] The New England gunsmith Seth Pomeroy, who knew him in the 1750s, described him as 'a man of large size, with a pleasant face, piercing eyes, ready communication, and pleasing manners though sometimes very abrupt'.[16] Anne Grant, who as a little girl met him during the same period, described him as 'an uncommonly tall, well made man: with a fine countenance; which, however, had rather an expression of dignified sedateness, approaching to melancholy'.[17] Both of these descriptions hint at a rather ambiguous presence, pleasing and courteous but sometimes abrupt, well made but with a touch of melancholy about him.

This combination created his charisma. He was big, strong, energetic and confident, and the Indians, who valued physical prowess very highly, were obviously impressed by these attributes. Yet his background had also given him a watchful quality that prevented his presence from being too blunt or direct. He had learned from childhood to accommodate himself to different kinds of people, to take stock of the company he was in, to listen before he spoke.

An anonymous description of him published in the *Gentleman's Magazine* in London in 1755 but clearly written in New York emphasised Johnson's ability, learned in his Irish Catholic youth, to adapt to any social environment:

He is particularly happy in making himself beloved by all sorts of people, and can conform to all companies and conversations. He is very much of the fine gentleman in genteel company. But as the inhabitants next to him are mostly Dutch, he sits down with them and smokes his tobacco, drinks flip, and talks of improvements, bear and beaver skins. Being surrounded with Indians, he speaks several of their languages well, and has always some of them with him.'[18]

This chameleon quality made him self-assured without being bumptious, able to converse with different kinds of people without becoming insensitive to those differences. Though he never spoke 'several' Indian languages, he did become reasonably fluent in Mohawk. He also either learned or already had the style of speaking of an Indian sachem: dignified, considered, never garrulous, but always eloquent. Anne Grant noted: 'He appeared to be taciturn, never wasting words on matters of no importance: but highly eloquent when the occasion called forth his powers.'

It is not insignificant that Johnson's family had a long tradition of providing distinguished churchmen, for the Europeans who had best mastered Indian modes of eloquence were the Jesuits. One Jesuit report to Paris from the mission to the American Indians noted: 'As these people are great haranguers and frequently make use of allegories and metaphors, our Fathers adapt themselves to this custom of theirs to win them to God.'[19] Johnson, coming from a culture in which shifts of language had created a particular sensitivity to words, was able to hit the right notes in Mohawk rhetoric.

He was, above all, unhampered by religious disdain. His experience of moving from one church to another for purely pragmatic rewards had left him without the prejudices of a devotee. While many English colonists regarded Indian religious practices and beliefs with fear and suspicion, Johnson was quite at ease with the general Mohawk religious attitude. For most of his Indian neighbours, Christianity sat lightly on top of their own creation myths, animist beliefs in natural spirits and elaborate rituals designed to keep grief at bay. Having grown up beside St John's Well, and among people whose practices were often seen as darkly satanic by their betters, Johnson would not have had any great aversion to this system of belief and behaviour. The rituals of initiation into the Mohawk nation would have held no fears for him.

In their decision to adopt Johnson, the Mohawks were seeking to make a firm friend of a man who was visibly prospering among them. His initial forays into trade had expanded by the early 1740s into a thriving operation. He now supplied traders about to make their way westward along the river to Oswego with the goods they would exchange for furs. On their return, he bought their furs and skins and sent them directly down the Hudson to New York, cutting the Albany middlemen out of the deal. He also sent the produce of his own and the neighbouring lands – wheat, flour, peas – down to the city and imported dry goods and rum in return. For Mohawks disgruntled with the Albany merchants, and looking for a new channel between themselves and the British, the evidence of Johnson's rise as a new and friendly force was heartening.

Though it is not possible to say when William Johnson was initiated into the Mohawk nation as a sachem, it is certain that some time between 1740 and 1745, probably around 1742, he was conducted by the warriors and sachems to the outskirts of one of the Mohawk villages. Already he had shaved his head and prepared a short song in Mohawk that he was to sing as he entered and the proper dance for the occasion. Now, his cheeks, chin and forehead were painted with vermilion mixed with bear's grease. Belts of wampum were hung about his neck. As he entered the village, the shrill shout went up that was used when a live person, rather than a dead scalp, was adding to the nation's spiritual strength. From the entrance to the centre of the village, he ran the gauntlet through gentle symbolic blows meant to banish any evil spirits that hung about him. Then the sachem, probably Hendrick, made a long speech of welcome before three young women led him down to the river and plunged him in. When he was immersed, they washed away his strangeness so that he could emerge as a new man with a new name.

The name chosen for him was Warraghiyagey. It meant, as Johnson would later tell his brother, 'A Man who undertakes great Things'. Because it would become one of the most famous Indian names across the North American continent, it would be assumed that it indicated from the start the choice of Johnson as a great political leader. Yet Johnson's son-in-law Daniel Claus wrote that Johnson was given the name because the Mohawks had watched him toiling to clear Peter Warren's lands and gave him 'a Name in their Language applicable or signifying a great & toilsome Undertaking'. A rough translation of the name might be 'Chief Much Business'.[20]

The Mohawks were never naive enough to believe that Johnson's induction into the nation made him simply one of them. Indeed, if Johnson had in fact become just another member of the tribe, his usefulness would have been greatly diminished. His value as a mediator was precisely that he knew how the English world worked, that he could translate their needs and demands into the terms that these awkward and often ignorant foreigners could understand. They needed him to be part of the imperial system. Yet they did also feel that a part of Johnson was theirs. Hendrick expressed this directly to Governor George Clinton in July 1751 when he explained that 'the one half of . . . Johnson belonged to His Excellency [Clinton] and the other to them.'[21]

8

Raw Head and Bloody Bones

Years of training made him alert even in sleep and now his mind registered the soft swish of snowshoes coming towards him. It was two o'clock on a cold northerly morning in March 1748, in the woods to the north of Mount Johnson. The Mohawk war chief Gingego was dozing lightly on the ground with two warriors of his own nation and three white men beside him. He woke the others in time to see by the flickering light of the fire the terrifying sight of thirty Indians moving to surround them. Most of them were Caughnawagas – Mohawks who had become Catholic and moved to Canada – so Gingego understood the language in which they shouted when his comrades began to flee through a thicket and the cry went up from the chief of the attackers: 'Pursue them, they have gone that way, we are men, we will have them all!'

Though he had hidden behind a tree with another Mohawk, Gingego was too proud not to reply and he called out, 'I am Gingego the Mohawk, a man who will not fly from you or mankind.' He gave his war cry of three great yelps and fired at the Caughnawagas. From the volley fired in reply, he was shot through the thigh and the body and the warrior who was with him was also hit. Their enemies cut their heads off, scalped them, flayed the skin from their faces, and then cut off their noses, ears and lips. They stuck the heads on stakes and held them to the fire, so that, when they were eventually found by their friends, they were half-roasted. The headless bodies were mutilated and mangled and planted shoulders down in the snow, their heels sticking in the air like the branches of dead, blasted trees. Of the rest of the party, one, a young Dutchman who lived on William Johnson's estate, was killed and scalped, and another was taken away as a captive.

Two of the six, one European and one Mohawk, escaped and made their way back to Johnson's house to tell what they had seen and heard. A large, heavily armed group, comprising about fifty whites and fifty Indians, went out to recover the remains. They came back to Johnson's house with the blackened heads and the raw, butchered bodies. The search party and the settlers and Mohawks who gathered to see the awful sight took their rage out on Johnson. All of this, they shouted, was his fault. The Mohawks were especially enraged at him 'for bringing us so far into the war', for sending them out in such small groups against a mighty enemy, and for failing to bring them the help that the British had promised. 'This Cruel Affair', a worried Johnson wrote to Governor Clinton, 'portends a Bloody Summer.'[1]

The war he had brought them so far into was a conflict between Britain and France sparked in 1744 by a dynastic dispute about the succession to the throne of faraway Austria. When Maria Theresa ascended the Habsburg throne in 1740, the Kings of Spain, Bavaria and Saxony all claimed the right to succeed. The subsequent power struggle gradually drew in France, Britain and Prussia and cost around 800,000 lives. That a few of them were Mohawk was, to a significant degree, Johnson's doing.

Johnson could have avoided direct involvement in the war, but his own interests and his family ties argued otherwise. He had spent eight years carving out his own fiefdom in upper New York, and stood to lose his lands, trade and influence in the event of a victory for the French and their Indian allies. Moreover, by November 1745 his younger brother Warren Johnson had joined their uncle Peter Warren in the British forces and was sailing to Boston. By July 1746 Warren Johnson, now a captain, was raising a company of a hundred Irishmen, called the Royal Irish Company, for a possible attack on Canada. At the same time, their cousin Mick Tyrell, who had been with Johnson in his first few years in New York, was now a naval captain and was gaining glory and riches by capturing French vessels and their cargo.[2] Most spectacularly of all, Peter Warren, commanding six ships of the line and five frigates, had successfully besieged the vital French fortress of Louisbourg on Cape Breton Island off the Canadian coast in the early summer of 1745. As a reward, he was made the first British governor of Cape Breton and a rear admiral.

This engagement of his wider family itself pointed to the broader context in which the Warrens and Johnsons were being presented with an opportunity to disavow, once and for all, their traitorous Jacobite heritage and stand forth as loyal subjects of Britain's Hanoverian kings. As a significant sideshow in the War of the Austrian Succession, the French supported Bonnie Prince Charlie's invasion of Scotland in August 1745, transforming the spectral Jacobite threat into a real challenge to the established order. The Jacobites, having rallied the Gaelic-speaking Highland clans, took control of Scotland and, by the end of the year, had pushed into England and got as far south as Derby. This was not a time for ambitious men with strong Jacobite and Catholic antecedents to hang back and remain discreet. Loyalty had to be declared and proven. Warren Johnson, who had slipped into military service through his uncle's patronage while still a Catholic, converted to Protestantism, on his return to Ireland in 1749.[3]

Even before the war broke out on the New York frontiers, there had been a constant background of paranoia about the loyalties of Irish Catholics. When fire swept through part of New York City in 1740, destroying official and military buildings, it was initially blamed on a conspiracy of black slaves, but the following year, the lieutenant governor informed the Board of Trade in London: 'It is now apparent that the hand of popery is in it, for a Romish Priest having been tryed was upon full and clear evidence convicted of having a deep share in it; we have besides several other white men in prison and most of them (it is thought) Irish Papists.'[4] While this was mere hysteria, there were in fact reasonable grounds for suspecting the loyalty of at least some Irish soldiers who ended up fighting the French in North America. One French military report from 1746 records the arrival of three Irish deserters from the British forces who claimed that 'more than 30 Irish soldiers were desirous to follow their example'.[5]

In this context of real and imagined treachery, the Johnsons had to declare their allegiance more loudly than most. Warren Johnson's Royal Irish Company, though a small gesture in overall military terms, was a richly symbolic affirmation, shadowing as it did the much larger Irish Brigade in the French army. William Johnson's first engagement in the war effort was in recruiting forty or fifty men from among his Irish tenants for his brother's company, among them James Rogers and Pat Flood, who were old friends from Warrenstown.[6] In August 1746, however, Johnson's involvement became much more significant. The New York governor George Clinton dismissed the Albany-based

Indian commissioners and appointed Johnson as 'Colonel of the Warriors of the Six Nations', with instructions to enlist and equip as many whites and Indians as possible for a campaign against the French and their allies.

The appointment of one man in the place of the commission that had always managed relations between New York and the Six Nations was official recognition of Johnson's unique standing. Explaining the move subsequently, Clinton's secretary and political ally Cadwallader Colden wrote: 'At that time Mr Johnson distinguished himself among the Indians by his indefatigable pains among them, and by his compliance with their humours in his dress and conversation with them.'7

It had become clear from the start of hostilities that the frontier war would be conducted by small raiding parties moving lightly over the lakes and through the forests to attack and burn settlements, take scalps and prisoners and withdraw. It would be, in other words, an Indian war. Native warriors, with their resilience, mobility, alertness and familiarity with hit-and-run warfare, were better at this kind of fighting than the European armies with their formal tactics, heavy regimentation and set-piece mentality. Johnson believed: 'It is a very unequal match between Indian and Christian, in this close woody country.'8 He told his brother Warren that he would 'almost reckon 300 Indians above a Match for 1000 Regulars, in the Woods, they are very great Walkers, bear fatigue and [are] quick sighted . . . Indians are not near soe much afraid of fighting against white people as against Indians.'9 This belief in the military superiority of Indian warriors over European regulars in North American conditions went against the grain of colonial assumptions, but it greatly fortified Johnson's respect for the importance of the Iroquois.

Johnson's understanding of the pivotal importance of Indian alliances in the unfolding conflict was borne out by the effectiveness of French and Indian raids into New York and New England, which gradually drove outlying settlers in the frontier country to take refuge in larger towns like Albany. Yet a response in kind to these attacks would have to overcome not only the Iroquois inclination to neutrality but also the tendency of the Albany traders to support such a policy.

Johnson's title as Colonel of the Six Nations was in fact rather fanciful, since the Six Nations as a whole had little interest in a war with the French. The confederacy had benefited from a thirty-year peace, during which it had developed a sophisticated policy of holding the balance of power between the French and the British while itself remaining neutral in the Europeans' disputes. The older sachems, moreover, remembered that the last time the British had recruited significant numbers of Iroquois warriors for an attack on Canada, in 1709 and 1711, the expeditions had turned into fiascos.

The overall tenor of Iroquois policy was still that articulated by the Onondagas at a league council meeting in 1709. Lying as they did 'between two powerful nations each able to exterminate them and both interested in doing so when they no longer needed their help', the Iroquois should try to keep both the French and the British 'always in necessity of conciliating them, and consequently preventing either from prevailing over the other'.[10] This strategy for survival demanded an active neutrality, in which the two imperial powers were appeased and flattered when necessary but in which wholehearted support for either of them made no sense. Johnson's task of recruiting the Six Nations as a whole onto the British side was in direct conflict with the confederacy's broader strategy.

Previous efforts to alter this strategy had failed. Governor Clinton had held a conference with the Six Nations in June 1744 and had urged them to abandon their various villages, gather together under British protection, protect the British trading post at Oswego, and expel all French agents from their midst. He received a polite but sceptical and evasive reply. The Iroquois speaker pointedly remarked that his people 'd[id] yet well remember' the abortive expeditions against Canada over thirty years previously. He declared that the confederates were 'inclined to Peace, till the Enemy attack some of His Majesty's subjects, and then we will join together to defend ourselves against them.'

In relation to Oswego, he complained: 'Goods are sold so dear at that place that we cannot say we think it advantageous to us.' As for expelling French agents: 'Shou'd we now take hold of any French that come among us, We shou'd be the Aggressors; Wherefore we leave it to you to do with the French that may come into our Country as you shall think proper.' Apart from a vague, and almost certainly insincere, promise to gather together as Clinton wished, the Iroquois had committed themselves to nothing.[11] Indeed, to balance this bland conference with Clinton, they had then gone to Montreal to meet the French governor there.

The clear reluctance of the confederacy was matched by a lack of enthusiasm among significant factions of New York colonial society. The economic interests of the Dutch traders at Albany argued against an open breach with New France. They carried on an illicit but flourishing trade with Montreal. The best-quality fur came from the coldest regions to the north, and these lay, of course, under French control. Furs were smuggled from Canada and traded for the English strouds that the Indians preferred and that in turn could be traded for more furs. In 1725 two Albany traders, John Groesback and Dirk Schuyler, estimated that 80 per cent of the beaver shipped from New York to Europe was obtained from French smugglers.[12] Even though the trade was illegal on both sides, there were extensive agency and credit arrangements between the two towns.[13] The principle middlemen in this trade, moreover, were the Catholic Mohawks who had settled in Canada. A war setting not just England and France but Mohawk against Mohawk threatened a fatal disruption of the clandestine trade. The Albany merchants therefore had, as Clinton reported in exasperation to the Duke of Newcastle, 'hopes as Dutchmen to have continued a neutrality with the French Indians as they did last war'.[14]

The powerful Livingston clan, whom Clinton denounced as a 'vile family', was equally loath to see its trading interests jeopardised by a war. To complicate matters even further, Philip Livingston, the colony's Secretary for Indian Affairs, was claiming and surveying a large tract of Mohawk land which he purported to have bought.

Hendrick's anger at Livingston's manoeuvres meant that the one person on whom Johnson ought to have been able to rely was also disaffected. Hendrick had been further infuriated by a sequence of events in the autumn of 1744, when a panic had spread through the Six Nations. The brilliant French agent Daniel-Marie Chabert de Joncaire, a half-Iroquois who lived among the Senecas, had spread a rumour that the British and the French were secretly plotting a joint assault on the Six Nations. The rumour had gathered strength even among the Mohawks, and Hendrick's normally pro-British position had been seriously undermined. He had sent a message to the Albany commissioners, demanding that they take steps to reassure the Iroquois, but had received no reply. The commissioners had intervened only in January 1745, when the Mohawks at Tionondoroga had actually begun to flee in fear of their lives, and then at the request, not of Hendrick, but of the Reverend Henry Barclay.[15]

Hendrick's rage at this snub was so strong and enduring that it burst out in incandescent and incoherent fury at a formal conference with Clinton and his officials in Albany a year later. Having raised the incident, he launched into a long rant which left the whites puzzled and the Indians uneasy. According to the official record,

The said Hendrick ran on for above an hour in an harangue which the Interpreter could make little or nothing of, and at which the rest of the Indians seemed to His Excellency and the Gentlemen present to be ashamed, of which opinion were both the Interpreters who were better acquainted with the behaviour of the Indians . . . neither head nor tail could be made of Hendrick's oration after a long pause and consultation, of which every one present was tired.[16]

While Clinton concluded that Hendrick was engaging in mere theatrics and had invented the whole story as a lever to prise more presents out of the colonists, the evident puzzlement of his fellow sachems suggests that he was genuinely enraged.

The particular resentments of the Mohawks and the determination of the other nations to maintain their neutrality meant that this second Albany conference of 1745 also failed to produce any firm evidence of Iroquois willingness to go to war against the French. If anything, the confederacy stressed its independence of the British, announcing its intention to send delegates to Canada to seek 'satisfaction for the wrongs they have done our Brethren' and only in the event of a refusal to 'use the Hatchet against them'.[17] While this might look on the surface like a commitment to eventually join the British war effort, it was in fact a clever formula for the continuation of negotiations with both sides.

With the confederacy determined to remain neutral, his Mohawk friends disaffected, the Albany faction working to maintain its Montreal trade and New York riven by internal political conflicts that made a coherent war effort impossible, Johnson had excellent reasons to avoid responsibility for the defence of the frontier. He had, however, even better reasons to get involved. The war presented him with both the imperative to protect what he had and the opportunity to acquire power.

Johnson's own economic and political interests were tied up with his ability to mobilise Iroquois resistance to French attacks. His growing wealth as a trader and land-holder was threatened by the insecurity of the borderlands. These private motives for repelling the French overlapped with the need to get some urgency into the British and colonial war effort. In order to recruit colonial power to the defence of the frontier, he needed political influence. In order to yield political influence, he needed to be accepted as a power in the land. To the meeting of all of these necessities, the Iroquois, and particularly the Mohawks, were crucial.

He was almost certainly active in private diplomacy with the Mohawks before his formal appointment as Colonel of the Six Nations. A group of Mohawks told Governor Clinton in July 1747: 'For these twelve months past and better, we have minded nor listened to nobody else' but Johnson.[18] His appointment resulted from the urgings of some of the Iroquois sachems, probably including Hendrick. Clinton referred, in a letter to the Lords of Trade, to Johnson 'being chosen by themselves to be their Colonel'.[19] It is surely not accidental therefore that the appointment coincided with a marked shift in the tone of the Six Nations' response to British requests for a military alliance. Clinton issued his formal letter of commission on 27 August 1746, which suggests that the arrangement had been agreed with Johnson some days before that. On 23 August, in a meeting in Albany with Clinton and a delegation from Massachusetts, the Six Nations had formally declared for the first time that they were now willing to go to war against the French and their Indian allies.

This conference had given Johnson the opportunity to display for the first time in colonial society his own status as an Indian leader. Though he had as yet no formal position in the colonial power structure, he contrived to arrive at Albany as a mighty war leader. He did this by announcing himself, not as a white settler and trader, but as a Mohawk war chief. He came dressed in blanket, loincloth, leggings and moccasins, his face painted with vermilion and verdigris, his hair drawn back and decorated with ribbons. The Mohawks followed him. Cadwallader Colden, who was present, described the scene:

When the Indians came near the Town of Albany, on the 8th of August, Mr Johnson put himself at the Head of the Mohawks, dressed and painted after the Manner of an Indian War-Captain; and the Indians who followed him, were likewise dressed and painted as is usual with them when they set out in War. The Indians saluted the Governor as they passed the Fort, by a running Fire; which his excellency ordered to be answered by a Discharge of some Cannon from the Fort; he afterwards received the Sachems in the Fort hall, bid them Welcome and treated them to a Glass of Wine.[20]

The carefully staged nature of this display suggests a done deal. Johnson presented his military leadership of the Mohawks as a fait accompli a fortnight before Clinton formally confirmed it. What seems to have happened is that Johnson had assured the Iroquois that he would lead them in raids against Canada and they in turn had agreed to renounce their neutrality in principle and allow at least some warriors to take part in these raids. There was probably a tacit understanding that the confederacy as a whole was not about to enter a full-scale war against the French. The Iroquois had granted Johnson a limited capacity to engage in a war of reprisal and counter-terror. He was not undertaking to engage in conventional battles, but to 'harass and alarm' the French and allied populations as reprisals for similar attacks on British colonial settlements in New York and New England.

This would be an Indian-style war, conducted outside the rules of European conflict. In some respects, it suited the Iroquois. In military terms, they would have the upper hand over Europeans in this hit-and-run mode of forest warfare. They could extract weapons, clothes and food from the British without having to operate directly under their command. In political terms, the small-scale fragmentary nature of the conflict addressed itself to the reality of a divided and even disintegrating confederacy. With the Senecas largely inclined to favour the French and the Mohawks drawn deeply into the British sphere of influence, a chaotic pattern of raids and counter-raids allowed individual nations to engage or to remain neutral as they saw fit. Johnson understood these terms and his appointment eased the way for some fitful involvement, especially by his Mohawk friends.

Johnson was able to influence the Mohawks towards engagement, not just because of the friendship and trust he had built up over the previous eight years, but because they had a real mutual interest. The decline in the Mohawk population had led to a diminution in their influence within the confederacy. Johnson could give them a reinforced position as Britain's favoured nation, restoring them to a position of power as essential mediators with the Empire. An alliance in which they appeared as the most faithful of Britain's friends, while the other confederate nations remained as lukewarm allies, actually suited these purposes. So did increased prestige for Johnson himself, which would give the Mohawks a more powerful protector to look after their interests.

More directly, Johnson and the Mohawks had the same economic gains to make in the war. The Albany fur trade with Montreal through the Caughnawagas was a rival to Johnson's fur trade through

Oswego. The war could draw the British more heavily into the Oswego region, force them to clamp down on the Albany merchants, and, if successful, end the Montreal trade altogether. For the Mohawks, this hope was spiritual as well as economic: if the Montreal trade was ended, they dreamed, their separated brethren the Caughnawagas would return to their ancestral homelands and the Mohawk nation would be made whole.

Given these shared interests, Johnson's formal appointment and the money for presents that came with it increased his standing among the Six Nations to an unprecedented level. Cadwallader Colden, who had completed a scholarly and sympathetic history of the Iroquois, was struck by 'the ascendancy he had gained over the Indians' and declared that with his title and resources 'he made a greater figure, and gained more influence among the Indians, than any person before him (so far as I have learned) ever did'.[21]

By the end of 1746 Johnson was organising raiding parties, fitting warriors with snowshoes, having lace-trimmed coats made for the sachems Hendrick and Seth, sending wampum belts to outlying nations urging them to join his war, feeding the wives and children of warriors so they would not suffer from the loss of the usual hunt. The numbers he was able to put in the field at any one time were small: twenty-four men sent on a raid into Canada, ten warriors who took part in a war dance, twelve men led on a raid by Nickus, a party of twenty-two sent out under a war chief called Isaac, and so on.[22]

Johnson was under no illusions about the atrocious nature of his mission. His instructions were to 'endeavour to send out as many Party's of the said Indians as you possibly can against the French & their Indians in Canada to harrass and Alarm their Quarters in all Parts and to take Prisoners for Intelligence as soon as may be, likewise Scalps . . . '[23] In essence, Johnson was being commissioned to carry out a terror campaign against French settlers and Indian villages in Canada. As he himself understood his mission, it was to 'go a Scalping' and to 'make the french Smart . . . by taking Scalping & burning them, & their Settlements'.[24]

The Indians of the north-eastern woodlands had long used scalps as props to prove the truth of a warrior's stories. In societies where a man's status depended on his deeds, it was important that heroic boasts be backed up with evidence. The scalplock taken from an enemy's crown and displayed in the village provided 'visible proofs of their valour' without which 'they are afraid that their relations of the combat and the account they give of their individual prowess might be doubted or disbelieved'.[25]

The scalp was also a token of spiritual power. The whorl of hair at the top of the head, braided and decorated, represented the soul. To lose that hair, even if one remained alive, was to lose control over one's personal identity. The scalp was thus an analogue of captivity. If a prisoner could not be taken to enhance the size of the nation, the scalp was a good substitute. When the Iroquois painted pictographs on trees or marked the handles of their hatchets, the same human figure symbolised both a prisoner captured and a scalp taken. As emblems of power, scalps could be worn as trophies, given to a family as a replacement for a dead member, sacrificed to the war god or offered to another nation as an inducement to go on the warpath.

Johnson himself used scalps in at least three of these traditional Iroquois ways. He does not seem to have worn them or displayed them at his home at Mount Johnson, though he did provide ribbons for the warriors to dangle their captured scalps, and he did use them to back up his stories of prowess, listing captured scalps carefully in his accounts to Governor Clinton as proof of the effectiveness of his raiding parties. He used scalps to symbolically replace lost warriors, sending a scalp to the Oneidas in June 1747 'in the Room of the Great Oneida Sachem Sciwatkis'. And he sent them to other Indian nations to try to persuade them to join him. In his accounts, for example, he lists a charge for '1 belt Wampum with the Scalp to the Messissageys Castle' and 'another with another scalp to the Oneidas' in December 1746.[26]

In this use of scalps, Johnson was using Iroquois culture for his own purposes. He was in fact usurping some of its structures of authority, taking to himself the traditional functions of the tribal councils in calling others to war and of the clan matrons in demanding the replacement through war of those who had fallen in battle. By purchasing scalps and disposing of them as he, rather than the nation as a whole, saw fit, he was changing the inherited system of values that gave meaning to warfare, even while he was making use of those very values.

The payment of bounties itself corrupted traditional notions of a warrior's valour. Johnson knew quite well that the victims of his raiding parties would not necessarily be armed combatants. The bounties were a licence to kill and scalp unarmed civilians of all ages and both sexes. In the absence of a serious military land campaign against French forts or towns, Johnson's war was tacitly understood by him and his superiors to be essentially the infliction of atrocities on vulnerable Canadian settlers. His instructions from Clinton to 'harass and alarm' the French could easily be translated as 'murder and terrify'.

In the minds of the colonial authorities, and probably of Johnson himself, the raids could be justified as a regrettable necessity imposed on them by the need to retaliate against French attacks. As the New York administrator Goldsbrow Banyar wrote to Johnson in a similar context a few years later: 'I abhor a cruel Thought but Mercy itself in many Cases is Cruelty, and lenity to a few the Destruction of thousands. If we must continue skirmishing with them . . . we should deal exactly with them as they do by us, destroy and scalp as they do: They set their Indians to scalping of our poor defenceless Inhabitants, in this the necessity pleads an Excuse for following so inhuman an Example, as the shortest way too perhaps to put an End to such Barbarities.'[27]

The knowledge that what was involved was inhuman barbarity nevertheless created an uneasy ambivalence. The New York authorities adopted a hypocritical posture in the face of the reality that they were ordering Johnson to organise and reward atrocities. On the one hand, the Governor's Council sought to exclude from the Scalp Act of 1747 bounties for 'Scalping or taking poor women or Children Prisiners'. On the other, the Assembly assured Clinton, who in turn assured Johnson, 'The Money shall be paid when it so happens, If the Indians insist upon it.'[28] It was a supreme act of moral evasion: women and children would be murdered or kidnapped, and the colonial authorities would reward those who did the deeds, but it would all be the fault of the Indians who 'insist[ed] on it'.

The attempts to distance civilised Christians from the barbarities committed in their name was, in the atmosphere of atrocity and counter-atrocity, bound to fail. Adult scalps were treated by white colonists as trophies of war. In July 1746 Richard Shuckburgh reported to Johnson from Albany that a Caughnawaga warrior had been killed and 'I had the pleasure of seeing his Scalp carried about [the] streets.'[29] Less openly, there was tacit official recognition of the practice of scalping children in the setting of a bounty of £5 – half the adult rate. Johnson was certainly a knowing party to this grisly practice. In July 1747 he paid out £365 in bounties for scalps and prisoners. Nine of the sixteen prisoners were 'under age'. More grimly, Johnson paid Gingego £15 for '3 Scalps under age'. He also paid full adult bounties for the scalps of women, as when he gave two Mohawks, David and Adam, £20 for '2 Scalps of a Man and a Woman'.[30]

One of the effects of these bounty payments was that Johnson's warriors seem never to have taken Indian prisoners. While the French did sometimes take Mohawk prisoners, some of whom were eventually released at the end of hostilities, Johnson's raiders took white captives, for whom he paid a bounty, but killed and scalped defeated Indians. After the war, the Governor of New France, the Marquis de la Galissonière, complained: 'I do not perceive that the life of one of our Indians has been spared, although it is sufficiently evident that some were taken alive.'[31]

Just as the colonial authorities could evade moral responsibility by blaming the Indians for excesses of violence, the Indians could blame the white men who had sent them out to kill. After one Mohawk raid on a Canadian mission village in 1748, the French governor asked an Iroquois delegation to explain the actions of their fellow warriors. They told him that they were 'surprised at the occurrence, and assured [him] that it could only be Colonel Amson [the French mishearing of Johnson] who could have induced them to make the attack'.[32] In the ragged frontier conflicts, it was becoming possible for both Europeans and Indians to set aside their different codes for the containment of violence and to disavow responsibility for allowing this to happen.

Johnson's first raiding party into Canada in 1746 divided into two groups, a war party that infiltrated to the north of Montreal and a diplomatic mission to the Caughnawagas led by Hendrick in an attempt to 'stop their Mouths'.[33] The latter group, on its way back from an apparently friendly meeting with the veteran French governor Charles de Beauharnois in Montreal, treacherously attacked a group of French carpenters who were building on Isle la Motte, at the north end of Lake Champlain, killing some of them and taking others prisoner. The French alleged that one of the latter, a Canadian named L'Esperance, was subsequently tortured by having his hand badly burned by a colonial officer 'in the presence of some Englishmen or Dutchmen, and not Indians'.[34]

In April 1747 Johnson sent two war parties 125 miles north towards the French stronghold of Fort St Frederic at the narrows of

Lake Champlain, which the British called Crown Point. Built on lands which the French claimed as part of Canada, and the Mohawks and British claimed as theirs, it had been the source of the most devastating French and Indian raids into New York and New England, notably an attack from the fort in November 1745 by a force of 600 whites and Indians led by Paul Marin that destroyed Saratoga and took around a hundred prisoners.[35] One of Johnson's parties, consisting of thirteen Mohawk warriors, attacked a party of twenty-seven French and Canadians and three Indians outside the fort, and killed eight men, including two officers and a sergeant, taking six scalps before they were chased away.

The skirmish provides an example of the breakdown of European military conventions in this kind of guerrilla warfare. One French officer, Johnson was told, was 'a young Man dressed in blue, with a broad Gold lace who fought with undaunted courage'. A brave soldier of this evidently high status would have expected to be spared when he was so badly wounded that he could no longer fight. This young man indeed 'called out for quarters in the Indian language'. However, as Johnson disingenuously expressed it, 'Perceiving his wounds were mortal, they dispatched him.'[36] The pretence that killing him was an act of kindness does not alter the evident reality that his scalp was worth £10.

Much less successful from Johnson's point of view was a raid in June 1747, in which Hendrick led a war party of white colonists, Mohawks, Senecas, and Oneidas into an ambush above Montreal, at the Cascades of the Saint Lawrence. Although Hendrick escaped, a number of leaders were killed and Karaghiagdatie (Nicholas or Nickus), a Wolf clan sachem from Canajoharie, was captured along with fourteen other Mohawk warriors.

In August, Johnson sent out three parties, two to Canada and one to the French fort at Crown Point, 'firmly resolved to Destroy whatever they meet of the Enemy either French or Indians'.[37] The third party scouted around Crown Point, which they found to be poorly defended, but returning by way of Lac Saint Sacrement they spotted a substantial French and allied force of about 500 or 600 men ready to thrust into New York. To head them off Johnson himself led 318 Indians, including some Senecas and Ottawas and about 400 colonial volunteers, 'in quest of a Body of French & Indians' to Lac Saint Sacrement.[38] He does not seem to have found his quarry, however, and the failure to bring back tangible trophies of war later led to allegations that the expedition had been a charade.[39]

Since these war parties, however mixed, were essentially Indian, the colonists who took part adopted native dress and tactics. Johnson, when he went to war, certainly adopted Mohawk dress and the Dutch and German volunteers seem to have done likewise. The Marquis de la Galissonière complained bitterly after the war that among the captives the French had taken were 'some Dutchmen . . . disguised like Indians'. This, he claimed, was 'a masquerade . . . unworthy of Englishmen and of all civilized nations, and can have no other object than to commit with impunity all sorts of cruelties and treacheries'.[40]

These raids and skirmishes were, however, a poor substitute for the concerted British attack on Canada which the Mohawks needed if their ultimate objective of bringing back the Caughnawaga refugees was to be fulfilled. They were frustrated that they had lost 'several of our Chief and principal Warriors' to no ultimate purpose. A delegation of Mohawks that accompanied Johnson to Albany as a bodyguard in July told Clinton: 'We are afraid you are not in earnest, for no other reason than that we don't see you do anything with your army as we expected, & wished for.'[41]

Johnson was convinced at that stage that he could 'bring 1000 Indian Warriours into the field' for a general assault on Canada.[42] His busy diplomacy had secured significant support from the Senecas, Oneida and Cayugas and he also believed that some of the western tribes could be induced to attack the French post at Fort Niagara, which controlled access to the west. An internal New York political crisis, however, made any kind of large-scale military action impossible. The official militia wouldn't go on any expedition without pay, and the Assembly had refused to vote funds for them. Time after time, Johnson was in the awkward position of stirring the Iroquois up for a fight, and then having no real fight in which to engage them.

The one serious European-style assault on Canada – the taking of Louisbourg in 1745 by Peter Warren's fleet and a New England colonial force led by Governor William Shirley of Massachusetts – merely added to the impression that the North American war was being conducted between France and Warrenstown. By May 1747, after he had helped to overpower the French fleet in the battle of Cape Ortegal off the northern coast of Spain, Warren was made a Knight of the Bath and then promoted to vice admiral.

For Johnson, though, Warren's fame merely made life more precarious. In November 1745 Johnson received a warning from a friend at Albany that 'the french have told our Indians that they will have you Dead or alive . . . that you are a Reallation of Captin War[ren] thier Great adveserey'. Johnson was in any case a target in his own right for the French, who now identified him, semi-accurately, as 'Colonel Johnson, Governor of Albany, who has influence among the Mohawk Indians'.43 He was urged to retreat to the town for the winter and offered refuge for himself and his servants. Albany itself was considered sufficiently vulnerable to attack for women, children and portable property to be sent down to New York,44 but Johnson's position was much more exposed. By late 1746 he seems to have become a formal target of French attacks. Governor Clinton reported to London that Johnson 'has run great hazards of loosing his life by the Governour of Canada offering a reward for his scalp'.45 Clinton subsequently complained to the Marquis de la Galissonière that 'a very large sum had been promised to the Indians to assassinate' Johnson.46

Johnson stayed on his estate, fortified with four captured French cannon from Peter Warren's farm and confident that 'the Mohawks will defend . . . me'.47 The very real sense of danger, however, was expressed in his decision to send Catty and their three young children away from Mount Johnson. He bought a two-storey brick house on High Street in Albany in 1748, and one in Schenectady around the same time or a little earlier, both almost certainly for their use.48 The likelihood is that they left Mount Johnson some time during 1746 and stayed in the meantime with some of his friends in either town.

Even if Johnson was relatively confident of his own safety, conditions were harsh and the stress of running a private war undermined his usual breezy optimism. He suffered sporadically from severe pain, probably due to the bowel complaint that affected him for much of his life and that may have been a form of chronic dysentery.49 He confessed to Clinton in 1747: 'I lead a most miserable life . . . at present,' and that he had 'more work than Man Can well bear'. He was 'pestered every day with partys returning with Prisoners and Scalps' and continually running low on essential supplies for the warriors and their families. His 'house & all my Outhouses' were 'Continually full of Indians of all Nations', and he was obliged almost daily to 'Sit five or Six hours in their Council to hear what they have to Say & Answer them in Every point'. The following year, he gave Clinton an exasperated description of his home life, complaining: 'My House was constantly full of Christians, as well as Indians, and Continues so still, that I have Scarce a Minutes time to do any thing, and then again this News of an Army coming against me, and the Mohawks River in Particular, has taken up my time much, by the People flocking about me, Women roaring & Clapping of Hands, begging for Shelter, so that I have a most miserable life of it, besides the great Risque I run of being hourly destroyed.'[50]

His misery was shared by the Indians, of course. A glimpse of their weariness and distress is revealed in a message from the River Indians of which he received a copy in early 1748: 'When I lie down at night I am afraid I shall not live till morning, and when I rise up in the morning I am afraid I shall not live till night; I am so harrassed with the War.'[51]

In June 1748 Clinton appointed Johnson Colonel of the New York levies, giving him, in addition to his duties as Colonel of the Six Nations, responsibility for the colonial militias stationed in Albany and on the frontier.[52] This was a particularly thankless task, because the New York Assembly consistently failed to vote sufficient money to pay or supply the militias. By the early summer of 1748 Johnson's situation was becoming desperate. The militias stationed at the Mohawk villages to protect them while the warriors were away fighting had deserted. The commander of the Schenectady garrison, Jacob Glen, who had helped Johnson on his first arrival in New York a decade earlier, resigned in disillusionment, and Johnson had to beg him to 'lay aside such thoughts'.[53]

The Mohawks, enraged by Gingego's grisly death in March, were blaming him for their losses and demanding that he get a large body of colonial troops to support them in a raid to avenge their war captain's death. At a meeting with the Mohawk council a few days after the return of Gingego's mangled body, Johnson was warned that

since we Can see no prospect of Your going against the Enemy to destroy them, as we Expected this long time You may no longer feed us with Promises of Assistance, but now give us Men who are fitt to go with Us, & we will endeavour what we Can, to revenge the Cruel and barbarous Usage we have (through Your Means) received from the French, & their Indians lately & lett them feel the effect of our resentment – Then we shall be thoroughly Convinced you have a Brotherly love for Us, as we have for you.[54]

Johnson had to intervene to stop the Six Nations sending a delegation to Canada to reach their own settlement with the French.

Johnson's fear was that Mohawk resentment at the non-fulfilment of the repeated assurances he had given them would make his own continued residence on the New York frontier untenable. He twice warned Clinton: 'Should things miscarry, it will be the intire ruin of me; for I can not pretend to live any where near them . . . they being a blood thirsty revengefull sett of people to any whom they have a regard for, should they be mislead or deceived by them.' He would, he said, be 'Obliged to leave my Settlements & make the best retreat I can, If I am not furnished & Enabled to fulfill my Engagements with those Savages'.[55]

He was saved, not by any great upsurge in the colonial war effort, but by the news of peace. Just as the war had been visited on the frontier by the machinations of competing powers in Europe, so it ended for reasons that had nothing to do with America. In July 1748 word reached New York that the contending powers had come to an agreement, and in October the Peace of Aix-la-Chapelle was signed. The murder and mayhem on the frontier had been completely pointless. The British and the French returned to the status quo of 1744. Even Peter Warren's great prize of Louisbourg was simply returned to New France. The only conceivable gain might have been a lesson to the Indians and colonists of North America on their small place in the great scheme of things. Yet even that lesson was useless, for the peace treaty involved no attempt to control the contention of two European powers for the lands of the indigenous peoples of North America. That struggle would continue, and make another war inevitable.

9

The Power of Absence

In August 1750 Hendrick, Abraham and other Mohawk sachems came to Mount Johnson with Nickus Karaghiagdatie, the Wolf clan sachem from Canajoharie who had been captured by the French on the disastrous raid into Canada in 1747 and who had now finally been released from Montreal under the terms of the peace. 'They entered [my house] in a great Passion,' Johnson wrote, and 'would not even shake hands with me.' When Johnson asked what they meant by this hostile behaviour, they told him that he and Governor Clinton 'were all French' and 'had endeavoured to bring the French Governour into [a] Plot' to destroy the Mohawks. Nickus claimed that while he was a prisoner in Montreal he had been shown a wampum belt from Clinton to the French governor inviting him to join in this supposed conspiracy to 'fall upon all the Indians on both sides and destroy them'.[1]

He alleged that he had corroboration of this vile plot from other sources, and that the French had assured him that they had rejected Clinton's overtures out of love of and concern for the Indians. Nickus's willingness to believe this fanciful story can be easily explained by his resentment at having been left in French custody for two years after peace was declared while the two empires haggled about the precise terms for the agreed exchange of prisoners. More puzzling is the apparent ease with which the wily Hendrick fell for the transparent French ploy to sow disaffection among Britain's most loyal Indian allies. According to Johnson, it took him three days of effort to bring Hendrick and the others to their senses and convince them that the plot did not exist.

The highly theatrical behaviour of refusing to shake hands with Johnson and assailing him with outlandish allegations suggests that the whole episode was an act. The allegation merely repeated the rumour that had spread panic through the Iroquois at the beginning of the war and Hendrick was far too experienced a politician to believe that the two European empires were capable of uniting in a sudden concerted assault on all the Indian nations. But the pretence that the Mohawk leaders as a whole were convinced by Nickus's delusions, until reassured by Johnson, was a useful device for reminding the New York government that, now that the war was over, it could take for granted neither its Indian allies nor their friend Warraghiyagey. Johnson's speedy and detailed report of the incident to Clinton suggests that he was not quite as displeased with the incident as he pretended.

Both Johnson and the Iroquois had reason to feel that their services in the war were not sufficiently appreciated. The Six Nations, and the Mohawks in particular, had suffered serious losses without the compensation of a significant victory and its accompanying rewards of booty and prestige. The only peace dividend was the reopening of trade at Oswego, and almost immediately the trade commissioners had proposed a new duty on goods sold to Indians, putting up the prices of these commodities. This, together with the long delay in redeeming Mohawk prisoners, created a general sense of being 'not so much taken notice of'.[2]

Johnson had even more reason to feel neglected. His wartime role as Colonel of the Six Nations had been converted into a formal appointment by Clinton as Commissary of New York for Indian Affairs,[3] but the title did not make him independent of the New York Assembly, which was controlled by the great oligarchic families and had the means to do him serious harm. He had conducted a private war on behalf of the northern colonies, using his own money to fund the presents and equipment that had put Iroquois war parties in the field and to sustain their families while they were away; but he had done this on commission from the New York government and on the understanding that his vast expenses, amounting to about £5,000, would be repaid. More than £2,000, plus his salary and interest, was left outstanding at the end of the war. His reasonable expectation that the money would be reimbursed became hostage, however, to factional rivalries that set him against his own family.

Johnson's assumption of the role of primary mediator between the colonies and the Iroquois had made him powerful enemies. The

Albany commissioners were outraged at the loss of office, not least because, as Cadwallader Colden reminded Clinton, Indian delegations coming to the town for negotiations used to 'go first to the Commissioners' who 'thereby gain a preference in the buying of Furs, and likewise make use of the Money allowed to them for Presents to the Indians, to trade with them preferably to others'. When Johnson, who had already drawn much of the Indian trade away from Albany, was appointed in their place, his new office enabled him to take most of the rest. In Cadwallader Colden's astute analysis:

Coll. Johnson is the most considerable trader with the Western Indians, and sends more goods to Oswego than any other person does; the people of Albany imagined, that his having the conduct of Indian affairs, gave him great advantages, for as he lives near the Mohawk Castle, and near forty miles from Albany, all the Six Nations, and the other Indians to the Westward stop at his house and were there supplied, and from that time few or none were seen at Albany. This touched a people, in the most sensible part, who have no other view in life, but that of getting money. 4

The rivalry between Johnson and the old Albany commissioners was complicated by both epic and intimate factors. Johnson had been appointed by the Governor, who represented the King. The early stirrings of colonial self-assertion, however, had created within the Assembly an embryonic radical faction bent on challenging the royal power by claiming the right to veto expenditures. The radicals would have had very limited sway, however, were it not for the cynical support of a powerful faction of merchants and oligarchs led by Peter Warren's brother-in-law James De Lancey.

The suave De Lancey had once been a protégé of Clinton's. As he gathered more power, however, becoming both Chief Justice and the chief spokesman in the Assembly for the Albany faction, he and Clinton came to heartily detest one another. De Lancey's dual role as Chief Justice and the holder at various times of senior political offices including Lieutenant Governor and Acting Governor made him a formidable figure. His arch-enemy Clinton wrote of the 'terror' he inspired: 'Chief Justice De Lancey's conduct makes all men afraid of the power he has by his office, and of his resentment, and to which every man in this Province may in some way or other be subjected.' Clinton was therefore continually urging De Lancey's dismissal and replacement as Chief Justice.

The rivalry between the two men reached into the British establishment. Clinton was connected through his sister-in-law to the Duke of Newcastle, who was secretary of state through all of this period, and to Newcastle's brother, Prime Minister Henry Pelham. De Lancey had been educated in England and boasted to Clinton that he had on his side the influence of both the Archbishop of Canterbury, who had been his tutor at Cambridge University, and Sir Peter Warren, 'which', Clinton spluttered, 'he had the assurance to tell me to my face was better than my interest'.[5]

According to the admittedly prejudiced Clinton, De Lancey's power was such that his brother Oliver could, with impunity, commit crimes such as threatening to rape a Jewish woman on the grounds that she looked like Clinton's wife, breaking the head of a poor man who got in his way, and stabbing a drunken man in a tavern.[6] The bitterness came to a head when a navy ship in New York harbour fired its guns to stop a passing vessel suspected of smuggling and accidentally killed a young woman on board. The commander of the naval vessel happened to be Clinton's son-in-law. De Lancey, as Chief Justice, attempted to prosecute him, but Clinton claimed that the naval service was outside De Lancey's jurisdiction.

Johnson was caught in the middle of this mutual loathing. In 1747, as part of the factional wrangle, the Assembly, led by De Lancey, supported the former Indian commissioners and attacked Johnson's position. It claimed, rather ludicrously, that the old commissioners 'were the principle inhabitants of that County, well known to the Indians, and had great Authority and Influence over them, which we doubt not would have continued, had it not through the Artifices of designing Men, who have private Views, been undermined by employing Private persons, [i.e. Johnson] to negotiate with the Indians'.[7]

This defence of the Albany commissioners was followed by a direct attack on Johnson. It would have been better, the Assembly maintained, if the Six Nations had been encouraged to remain neutral and the colony been 'left to fight our own Quarrel with the French than to have treated with them to enter into the War'. Johnson had aroused among the Iroquois 'unreasonable Expectations'. Johnson's belief that the Albany merchants were continuing to trade with Montreal 'never had any other Existence, than in the Imagination and Invention of his own brain', they said. They implied that Johnson and Clinton had stolen the money they claimed to have disbursed on presents to the Indians.

The charges were absurd. The Assembly's stated desire to have fought its own war with the French was hardly consistent with its failure to raise either an army or the money to pay for one. Without the Iroquois, and the colonial volunteers Johnson deployed alongside them, there would have been no resistance to French incursions into New York. Moreover, the Albany merchants were indeed manoeuvring to keep their Canadian trade open. And far from pocketing an alleged surplus, Johnson had used thousands of pounds of his own money to keep the Indians in the field.

Clinton claimed that these attacks on Johnson came 'not from the Members of the Assembly, but from other Persons who were known to be principal compilers of their Representation', in other words De Lancey and his cronies.[8] Johnson for his part was contemptuous of the previous Indian commissioners: 'Their own letters testify their inability to make the Indians any way tractable in the Service I believe in a great measure owing to the contempt the Indians must consequently have of a set of Men who were more concerned in buying and selling than in advising or consulting them . . . or the Wellfare of a usefull body of men, so absolutely necessary, as the only Barrier, against so bad a neighbour [as] the French.' He made clear the kind of office he would like to have. He wanted 'some appointment from home' (i.e., London) that would make him independent of the whims of the Assembly. He suggested that this appointment should be a royal one, since 'the Indians . . . tho called subjects, are a foreign people, and are to be treated with as immediately from the King'.[9]

In the absence of such an appointment, Johnson was at the mercy of the factional politics of New York. The financial penalties on Johnson began even during the war with a refusal by the Assembly to alter the terms of his contract to supply the garrison at Oswego. The contract had been signed in peacetime, but the war dramatically increased the cost of the goods he supplied. He expected the colonial government to make up the difference, but in September 1747 the Assembly voted 'that no additional allowance should be made to the Contractor for victualling the Garrison at Oswego'.[10]

His expenses had continued to mount even after the end of hostilities. He took thirteen French prisoners from the Indians at the end of the war and 'Cloathed them ever Since, and keep them at my own House, as if they were my own family, which no Body else would ever have done, nor would Attempt it'. He also arranged delegations to go to Montreal to get the Mohawk prisoners released. The New York Assembly failed to pay these expenses as well. It contributed nothing to the upkeep of the French captives, and 'refused to provide for the necessary expense of sending to Canada for the liberty of the Prisoners there'.[11]

In October 1748 Governor Clinton asked the Assembly 'to pay the large sums due from the province to Coll. Johnson for which the honour of the Government was engaged'. The following month, he laid Johnson's accounts before the Assembly and asked for the debt to paid 'as soon as possible'. But the Assembly claimed not to have received Johnson's accounts and gave this as the reason why payment to him was 'postponed'. Two years later, in September 1750, Clinton was again reminding the Assembly of the debt owed to Johnson, and again being ignored.[12] The Assembly used various devices to prevent the money being paid: ordering payment from funds known to be exhausted, paying debts of a later date to other creditors until available funds ran out, disallowing parts of Johnson's claims without specifying which parts or why they were invalid.[13]

Johnson was protected to some extent by the evident admiration of the Lords of Trade in London, and in 1750 he was appointed to the New York Governor's Council. The following year, in the Privy Council's 'Report Upon the State of New York', which gave an official overview of the political crisis in the colony, he was defended against the charges of the Assembly and declared 'a very diligent, honest and able Officer'.[14] These kind words and honours did nothing to get Johnson his money, however. As Clinton explained, Johnson was being punished for his temerity in challenging the interests of the oligarchs: 'As he will not be a tool to them, they always take care to put him off in some scandalous manner.' Johnson could do nothing but rail against the injustice of it all: 'They kept me out of my Money, Disbursed for the Service of the province and at Risque of my life & fortune, & at a time when no one Else here would dare to undertake it . . . they must be all sensible that it has been a great loss to me in my way of Business.'[15]

Especially galling to Johnson in all of this was the part played by his one-time surrogate father Peter Warren. The admiral, having attained the pinnacle of his navy career, had developed political ambitions and had been elected as the member of parliament for the prestigious Westminster seat in 1747, even though he was at sea at the time. He had his eye on the governorship of New York, and with his brother-in-law De Lancey exercising a virtual veto over the administration of colonial power, he was anxious to keep well in with the De Lancey faction.

As Governor Clinton saw it, Warren was plotting either to become governor himself or to put De Lancey into that position. The latter, he complained to the Duke of Newcastle, was 'incouraged by the assistance he knew Sir Peter would give him, and it was given out here that Sir Peter had given assurances that no application should be wanting to bring the Administration of government into the Chief Justices hands. It was with this view and to serve this purpose that the schemes were laid which have since given me so much trouble.'[16] By early 1751 Clinton was in 'a very ill state of health' and intended to leave New York. In June, he even heard that 'Sir Peter Warren's commission for Governour of this Province was actually made out.'[17]

Clinton's information was wrong, but Warren's political ambitions certainly influenced his behaviour. The admiral urged Johnson to resign as Indian commissioner and give the job back to the Albany men. Cadwallader Colden heard that:

Sir Peter Warren has advised Col. Johnson who is his Nephew no longer to assist Governor Clinton in the Indian affairs & to decline all public business & to attend only to his own private affairs. It is so much Col. Johnson's interest to please his Uncle that it is expected he will submit to his Desire which the ingratitude of the Assembly might make him likewise incline to do. The Faction hereby hopes that the Indian affairs will return into the old channel of Commissioners at Albany.[18]

Thus, Peter Warren was promoting De Lancey's interests while De Lancey's enemy Clinton was promoting Johnson. In February 1747 Clinton had written to the Duke of Newcastle condemning De Lancey's 'insatiable thirst of power'. He had also complained about Warren's having 'concerned himself much in the recommendation of Mr De Lancy to your Grace's favour . . . In this I think Sir Peter has been highly partiall, because he is his brother in law, and has gone [to] too great lengths, consistant with prudence to interfere himself with any appointments in my government without my consent or approbation.' Clinton went so far as to recommend that Vice Admiral Warren 'may not be allowed to apply for any more places in this Province during my administration, in which he has taken too many freedoms to my disadvantage'.[19]

Almost at the same time as he was trying to stop Warren's advance, Clinton was singing the praises of Warren's nephew. He wrote to the Duke of Newcastle a month previously recommending 'Coll. Johnson's great services among the Indians, who remains still with them at great expence, fatigue & trouble, & runs a great risque of his life & fortune'.[20]

The De Lancey/Warren faction, for their part, continued to defy Clinton, organising the appointment by the Assembly of Robert Charles as agent for the colony 'being recommended by Sir Peter Warren', and authorising him to act independently of Clinton. The Governor believed that Charles would be a tool of the De Lancey faction and that the Assembly had privately given him 'this general instruction, to follow Sir Peter Warren's directions in every thing'.[21]

In 1751, worn out by his labours, infuriated by the Assembly's refusal to pay what it owed him and embarrassed by his uncle's support for his enemies, Johnson played his last card. Without telling Clinton, he sent a belt of wampum around all the villages of the Six Nations, informing them that he 'no longer took care of their affairs'. This, wrote Cadwallader Colden, 'was a very odd step, such as nothing of the kind had ever been done before, & occasioned extraordinary speculations among the Indians, of which it is supposed the French emissaries took advantage'.[22]

Johnson's resignation left relations between New York and the Six Nations in disarray. There was now a vacuum that could not be filled. On the one hand, the Assembly would grant no money for presents to the Indians unless they were to be dispersed through the old commissioners whom Clinton would not reappoint because 'by their past conduct [they] appear no way proper to be entrusted'. On the other hand, Johnson's influence with the Six Nations was still such that 'they insist on his continuing and will be dissatisfied with any other appointment'. Both sides, as Colden noted, 'seem to have in view, in opposition to each other to make it impracticable to carry on the Indian affairs, unless the one be separately employed, exclusive of the other, and thereby the Governor is disabled to imploy either, or any other'.[23]

As Johnson surely anticipated, the Iroquois, from the moment of his resignation, agitated for his return. At a major conference in Albany in July 1751, between the Six Nations and senior representatives of New York, Connecticut, Massachusetts and South Carolina, the confederate speaker, probably Nickus, the Mohawk sachem, demanded that 'the King our Father would reinstate Coll. Johnson amongst us'. Clinton promised: 'I shall . . . on my return to Court, Lay before the King your Father what you have desired me to say in relation to Coll. Johnson.' The Six Nations, in an ominous parting shot, repeated their demand that Johnson be reappointed and warned that a delegation of Iroquois had gone to Canada to discuss with the French their erection of a fort at Niagara. If Johnson were not reinstated, they said, the colonials 'Cannot Expect to hear' what would transpire in those discussions.

In June 1753 Hendrick led a delegation of seventeen Mohawks to New York City, where they met with Clinton, the city's mayor and members of the Assembly and of the Council, including Johnson. Hendrick cited Johnson as witness to the Mohawks' loyalty in the last war, in which, if it had gone on longer, 'we would have torn the Frenchmens Hearts out'. The Assembly and Council, he charged, 'don't care what becomes of our Nation'. Land was being stolen from them by fraud. If their grievances were not addressed, 'the rest of our brethren the Five Nations shall know it and all Paths will be stopped'.

When Clinton assured him 'the Management of your affairs is now put on the same footing as formerly for Commissioners have been appointed and Provision is now made for them', Hendrick reacted furiously. He and his people, he said, knew the Albany commissioners well: 'We will not trust to them, for they are no people but Devils, so we rather desire that you'll say, Nothing shall be done for us.' Dramatically, he announced that he was returning home to inform the other Iroquois nations that the Covenant Chain binding the Six Nations to Britain was now broken. 'So brother you are not to expect to hear of me any more, and Brother we desire to hear no more of you.' With this magnificent peroration he stormed off with his delegation.[24]

Hendrick's flamboyant gesture demonstrated more powerfully than any action that Johnson could have taken the position he had now attained. Without the Mohawks, there could be no Iroquois alliance for the British Empire. Without Johnson, as Hendrick had made clear, the British would have no alliance with the Mohawks. Beaten in the game of colonial politics, humiliated by the Assembly and betrayed by the man who had been his 'only Father in this part of the world', Johnson had now been granted, by the Mohawks, both an indispensable political function and a set of unshakeable allies. The Mohawks had railed against him at times during the war. They made him, at its lowest point, fear the revenge of a people who might come to feel that they had been deceived by him. Yet even then, the resentment he had feared was the special kind they reserved for those 'whom they have a regard for'. The Mohawks had come to feel that he was one of their own, and so long as they felt that way, his place in their valley was secure.

10

Force, Motion and Equilibrium

There was a game that some American gentlemen liked to play, a game of power in which loyalty and treason, those deadly serious forces for which men killed and died, became funny, wicked and absurd. The game was called the 'magical picture' and instructions on how to play it circulated widely among enthusiasts for the emerging science of electricity. You got a large print of King George and carefully cut a border. You pasted the border to the glass of the frame. You filled up the space behind it with gold leaf or brass, and gilded most, but not all, of the frame as well, arranging the whole thing so that the operation was invisible to the casual viewer. You then put a small gilt crown on the King's head, connected the picture to an electrical apparatus and announced a test of loyalty.

You called in those who were to be tested and made sure that they held the picture by the gilded part of the frame. When they tried to touch the crown, they got a severe shock. When the person who set up the experiment, holding the frame by the ungilded part, touched the crown, there was no shock. You told them that they had been punished because, in their hearts, they were traitors. You, on the other hand, had been spared because your heart was free of seditious impulses.[1] The violence and strangeness of politics were transformed into a trick, and you, the operator, were one of the few who could perform it.

William Johnson loved playing with electricity. He wanted to know how the world worked. Like most of the emerging American elite, he was fascinated by the discovery that the universe was controlled by invisible forces which, once understood, could be tamed and put to work. Amid the chaos and violence of these years on the frontier, he

98

made time to teach himself the new physics and to test the new laws of force, motion and equilibrium. He wanted to see for himself the power of electricity.

When he held a metal sphere in his hand and rubbed it with fur, there was no glow or spark of static electricity. The charge was generated but immediately dissipated through his body. But if he suspended the sphere from the ceiling with silken wires, or put it on a wooden platform, and then rubbed it without touching it with his hand, it would become electrified. He was studying the work of the man who had discovered the difference between a 'body electrical' and a conductor through which electricity passes on to other bodies. It must have amused him to confirm that he himself was a conductor, a mediator that energy passed through on its way from one object to another.

Around 1750, William Johnson ordered from London *Mathematical Elements of Natural Philosophy, confirmed by experiments – or an introduction to Sir Isaac Newtown's Philosophy; translated into English by the late J. T. D. Desaguliers* and the second edition of *Doctor Desaguliers Course of Experimental Philosophy, adorned with 78 copper plate*s. These books, by Isaac Newton's collaborator and populariser, the English Huguenot scientist John Théophile Desaguliers, were a gateway into the new knowledge for those who could not follow the complex mathematics of the master's own works. For many intellectually curious eighteenth-century gentlemen, among them, in America, Benjamin Franklin, John Adams, Tom Paine and Thomas Jefferson, they generated a powerful charge of hope and excitement.

Johnson wanted to see beyond visible surfaces. He had at Mount Johnson a prism and a microscope, which he taught himself to use with *Baker's Microscope Made Easy* ordered from London.[2] He asked for a telescope to be sent up from New York in 1755.[3] He obtained a camera obscura in 1771.[4] What concerned him most, though, was the flow of unseen power.

Johnson's strong and abiding interest in electricity would last almost his entire adult life. Some time in 1752 he wrote a note reminding himself about getting 'A globe for the electrical machine'.[5] This was probably a replacement for the 'good Globe to Hang in a Hall with light' he had ordered from London in 1749 or 1750.[6] Letters since destroyed by fire at the New York State Archives included one from the merchants Baynton, Wharton & Morgan in Philadelphia in

June 1765 about 'electrical apparatus and seals to be forwarded' to him, another from Lieutenant Augustus Prevost at Albany in November 1765 'about a box containing electrical apparatus which has gone astray' and a third from the same source a month later also 'concerning a lost box containing electrical machines'.[7] In 1766, Thomas Barton was promising to send him 'the Jet D'eau' and wishing he could 'assist you in fixing up some little philosophical Aparatus, that might amuse you in your Hours of Leisure and Retirement'.[8]

This electrical equipment was so important to him that when he eventually built the house he wanted, he had a separate east wing constructed to house the machinery. Local memories recorded that it 'contained a *philosophical apparatus*, of which he died possessed. The room in which the apparatus was kept, was called his own *private* study.'[9]

Behind this fascination was the search of a way out of chaos. He had come to live a life in which multiple historical forces – the fall of Gaelic Ireland and the rise of Protestant Britain, the ambitions of a European exile and the Iroquois struggle for survival, the reality of conflict and the dream of civility – were in constant motion. Competing visions of the world spun around him. They met but did not always cohere, and were kept from collision only by the force of his own multi-layered personality.

The new 'natural philosophy' held out the promise that all the world's apparent chaos was a mere illusion, and that beneath the surface there was in fact a clear and rational structure in which all things were governed by the same laws of cause and effect. Everything from the motion of the planets to the swing of a tomahawk, from the flight of a musket ball to the circulation of the blood, from the behaviour of static fluids to the reflection and refraction of light on the surface of the turbulent lakes of upper New York, from the fall of a wounded body to the fall of night, had a mechanical explanation that could be codified in an elegant and enduring formula.

The fuss of religious identities, whether Catholic, Protestant or animist, could also be calmed by the Newton's revelation of God as the benevolent but distant artisan who had set the machine in motion and then left it to its own rational workings. As John Harris explained in his *Lexicon Technicum*, 'It is the chief End, Design, and Business of natural Philosophy to consider Effects; and by reasoning upon them and their various Phaenomena, to proceed regularly at last to the Knowledge of the First Cause.'[10]

Studying Desaguliers, Johnson would have seen the glory of machines like the 'virtual orrery', in which the relative positions and motions of the bodies in the solar system that he himself spied through his telescope were represented by the revolution of metal balls in a clockwork apparatus. He learned how to make his globe light up with electricity. He re-enacted experiments like Desaguliers's famous demonstration that a cork hundreds of feet away could be electrified by connecting it with metal wire to a glass tube which he then rubbed to generate a charge.

The *Course of Experimental Philosophy* also contained images of the way humans could survive outside their natural element. For an amphibious creature like Johnson, there would have been a particular fascination in Desaguliers's illustrations of diving bells with little men inside, suspended above the ocean floor and talking away, undrowned; and of little warriors with axes and spears walking on the seabed wearing helmets from which long tubes stretch upwards to an unseen surface.[11] They could move through strange and hostile places, where the old familiar atmosphere did not exist, and yet breathe easy.

The Late Emperor of Morocco

The story goes that the young Irishwoman, from somewhere near Warrenstown, married an officer in the English army and went with him to New York. He was killed in the fighting against the French and his corpse dumped in a mass grave in the forest. His distraught wife could not bear to go on living unless she saw his body one last time. She hired Indian guides to take her to the spot. When the grave was opened, there was just the stench of putrefaction and the grotesque sight of the undifferentiated flesh of many cadavers melting into a decomposed mess. Her guides ran away. She wandered, half-crazed and starving, alone in the dense wilderness, until, by chance, she stumbled across William Johnson and a party of Mohawks on the warpath.

Johnson called her his dear countrywoman, embraced her like a long-lost sister and chivalrously offered his tent to the recuperating lady. When he came to see her he told her that he would send her back to his mansion at Mount Johnson while he was on the warpath and give orders that she was to be cared for by 'his women'. The phrase sent an undercurrent of alarm through her delicate frame. She asked what he meant. He put it as delicately as he could:

'They serve me in the natural capacity of women, while they please to continue with me. I do not desire any other service from them.'

'I presume, Sir, you mean that they wait upon your lady, or perform the other domestic offices of your family, in which women servants only are employed.'

'No, really, Madam, I have no lady for them to wait upon; nor do they live so immediately in my own family as to have any domestic employment in it.'

'How, Sir! Are you not married?'

'Not particularly to any one person, Madam.'

'That's strange. That is really very strange. And pray, Sir, are these ladies *Europeans*? I suppose they are the unhappy widows of such officers as have fallen in the service, to whom you have shown the same politeness and humanity as I now experience from you.'

'I am sorry, Madam, to be obliged to undeceive you in an opinion so favourable to me; they are all native *Americans* by whom I have had children and in whose unfeigned affection, and easy complying tempers I find such satisfaction that I never shall quit them to attach myself solely to one woman, however superior to them in advantages of beauty and education.'

He has left her with no room for polite evasion. He has bluntly told a decent European woman not only that he sleeps with numerous Indians but that he has no intention of ever giving up this acquired taste. She flips her chin up to its haughtiest angle and makes a coldly formal curtsy: 'I am much obliged to you for your civil offer, Sir!, but I cannot accept of it. I have not the least desire for the conversation of *Squaws* and am in haste to leave this savage place.'

Johnson kindly arranges an escort to take her safely to the city. As soon as she is out of his sight she begins to rage: 'Insensible brute! Not quit his odious *Squaws* for any woman! And to have the rudeness to tell me to my face! It shows his gross, low taste, for which such animals are fittest.' But when she has travelled on another while, moved another mile from this magnetic creature, she begins to sigh and moan in a lament compounded of grief and arousal: 'What a charming figure! Such a size! Such strength and ease in every motion! And then the manly beauty in his looks! Had I but the polishing of him! I was too hasty. I should have waited to insinuate myself into his heart by degrees.' It is too late now, though. She has lost the great playboy of the western world.[1]

The story is fictional, part of Charles Johnstone's novel *Chrysal*, which went through several editions in William Johnson's lifetime. It represents accurately, however, the strange position that Johnson came to occupy in the imperial imagination. He became the fixed point around which a storm of contradictory emotions could spin. He inspired disgust and envy. He embodied the fear of pollution and the excitement of erotic freedom; base abandonment to the unregulated desires of the savages and the natural, fecund impulse of life amid the putrefaction of war and death.

The Johnson of *Chrysal* is testament to the real man's elusive power. He is courtly and chivalrous, a perfect gentleman encountered amid the dark of a forest that owes more to the psychic landscape of European folktales than to the geography of northern New York. He is the good prince who rescues the damsel in distress, the woodman who saves the lost girl from the wolf. He has a natural grace and charm which want only 'polishing' to make them shine in civilised society. Yet he is also an animal, brought down by the savage natives to their own uncivilised level of promiscuous sexual anarchy, populating the vulnerable frontiers of empire with his half-breed children. He is both Prospero and Caliban.

Mythic stories of the tension between political control and sexual freedom, in which the natives are both dangerous and desirable – from Solomon and the Queen of Sheba to *Mutiny on the Bounty* to Rudolf Valentino in *The Sheik* – have always thrilled imperial societies. Johnson was thrilling in precisely this way. His double image reflected a wider fear of and lust after non-European peoples. As his fame grew, it carried this erotic charge.

Johnson's reputation as an awesomely sexual figure, the literal father of the Mohawks, was so well established by early 1756 that the former New York governor George Clinton, now safely returned to London, could write to him from there that one of the 'things I have been asked about and very often repeated to me which is the Number [of] Indian Concubines you had and as many Children they had fixed upon you as the late Emperor of Merocco Muli Ishmale which I think was 700'.[2] This image of Johnson among the Mohawks as a grand sensualist from the southern Mediterranean was later repeated by his sometime comrade-in-arms Colonel Henry Babcock, who wrote that Johnson, 'like Solomon has been eminent in his Pleasures with the brown Ladies'.[3]

The notion of Johnson as a Biblical king or an Islamic potentate with an enormous harem was qualified by *Chrysal*'s version of an apostle of free love with a range of voluntary and temporary liaisons. The truth lies somewhere between the two. Johnson's relations with Iroquois women had a strong political dimension and reflected his power and status. Those women were also, however, independent and active individuals with minds and desires of their own. These relationships, moreover, were more than sexual. They formed some of the ties that bound William Johnson to the Mohawks and made them think of him as belonging at least in part to them.

There is no reason to suppose that when Johnson left Ireland in his early twenties he was not already sexually active. The repression of the Catholic Church as an institution and the refusal of the majority of the population to join any other left Irish society relatively free from the moral strictures of the clergy. Gaelic poetry and song from the eighteenth century are vigorously earthy and tend to envisage women as passionate and sexually aware. There were certainly men and women who broke the rules. A late seventeenth-century ordnance by the Catholic Bishop of Meath sets out rules for the ritual purification of women who have given birth out of wedlock and makes specific provision for up to three such children.4

Even if it is likely that a young man of Johnson's strong sexual appetites did not leave Ireland a virgin, the Mohawk valley nevertheless offered him a completely new sense of freedom. Not only was he far from the censorious eyes of his parents and his clerical uncles, but he was among people who had a much more sophisticated attitude to sex. Iroquois wives and husbands were expected to be faithful to each other. Unmarried women, however, were free to form sexual relationships. Sex was sometimes regarded as a normal part of the ritual exchange involved in trade and the giving of presents. Johnson was not at all displeased by these courtesies, as is evident from a later letter of his teasing the colonial administrator Goldsbrow Banyar that he would introduce him to a 'Princess of the first Rank' provided he would not insult the woman by failing to discharge 'the necessary Duty, which men of years and infirmities are seldom capable of'.5

In 1742, the year his son John was born to Catharine Weissenberg, Johnson also had his first identifiable Mohawk child. The mother was Elizabeth Brant, daughter of a Wolf clan sachem Brant and his wife Jacomine, and then about twenty-two years old. The boy was christened Brant and given the Mohawk name Keghneghtago, or Quahayack, which means either 'on the bed' or 'in the gun'. In 1744, the year his daughter Mary was born to Catharine, he and Elizabeth had another Mohawk son, Thomas. They seem to have had another son, Christian, the following year, which suggests, since Mohawk women spaced their pregnancies every three years or so unless a baby died, that Thomas did not live long. Christian, too, died in infancy.

The birth of these Mohawk children involved Johnson in a wider set of familial relationships. Since he did not wish to be recognised as their legal father in the colonial world, they were listed by the Reverend Barclay in his register of baptisms at Fort Hunter as the children of other Mohawk couples. Brant and Thomas were recorded as the children of the Turtle clan sachem Brant Kanagaradunkwa and his wife, Elizabeth's aunt Christina, which must have raised some suspicions in Barclay's mind, since Christina was then in her fifties and almost certainly past child-bearing age. Barclay indeed made his suspicions obvious by listing Christian as the 'adopted son of Brant'.[6] But these evasions were not simply fraudulent. In Mohawk terms, the mother was the most important parent, and Brant and Christina would have genuinely seen Johnson's Mohawk children as part of their family.

This relationship took a poignant twist in 1746 when Johnson, in his official role as Indian Commissioner for New York, supplied Brant with black cloth, a pair of stockings and a shirt 'to Clean Brant's house after the Decease of his Son before he could keep Council in his House'.[7] Almost certainly this son was Johnson's own child Christian.

Around 1750, Johnson had a son by another Mohawk woman. Named William after his father, the boy's Mohawk name was Tagawirunta.[8] His mother was probably also a relative of Brant Kanagaradunkwa, and possibly was Elizabeth's younger sister Margaret.

Johnson seems to have been particularly fond of William/ Tagawirunta. The New York colonial official John Catherwood, writing in April 1750, expressed his hope that 'little Will behaves well and improves', showing that Johnson had advertised his birth even in government circles.[9] In 1769 he was included in a Mohawk grant of land at Canajoharie to Johnson.[10] In his will Johnson linked William/ Tagawirunta with Brant/Keghneghtago as the 'two Mohawk Lads' he implicitly acknowledged as his sons, and left each of them £100 and 1,000 acres of land. He had also set aside for them two horses, two cows, two breeding sows and four sheep each.[11]

Other Mohawk relationships are hinted at in a letter from Johnson's friend Joseph Chew in 1749, in which he hopes 'the young Ladys at the [Indian] Castle are well' and sends his 'Compliments to little Miss Michael at the Mohaw[k]s & madam Curl'd locks at Conejesharry' [Canajoharie].[12]

So it seems clear that Johnson had more than one sexual relationship active at any one period of his life in America. According to Jeptha Simms, who collected Mohawk valley folklore in the early nineteenth century, Johnson was 'on very intimate terms' with Susannah and Elizabeth, two daughters of Henry Wormwood who lived near a fishing lodge he had built in the woods. The Wormwoods certainly had some relationship with Johnson. He bought cattle from the Wormwood family in the 1740s and 1750s. More intriguingly, according to an account book, he paid nine shillings for a pair of shoes for Henry in August 1771 and six shillings for a parcel of salt that December, gifts that suggest a degree of intimacy beyond a mere business relationship.[13]

Simms records that Johnson was particularly close to Susannah, 'a beautiful girl, of middling stature, charmingly formed, with a complexion fair as a water lily – contrasting with which she had a melting dark eye and raven hair'. He claims that Johnson arranged a match for her with an Irishman, Robert or Alexander Dunbar. There certainly was an Alexander Dunbar around Johnson's second house, Johnson Hall in 1772, where he seems to have worked as a carpenter or builder.[14] According to Simms, Susannah's marriage to Dunbar lasted only a short while, leaving her, at around twenty years of age, a 'grass widow' with one child. After this, she became Johnson's semi-regular companion when he stayed overnight at the lodge he called the Fish House.

In passing Wormwood's dwelling, some half a mile distant from his boat at the nearest point, if he desired an agreeable companion for the night, he discharged his double-barrelled gun, and the two shots in quick succession was a signal that never failed to bring him a temporary housekeeper. Susannah was his favourite and so pleased was she with his attentions, that she often arrived on foot at the Fish House before he did, especially if he lingered to fish by the way.[15]

The folkloric nature of these recollections is clear from an anecdote told about a conversation between Henry Wormwood and the wife of his more genteel neighbour Godfrey Shew. Wormwood's arm was sore and Mrs Shew suggested that he had made it lame by sleeping on the floor of the Fish House. 'No I haven't', said Wormwood, 'I slept on a good bed, for Sir William brought down from the point a very nice wide one, which was plenty large enough for four.' 'Four?' gasped Mrs Shew. 'Pray how did you manage to sleep four in a bed?' 'Oh, easy enough. Susannah made it up very nicely on the floor, and then Sir William told us how to lay. He first directed the women to get in the middle, and "Now," said he to me, "you get on that side and take care of your old woman next to you, and I'll get on this side and try to take care of Susannah."'[16]

Such vivid tales are not evidence of actual incidents, though Simms had the story from Mrs Shew's son Jacob. What they do suggest, however, is the kind of tale that circulated about Johnson among his ordinary tenants. They conjure up a figure of half-scandalous fascination, a thrilling rogue, a sexual trickster to whom the normal laws of propriety don't apply. The man who can make love to a woman while her parents are beside them in the bed is a Lord of Misrule, with both the hedonistic energy and the commanding authority that the term implies.

Even in the dangerous and distressing circumstances of the war of the 1740s he found time for sexual pleasure. While Catharine and the children were away in Albany and Schenectady where he had sent them for their safety, he took up with an Irishwoman called Mary McGrath. She was the widow of an Irish soldier at Fort Hunter, Sergeant Owen Connor. Her second husband, Christopher, 'Native of Dublin in Irland',[17] was taken prisoner by a French and Indian war party in 1746 and held in Quebec until 1750.[18] She probably sought Johnson's help after her husband's capture and they clearly established a relationship.

Johnson helped to get money to Christopher McGrath in Quebec in early 1749, and after his return urged the New York Assembly to reward his unshakeable 'Loyalty and Steadfastness'.[19] That he himself enjoyed the lack of similar qualities in McGrath's wife is apparent from the acknowledgement of her daughter, also Mary, in his will, where she was left 200 acres of land.[20]

12

Master of Ceremonies

===

In June 1755 William Johnson ordered the trimmings of a fine topcoat and jacket and an elaborate waistcoat from the New York merchants Colden and Kelly. His demands were very specific: strips of silver lace an inch wide, 'the genteelest you Can get there'; thirty-six white buttons for the coat and thirty plain and wrought gilt buttons for the jacket; thin green velvet for the lapels and cuffs; green alpaca to line all three garments.[1]

This genteel raiment was ordered alongside the more mundane equipment of a military commander: Indian corn, writing paper, quills and ink, 'a verry good Tent made for my own Use of the best Stuff to keep out the rain', fuses and flints, mortars and mallets, pitch and powder horns, shovels and spades, axes and adzes, knapsacks, grindstones and bullets. But the elaborate new clothes were in their own way necessary implements of war. An outward show of distinction sufficiently lavish to impress a new range of people, from gawky farm boys to big-city lawyers and from God-bothering Puritans to raw young warriors. For he was now General Johnson, commander of a whole front in Britain's renewed war against France.

Johnson himself had been among the first to feel the earliest rumblings of this new conflict. In December 1750 George Clinton in New York City received a letter from Johnson on the Mohawk and immediately sent an urgent despatch to the Lords of Trade in London. Johnson's letter informed Clinton that he had been given a 'Plate of Lead full of Writing, which some of the upper Nations of Indians stole from Jean Coeur the French Interpreter, at Niagara, on his way to the River Ohio, which river and all lands thereabouts, the French claim as will appear by said writing. It gave the Indians so much uneasiness that they immediately dispatched some of the Cayuga Cheifs to me with it, telling me . . . their only reliance was on me.'[2]

Johnson translated for the Cayuga sachems the 'Devilish Writing' on the lead plate. It stated in French that the plate had been buried on 24 July 1749 near the Ohio River 'as a monument of the renewal of possession which we have taken of the said River Ohio and of all those that therin fall, and of all the lands on both sides as far as the sources of the said rivers'.[3] Johnson sent the plate to Clinton, who in turn sent it immediately to London.

The reaction to this bold claim to the Ohio valley and with it in effect to the immense, and to Europeans still unknown, reaches of the American West, was at first slow. The colony of Virginia sent a young officer, George Washington, to the Ohio country to demand the removal of the forts which the French were building there. The French commander at Fort LeBoeuf, Jacques Legardeur de Saint-Pierre, offered him a polite but firm rebuff. In May 1754 Washington attacked and massacred a small French force and was then roundly defeated himself.

In preparation for the coming war, Johnson began the process of fortifying the new stone house he had built at Mount Johnson as soon as the last one ended, a quarter of a mile upriver from the wooden home he had had occupied since 1739. His decision, in late 1748, to construct a fine Georgian-style mansion '60 foot long, by 32 Wide two Story High, all Stone', was in part a declaration of his permanent presence in the Mohawk valley.[4] With four large rooms downstairs – a living room, a dining room, a kitchen and an office – and four bedrooms reached by an elegant staircase, the new Mount Johnson was an imposing statement of the arrival of European gentility in the woodlands. Johnson's prominence in the war of the 1740s had raised his social status to such a level that the Dutch schoolmaster in Schenectady, reaching for an appropriate form of address, came up with 'Myn Heer Janson Consul van syn majt. Van Groot Britt.' – Mr Janson, Consul of His Majesty of Great Britain.[5] A consul needed to live in something better than a log cabin.

Yet the need for a strong stone house was also testament to the continuing threat of violence. As the 1750s advanced, Mount Johnson gradually became Fort Johnson. A report from a French spy describes Johnson's physical situation halfway through this process, after the addition of a parapet but before the construction of further defences:

Col. Johnson's mansion is situated on the border of the left bank of the River Mohawk; it is three stories high; built of stone, with loopholes *(crénelés)* and a parapet and flanked with four bastions on which are some small guns. In the same yard, on both sides of the Mansion, there are two small houses; that on the right of the entrance is a Store, and that on the left is designed for workmen, negroes and other domestics. The yard gate is a heavy swing gate well ironed; it is on the Mohawk River side; from this gate to the river there is about 200 paces of level ground. The high road passes there. A small rivulet coming from the north empties itself into the Mohawk River, about 200 paces below the enclosure of the yard. On this stream there is a Mill about 50 paces distance from the house; below the Mill is the miller's house where grain and flour are stored, and on the other side of the creek 100 paces from the mill, is a barn in which cattle and fodder are kept. One hundred and fifty paces from Colonel Johnson's Mansion at the North side, on the left bank of the little creek, is a little hill on which is a small house with port holes where is ordinarily kept a guard of honour of some twenty men, which serves also as an advanced post.[6]

Eventually, Johnson would find it necessary to add 'two Blockhouses upon the most convenient ground to serve as Outworks, & cover my house'.[7] Bit by bit, he was forced to become at home with war.

These changes were made necessary by the onset of conflict. In response to French success in defending its claim to the Ohio valley, the British government sent Major General Edward Braddock to America with two Irish regiments and a wide authority over the colonial governors. Initially, his orders were to raise what colonial troops he needed and mount four successive expeditions. First he was to uproot the French from the Ohio valley. Then he was to move north and dislodge the French from Fort Niagara on Lake Ontario, which controlled the communications between Ohio and Canada. From there he was to shift his attentions to the New York frontier and destroy Fort St Frederic, which the French had maintained for two decades at Crown Point on Lake Champlain, guarding territory that was claimed by the Iroquois and therefore by the British. Finally, Braddock was to push the French out of the forts they had constructed on the isthmus connecting the Nova Scotia peninsula to the Canadian mainland.[8]

From the safety of London, however, the British government began to feel that this initial, carefully staged, plan was insufficiently aggressive. Braddock's orders were revised to encompass a much more ambitious strategy of four simultaneous attacks: one against the Ohio forts; one against Fort Niagara; one against Crown Point; and a fourth against the Nova Scotia isthmus.9 The hope was that making simultaneous war on these four fronts would stymie the ability of the French to reinforce their garrisons and the British advantage in colonial manpower could be brought to bear.

This division of forces raised an obvious problem of command. In the initial plan for serial campaigns, Braddock would have charge of each stage of the war. In the new plan, while he would remain as commander-in-chief and lead the attack on the Ohio forts, leaders were required for each of the other expeditions.

In mid-April 1755 Braddock summoned William Johnson to his camp at Alexandria, Virginia, where he was preparing his own assault on the Ohio forts. There he announced the new command structure. The Nova Scotia campaign would be led by Brigadier General Charles Lawrence. The expedition against Fort Niagara would be under the command of Governor William Shirley of Massachusetts. To his surprise, and not entirely to his delight, Johnson had been chosen to command the attack on Crown Point. Braddock also gave him a formal commission as Sole Superintendent of 'the affairs of the United Nations of Indians, their allies and dependants'.10 On 16 April Johnson was commissioned as major general in the provincial army11 and commander-in-chief of the colonial forces raised for the Crown Point campaign in New York, Massachusetts, New Hampshire, Vermont, Connecticut and Rhode Island.12

In some respects Johnson was a logical choice. A month before, he had himself urged the most influential colonial governor, William Shirley of Massachusetts, to plan an attack on Crown Point as the best way of bringing the Iroquois into the conflict on the British side. Shirley had forwarded these recommendations to London with his own strong support, adding that Johnson was 'the best judge in America' of the disposition of the Iroquois.13 The Lords of Trade had been hearing Johnson's praises sung by Clinton for the past eight years.14

The strong evidence of Iroquois loyalty to him after his resignation as Indian Commissioner showed that he had the trust of at least one colonial force that would have a crucial role in an attack through the rugged wilderness terrain of northern New York. That he had the support of the Governors of Massachusetts and New York, who would have to contribute militia for his expedition, was also obvious. Johnson, moreover, had sent scouting and scalping parties as far as

Fort St Frederic in previous years and had himself in 1747 led a small force to Lac Saint Sacrement, from which any assault on Crown Point would have to begin.

On the other hand, though, Johnson was no soldier. As he put it himself: 'I was not bred to Military Life, nor do I claim the knowledge of an experienced officer.'[15] What military experience he had was in the organisation of Indian guerrilla warfare. He was now being asked to undertake what was in effect a European military campaign: cutting roads, hauling cannon, building stockades and then besieging a very substantial French fortress. All of this was to be done, however, in a rough and decidedly American environment. The task would have been daunting even for a hardened military aristocrat with a special knack for logistics.

He himself was all too aware of his limitations and that of the colonial militias who began to gather in Albany for the campaign. 'I am', he wrote to Braddock from Mount Johnson in May, 'truly sensible of my own Inability to be at the head of this undertaking, & I am afraid I shall have but few to assist & strengthen my Incapacity. None that can be called an Engineer, their Artillery in bad order & no Carriages yet provided, their Shells not fit for Service, No Man of Military Experience that I hear of amongst them.'[16]

The absurdity of his situation as the commander of a front in a major imperial war is reflected in a note of 24 May that he kept in his papers. Headed 'Some Hints for a Commanding Officer' and copied out in someone else's hand, it has the feel of a crash course in generalship-made-easy:

Make sure of a safe retreat in case of accidents; the Battle is not always to the strong.
If you gain a Victory, be more upon your guard.
If you loose dont despair.
Let nothing ruffle your Temper, be always cool, happen what will.
Let no disappointment cool your Courage, but on the Contrary exert yourself the more, disappointments create experience, and this an officer.
At no time shew any diffidence or fear in your Countenance.
By all means get the esteem and affection of your officers and Men, but they ought at the same time to know you Command; there is a difference between power and authority.[17]

Johnson, though, wasn't alone in his inexperience. Apart from the very able Captain William Eyre, an experienced British army engineer sent by Braddock in response to his pleas, Johnson's army had no soldiers. He was given no regular troops. His second-in-command, Phineas Lyman of Connecticut, had been a tutor at Yale College and more recently a lawyer. Most of the rank-and-file were farmers and farmers' sons, who wore their own clothes and brought their own guns. 'They came chiefly from plain New England homesteads – rustic abodes, unpainted and dingy, with long well-sweeps, capacious barns, rough fields of pumpkin and corn, and vast kitchen chimneys, above which in winter hung squashes to keep them from frost, and guns to keep them from rust.'[18] Instead of bayonets, they had hatchets stuck in their belts.

The troops who were gathering at Albany for the expedition were, as Johnson afterwards told his brother Warren, 'raw and undisciplined'.[19] Some of them had fought during the 1740s, but even in formal combat like the siege of Louisbourg they had not learned to behave like military automatons. 'Those who were on the spot', recorded one contemporary historian of the militia at Louisbourg, 'have frequently, in my hearing, laughed at the recital of their own irregularities, and expressed their admiration when they reflected on the almost miraculous preservation of the army from destruction. They indeed presented a formidable front to the enemy; but the rear was a scene of confusion and frolic. While some were on duty in the trenches, others were racing, wrestling, pitching quoits, firing at marks, or at birds . . .'[20]

All of this made it crucial, both for Johnson's self-confidence and for the success of the campaign, that a decent contingent of Iroquois warriors should be persuaded to join him. It was not just that the French would have strong Indian allies or that the terrain demanded Indian military skills. The Six Nations could supply fighters far more experienced and far better led than anything Connecticut, New York or Rhode Island could muster.

When he summoned the Six Nations and their allies for a conference at Fort Johnson on 21 June, the response seemed promising. A huge crowd of over 1,100 men, women and children assembled at his house. While the Senecas, among whom French influence was strongest, were under-represented, there was significant compensation in the form of 130 Delawares, the arrival of a Mississauga chief sachem, and a supportive letter from Scarouday, leader of the Iroquois interest in the upper Ohio valley.

The orchestration of this huge gathering demanded both money and ingenuity. Johnson laid in huge quantities of cloth, blankets, guns, gunpowder, make-up, frying pans, combs, hawk's bells, knives, razors and Jew's harps to distribute as presents. He prepared pipes and tobacco, punch and belts of wampum for the ceremonial exchanges and diplomatic rituals. He got high-quality clothes ready to present as parting gifts to ninety-seven sachems from eleven different nations in anticipation of a successful outcome. Beef, pork, corn, bread and tea were ordered for the feasting; and most important, he curried the favour of strategically important sachems with £155 in private presents, and greased the palms of three important Oneida warriors – 'very great friends of mine' – with presents of around £2 each.[21]

As ever, Hendrick was deeply involved in the planning of Johnson's strategy for the public conference. He and his brother Abraham came to stay at Fort Johnson with their families a full ten days before the proceedings began. Officially, they were there to help Johnson translate his speech into Iroquoian, but the careful and elaborate nature of the subsequent proceedings makes it clear that Hendrick was in fact engaged in preparing a scenario for Johnson's appeal to a sceptical audience.

This conference was Johnson's reintroduction to his abandoned role as the leading Indian diplomat, and he had to make a good impression. By now, Johnson had learned much of the art of Iroquois rhetoric. The kind of speech he would have to give to this public gathering had an important place in the culture of the confederate nations, and his audience had high standards of performance. For elaborate public speeches, sachems had what one of the early Jesuit missionaries called a 'Captain's tone'. The flow of speech was maintained with the help of mnemonic devices like a marked stick, or, at crucial moments, a belt of wampum. The speaker walked back and forward 'like an actor on a stage'. At one conference, the Mohawk chief Kiotseaeton was noted as striding 'about that great space as if on the stage of a theatre; he made a thousand gestures; he looked up to heaven; he gazed at the Sun; he rubbed his arms as if he wished to draw from them the strength that moved them in war'.[22] This was the high style that Johnson would have to emulate, and Hendrick probably gave him some coaching.

The first test, though, was of his patience. Many of the warriors arrived on horseback and, since he was the suitor, Johnson could not risk insulting them by asking them not to use his garden and meadows as gallops. He bit his tongue while they 'spoiled my Meadows & destroy[ed] every Green thing about my Estate'.[23]

French influence among the Iroquois had grown during the five years of Johnson's absence and official neglect. Johnson's priority at this conference was therefore to at least ensure the neutrality of those nations who were not inclined to take an active part on the British side. But he also hoped to persuade a substantial number of warriors to join the British expeditions, particularly, of course, his own.

Johnson knew that diplomatic negotiations before such a large and volatile audience had to be handled with extreme care. The ground could be laid in what he called 'private Conferences with the chiefs where the principal matters are first resolved on'.[24] His preparations focused largely on an influential Onondaga sachem Kakhswenthioni, also called Sequaresere and known to the English as Red Head.[25] This chief was crucial, not because he was regarded as being pro-British but precisely because he had been seen for some years as sympathetic to the French. As early as 1751 Johnson had identified him to the New York State Council as 'well known to be the most attached to the French' and as having gone to Canada at the invitation of French agents.[26] Johnson befriended him and brought him over to his own side, presumably with the help of substantial presents like the stockings and buckles he gave him during the conference and the gold locket, coat, gun and £4 in cash he gave him shortly afterwards.[27] Before this great Indian audience, he could now get Red Head to play out the role of known French sympathiser persuaded by the arguments, generosity and charisma of the great Warraghiyagey to shift his allegiance and return to the true faith. Red Head played his part to perfection.

Johnson made sure that his closest allies were fully aware of his strategy. Before he delivered his opening speech, he had Daniel Claus, a young German who was fluent in Mohawk and who had joined Johnson's service, read it in Iroquoian, for their approval, to the chief sachems of the Oneida and Onondaga nations. He then delivered in English a harangue designed to re-establish himself as the great mediator between the British and the Iroquois.

He began with the metaphor of himself as the Sole Superintendent being a tree that had been planted among them to provide 'a comfortable and extensive shade for you and your allies to take shelter under it'. He compared the regime of the old Albany-based Indian commissioners to a weak fire whose embers had now been removed to Fort Johnson, where it had been rekindled so as to give the 'clearest light and greatest warmth' to those who wished to light their pipes at it, but also to 'dazzle and scorch' its enemies.[28]

In the hope of using a conference at which he had a majority of his sympathisers to bind those more doubtful leaders who had stayed away, he enacted a parable of unity that had clearly been pre-arranged with the Onondaga speaker Red Head. First Johnson proclaimed: 'Brothers joined together with love and confidence are like a great Bundle of sticks which can not be broke whilst they are bound together, but when separated from each other, a Child may breake them.' While he spoke these words, he passed a bundle of sticks to Red Head, who, with elaborate formal gestures tried and failed to snap them in two, then, separating one out from the bunch, split it with extravagant ease. Red Head then formally passed the sticks to one of the other sachems, presumably a representative of one of the more sceptical factions. As Johnson had intended, the dumb show produced a huge roar of approval.

Even when Johnson finished, however, the performance was not over. Usually, when a speech was delivered in English, one of the interpreters translated it paragraph by paragraph. This time, through, Johnson had concocted a performance in which he could present himself, not just as an emissary to the Iroquois, but as one of them. He wanted the audience to feel that his own words were passing through them and emerging from the mouth of an Indian leader. First, in a low voice, Claus read the translation of Johnson's speech a paragraph at a time to one of the Oneida sachems. He in turn prompted Red Head, who recapitulated the paragraph aloud in Iroquoian before the entire audience.

For that audience, highly attuned as it was to the forms and gestures of rhetorical exchange, this elaborate performance carried its own meanings. They watched Johnson's words being carried through a series of voices, thus experiencing them as a verbal version of the Covenant Chain which this conference was designed to re-forge. And the words spoken in English were transformed so that they carried to the audience through the voice of the speaker of the Onondagas, keepers of the great council fire of the confederacy. Johnson's authority and that of Iroquois tradition were being made to speak with one voice.

This staging of the spectacle continued two days later when the sachems arranged to give their reply. Usually, the forms and conventions of an Iroquois conference were taken for granted. Hendrick, presumably in agreement with Johnson, saw the opportunity provided by the presence of large numbers of children and young warriors, who did not usually attend conferences, to turn the meeting into a demonstration and renewal of the traditional rituals. When he began his formal reply, he addressed it, not as was usual, simply to 'Brothers' or 'Brother Sachems' but (in Claus's rather clumsy translation) to 'Brother Sachems and You Warrior my children!'.

Speaking to the uninitiated youngsters, he then explained: 'We are now assembled to reply to our Brother Warraghiyagey. I will therefore acquaint you with the method that has always been observed by our Forefathers on these occasions.' What followed was thus not just as a particular response to Johnson's requests but the re-enactment of a time-honoured tradition, again placing Johnson symbolically at the heart of Iroquois political identity. And to this clever manipulation of the conventions, Hendrick added another twist. Having stepped forward as the speaker who would deliver the reply, he then announced that it would be delivered, in fact, by Red Head.

Just as this echoed Johnson's previous drama in which Red Head became his voice, so Red Head now delivered a speech that echoed the imagery of Johnson's speech. Johnson had spoken of himself as a tree whose branches would shelter the Iroquois and their allies. Red Head replied: 'We were grieved and distressed whilst the Tree lay down . . . We are universally rejoiced to see this Tree replanted.' Johnson had spoken of the fire that would warm the Iroquois and scorch their enemies. Red Head replied that the King had restored a 'clear and comfortable light' by bringing back Johnson 'whom we look upon as our own flesh and Blood'. To dramatise the image, he enacted the kicking away with his foot of all other fires 'as unnatural and hateful to us' and, with three low bows, presented Johnson with a belt of wampum. He then thanked Johnson 'for renewing our ancient forms'.

All this was designed to present Johnson, not as a European outsider, but as a cornerstone of the Iroquois's own system of authority. To further reinforce this image of Johnson as the guarantor of continuity for the Iroquois confederacy, Red Head was followed by the Oneida chief sachem who announced that another of their sachems, Connochquisie, had died. He then brought forward the boy who was to take Connochquisie's place and presented him to Johnson, who 'took the Lad by the hand' and promised to clothe him the next day in an outfit proper to a sachem.

Having prepared the ground with these expansive performances, Johnson used his reply the following day to get down to business. Knowing that the French had been spreading rumours that the English preparations for war were in fact intended for hostilities against the Iroquois, he swore that this propaganda was false, using Indian forms to speak on behalf of the English: 'I call that Almighty Spirit above to witness, who made us all, and knows our hearts, who created the sun which shines upon us, and in whose hands are the Thunder and Lightning, That we your Brethren have no ill designs whatsoever against you.'

He then asked directly for warriors to join the campaigns against the French: 'If you treat me as your Brother, Go with me. My war kettle is on the Fire, my Canoe is ready to put in the water, my Gun is loaded, my sword by my side and my Ax is sharpened. I desire and expect you will now take up the Hatchet and join us your Brethren, against all our Enemies.'[29] A day later, he delivered a harangue on behalf of General Braddock and then threw down a war belt which was taken up by the Oneida sachem. This was the signal for one of the interpreters, Arent Stevens, to begin a war dance and for Johnson to break out a large tub of punch made with five bottles of claret.[30]

Even all these histrionics and revelries, designed as they were to sweep the Iroquois back into the arms of the British, were not strong enough to counteract the effects of years of disappointment. A combination of the festive atmosphere of such a large gathering of different nations and the stress of making a decision on which the survival of the confederacy itself could depend caused many of the sachems to take to the rum. It was four days before they were able to deliver a reply. It was, in its rhetoric, as positive as Johnson could have hoped, with promises of renewed friendship and alliance.

There were, though, two carefully placed hesitations. To the agreement to join in the war was added a rider: 'We have not yet determined what particular numbers will go from each Castle' – a hint that the ultimate level of engagement would depend on evidence of effective British organisation; and, in a clever play on Johnson's original performance with the bunch of sticks, Red Head turned the metaphor around. Holding out the bundle, he addressed Johnson and told him that the lesson he had drawn from it was already taking effect. But, he added, there was a lesson too for the English, some of whom showed, by continuing to trade with France, that they put their own wealth before the common good: 'Your people are very faulty, they are too thirsty for money.'

Red Head's point was astutely made. The British, as Johnson well knew, were very good at using the rhetoric of brotherhood but not so good at putting it into practice, even among themselves. The Iroquois had watched the colonists long and hard enough to know that money, power and jealousy could override all their stated intentions. And just when Johnson seemed to have ended his exhausting nine-day public performance with apparent success, he was about to discover the truth of Red Head's lesson.

13

An Upstart of Yesterday

═══

Matthew Farrell was a friend of the Johnsons from Warrenstown. He had come to Mount Johnson in 1751, having been 'obliged to give up Business & advised by our Friends in County Meath' to go to Johnson for 'protection'.[1] He received, not just protection, but the hand in marriage of Johnson's sister Catherine, who had also come to live with him around the same time. Johnson employed him in the Indian trade and, as the plans for war were set in train, as a leader of Mohawk warriors. In July 1755 Farrell and Johnson's assistant and future son-in-law Daniel Claus went to the Mohawk village at Canajoharie. Their purpose was to hold a 'Frolick' for the warriors who had agreed to join the major military expedition to be led by William Johnson against the French. They supplied meat and drink and were invited to an all-night war dance at the house of Brant Kanagaradunkwa's son Thomas.

The party was joined, however, by John Henry Lydius, a trader and adopted Mohawk, who was trying to recruit the Mohawks to join the rival military expedition to be led by the Massachusetts governor William Shirley. In the middle of the celebration, a row broke out between Lydius and Farrell. Lydius's Turtle clan brother, the war chief Aaron Oseragighte, pushed Farrell to the floor and poured hot ashes over his head. It was a deliberate and flagrant insult to Johnson.[2]

When William Shirley had to suggest a commander for the expedition against Crown Point, his natural instinct had been to look to his own political constituency among the gentlemen of Massachusetts. Now sixty-two, Shirley had been born in Sussex and, in spite of many years in Boston, remained very much an Englishman and a royalist with little sympathy for the dissenting culture of the colonists whom he governed. 'Artful, needy and ambitious',[3] he substituted for popularity a brilliant use of patronage that had kept him in office as governor of the wealthiest of the colonies since 1741. His own Massachusetts circle contained, as he told James De Lancey, 'Officers of Rank, & Experience, out of whom I could have Nominated' a general to lead the attack on Crown Point.

Yet Shirley decided to put forward instead the name of William Johnson 'preferably to any Gentleman in my own Government',[4] an act he considered to be a token of his great selflessness and patriotism. He understood that much of the point of the expedition was to restore English influence with the Iroquois. To that end, 'It would be an Unspeakable advantage to Us at this Conjuncture if we could engage any of them in the proposed Service.' This being so, he said, 'the great Influence he hath for Severall Years maintained over the Indians of the Six Nations is the circumstance which determines me in my Choice' – of Johnson. The irony of the bitter dispute that began to erupt immediately after the Fort Johnson conference was that Shirley now set about attempting to destroy that very influence.

Shirley's choice had not, in fact, been entirely selfless. He disliked James De Lancey and the Albany merchants, both for their lack of enthusiasm for the war and for their tendency to award lucrative war contracts to their own protégés rather than his. Shirley was astute enough to understand that, in spite of his family connections, Johnson was at best an extremely uncomfortable ally of De Lancey's. By being seen to promote Johnson himself, he could hope to bring him and his Indian connections within his own circle of influence.

Shirley had good reason to believe that Johnson could be brought into that circle and out of De Lancey's. He knew, of course, that Johnson was the nephew of Sir Peter Warren and that Warren was married to De Lancey's sister. But he also knew that De Lancey and Warren had conspired to undermine Johnson's previous term as Indian Commissioner and to ensure that he was not paid the debts that were still outstanding from the 1740s. He may also have gathered that Johnson had since been given a further reason to be embittered against the Warren/De Lancey faction.

Johnson had believed when he left Ireland that Peter Warren would reward him well for his hard work in clearing and settling the latter's estate in the Mohawk valley. He felt that he had been assured, at least implicitly, that most of this land would eventually be left to him in

Warren's will. Shortly before he died, after a short illness, in Dublin in July 1752, however, Warren changed his will to say, not merely that Johnson was to get nothing, but that he was to repay the supposed debts he had incurred in settling Warren's estates and establishing himself as an Indian trader. In an especially malign twist, Warren then left this money to Johnson's brothers and sisters in Ireland, so that he could not contest the will without seeming to harm his own family.

This new will, of which De Lancey was made an executor, seems to have been motivated by pure spite. Warren died a very rich man, and left a fortune of £160,000. Johnson's supposed debts to him amounted, in this context, to a pittance. The new will, moreover, changed a previous document in which Johnson, though not in fact left the New York estate, was absolved of his supposed debts to Warren. De Lancey's brother Oliver later expressed to Johnson his puzzlement at Warren's decision to alter his will: 'Who had Influence over him in Ireland I cant Say at the time of his Death, It could not be his Lady who was in England and was not So well considered as in his former Wills.'⁵ Johnson himself was sure that neither his own family nor Warren's had any part in the affair: 'I do not suspect that I had any Enemys about him of my own family, as they did not partake of any benefit from his Last Will, nor can I believe the family into which he married would concern themselves about it.'⁶ The only reasonable conclusion was that Warren had used the will to express his resentment at Johnson's temerity in carving out an independent career for himself. Governor Shirley may not have known the details of this family feud, but he was certainly well connected enough to know that Johnson's ties to the De Lancey/Warren faction were weaker than they had ever been.

These considerations were very much alive as the war effort was gearing up. As soon as he left the conference in Alexandria, Virginia, at which Braddock had appointed Johnson to the command, Governor Shirley headed for New York, accompanied by the Governor of Pennsylvania, Robert Morris. There, the two men set about awarding the contracts to supply Shirley's Fort Niagara expedition. This gave them a bountiful font of patronage which they directed towards Boston merchants like Thomas Hutchinson and Morris's supporters in Philadelphia. Brazenly, however, they also gave contracts to a firm in New York headed by Morris's nephew and a member of the Livingston faction, who were De Lancey's greatest enemies. Not only were De Lancey and his cronies cut out of the business, but they had to watch the wonderful opportunities for profiteering flow to their opponents.[7]

None of this need have affected Johnson. He had more than enough on his hands with the huge and interminable Indian conference at his house and his raw colonial recruits pouring into Albany. The conference at Fort Johnson seemed to have reached a conclusion on the night of 29 June, when Johnson began the war dance around the fire and Red Head and many leading warriors joined in.

On the afternoon of 1 July the yard beside the house was filled with the clothes, guns, kettles, frying pans and trinkets that were the usual presents to mark the first stage in the leave-taking of the sachems and warriors. Two days later, the sachems and warriors assembled to give their final reply to Johnson's farewell speech. Having gone through the usual formalities, however, Red Head suddenly launched into a bitter denunciation of fraudulent land deals concocted by greedy colonists: 'You desire us to unite and live together and draw all our Allies near us, but we shall have no land left either for ourselves or them; for your people, when they buy a small piece of land of us, by stealing they make it large.'[8]

The cause of this passionate outburst was the arrival at Fort Johnson of John Henry Lydius, the trader whom Governor Shirley had engaged to recruit Indians for his projected expedition against Fort Niagara. Shirley had probably commissioned Lydius in good faith even though he knew as early as 1747 that Johnson resented his tendency to use Lydius on Indian business. Back then he protested that he had employed Lydius in the belief that 'he stood extreamely well with Col. Johnson'.[9] In fact Lydius was despised both by Johnson, who regarded him as 'a Man extreamly obnoxious to the public in general and to me in particular',[10] and by the Six Nations.

In Johnson's early years in America he did business with Lydius and the two enjoyed reasonably friendly relations. Lydius, ten years older than Johnson and the son of a Dutch minister in Albany, had established close relations with some of the Mohawks, initially as a preacher and then as a fur trader. In 1732, after his induction into the Turtle clan, he had succeeded in persuading his new brothers to grant him an extensive tract of land at Wood Creek on the upper Hudson River. When Johnson first arrived in the Mohawk valley and began to trade, he used Lydius as his Albany agent.

As Johnson's standing with the Mohawks grew higher, however, the two men began to see each other as rivals. In the autumn of 1744 a series of rumours swept through the Mohawk villages to the effect that the people of Albany and Schenectady were plotting to attack them and drive them off their lands. The panic had a dangerous effect on Mohawk–colonial relations at a time when war between Britain and France was threatening the peace of the frontier. The Commissioners for Indian Affairs set up an investigation to discover the source of the rumours. One of Lydius's neighbours, probably at the latter's instigation, named Johnson as the culprit.[11] Though the allegation was not taken seriously, it turned Johnson's antipathy to his rival into a feud that now had larger political consequences.

By the 1750s the Iroquois as a whole shared Johnson's contempt for Lydius. The cause of this antagonism quickly revealed itself. Immediately after Red Head's philippic, the Oneida speaker Aguiotta got to his feet and said that Johnson had promised to keep the place where such councils were held 'clean from all Filth and that no *Snake* should come into the Council Room'. He then pointed at Lydius and said, 'That man sitting there is a devil and has stole our Lands, he takes Indians slyly by the Blanket one at a time, and when they are drunk, puts some money into their Bosoms, and perswades them to sign deeds for our lands upon the Susquehanna.'[12]

Johnson was already appalled by Shirley's attempts to recruit and organise Iroquois warriors for his own expedition against Fort Niagara, as if they were European or colonial troops. Shirley was offering them pay by the day, and tried to organise them into militia-style companies. Johnson objected: 'To establish the Indians into Companys of 100 Men each with Captains, Lieutenants & Ensigns is impossible, that sort of regulation cannot be obtained amongst those People, their officers must be Interpreters and take care of them in all respects besides their Duty as officers.'[13] But these tensions must have seemed manageable until the presence of Lydius suddenly threatened to undo all the hard-won amity of the previous fortnight.

Johnson, in his reply, made no attempt to defend Lydius, but in fact accepted the essential truth of the Indians' complaints. He pointedly acknowledged that he had indeed promised that no snakes would be allowed to come into the council room, and explained that while he was sorry if Lydius's presence had caused offence, 'he came of his own accord without any invitation from me'. He added: 'If Col. Lyddius hath done as you represent, and which I am affraid is in great measure true, I think he is very faulty.'[14]

From Shirley's point of view, this open disavowal of his agent was infuriating enough. To make matters worse, Johnson's secretary, Peter Wraxall, inserted into the official record of the conference an explanatory note to the effect that while Lydius had been 'privately' trying to persuade the Six Nations warriors to join Shirley's expedition, he had shown Johnson Shirley's orders for the recruitment of Indians and Johnson 'forbid him . . . to interfere any further with the Indians as it had and would occasion an uneasiness amongst them which might be prejudicial to the service in general'.[15] This record of the conference was sent both to the governors of the colonies and to the Lords of Trade in London. They were thus being informed in an official document that Shirley's attempts to recruit among the Six Nations were against the British interest and, even more humiliatingly, that Johnson had in effect countermanded Shirley's orders to Lydius.

Shirley confronted Johnson on the subject on 15 July in Albany, and demanded that all references to himself be expunged from the record of the conference. This was done, but the record sent to London still contained most of Wraxall's explanatory note and made it perfectly clear that Johnson had disavowed Lydius and countermanded Shirley's orders. Shirley was enraged. He felt, as he wrote to Johnson, 'that the only Intent [of the note] is to raise a Reflection upon me; and every word in it is pointed for that purpose'.[16]

His rage spurred Shirley to question the whole basis of Johnson's independent power as the sole manager of military relations with the Indians. 'I don't understand your Commission in the same manner you seem to do . . . or that you should assume to yourself a Power to engage all the Indians to go with yourself to Crown point.' It was, he curtly informed Johnson, 'your Duty to comply with my Demand of a Number of Indians to go with me; and not forbid all Persons to speak to any Indians for that Purpose'. To underline this demand for submission, he immediately ordered Johnson to supply him with sixty or seventy Indians to escort him to Oswego.[17]

This was a direct test of Johnson's nerve. There was no real need for such an elaborate escort through the territories of the Six Nations and it seems clear that the purpose of Shirley's order was simply to command obedience. Johnson understood this and abruptly refused. 'I told him that as his whole way to Oswego lay thro' the Indians

Country there was no fear of his being attacked by Enemy Indians in going hither.'[18]

Shirley retaliated by trying to humiliate Johnson before the Six Nations. He told the sachems that he had given Johnson £5,000 for them[19] and ordered military appointments and wages for their warriors, and that Johnson had concealed these generous bounties from them. He denigrated Johnson's position as commander of the expedition against Crown Point, suggesting that his was 'no more than a Militia commission'. He also told them, as Johnson put it, that 'it was him made a great Man of me', implying in effect that Johnson was a mere minion of his own who could be disposed of at the snap of his fingers.[20]

Johnson was particularly insulted that Shirley's secretary, William Alexander, forcibly pressed two of Johnson's own servants into his service. As Matthew Farrell at Fort Johnson informed Johnson at Albany in late July, 'They tould him they were your Servants and was to go to Crown point along with you he said he did not Care for you yourself must go where some ever Govenor Shirley orders you.' Both servants soon escaped from Shirley, but the point of the insult had been thrust home: Shirley was Johnson's master.[21]

Johnson's fury exploded in a letter to James De Lancey:

General Shirley's Conduct with regard to the Indians is in my Opinion extremely Culpable, will not only be very hurtful to the public Interest, but in the end obstruct even his own Designs. My Character and Conduct has been vilified to them without any regard either to facts or truth. By a Lavish bribery, a constant Licentious festivity, by Falsehoods, by Flattery, by threats, they have raised such a Confusion, such Corruption, such extravagant Expectations, among the Indians as not only greatly embarrasses the public service at present, Loads it with many great & additional Expenses, but will I fear be of lasting ill Consequence. Their sachems have sent me down word, that they are all in Amazement, that they cannot comprehend what is the meaning of these opposite Proceedings they desire I will clear up and explain matters to them, that their Castles are tore to pieces with Discord Faction & riot etc etc.[22]

The split in the British camp was deeply disconcerting for the Iroquois. Their relationship with the British was mediated through Johnson. It was his position as a partly Indianised European and his long cultivation of reciprocal friendships that made the alliance personal. Now, when the alliance itself was under such strain and the military incompetence of the British was generating a deep fear of defeat and abandonment, the deliberate undermining of Johnson's authority was likely to be disastrous.

Governor Shirley, however, made matters even worse by visiting the Mohawks at the Upper Castle and telling them, as Hendrick recalled, 'that though we thought [Johnson] had the sole management of Indian affairs, yet that he [Shirley] was over all; that he could pull down and set up . . . that he had always been a great Man and that . . . Brother Warraghiyagey was but an upstart of yesterday . . . and When I please I can take all his power from him'.[23]

In thus contrasting himself as a Great Man with the upstart nobody Johnson, Shirley was touching the tenderest of nerves. Irishmen in general were not inclined to be amused at English claims to superior status. For someone of Johnson's class, the dispossessed heirs of Gaelic landowners who compensated for their present penury with high notions of a noble past, this contemptuous dismissal was all but unbearable; and to express this contempt in front of the very people for whom Johnson knew himself to be a great man was to inflict an unforgivable wound.

The insult to the Iroquois was almost as flagrant. According to Hendrick, 'These Speeches made us quite ashamed and the Five Nations hung down their heads and would make no answer.' The silence of a great orator like Hendrick is itself eloquent. To him and the other Mohawk sachems, Johnson was important, not just because of his ability to deal with them on their own terms, but because he seemed to be the personal representative of the distant power of empire. Yet here was Shirley telling them, as Hendrick in turn told Johnson in front of his officers, 'that I was an Upstart of his creating, that it was he supplied me with money and that he could pull me down'.[24]

Johnson had to assure the Iroquois that 'it was not Governor Shirley who raised me up' but the King himself. He also had to deny that he was withholding from them the £5,000 that Shirley had supposedly given him for their use.[25] But the very need to make such explicit denials was a mark of the damage that had been done to his standing with the Six Nations.

Johnson was also aware that he had now acquired a very powerful antagonist. If Shirley had been influential enough to have him appointed to the command of the Crown Point expedition in the first place, he would also be powerful enough to do him immense harm. He therefore moved to protect his own position by denouncing Shirley to the Lords of Trade as a man who 'does not wear power with generous ease and true dignity'. In a long letter, he set out his version of events, and warned that Shirley was his 'inveterate Enemy' and would be trying to blacken his name.[26] He now knew that his own expedition against Crown Point and Shirley's against Fort Niagara would be not just military crusades but propaganda battles in which his and Shirley's factions would compete for the moral high ground. If Johnson's own rather unpromising campaign were to end in defeat, Shirley would have the opportunity to destroy him. 'I perceive plainly from the Stile, Temper & Character of the Man', he wrote to Thomas Pownall, an English ally of De Lancey's, 'that I may expect every thing that can be executed by a bad Man abandoned to passion & enslaved by resentment.'[27]

The dispute itself made failure more likely. Most of the Iroquois, appalled at the wrangling within the British camp and anxious about Johnson's true status, decided not to join his forces on the march to Lac Saint Sacrement. Back in 1747 Johnson had confidently claimed that he could 'bring a thousand Indian Warriors into the field'[28] against the French. Given the disappointments and failures of the intervening years, his expectations were now much lower, but he still anticipated that 'upwards of 300 will join me in my March towards Crown Point'.[29] Now he would be hard put to bring any at all.

Shirley, meanwhile, diverted 1,000 members of the Massachusetts and New Jersey militia from Johnson's forces to his own.[30] Competition between the two armies for cannon, wagons, boats and other supplies became quite overt. Morale among Johnson's own forces was also bound to be affected by the open nature of the row. By early August the split between Shirley and Johnson was common knowledge. Goldsbrow Banyar wrote to Johnson on 5 August that 'the difference between you and Mr S. begins to be talk'd of'.[31] The prospect of waging war simultaneously against the French and Shirley, while trying to discipline his raw recruits and overcome his own lack of military experience, seemed rather bleak.

14

The Precarious Salvo of Applause

When Johnson's army finally began to move northwards from Albany, it was already August, and the summer campaigning season was half over. It had to literally cut a path through the thick forests, creating roads wide enough for the heavily laden carts to follow if and when the wagoners who were left behind with the bulk of the supplies in Albany were persuaded that someone would pay them. Many of the shallow boats (known as *bateaux*) that were to carry Johnson's forces along Lac Saint Sacrement had been found to be leaky, and the general had to stay behind to get them repaired. Even when he got on the road with the rest of his troops, progress was slow. As Thomas Williams, surgeon to a Massachusetts regiment serving under Johnson's command, wrote to his wife: 'The expedition goes on very much as a snail runs; it seems we may possibly see Crown Point this time twelve months.'[1]

Most of Johnson's raw recruits were from the Calvinist heartlands of New England. A sense of religious purpose animated many of the volunteers who filled Johnson's ranks. Mary Pomeroy wrote to her husband, Seth, a gunsmith and lieutenant colonel in the Massachusetts Militia, on 9 August, for example, that 'after the defeat of the Lord's people at Ai, the kings of the land combined together, and thought they would cut them off, but the Lord had other thoughts about them. Such things he has done for his people and will do again. I commend you all to Him who knoweth the end from the beginning.'[2]

Discipline was not helped by the tendency of some of the more puritan commanders to enforce religious, rather than strictly military, rules. In early August, while the army was at Saratoga, 'A soldier, one Bickerstaff, was whipt for Profane Swaring & a Sodomittical Attempt, with one hundred lashes, and drummed out of the army with a rope about his neck, and ordered to be sent to a convenient place, and there to be kept till the Crown Point expedition is over.'3

Some of these tensions gathered around Johnson's relaxed attitude to the presence of women in the camp. The New Englanders, whose idea of training was 'sermons twice a week, daily prayers and frequent psalm-singing',4 regarded war as men's work. The New York, Rhode Island and Six Nations contingents, however, were all accompanied by wives, laundresses, nurses and prostitutes. The question was all the sharper, however, because it crystallised New England distrust of Johnson, consort of pagan savages and notorious womaniser, who was known to be in dispute with Governor Shirley.

For those who felt themselves engaged in a holy war against French Catholics and their heathen savage allies, the risk of moral contamination from service under a sinner was a matter of real discomfort. The possibility of prostitutes being among the camp followers was especially horrifying. Phineas Lyman complained to Johnson that the presence of such women 'g[ave] a very great uneasiness to the New England Troops', who feared 'Sacrificing all our Carracter' so much that they had threatened to 'either mobb or privately destroy' them.5

Johnson had prepared himself for the task of catering to the religious tastes of the New Englanders. In the 'Hints for a Commanding Officer' he had drawn up in May, he reminded himself: 'Prayers have often a good effect, especially among New England men, a well gifted New England Parson, might therefore be an usefull implement.'6 And while the puritans might have been highly insulted at his notion of a man of God as merely a useful implement of military command, he was careful to keep his cynicism to himself.

Johnson was forced to adopt a high moral tone that did not come naturally to him and assured Lyman: 'As to bad Women following or being harboured in our Camp I shall discountenance it to the utmost of my Power.' He saw no difficulty, though, with wives accompanying their husbands in the camps: 'As to Men's Wives while they behave Decently they are suffered in all Camps and thought necessary to Wash & mend.'7 The objections of the New Englanders were so strong, however, that Lyman eventually got his way. At a council of war between Johnson and the provincial commanders in mid-August, Lyman proposed 'that all the Women in the Camp should be removed from the same and forbid to return'. It was unanimously agreed 'that they be sent away by the first Conveyance to Albany'.8

Alerted by such disputes to the probability that many of his troops had heard stories of his immorality that were not to their taste, Johnson mobilised all his resources of charm, courtesy and geniality. Ironically, the skills he had acquired in Ireland and developed as a diplomat among the Iroquois – the ability to understand the conventions and culture of other people – now served him well with New England puritans, for whom the Iroquois were devil-worshipping savages.

Such men were never going to understand fully Johnson's relationship with the Indians. The sight of their general dressing occasionally in Indian clothes with his face painted was bound to be confusing, and some of the codes and gestures he employed in his role as Colonel of the Six Nations were literally incomprehensible to them. He gave instructions to the colonial militia, for example, that they would know a friendly Indian encountered on the march because he would call out Johnson's Mohawk name 'Warraghiyagey'.9 To many of the colonials this crucial password was heathen gobbledygook and impossible to remember. In the journal of James Gilbert, a Massachusetts volunteer, it turns up as 'Dewoveiaygo'.10

Johnson managed nevertheless to charm his troops. His success in overturning the prejudices and expectations of these sober middle-class believers is summed up in a letter from the Massachusetts surgeon Thomas Williams describing Johnson to the folks back home: 'I must say he is a complete gentleman & willing to oblige & please all men, familiar and free of access to the lowest Centinel, a gentleman of uncommon smart sense & even temper; never yet saw him in a ruffle, or use any bad language – in short I never was so disappointed in a person in the ideal I had of him before I came from home in my life.'11 Seth Pomeroy, likewise found Johnson 'a gentleman of great modesty, yet free and pleasant'.12

Though the thought would have disturbed the puritan officers, Johnson was really employing a manner he had learned from Irish papists and Iroquois sachems. In Indian society, a chief maintained his position, not through the fear of authority, but through personal magnetism, the careful distribution of generosity and the ability to project oneself as the first among equals. Appearance was important – just as the Mohawk sachem dressed himself in the best available finery, Johnson's genteel jacket with its thirty gilt buttons and green velvet lapels was the costume for the part he needed to perform. The performance itself required him to cultivate an air of dignity, censoring the bawdy jokes that usually accompanied his style of male intimacy, but yet avoiding any hint of stand-offish hauteur. It was a hard trick, but Johnson was as well schooled in these subtly calibrated manners as he was ignorant of the conventional arts of European command.

The style of his command was vital, because Johnson lacked its substance. Not only was Governor Shirley undermining his authority with the Iroquois, but the colonial war effort was chaotic to the point of anarchy. Johnson was privately appalled at the democratic conduct of the New England militiamen, who insisted on electing their own officers. 'A Popular choice in Military Life', he wrote, 'and that by new Levies is founded in Ignorance & will be guided by caprice, such officers will in all probability be like the heads of a Mob, who must support their preheminence by unworthy Condesensions, & Indulgences subversive of order & of the very Existance of an Army.'[13]

Discipline was in fact so weak that there were real fears of outright mutiny. Courts martial were held to hear charges of 'supporting & exciting a Mutinous Disposition in certain Soldiers', refusal to obey orders, fighting, sleeping on sentry duty, desertion.[14] Yet the democratic nature of the militia made the punishment even of serious military crimes almost impossible. Even those found guilty of encouraging mutiny were merely ordered to acknowledge their crimes and promise future good behaviour.

The one great hope for lifting morale was the rumour that General Braddock had won an easy victory against the French on the Ohio valley. Daniel Claus had written on 10 July: 'I wish to God the Report was true we had from Ohio that General Braddock took the french Forts with the loss of only 500 men, and the French lost double the Number. If once this will be the Case all the Indians will flock over to the English, and the rest of the Expeditions won't want of Success.'[15] On 15 July Seth Pomeroy wrote to his wife from Albany, where he was with Johnson's forces: 'Upon the whole that I hear, I think there is the greatest probability that Braddock is master of the Ohio before this time.'[16] On the same day Johnson in Albany sent Braddock a long and detailed account of his conferences with the Iroquois and the state of his colonial militias and ended by sending the commander-in-chief 'my most sincere Wishes that every Species of Felicity may Attend you'.[17]

Whatever felicity was attending Braddock now was in the afterlife. He had been buried the day before Johnson wrote to him, on a dirt road through a forest, having died of a chest wound received when his army was routed by a combined French and Indian force just beyond the Monongahela River, a tributary of the Ohio, ten miles from his objective of Fort Duquesne. The column that had wiped out two-thirds of Braddock's army on 9 July was mostly made up of Ottawa, Shawnee, Mississauga, Wyandot and Potawatomi warriors – a devastating demonstration of the effectiveness of Indian troops against European regulars and a horrible reminder of the potential cost of Shirley's deliberate disruption of Johnson's efforts to forge a broad alliance with the Indians.[18]

The disaster on the Monongahela had the unfortunate side effect, from Johnson's point of view, of both further embittering and further empowering Shirley. Braddock's personal secretary, Shirley's son William Jr, had been shot through the head during the battle. Alongside these terrible personal tidings Shirley also received the news that, with Braddock's death, he himself was now acting commander-in-chief of His Majesty's forces in North America.[19]

The other consequence of the defeat in Ohio was that Braddock's papers, which contained the complete plans of all the British campaigns, had been abandoned on the battlefield. It was therefore almost certain that the French knew all about Johnson's expedition against Crown Point and would have plenty of time to reinforce their position there.

With a commander-in-chief who was waiting for him to fail ignominiously, an official enemy who had ample advance notice of his plans and the summer campaigning season rapidly petering out, Johnson could be forgiven for being in no great rush to hurl himself into the abyss of defeat. Even had he been inclined to hurry forward, however, the logistics of pushing an amateur army through miles of pathless forest enforced slow motion. When his Connecticut and New Hampshire militia reached the strategic portage at the Great Carrying Place beyond Saratoga, between the falls on the upper Hudson River and Lac Saint Sacrement, they built, on his instructions, a wooden military storehouse. The Connecticut men named it Fort Lyman, after their commander. Johnson, who saw a different kind of strategic opportunity, called it Fort Edward, 'in honour of the Second Pri[nce] of the Blood of that name'.[20] This ostentatious declaration of his own loyalty to the Hanoverian royal family was soon trumped by a more significant and, in the event, permanent act of renaming.

The long narrow lake that flowed northwards towards Crown Point, Lake Champlain and thence towards the heart of New France in Canada was to be the principal staging point for Johnson's ultimate attack. The plan was to sail up this natural watery highway to Ticonderoga on its western shore, where the French were planning to build a fort, cross the narrows connecting it to Lake Champlain, and then proceed north to assault Crown Point.

Leaving five companies under Colonel Joseph Blanchard of New Hampshire to complete and garrison Fort Edward, Johnson moved sixteen miles towards the base of Lac Saint Sacrement at a leisurely pace and, having noted in his Hints for a Commanding Officer that 'A General officer must keep a good Table', treated his New England officers almost like guests at his house who had been taken out for a picnic. 'We went on about four or five miles,' wrote Seth Pomeroy in his journal, 'then stopped, ate pieces of broken bread and cheese, and drank some fresh lemon-punch and the best of wine with General Johnson and some of the field-officers.' The next day they 'Stopped about noon and dined with General Johnson by a small brook under a tree; ate a good dinner of cold boiled and roast venison; drank good fresh lemon-punch and wine.'[21]

When he reached Lac Saint Sacrement at the end of August, Johnson lost little time before making a grand gesture that had both public and private significance. He changed its name to Lake George, 'not only in honour to his Majesty but to assertain his Dominion here'.[22] The political meaning of the gesture was obvious enough. The lake stretched thirty-two miles northwards into territory claimed by both Britain and France. Naming it after the British monarch turned this thin, sharp stretch of clear water into a symbolic dagger thrust towards the enemy.

If Johnson had made a heavy-footed progress towards Lake George, the French, on the contrary, had every reason for urgency. Their new military commander Baron Jean-Armand (or, in his original German, Ludwig August) de Dieskau had arrived in Quebec on 23 June with 2,500 professional troops from France. Buoyed up by news of Braddock's defeat and alarmed at exaggerated reports from spies of Johnson's advance, he moved rapidly down to Fort St Frederic at Crown Point. From there, receiving more accurate reports of Johnson's relative weakness, he decided to leave the bulk of his regulars at the fort, and strike southwards with a mobile irregular force.

In contrast to Johnson's amateur army, this French force was, as Cadwallader Colden wrote shortly afterwards, 'commanded by experienced officers & one third of them were consisted of the best troops in France & the Canadians were all picked men the choice of all their Militia'.[23] While Colden's proportions were wrong, Dieskau had indeed, alongside 600 Canadians and 700 Abenaki and Caughnawaga warriors, a hard core of 216 regular grenadiers of the Languedoc and La Reine battalions, whose white uniforms, glistening bayonets and disciplined movements proclaimed their status as an elite force.

Dieskau's adoption of fast-moving, guerrilla-style tactics was unusual for a European commander of the day, especially a tough old veteran of so many formal battles; but he was a former protégé and aide-de-camp to the great Marechal Arminius Maurice, Comte de Saxe, who had pioneered the successful use of partisans and irregulars against the British army in Flanders during the War of the Austrian Succession.[24] His decision to push against Johnson with such a force was certainly bold, but it also showed a far quicker grasp of the conditions of woodland warfare in North America than most of his English counterparts.

Rather paradoxically, however, Dieskau had a particular contempt for North American militia. Even though he had never fought with or against such troops, he confidently declared them 'such miserable soldiers that a single Indian would put ten of them to flight' and 'the worst troops on the face of the earth'.[25] While this distrust may not have encouraged him to put much faith in his own Canadian irregulars, it certainly boosted his belief that Johnson's army, composed entirely of such dross, was nothing to fear.

His progress towards that army was indeed fast. By 4 September, Dieskau and his men had advanced to the confluence of Lake George and Lake Champlain, the area the British knew as Ticonderoga and the French as Carillon. From there they paddled down to South Bay, hid their canoes and pushed on through the woods towards the still unfinished Fort Edward. On 7 September Dieskau emerged from the forest three miles north of Fort Edward and onto the portage road that Johnson's troops had cut.

In Johnson's camp, meanwhile, there was a gathering feeling of unease. On Saturday, 6 September, 'One of the Sachems dreamed a dream, and ordered prayers to be read (a prayer was read in the Indian Camp) and the Sachems ordered no person to go out on the left of the camp, which was obeyed.'[26] On the evening of Sunday, 7 September, some of Johnson's Mohawk scouts returned to the camp. Hendrick announced their news that roads had been cut into the forest around the south of the lake and that there was 'a great Body of Men . . . which we judge were march[ing] towards the Carrying Place'.[27] Johnson sent a wagoner called Jacob Adams, followed shortly afterwards by two Indians and two militiamen, with a warning to Blanchard at Fort Edward and instructions to withdraw all his men behind its defences. Around midnight, word came back from others who had been attempting to desert that, about four miles from the Carrying Place, they had heard gunfire and Adams 'Call upon Heaven for Mercy', indicating, apparently, that the French were already at Fort Edward and that his warning had come too late.

In fact, Johnson had drawn too many conclusions from these two reports. Dieskau's forces were indeed on the move and the unfortunate Adams had indeed run into them. Johnson assumed, however, that the immediate object of the French attack was Fort Edward. He realised that he had left his men at Fort Edward in a dreadfully vulnerable position, with many of them working on the fortifications and still camped out in the open. As he admitted shortly afterwards, an attack on the fort by Dieskau 'would have found our Troops separately encamp'd out of the works, and no canon there and his victory would probably have been a very cheap one'. Having annihilated the British forces at Fort Edward, Dieskau could then have turned his attention to Johnson's encampment. Victory at Fort Edward would, as Johnson admitted, have 'made way for another here'.[28]

Fearing exactly this outcome, Johnson made the somewhat panicky decision to divide his forces yet again. At a council of war the next morning he resolved, with the agreement of the other commanders, to send out two parties of 500 men each 'to Catch the Enemy in their Retreat from the other Camp, either as Victors or defeated in their Designs'.

This was a serious mistake. Dieskau had not yet attacked Fort Edward and Johnson's warning message, captured when Adams was shot, had alerted the French commander to the presence of another British encampment. The capture of two more deserters added the information that Johnson's force, although large, was encamped without walled defences and exposed on one side, and therefore seemed to offer a more tempting target than the fort. Though Dieskau himself was still inclined to attack Fort Edward first, he was dissuaded by the reluctance of his Indian allies to assault what they assumed to be a well-fortified fort armed with artillery. He agreed to move first against Johnson's encampment.

This camp backed on to the lake but was open at the front. Johnson ordered a rough barricade to be erected from the trees that had been felled in clearing the area, *bateaux* hauled up from the lake shore and provision wagons tipped onto their sides. Overall, the barricade was not especially formidable: Dieskau described it as being 'of very trifling height' – in places no more than knee-high.[29] It did, however, form a clear line of defence for troops who were not used to military manoeuvres.

Johnson did not know that Dieskau was now advancing towards his camp and that the relatively small detachment he was sending to reinforce Fort Edward was in fact heading straight for this oncoming French force. Hendrick was the one leader to object to this ill-considered manoeuvre. In the face of his protests, Johnson had agreed to unite what he had initially planned as two groups of 500 men each into one force. It was still foolish to send a thousand troops into terrain that Johnson knew to contain 'a very Considerable Number of the Enemy'. As Hendrick eloquently expressed it, 'If they are to be killed, they are too many; if they are to fight, they are too few.' Hendrick himself nevertheless agreed to lead the Indian part of this detachment. Johnson, knowing that his old friend, now about seventy-five, was too old and slow to go on foot, gave him a horse.

Dieskau learned from two prisoners that this party, under Colonel Ephraim Williams, was approaching. He moved his force along the road into a deep ravine about four miles from the lake. To the west of the road, a thirty-foot-high embankment ran for a mile and a half along the ravine, giving perfect cover for an ambush. To the east, along the slopes of French Mountain, there was dense woodland. Dieskau ordered the Indians and Canadians to move 300 paces ahead, conceal themselves silently in the woods and not shoot until his French grenadiers, whom he left in view on the road, began to fire. He hoped in this way to draw the British force fully into a trap which, when closed, would leave them surrounded.

The plan partly failed, however, when, at about ten o'clock in the morning, some of the Caughnawaga Mohawks in Dieskau's troop spotted Hendrick and his Mohawks at the head of the British column.

According to Johnson, 'one of the enemys Musketts by accident went off, which allarmed our People and discovered the enemy',[30] allowing Williams to halt his march before the trap was fully closed. There was then a shouted dialogue in the Iroquois language between Hendrick and an Indian leader with the French party, in which each urged the other to keep out of the way, as they had no desire to fire on fellow Indians. One of Hendrick's young warriors, however, fired at the French Indian spokesman, and everyone else followed suit.[31]

The British force was unprotected on the road, with fire coming from three directions – the Indians on their left, the Canadians on their right, and the French regulars straight ahead. In panic, the British ranks, as Dieskau afterwards recalled, 'doubled up like a pack of cards'.[32] In the midst of this confusion, Hendrick, on horseback and too old and stiff to jump down and hide in the bushes, was left exposed. He tried to ride back towards the camp at the lake, but somehow galloped into a group of Indian women and boys who were accompanying Dieskau's men and had stayed with the baggage train. He was surrounded and 'stabbed in the Back with a Spear or Bayonet'. He was then scalped, 'the scalp being taken off not larger than an English crown', suggesting that the job was done by a woman – an ignominious end for the proud sachem.[33]

Williams, most of his officers and about fifty of his men were also killed in the ambush, which soon became known as the Bloody Morning Scout. The survivors fled, more or less in disarray, back towards Johnson's camp. The French, however, also took a significant loss. Jacques Legardeur de Saint-Pierre, the most accomplished French-Canadian leader of Indian warriors and the man who had defied George Washington's threats at the start of the war, was killed in the fighting. His death caused confusion among the Caughnawagas, and their reluctance to press on led to disputes with the Abenakis and Canadians that prevented Dieskau from following up his victory with the speed he desired.

Johnson and his men were very lucky, indeed, that Dieskau's forces were somewhat slow to pursue the fleeing remnants of Williams's detachment. As Johnson himself admitted shortly afterwards, 'The enemy did not pursue vigorously, or our slaughter would have been greater, and perhaps our Panick fatal, this gave us time to recover & make dispositions to receive the approaching enemy.'[34] The crucial disposition was Captain Eyre's placing of his four siege cannon, including one thirty-two-pounder, within easy range of the road. Johnson was also able to send out a party of 300 men to cover the retreat of the fleeing troops.

For most of Johnson's troops, still in the camp, the first sight of battle was the terrifying spectacle of their own comrades running back towards them, 'bringing wounded men with them, and others soon flocked in by hundreds, a perpetual fire being kept up and drawing nearer and nearer, till nearly 12 o'clock when the enemy came in sight'.[35] Johnson needed all his force of personality and his rhetorical skills to steady nerves and make orderly lines from the anarchic bustle.

Dieskau's regulars marched towards the barricade in close order. Arranged in rows of six, they fired in platoons, until Eyre's artillery forced them to break ranks. As one of Eyre's gunners wrote to his cousin after the battle, 'The French thought to go thro' all, but was much surprised with our Artillery which made Lanes, Streets and Alleys thro' their army.'[36] The Indians and Canadians, meanwhile, had veered off the path into the forest and fired from behind the trees. While Dieskau later claimed that these Indian and Canadian allies effectively deserted him, Johnson insisted that this was not so and that 'they continued at the attack till all was near decided, and the last push was made by some of their Indians'.[37]

With the repulse of Dieskau's regulars, the most dangerous fire was coming from the Canadian snipers whom the marshal had deployed in large numbers on the fringes of the woods. Two hours into the battle, at about two o'clock, Johnson stiffened suddenly. His aide-de-camp Peter Wraxall, who was beside him, thought he saw a shot enter the small of Johnson's back and feared that his leader was mortally wounded. In fact, the ball had entered his thigh just below the hip. Wraxall took him to have the wound dressed, and though stiff and in pain, Johnson seems to have been able to resume command.[38]

Johnson later told his brother Warren that the indiscipline of his troops 'obliged him to Expose himself greatly in Action' and that 'he was soe hoarse in the Engagement with calling to the Troops, & running along the Lines, as not to be able to speak, untill he got a Lemon, & sucked the Juice, & Nothwithstanding his wound . . . did not keep in his Tent, but was very active'.[39] Seth Pomeroy, who seems a reliable and fair-minded witness, wrote to his wife the day after the battle that Johnson and Lyman 'both behaved with steadiness and resolution'.[40] At the same time, Lambert Moore, the Deputy Secretary of New York, reported that Johnson 'behaved in all respects worthy his station and is the Idoll of the army'.[41]

Evidence that Johnson was in fact still in command late in the battle comes from the account of the anonymous gunner who wrote to his cousin that when the French force tried to come through the trees towards the rear of the camp, 'the General perceiving danger, ordered me to throw some shells, which accordingly I did, and some 32 pounders, which soon made them shift births [sic]'.[42] Peter Wraxall, who was with Johnson when he was wounded, wrote: 'Our General was wounded in the Hip, yet kept the field, altho' in great pain.'[43] Surgeon Thomas Williams wrote after the battle: 'He is almost universally beloved & esteemed by officers & soldiers as a second Marlborough for coolness of head & warmness of heart.'[44]

As the French assault bogged down, an increasingly frantic Dieskau ventured too close to the breastwork and was hit three times in the leg. He crawled behind a tree and ordered his second-in-command Major General Montreuil to assume command and arrange an orderly retreat. According to the anonymous gunner, Dieskau's last words of command were: 'Fight on, boys, this is Johnson, not Braddock,' meaning, presumably, that they could still win against an amateur commander.[45]

By around four o'clock the French had begun to pull back in disarray and Johnson's men to emerge cautiously from behind the breastwork. They did not give chase into the woods. In the ravine where the morning's ambush had taken place, however, a group of about 400 French, Canadian and Indian troops who had gone to collect prisoners they had tied up there were themselves set upon by a party of colonials coming from Fort Edward. They had heard the noise of battle and been sent to help Johnson. They attacked the disorganised and weary enemy and inflicted severe casualties. Part of the blood-price was paid, however, by the Mohawk and colonial prisoners who were shot and scalped by the Abenakis before they fled.

After this gory engagement, there was a grisly parody of Johnson's grand gesture in renaming Lac Saint Sacrement as Lake George. The rank, sedgy pool into which the torn corpses of the dead were thrown was known ever after as Bloody Pond.

15

Unspeakable Perplexity

===

Along with the ball that remained in his hip for the rest of his life, Johnson received two severe wounds at Lake George. The loss of Hendrick, who had been his friend and ally since his early days in America, was a severe toll on victory; and his fellow Irishman and brother-in-law Matthew Farrell, a captain in the New York militia, had also been killed. He was with Hendrick's Mohawks when they were ambushed in the Bloody Morning Scout and was killed along with the great sachem.[1]

In strictly political terms, however, these losses were to some degree compensated for by a living body Johnson had taken from the field of battle: Dieskau. The French commander had watched and listened to the repulse of his forces from behind the tree where he had crawled after being wounded. Two Canadians had been sent to rescue him, but one had been killed instantly and fallen over Dieskau's legs. The other went to fetch some more help, but in the meantime Dieskau heard the retreat being sounded and was left alone, abandoned as the jetsam of war. After half an hour or so, he saw a soldier taking aim at him from behind a nearby tree and made signs not to fire. The man fired anyway, the shot passing through one of the marechal's hips and out the other. When Dieskau shouted at him in pain and anger, demanding to know why he had fired at a wounded man, the soldier, a Canadian who had deserted a decade earlier, replied in French: 'But how did I know but you had a pistol? I prefer to kill the Devil than that the Devil kill me.'

Shortly afterwards, a group of other soldiers stripped Dieskau and brought him to Johnson. What happened next became an important strand in the weaving of Johnson's image. Dieskau himself told the story in an imaginary dialogue in the Elysian Fields with his mentor the Marechal de Saxe:

On learning who I was, he [Johnson] had me laid on his bed and sent for surgeons to dress my wounds, and, though wounded himself, he refused all attendance until mine were dressed. Several Indians entered his tent soon after, who regarded me with a furious look, and spoke to him a long time, and with much vehemence. When they had departed, I observed: 'Those fellows have been regarding me with a look not indicative of much compassion.' 'Anything else but that,' he answered; 'for they wished to oblige me to deliver you into their hands, in order to burn you in revenge for the death of their comrades, and of the three Chiefs who have been slain in the battle, and threaten to abandon me if I do not give you up. Feel no uneasiness. You are safe with me.'

The same Indians returned some time after to the tent. The conversation appeared to me animated at first, and became more moderate at the close, when, smiling, they took my hand in token of friendship and retired. General Johnson afterwards told me that he had made my peace with them, and that they had abandoned all their pretensions. I observed, that as he was wounded himself, I was afraid I incommoded him, and requested him to have me removed elsewhere. 'I dare not,' he answered, 'for were I to do so, the Indians would massacre you. They must have time to sleep.'[2]

Johnson's compassion for Dieskau was undoubtedly genuine and a deep affection developed between the men in the nine days after the battle when they were both recovering from their wounds in the camp. Dieskau was then taken to Johnson's house in Albany, where he was cared for by Johnson's sister and Matthew Farrell's grieving widow, Catherine, for the next month. Catherine Johnson Farrell cared for Dieskau with a kindness which, as he told Johnson, 'exceed[ed] perhaps all that I could have hoped for in the bosom of my family'[3] even though her own husband had been killed in the battle by Dieskau's men. The marechal was sensitive to the dignity with which she attempted to conceal her grief from him.[4] She herself was taken ill by early November and died later that month or in early December.[5]

This bond between Dieskau and the Johnsons, however, developed after the famous initial encounter in which Johnson saved Dieskau from the wrath of the Mohawks bent on vengeance for the death of Hendrick and their other brethren. His exemplary chivalry towards his fallen enemy had other motives beyond simple compassion. He instinctively understood that Dieskau was a very valuable prize, a high-class vehicle in which to carry his own reputation far beyond the forests of New York.

Johnson knew from his conduct of a war of terror a decade before that the kind of fighting he was most deeply engaged in was a dirty business. In the ideology of European warfare, honourable enemies were to be treated honourably even in defeat. The dead were not scalped. Living prisoners were allowed to keep their personal effects and, especially if they were gentlemen, were eventually exchanged or paroled. These forms, though not always adhered to, were not entirely hypocritical. As arms had become an established profession, the enemy could be seen as fellow professionals. When the job was done, it was in the mutual interest of both sides to behave well, not least because the same conventions would apply to today's victors when they became tomorrow's vanquished.

Indian warfare was different. Indian warriors were not paid professionals. They fought to bring honour to their nation and the tangible proofs of honour were plunder brought back to the village, trophies to support their stories of prowess and valour, and captives to sacrifice or adopt as replacements for dead brothers, or perhaps to hold for ransom. Booty, scalps and prisoners were the point of the fight, and to return without them was to be defeated, even if their European allies claimed victory.

At the end of his first real battle, Johnson found himself occupying each of these conflicting European and Indian positions. As General Johnson, he was a representative of the British empire, one European holding the field of battle against others. As Warraghiyagey, he was a Mohawk war captain, expected to send the tokens of victory back to the villages of Iroquoia. If he allowed his Indian allies to scalp prisoners or take European captives to replace their dead, he risked being seen as a savage. If he did not, he risked his prestige with the Indians, who were still the source of his power.

His extreme chivalry towards Dieskau was a brilliant escape from this dilemma. It created a dramatic story of European civility restraining the vengeful savagery of the red man. And this tale, carried back to Europe on Dieskau's own lips, was also a cover story. It diverted attention from the fact that Johnson allowed his Iroquois allies to behave according to their own lights. When his men went to bury the dead, they found it virtually impossible to tell their own comrades from the French, since so many of the bodies had been stripped and scalped. Even while he was protecting Dieskau, moreover, Johnson was secretly handing other French prisoners over to the Mohawks.

Most probably, the calming words that Dieskau heard Johnson

delivering to the warriors who had come to kill him were a reassurance that, if they left Dieskau to him, he would make sure they got prisoners to replace their dead. Two months after the battle, he was retrieving French captives he had sent down to Albany, 'who I now wish to have again, in order to give them in the Room of those Indians killed, as it is much expected by them, and will ease their Minds a good deal'. Significantly, he wanted this to be kept secret from his commander-in-chief: 'I would not have Mr Shirley know anything of it, at least he might overset it.'[6]

In a scene that would have astonished most Europeans, he performed a ritual handover of six French prisoners to the Iroquois before a gathering of almost 600 Indians at Fort Johnson in February 1756 to replace Hendrick and others who had died at Lake George: three Mohawks – Waniacoone, Skahyowio, and Onienkoto; Nicaanawa, son of the so-called Half-King of the Ohio; and Cayadanora, a Tuscarora. With all the requisite grandiloquence and delicacy he announced: 'By constant experience we discover that the life of man is as the flower of the field; in this transitory scene, therefore, resignation becomes us under the loss of our nearest and dearest friends: comfort yourselves, therefore, under the losses you have sustained, as becomes reasonable creatures. With this belt [of wampum] I cover all your dead, that they may no more offend your sight.'

Then, according to the official record, 'six French prisoners, some of those who were taken at the late battle, near Lake George, were delivered with great ceremony to the Indians . . . They received the prisoners with the greatest marks of gratitude and satisfaction; every nation giving a shout of approbation, and then carried the prisoners off to their respective families.'[7] Some of these prisoners were probably ransomed back from the Indians at the end of the war.

The Onondaga speaker Red Head returned the ritual words of thanks: 'Brother Warraghiyagey, the six united nations, as one body, do with the greatest thankfulness acknowledge your brotherly affection, in thus effectually cleansing and purifying all our habitations from all the blood and defilement, which they had contracted by the death of so many of our principal men.' Johnson had thus managed to fulfil the highest demands of courtesy in two contrasting cultures.

If his kindness to Dieskau allowed Johnson to execute this tricky cultural manoeuvre, the French commander also had another, simpler value. Johnson had won the battle in the narrow sense that his forces held the field; but in strategic terms the victory was equivocal. The losses on both sides were roughly equal, with 339 French and allied fighters killed, wounded or captured, compared to 331 on Johnson's side.[8] Dieskau's claim that 'the English . . . lost a much greater number of men than I, without gaining an inch of territory' was, though exaggerated and entirely self-serving, not wildly wrong.[9]

While Dieskau's attack had been repulsed, he had in fact succeeded in his primary aim of preventing a British attack on Crown Point. Almost immediately after the battle, Johnson's Indian warriors went home to perform their condolence ceremonies and to prevent further losses in their already thin ranks. At the same time, his colonial troops also decided that one hot battle was enough for any campaigning season and were determined to get home as soon as they could. The best Johnson could do was to consolidate the position by building a fort at Lake George. He knew that by the time that was done, the winter would be approaching and there would be no hope of continuing the attack.

After the initial euphoria of the battle had evaporated, he realised that he could easily find himself taking the blame for a failure, especially in the face of Shirley's enmity. As he wrote to the Massachusetts politician Thomas Hutchinson from the camp at Lake George, 'Whenever I consider the Great Expence of the Colonies, & that uncommon exertion of themselves which has appeared in favour of this Expedition I am apprehensive the Events of this Campaign will not be equal to their Hopes, & perhaps all that has been done will to the generality appear of little consequence & merit, because all was not done.'[10]

He was, as he put it, 'exposed to too much & to too little Fame', meaning that the event at Lake George was now world news but its significance was still undetermined. A confused six-hour, three-stage battle, with fighting spread between the Bloody Morning Scout, Johnson's camp and Bloody Pond, did not lend itself to an easy calculation of defeat and victory. Except, of course, in one simple respect: Johnson's possession of Dieskau.

The French immediately understood the significance of Dieskau's capture, even before they knew whether he was alive or dead. That his death was the preferred option is clear from the letter to Paris of the new governor of New France, the Marquis de Vaudreil-Cavagnal, giving the news of the battle and of Dieskau's loss: 'I feel intense interest in his fate. If, as several of our Indians assert, he has been killed, he will not have been recognised. He had no mark of distinction nor papers on his person; but if taken prisoner, the enemy will cite the abandonment of this General as a proof of their triumph.'[11]

On the other side, as Goldsbrow Banyar subsequently reminded Johnson, 'Dieskau bears the Character in England of a very considerable Officer.'[12] As not merely the supreme French military commander in Canada but the protégé of Saxe and veteran of the latter's stunning defeat of the British at Fontenoy, he was a respected and formidable foe. The corollary – that his vanquisher must also be a redoubtable man – was a great enhancement to Johnson's reputation in England.

Though he was in pain from his wound and furthered weakened by a severe infection in his face, throat and ear, Johnson was fully aware that the end of the shooting was merely the start of the battle to defend his victory against the besieging forces of Governor Shirley.[13] Just a few days before the battle, he had begun to orchestrate a propaganda offensive from the remoteness of the camp, asking Thomas Pownall to put an article favourable to his conduct of the campaign, and by implication disparaging Shirley, into Benjamin Franklin's *Pennsylvania Gazette*.[14] Now, he drew on Pownall's skills to turn a bloody draw into a great victory.

Thomas Pownall was a great asset to Johnson's cause, not least because his brother John was secretary to the Board of Trade in London. Thomas had come to New York in 1753 as private secretary to Sir Danvers Osborne, who had been appointed to replace George Clinton as governor. When Osborne committed suicide six days after his arrival, Pownall was left adrift and alone. Such were his skills at making friends, however, that he went to Philadelphia and within a month was on affectionate terms with many of its power-brokers, including Franklin. He had been invited to join the Pennsylvania delegation to the conference in Albany in June and July 1754 at which the colonies had sought to repair their relations with the Six Nations, and Franklin had presented his famous plan for a unified colonial government. Johnson had also attended in his capacity as a member of the New York Council, and had got on well with Pownall and Franklin.

Four days after the battle, from the New York City front in the propaganda war Thomas Pownall sent a dispatch to Johnson at Lake George. It gives a strong flavour of the urgency with which Johnson and his allies were already preparing for the expected onslaught from

Shirley's partisans: 'All is right in Your favor. – the Governor has received from *Your freinds* [italicised in the original] all the Impressions in Your Favor That Your Virtue Deserves. There are two things upon which every Man must rest his Merits, one his own right conduct, the other the Reality of his Freinds. The First is in your own Breast & You will command it. – the Other give me leave to assure You off, Your interest in this latter is and shall be secured.' Pownall asked Johnson for as much ammunition as he could supply, in the form of accounts of the victory, so that he could carry the fight with him on a projected visit to London.[15]

The necessity for ammunition was very real. Almost as soon as he got the news of the battle, Governor Shirley was suggesting to Johnson that, since he was wounded, Lyman or Colonel Timothy Ruggles could take over his command.[16] Shirley was also insisting that Johnson should immediately proceed against Crown Point and forget about constructing a fort at Lake George. He probably knew that was now impossible, but by issuing these orders he was cleverly putting Johnson in the position of an insubordinate who lacked the capacity or the will to complete a victory that was there for the taking.

Johnson, in return, had a circular letter with his account of the battle printed and dispatched to all the colonial governments and to London. He sent Dieskau's order of battle, captured with the rest of his papers, to De Lancey to be 'immediately printed at New York for the Entertainment of the public'. This, and an account of the battle by Peter Wraxall, were published in the New York newspapers before they were sent to the Massachusetts colonial government, to which Johnson was officially responsible.[17] On 22 September, Johnson's long account of the battle was published in the *New York Mercury*. It was quickly reprinted in the London *Gentleman's Magazine*.

This careful manipulation of public opinion was enhanced by assurances that he had no interest in public opinion. Even while the press campaign was at its height, Johnson was protesting his indifference to patronage and high-level approval, and insisting that he had no interest in fighting for his reputation. In early October, he wrote to Spencer Phipps, the lieutenant governor of Massachusetts, from the camp at Lake George: 'From selfish or Ambitious Views, I make my court to no Government having no political Schemes to carry, & resting every future Plan of my Life on a private Bottom. A lesson which mortifying Experience has taught me.'[18] At the same time, he was telling Thomas

Hutchinson: 'I prefer the inward conviction of my own rectitude to every precarious Salvo of applause.'[19]

Shirley's counter-attack began with a letter from Johnson's second-in-command Phineas Lyman dated 8 September 1755 and published in the *New York Gazette* on 6 October claiming that 'General Johnson was shot thro' the thigh near the beginning of the Battle and retired to his tent' and suggesting, in effect that Lyman himself was therefore the effective commander and the true hero of Lake George. This claim was in turn countered by a letter from Lieutenant-Colonel Edward Cole who had led the Rhode Island regiment at Lake George and who afterwards settled near Johnson to be close to 'My Good Friend and Patron'.[20] He suggested that the previous letter could not really be from Lyman because he could not 'reconcile such a Compilition of Nonsense and Falsities with the Character that Gentleman has borne in the world' and that it must really be the product of 'some one of his mean, ignorant Camp Flatterers . . . endeavouring to load him with Honours which he never could, nor surely never would have claimed'. He accused this anonymous flatterer of ascribing to Lyman 'the Glory of that day's Victory, which is solely due to General Johnson'.

According to Cole, Johnson had not been wounded at the beginning of the battle but 'from the authority of Dr Hunter, our Surgeon, who dressed him; of Capt. Wraxall, the Aid de Camp who led him off, and of many others, he did not receive his Wound till about two o'Clock in the afternoon; and no sooner was he dressed than immediately he again appeared among the Men, and gave the proper Orders in person'.[21]

With the failure of the attempt to imply that Johnson had been out of the action from early in the battle and was therefore due no credit as a commander, Shirley, who learned in early November that he had been formally appointed as commander-in-chief in succession to Braddock, tried another tack.

Shirley's own position was becoming vulnerable because his own part of the four-pronged campaign, the planned assault on the French fort at Niagara, was going nowhere. With the same tortuousness that had marked Johnson's march to Lake George, Shirley had eventually moved his force westward to the Oswego, the fort and trading post on Lake Ontario that Johnson had long supplied. This was to be the jumping-off point for his attack on Fort Niagara, but it gradually became clear that it was in fact the terminus. Short of provisions and money, and finding Fort Oswego a ramshackle and virtually indefensible structure, Shirley could do little more than repair the buildings and prepare winter quarters for his increasingly disaffected troops.

This embarrassment gave him, however, an added incentive to resume the war against his upstart and insubordinate rival. In the hope of simultaneously saving his own reputation and discrediting Johnson, he claimed that the latter's failure to supply Indians to Shirley's army was the reason for the failure of the Niagara expedition. Thomas Pownall told Johnson in confidence that 'General Shirley and party were his declared enemies and going to make serious & heavy Complaints to the king and ministry against him laying the whole Blame upon Him for not having done anything in their Expedition against Niagara on Acct. of his having sent a Belt of wampum to the Six Nations clandestinely that not a man of them would join General Shirley's Expedition . . . & that he, Genl. Johnson had diametrically acted contrary to his orders, [and] Instructions, of which he should acquaint the Kings Ministers.'[22]

Shirley did indeed write to London in December that 'The Construction which Colonel Johnson made of his Indian Commission, was that it Excluded me from Employing any Person whatever to Engage any Indians to go with me to Niagara.'[23] Johnson had 'Secretly Endeavour'd to prejudice [Indians] against going with me'. Yet, to Shirley's 'further Mortification', he now found that Johnson's 'wrong Notions' about his power as Indian Commissioner were supported by De Lancey.

Shirley acted on his resentment by revoking Johnson's commission as Indian Commissioner and issuing him another, which deleted his designation as Sole Superintendent. He admitted to London: 'Whether he will Act under this Commission, or at least follow my Instructions (which last will satisfy me) I know not yet.' Knowing in reality that Johnson would never accept this demotion, Shirley at the same time suggested that in this event he should be replaced. He had a candidate: 'the Noted Conrad Weiser, who besides being a Person of the most Universal Influence over, and knowledge of all the Indians of the five Nations, of any one upon this Continent, is an adopted Sachem among them, and Constituted a Member of their General Council at Onondago [sic].'[24]

While all of this was going on, Johnson was stuck in the swamps around Lake George. The dispute between him and the De Lancey faction of New York on the one side and Shirley and the Massachusetts partisans on the other was mirrored by literal in-fighting among his colonial troops. Just weeks after the battle, fierce fighting had broken out again at Lake George, but this time within Johnson's camp. It was described from a Massachusetts point of view by Captain Nathaniel Dwight:

One of our men sold a Yorker a mug of Beer and he run away and would not pay for it. The man run after him and the Yorkers fell upon him and Coll. Pomroys regiment. Men run to relieve him . . . The Fight came to Clubs and naked Cutlashes and they struck one of our men and half Scalped him and drove into our Regt and Come with Swords and Clubs and Com[e] Like Hornets out of their Nests Swearing and Cursing in the Most Helish Manner. If the Devil and all he could raise had been Let Loose it wouldn't look more Dreadfull. They wounded two of our men with cutlashes one with a Club and many Slityly beside . . . Genl. Johnson was soon called up and he pasifyed the Yorkers, but it was hard pasefying our men that recd. So much Damage by them.[25]

Johnson's ability to keep order among his militia had been tested to breaking point and he complained bitterly of 'The Want of due Subordination the little respect which is daily paid to my Orders, the Democratical . . . Fabrick of this Army in general', all of which had given him 'unspeakable perplexity'.[26]

The one point of universal agreement at the camp had been the impossibility of proceeding against Crown Point. Faced with 'a general indisposition amongst the Troops to proceed further, arising from the severity of the Season, a surfeit of Military Life its fatigues and hardships, & an extreme fond inclination of returning to their more comfortable homes & the endearments of Family tyes',[27] Johnson had quickly decided to build and garrison a fort at Lake George, which he named Fort 'William Henry after Two of the Royal Family' in another conspicuous declaration of his loyalty to the Hanoverians, and then to disband the rest of his force.[28]

Even securing agreement to construct a substantial stronghold was difficult. Shirley was against it, and the colonial commanders in his army were reluctant to commit their regiments to the laborious construction and expensive garrisoning of a fortress formidable enough to withstand a serious French assault. Johnson scored a significant political victory by gaining approval for an earthen fort large enough to garrison 500 men. Even so, the work stuttered forward at a frustrating pace. Young men who had escaped the farm to fight papists and savages were not happy to find themselves hauling timber and digging ditches. On 20 October a Massachusetts captain mentally divided the troops into five roughly equal segments: one on guard duty, one sick, one busy cooking the temporarily plentiful food, one working on the fort 'or mountain of sand they are making . . . and the Rest cheating and hulking about some friend sick. Some have overeat themselves and a Great number Confounded Lazy which Dogg about hear and there.'[29]

Snow and rain in late October raised the level of the Hudson and made water-borne supplies more difficult to obtain, leading to a shortage of bread and, even more seriously, of rum. By the second week in November, 500 remaining Connecticut troops refused duty and threatened to leave with some of their comrades who had reached the end of the term for which they had enlisted. Twenty New Yorkers deserted and were brought back without being punished. Literally sick and tired of army life, Johnson had no sooner seen the completion of the fort and the withdrawal of the bulk of the army from Lake George than, at the beginning of December 1755, he formally resigned his position as major general and declared his 'disinclination to act any longer in that Capacity.'[30] The word 'disinclination' was at this point a masterpiece of understatement.

Yet, though he did not yet know it, he was in fact an official military hero of the British Empire, triumphantly victorious not just over France, but over Shirley. The delay in the transmission of correspondence between America and England meant that Johnson's complaints against Shirley and Shirley's suggestions that Johnson be replaced were reaching London alongside the reports of Johnson's apparent victory at Lake George and Shirley's failure to mount an attack on Niagara. After a dreadful year in the war, the crown needed a glorious triumph to celebrate and Lake George fitted the bill far more neatly than any other event. It was decided that Johnson had indeed won a great victory and that he was therefore a hero. It followed that Shirley, whose denunciations of the hero were flowing in, was a villain.

By mid-November King George, having been given Johnson's report of the battle, had been so filled with admiration for his 'prudence, spirit and resolution' that he was 'graciously pleased to confer upon you, as a distinguishing mark of His Royal favor and approbation of your conduct, the dignity of a Baronet of Great Brittain'.[31] He was now to be Sir William Johnson, first Baronet of New York. The Lords of Trade were naturally unhappy to learn that the conqueror of Dieskau 'should have been obstructed in your endeavours to engage the Six Nations of Indians . . . in His Majesty's interest' by Shirley.[32] Johnson's baronetcy was announced in London on 18 November, and had Shirley known of it, he would surely have tempered his attacks on the now-official hero. As it was, he fell headlong into the communication gap.

On the day before New Year's Eve 1755, dozens of New York City gentlemen mounted their horses and rode six miles through Manhattan Island to meet and salute the victorious general who was making his way down from Albany. After their rendezvous and an exchange of greetings they turned back and, accompanied now by a cavalcade of coaches and chairs, conducted the hero to the King's Arms tavern, where 'most of the principal Inhabitants were assembled to congratulate him on his safe Arrival'. As they passed the waterfront the ships in the harbour sounded their foghorns or fired off guns in exuberant salutation. The streets rang with 'the Acclamations of the People'. That night houses throughout the city were illuminated in honour of General Johnson.[33]

Johnson's triumphal entry into New York was planned in advance to mark his double victory over France and Massachusetts. Colden and Kelly, the merchant company that handled much of Johnson's trade through New York port, had informed him weeks before that six merchant ships would hail his arrival 'in so audible a manner as to make it both grating & Irksome to the few here whose private piques and late Contracted dirty party Prejudices would wish you a different reception'. William Smith, a partisan of Shirley's, was successfully irked, noting that the cavalcade, salutes and illuminations were 'a party Business to put Contempt upon Mr Shirley . . . those who were no friends of Shirley illuminated their Houses in the evening'.[34]

In London, on 7 January 1756 the Duke of Halifax, President of the Board of Trade, proposed to the cabinet that Shirley be replaced as commander-in-chief and that William Johnson be given a new commission as Sole Superintendent of Indian Affairs for the northern colonies and Colonel of the Six Nations, this time directly from the King. (At the same time, the Carolina trader Edmund Atkin was appointed Indian superintendent for the southern colonies.) This new office, which carried with it a handsome annual stipend of £600 sterling, conceded exactly what Johnson had been asking for since the late

1740s: that he no longer be 'subjected to or controlled by any Governor'.[35] He would now be effectively on a par with the colonial governors themselves, answerable directly and solely to the imperial government in London. Just to complete his apotheosis, the Westminster parliament voted to award him a gift of £5,000 as a mark of its appreciation.[36] To add sauce to the dish, Shirley had to arrange for the payment of this money.[37]

This triumph for Johnson was a result partly of the romantic charisma of his reputation and the prestige of having captured Dieskau, but largely of the political connections of the De Lanceys and the dark arts of Thomas Pownall. Having peppered senior politicians with letters denouncing Shirley, Pownall went to London in late December to exert a more direct influence. Around the time of his arrival, four letters written in America and addressed to the Duc de Mirepoix, the French ambassador to the court of Saint James, were intercepted by the British. Written by someone calling himself 'Filius Gallicae', they contained accurate information on the disposition of the military in North America and seemed to promise treason in return for money. They were almost certainly a hoax, intended to be intercepted. Whether or not the letters were part of Pownall's scheme, he certainly exploited their impact by suggesting that Shirley, who had a French wife and had spent several years in Paris, was the anonymous 'Son of France'.

On 31 March, the Secretary at War Henry Fox wrote to Shirley curtly ordering him to 'repair to England with all possible Expedition', pausing only to deliver to the new commander-in-chief 'all such papers as relate to the King's Service'.[38] It was part of a clean sweep for Pownall and the De Lancey faction. Shirley's ally Governor Robert Morris of Pennsylvania was dismissed. An inquiry into the awarding to Morris and Livingston of the contracts to supply the New York militia was established. The contracts themselves were transferred to a London company whose New York agent just happened to be Oliver De Lancey, younger brother of James De Lancey; and in looking for a replacement for Shirley in Massachusetts, the cabinet could find no one more able and public-spirited than Thomas Pownall.[39]

Shirley's partisans were still trying to tear the laurels from Johnson's head in 1757 when they published in London the anonymous pamphlet 'A Review of the Military Operations in North America: A Letter to a Nobleman', claiming that Johnson himself had admitted after the battle that Lyman was the real hero and again blaming Johnson for the failure of Shirley's campaign against Fort Niagara because he had failed to supply the necessary Indians. By then, however, Johnson was firmly established as a necessary imperial hero.

For the Indians who had fought alongside him, the aftermath was not so pleasant. Two months after the battle, the Mohawks in their village at Canajoharie received a message for Johnson from their Iroquois brethren at Oneida. An Onondaga who had been in Canada reported that 'The French Governor made Inquiry of the Indians who had taken the French General [Dieskau] prisoner, upon which they answered the Oneidas. O says he, that is all I want to know, I can take them likewise.' A month later a Tuscarora speaker, Tawontha, expressed the same fears to Johnson: 'As we, the Oneidas & the Mohocks are said to be the People who killed the French general & defeated [their] Army, the French have said they are making Snow Shoes & preparing every thing for a Winter expedition, being determined to have Revenge for the blood which we have spilt.'[40]

This sense of foreboding, though not immediately justified, came from an understanding of violence and vengeance in which every triumph brought the fear of reprisal. Revenge, as Johnson and the Indians knew, had a visceral power that was not to be denied by the high political manoeuvres of the Pownalls and De Lanceys.

In May 1758, nearly two and a half years after the battle, Captain Jacob, a Stockbridge Indian war chief, arrived at Johnson's house in Albany. He had a present for Brother Warraghiyagey: four fresh French scalps. He asked for one to be delivered to his wife's uncle, a Mohawk at Canajahorie to replace his dead sister, and another to replace another dead female relative. The other two were to make up for two of the dead at Lake George. One, which he held up on a stick tied with a string of black wampum, was to replace Hendrick, who had seen *Macbeth* in London and knew that 'blood will have blood'. The other was a gift from Jacob's cousin to replace the young son of the Mohawk sachem Nickus, 'who was killed at the battle of the Lake under your command'. It was a small bundle of flesh and hair, wrapped in a string of black wampum, the scalp of a child.

16

The Largest Pipe in America

===

Shortly after Johnson got the news of his new appointment as Sole Superintendent of Indian Affairs, a devout family in the French ship-building town of Saint Malo approached an Irish priest, Father James McDonnell. They wanted to know what to do with two small chests that had belonged to some of McDonnell's fellow Franciscans more than fifty years before, when the order had had a house in the town. The chests, now old and half-rotten, with no locks, had been left in their family's keeping and then forgotten. When McDonnell went to see them he found one full of dusty prayer books and tomes of theology, most of them printed in Italy. The other contained mouldy, moth-eaten relics and scapulars, with five pairs of rosary beads, two of them made of agate, and a bunch of brass medals of Jesus and the Virgin Mary. It also contained a worm-ravaged letter giving permission to a named Irish priest 'to read prohibited books in Ireland'.

From this letter and from documents accompanying the books, it was clear to Father McDonnell that the chests had been filled by the old Franciscan provincial Father Peter Warren and that the contents had been intended for surreptitious transport to Dublin, where they were to be used by the order's convent. Though McDonnell did not make the connection, he was looking at the dank, grimy remains of a forgotten history. The Father Warren who had packed these crates with forbidden words and symbols to sustain the beleaguered followers of his faith with encouragement from Rome and France was undoubtedly the illustrious Franciscan well known to two heroes of Protestant Britain. His namesake and nephew, Admiral Peter Warren, was probably named after him. The new Sir William Johnson was his grand-nephew, and must surely have been taken to see him in the mid-

1720s, when Johnson was a boy and the priest was Guardian of the Franciscan friary at Multyfarnham in nearby County Westmeath.

It did not strike Father McDonnell that there was any irony in sending those of the books that he could salvage belatedly to Dublin. Writing to Louvain to report his find and his intentions, he complained of the cruelties of the heathen Protestants and prayed for their defeat: 'I am informed that there is an act of parlimint for banishing the regular clergy of Ireland. Pray let me know if it is true . . . We daily expect a declaration of War against England. Really they deserve to be punished for their piratry . . .'[1]

A formal declaration of war between France and England was indeed to follow in May and June 1756, but in the American context it was a grotesque irrelevance. Three weeks after McDonnell wrote his letter a large party of French and Indians appeared suddenly outside the palisade of Fort Bull at the west end of the Great Carrying Place, the portage road between the Mohawk River and Wood Creek.[2] Johnson, who had heard reports of the approach of this force, rushed to the fort with about 500 militiamen and Mohawks. At the Great Carrying Place he was met by a hundred Oneidas and Tuscarora warriors and led the combined party to Fort Bull:

I found within the Fort twenty three Soldiers, two Women and one Battoe Man, Some burnt almost to Ashes, others most Inhumanly Butchered, and all Scalped, without the Fort, I found three Soldiers Scalped, who I think were blown over by the powder which was in the Magazine, as they were very much Scorched. About 200 Yards from the Fort, One of my Party (a German) found an Indian in the Woods dead, whose Scalp he brought me. He was well known to our Indians, they say he was a Messissagey who married an Onondaga Squaw & lived at Swegatchey, a Man of considerable Interest among them . . . The Whole Number killed, & missing is 62 thirty of which I found and buried.[3]

Johnson's attempt to rescue the fort, for which his reward was this appalling spectacle, was evidence that his resignation as major general of the combined colonial forces did not mean that he was disengaging from the war. Indeed, this bold French and Indian raid into New York and across Johnson's familiar trading route showed that he could not avoid the war even if he wanted to.

The fact that, in his stunned description of what he had seen at Fort Bull, the death of the Mississauga was given far more attention than the massacre of the Europeans was in itself an indication of his train of thought.

Not merely was he preoccupied with the use of his new authority as Sole Superintendent for the Indians of all the northern colonies, but he had conceived a remarkably ambitious plan. For even as he was still recuperating from the battle and the tense struggle with Shirley, he was planning a manoeuvre of great scope and ambition, a bold response to the loss of Hendrick: nothing less than the refurbishment of the Iroquois confederacy with himself at its centre. With his new powers and the greatly enhanced prestige of his name, he saw the opportunity to move beyond his old role as a mediator between the British and Iroquois. He could now reshape the Iroquois polity in his own image.

His aim was nothing less than the establishment of William Johnson as the ultimate arbiter of Iroquois traditions. Over time, he would arrive at a point where he could challenge the sachems on the grounds of their own inherited forms and customs. It would take him the best part of twenty years to achieve this status explicitly, and to feel free to lecture a council of the Six Nations about the proper Iroquois protocol, as he was to in 1773. On that occasion, he complained of the way the council at Onondaga engaged in diplomacy with a dependent tribe: 'I do not doubt, but that in this, you imagine you act right, and agreeable to ancient custom; but you must be sensible that I do well know all your ancient customs, that I cannot be mistaken in them, having committed them all to writing an age ago, when they were better understood than they are at present . . .'4 Johnson, in other words, knew Iroquois customs better than the Iroquois. His interpretations of their laws were infallible.

This was the terminus of a journey he began in the mid-1750s. The opportunity arose, rather paradoxically, from the decayed state of the confederacy itself. The old policy of neutrality which Johnson had undermined in the mid-1740s had helped to hold the pro-British and pro-French factions of the Great League together. Johnson's success in drawing the Mohawks and some members of the other nations into action on the British side had, however, shattered the facade of unity, and by 1755 the pretence of a single political strategy was gone. The Mohawk villages, under Johnson's influence, were staunchly pro-British. The Oneidas were split down the middle. Pro-French or neutralist sachems prevailed at Onondaga, the ritual centre of the league. The Cayugas and Senecas favoured the French and tended increasingly to identify with their émigré kin who had moved into the Ohio valley, where, as Braddock's defeat had shown, British military power was almost non-existent. As a force for the co-ordination of political and military strategy among the nations, the confederacy was effectively dead.

The near-demise of the league was, for Johnson, a threat as well as an opportunity. Disunited, the Iroquois could no longer hold the balance of power between the British and the French. The centre of political gravity, moreover, was shifting away from upper New York and towards the tribes in the Ohio, Delaware and Susquehanna valleys. Traditionally, the Iroquois had enjoyed a formal hegemony over these western nations, and had controlled much of the trade between them and the British. Conditions of war and competition for their favour between the French and the British had, however, gradually given the western nations the confidence to declare their independence.

This threat to Iroquois hegemony was clear for at least a decade. The government of Pennsylvania, for example, had long refused to deal directly with the nations on its borders, including the Shawnees, Delawares and Conestogas, preferring to recognise the semi-fictional supremacy over them of the Iroquois, with whom it was easier to negotiate. By the late 1740s, however, the Pennsylvania nations seemed so effectively subdued that the colonial government no longer thought it necessary to flatter the pretensions of the Six Nations.

At the same time, groups of Indians from different nations who had migrated into the region between the Ohio River and the Great Lakes and formed independent republics were asserting themselves. What had begun in the early years of the century as a scattered migration from different directions – Cherokees from the south, Mascoutens and Kickapoos from Illinois, Miamis and Wyandots from the Great Lakes, Iroquois, Delawares and Shawnees from the east – had developed into a formidable military power. By 1750 it was estimated that the Ohio nations could put between 1,500 and 2,000 warriors into the field, making them a bigger force than the Six Nations.[5] While Iroquois migrant leaders in the Ohio country like Scarooyady and the so-called Half-King Tanacharisson provided loose, informal ties to the confederacy at Onondaga, they neither blindly obeyed the Six Nations nor were themselves meekly followed by the Ohio villages. By 1747, moreover, the Ohio Indians had lit their own council fire and opened diplomatic relations with both the British and the French, independent of Onondaga.[6]

Most alarmingly, from a colonial point of view, the Ohio nations had been driven into open revolt against the British and alliance with the French. In 1747 a number of prominent Virginia planters, including George Washington, formed the Ohio Land Company, primarily to invest in lands to the west of the Appalachian Mountains. They hoped both to purchase a large tract, subdivide it and sell portions to settlers, and to lure the fur trade away from the French, who ultimately responded by building a string of forts in the Ohio country, including Presque Isle on the south shore of Lake Erie, Fort Machault near the Delaware village of Venanago on the Allegheny River and Fort Duquesne at the forks of the Ohio River. At the Albany congress of 1754, the Pennsylvania agents had persuaded some Iroquois sachems to sign a deed granting that state a huge tract of Ohio lands.

Infuriated by these encroachments, the Ohio nations launched an aggressive war in the Pennsylvania back-country that had claimed, by 1756, the lives of 2,500 Anglo-American settlers. Though this revolt was conducted in tandem with the French, its ultimate aim was to secure complete independence from Britain, France and the Iroquois. As Daniel Claus informed Johnson from Philadelphia in April 1756, the Delaware sachem Shingo told a prisoner who subsequently escaped: 'If we only Subdue the English first, we may do afterwards what we please with the French.'7

Many of the unfortunate back-country settlers exposed to the terrifying raids of the Ohio Indians clung desperately to the belief that the Iroquois still controlled their assailants and that the great Sir William Johnson could simply use his influence with the latter to turn off the violence. He received, for example, a pathetic letter from the mostly Dutch Corporation of Kingston in January 1756:

The People Daily See Nothing but Fire and Sword Devastations and Desolations before Their Eyes, and Dread to become a Victum to an Inhuman Enemy, they have Laid Waste and Made Desolate about Sixty Miles In Length Upon Delaware River, as We Always Understood That The Delaware and Shawanose Indians Was Subject, or at Least Tributary, to The Mohawk Indians We Desire That you'll be pleased to Lay our Case before Them And to Endeavour If The Mohawks Will Order or Direct the Delaware and Shawanose Indians To Cease Commiting Any Further Hostilities Upon The Inhabitants . . .8

The very hopelessness of such appeals merely underlined the declining influence of the Iroquois. For Johnson, personal, political and imperial motives all combined to urge on his project of re-creating the confederacy and restoring its authority. His greatest influence, and thus his private power, still lay with the Mohawks and, through them, with the Iroquois in general. A collapse in their prestige threatened his. In the broader imperial struggle, meanwhile, British claims to the west depended crucially on their internationally acknowledged status as protectors of the Iroquois. The Ohio revolt was both a military and an ideological challenge to imperial power. If he could refurbish the Great League, Johnson could at once strengthen British rule, re-focus imperial attention on his Mohawk friends and make himself indispensable.

Johnson had began his assumption of Iroquois power at the major conference he hosted in April 1755, when he symbolically quenched the fire in Albany around which diplomatic councils between the British and the Iroquois had been conducted, and rekindled it at Fort Johnson. By shifting the meeting place between the Empire and the Six Nations onto his own ground Johnson solemnised his ascendancy over the old Albany commissioners. But he was also laying claim to a kind of apostolic succession that could be traced back to the legendary founding of the league. As the Mohawk sachem Abraham explained, 'Our Forefathers kindled the first Fire at Onondaga from whence they carried Fuel and made another at the Habitation of Quider [Albany].'⁹ This fire in turn had now been rekindled at Johnson's house, making him the symbolic descendant of Deganawidah.

The Crown Point campaign and its immediate aftermath had prevented Johnson from following through on this strategy of remaking the confederacy, but he got it going again in February 1756, with a large conference at Fort Johnson attended by 586 Indians from each of the Six Nations, including at least fifty warriors 'from the most remote parts of the Seneca's country who never came down before to any meeting'. To mark this important occasion, Johnson produced two symbolic objects.

One was 'the largest pipe in America, made on purpose' – evidently a huge calumet (peace-pipe). To underscore its significance as a way of placing Johnson himself at the heart of the league he presented it with the words: 'Take this pipe to your great council chamber at Onondaga, let it hang there in view; and should you be wavering in your minds at any time, take and smoke out of it, and think of my advice given with it, and you will recover and think properly.'

The second object, presented in return to Johnson by Red Head 'as a pledge of our inviolable attachment to you', but probably commissioned and supplied by Johnson himself for this purpose, was a 'prodigious' belt of wampum. It was 'the largest ever given! Upon it was wrought the sun, by way of the emblem of light, and some figures representing the six nations; it was intended to signify that they now saw objects in their proper light.'[10]

The creation of these outsized versions of traditional objects symbolised Johnson's intention to create a larger version of the old league. In June and July 1756 this process continued with his long ritual journey to and from Onondaga, where he performed the condolence and re-quickening ceremonies to mark the death of Red Head.[11] The journey, because of the danger of French attacks, was extremely risky – so much so that a delegation of Mohawks pleaded with him not to go: 'We are extreamely alarmed & uneasy about it & are absolutely against your venturing up thither. If harm should happen to you We are a lost & ruined people – you are the principle Tie that keeps the 6 Nations together. We cannot comprehend why the Onondagas are so very urgent for your going up when the road is so dangerous.'

For Johnson, however, the risk was worth taking. He shrugged off the Mohawks' fears with a blustering claim: 'If I had called the 6 Nations down here to a meeting & any French Man had dared in my presence to have threatened their safety, I would have drove my ax into his head.'[12] Behind the bravado, though, there was a much subtler sense of purpose.

Johnson's performance, in which he led elaborate and large-scale ceremonies, involved a chanted repetition of the mythic formulae through which the Great League was renewed. As he approached Onondaga, he placed himself at the head of a procession of 'Sachems singing the condoling song which contains the names laws and Customs of their renowned ancestors'.[13] This was no mere lip service to established protocol. It was in fact a far bolder act: a re-creation of forms that were becoming archaic.

Twelve years earlier, in 1744, when the veteran Pennsylvania Indian agent Conrad Weiser went to Onondaga to investigate the panic that had spread through the Mohawk villages at rumours that the English were about to destroy them, his ceremonial approach had been highly European. He was accompanied into Onondaga by a parade led by Indians playing violins, flutes and drums.[14] When Johnson himself had first visited Onondaga in his official capacity as Colonel of the Six Nations in 1748, his reception had been marked with a volley of rifle fire from a group of warriors and sachems lined up in order of rank which was returned by Johnson's Mohawk guard – again a heavily Europeanised ceremony.[15] By reverting now to more archaic forms, Johnson was harnessing the power of tradition for what was in fact a revolutionary innovation: the reinvention of the old structures with a European at their centre.

Two weeks later, at the end of the conference, he was confident enough to present his own pre-eminence within the league as a *fait accompli*. The condolence council reaches a climax with the holding up of the face of the new living sachem who will take the place of the dead man. Johnson took this role to himself. As the Onondaga speaker thanked him for the presents he had bestowed, Johnson made him a sachem by placing a medal around his neck. This innovation was so far accepted that in Iroquois ritual today, the giving to a member of one clan a name borrowed from another is referred to as 'a name hung round the neck'.[16]

Why did the Iroquois accept Johnson's effective usurpation of traditional ceremonial roles? For the majority of the Iroquois sachems who still wished to preserve a policy of neutrality, Johnson's eminence within their ranks was deeply problematic. Around the time that Johnson was at Onondaga, a delegation of 150 Oneidas and Onondagas was in Montreal, meeting with the French governor, Vaudreil. He openly taunted them with their subservience to Johnson: 'None of your nation dare say a word to the English. Colonel Johnson's word makes all your villages tremble.' They defended themselves by claiming: 'We, the Five Nations, fear no man on the face of the earth . . . and a proof of that is that we have come in spite of Colonel Johnson, who has done his best to retain us in our villages.'[17] Yet Vaudreil had obviously touched a nerve. By hinting that the once-proud Iroquois confederacy was allowing itself to become a tool of Johnson, he had given it a reason to resist his stratagems.

Why did they not do so? The answer is partly political. The annihilation of Fort Bull had just demonstrated the vulnerability of the New York frontier and of the British trade that was so important to the Indians to attacks from Canada. Even for those who were not explicitly pro-British and wanted to retain the old policy of neutrality, the power of France and its alliance with the Ohio Indians demanded a counterbalance. Johnson, with his massively enhanced prestige as the sole authorised intermediary with the British, was now more personally important than any single French agent, and as such a necessary

figure. The more he could be drawn into the councils of the confederacy, the more likely he was to represent its interests.

As Johnson understood, however, the answer was also partly cultural. The body of etiquette and protocol that had developed around
the league was formidable and hard to master. The ability to observe
and renew the forms was itself one of the marks of chieftaincy. A ritual sachem of the Onondaga council – as opposed to the village headmen who conducted day-to-day business – was above all a performer,
a man who could embody and give voice to the old forms. Johnson
had become a formidable actor and rhetorician, and by refurbishing
and demonstrating his mastery of the forms, he was demonstrating
chieftainship. To the Iroquois, his skilled performances represented,
not an affront, but great courtesy. Journeying home from Onondaga,
Johnson came to an Oneida village where a death had occurred. He
again performed the condolence ceremony. In thanking him, the
Oneida sachem commented that his actions were convincing proof of
his genuine regard for them, because he had not neglected the necessary rituals even though they knew he was extremely busy.[18]

Johnson's assumption of the role of a sachem in the confederacy
was not, moreover, a threat to the traditional structures. The Iroquois
had long recognised the usefulness of incorporating into the leadership
structure talented individuals who had no hereditary claims. The rules
of the league, as they were codified more than a century later, state:

Should any man of the Nation assist with special ability or show great interest in
the affairs of the Nation, if he proves himself wise, honest and worthy of confidence, the Confederate Lords may elect him to a seat with them, and he may sit in
the Confederate Council. He shall be proclaimed a *Pine Tree sprung up for the
Nation* and be installed as such at the next assembly for the installation of Lords.
Should he ever do anything contrary to the rules of the Great Peace, he may not
be deposed from office – no one shall cut him down (because his top branches
pierce the sky and if his roots are cut he will not fall but hang upright before the
people) – but everyone thereafter shall be deaf to his voice and his advice. Should
he resign his seat and title no one shall prevent him. A Pine Tree chief has no
authority to name a successor nor is his title hereditary.[19]

The constant references by Iroquois speakers to Johnson as 'a Tree
that grew for our use', or similar formulations, suggests that this is the
way his position was understood. Yet Johnson also manipulated the
imagery to extend his prestige. The Pine Tree chief who had sprung up
for the Six Nations also identified himself with the Tree of Peace that
symbolised the confederacy itself. On certificates he gave to Indians

around this time as testimonials to their loyalty and passports through British territories, he had printed an illustration of the Tree of Peace hung with the Covenant Chain. On each side sit delegations of colonials and Indians. In the centre, around the council fire, is Johnson presenting a medal to an Indian whom he is making a sachem. By a clever visual analogy, Johnson was extending his remit from honest advisor to the council at Onondaga to embodiment of the council itself.

When several Oneida and Tuscarora warriors visited him in 1757 and the Oneida sachem Conochquiesa told him that one young Tuscarora man intended to travel south, he replied: 'I am glad to find that it was not a Resolution of your Council that the Tuscarore Young Man should go to the Southward without my Approbation. I must now tell you again, that none of you go to the Southward or elsewhere far distant without my knowledge & Passport, for two reasons; The first is, it will not be safe for you at this time. The other is, I may have some Errand to send by you or Business to transmit there.'[20] His demand for control over the movement of Iroquois warriors was founded on military necessity but also on the visual message of the passports: that Johnson's business was also that of the league itself.

Above all, Johnson was now able to combine the two kinds of chieftaincy in his own person. He had shown that he could be a ritual sachem of the confederacy; and he was also the supreme chief of the more pragmatic kind, the essential function of this kind of chief being to gain goods and distribute them to his village. Johnson was now at the pinnacle of the system of chieftaincy because he could not only supply goods but also choose which sachems to give them to. In this, he was the one who made their performance of the duties of chieftainship possible. As well as bringing his charismatic performances to Onondaga, he also brought eighteen horses laden with presents and a small herd of oxen.[21]

Refurbishing the confederacy was not, in itself, a sufficient response to the French challenge. The emergence of the Ohio nations and villages as an independent force meant that things had changed. Both the short-term aim of stopping the attacks on the western frontier settlements and the long-term goal of creating a durable new alliance required a new approach. It was no longer enough simply to assert that all of these nations were vassals of the Six Nations and should do as they were told. Johnson understood that this very sense of subordination to the Iroquois was one of the driving forces behind the violence. A refurbished confederacy would have to be broader, more inclusive and less humiliating to its supposedly dependent allies.

Johnson therefore combined his assertion of power within the confederacy with an equally adventurous gesture towards the Ohio tribes. Just as the Onondaga conference was breaking up, a delegation of Susquehanna Delawares with some Shawnees arrived. Significantly, Johnson chose not to treat with them at Onondaga. He invited them to accompany him back to Fort Johnson. He wished to perform a ritual that would be most powerful on his own ground, away from the centre of the old Iroquois confederacy.

Johnson knew that the Ohio violence was driven by the desire of the Pennsylvania Indians to shrug off old humiliations. The Six Nations asserted their dominance over the Delawares in starkly sexual terms:

Cousins the Delaware Indians: You will remember that you are our Women, our Forefathers made you so, and put a Petty Coat on you, and charged you to be true to us, and lye with no other Man; but of late you suffered the string that ty'd your Petticoat to be cut loose by the French and you lay with them and so became a common bawd, in which you did very wrong and deserved Chastisement, but notwithstanding this we have an Esteem for you and you have thrown off your Piece, and become stark naked which is a shame for a Woman we now give you a little Prick & put it in your private Parts and so let it grow there, till you shall be a compleat man. We advise you not to act as a Man yet but be first instructed by us and do as we bid you and you will become a noted man.[22]

These insults, employing notions of virility and masculinity to paint the Delaware warriors successively as concubines, whores, and pre-pubescent boys had long created a sense of shame that found release in the extreme violence of the attacks on white settlers. In a culture where masculinity was expressed in battle, the Delawares tried to prove they were men by the ferocity of their assaults on the whites, which was much more intense than the normal pattern of Indian aggression.

While on the surface Johnson's interests might seem to have been best served by reinforcing this imagery of dependence and subjection, he was astute enough to realise that it was itself a large part of the problem. He had been sent a copy of a letter from the Lieutenant Governor of Pennsylvania Robert Hunter Norris to William Shirley reporting that the Western Nations had 'proclaimed War with great Solemnity against all the English & threaten not to Leave one of them alive; & assign, as a Reason for this, that they have been too long treated by the Six Nations, to whom they are subject, as Women, but will now show them that they are Men'.[23]

With his sharp feeling for the value Indians placed on self-respect, and a growing skill in manipulating the gender politics of Indian cultures, Johnson understood that the Pennsylvania war was motivated as much by a male desire for dignity in the eyes of the Six Nations as by resentment of British encroachments. He therefore decided that he, as a representative of both the Six Nations and the British, could symbolically heal the wound and remove the stigma. What was called for initially was not a diplomat negotiating a treaty but a shaman lifting a curse.

Before the Delaware and Shawnee sachems, and some non-commital Mohawks, Johnson intoned the necessary incantation: 'I do, in the name of the Great King of England, your father, declare that henceforth you are to be considered as men by all your brethren, the English, and no longer as women, and I hope that your Brethren the Six Nations will take it into consideration, follow my example, and remove this invidious distinction – which I shall recommend to them.'[24] For this audacious sex-change operation, Johnson had no sanction from Onondaga, but if the Great King of England had declared the Delawares and Shawnees men, the Six Nations could hardly continue to claim otherwise.

Johnson followed up his ritual freeing of the Shawnees and Delawares by sending George Croghan, an Irish trader whom he had appointed as his deputy, to Pennsylvania to investigate the grievances of the Ohio nations and 'assure them, that if they will come and let me Know wherein they are injured, I will endeavour to have Justice done them, so that, that unhappy Difference may be settled'.[25] He meanwhile pressed the Lords of Trade in London to rescind the grant of Ohio land that the Iroquois had made to Pennsylvania at Albany in 1754, and in December 1756 the proprietors of Pennsylvania agreed to renounce these purchases. After tedious negotiations in late July and early August 1757, involving representatives of the eastern Delawares under their leader Teedyuscung, Croghan secured a partial peace treaty and a truce.

In freeing the Ohio nations from their status as women, Johnson had effectively usurped the role of an Onondaga council. He was not really recognising their independence, merely attempting to change the nature of their dependence. If, hitherto, they had been in theory under the protection of the Iroquois, now, since Johnson had placed himself at the centre of the confederacy, they would be under his. By inviting them to see him as the person to whom they could appeal for justice and the settlement of differences, he had strongly implied that he himself stood at the apex of Indian politics not just in New York but in the Ohio valley as well. Grandiose as this gesture may have been, he had also taken steps to strengthen in the most intimate way possible his ties to Iroquois culture.

17

Miss Molly

The beautiful young Mohawk girl is watching the strut and colour of a regimental militia muster in Albany. She catches the eye of an officer, who flirts with her. Flirting back, she asks if she may climb up behind him on his prancing, headstrong horse. As a joke, he tells her to try, not supposing for a moment that she could make it. She grabs the horse's crupper and leaps with the agility of a gazelle to land neatly behind him. She digs in her heels and the horse races around the parade ground at full gallop. Her long black hair streams behind her and her blanket billows and parts. The crowd cheers. The watching William Johnson falls for her and takes her home to Fort Johnson.[1]

This legend lingered in the folklore of the Mohawk valley for more than a century, providing a suitably colourful beginning to the larger story of Johnson's long relationship with the Mohawk woman, Mary (Molly) Brant. Molly, whose Mohawk name was Degonwadonti ('Several Against One') was born around 1736, making her about twenty years younger than Johnson. Her parents, Peter Tehonwaghkwangeraghkwa and his wife Margaret, were Mohawks from the upper village of Canajoharie, but possibly because they were both members of the Wolf clan and their marriage violated the rule of clan exogamy, they had moved west to the Ohio valley, where Margaret seems to have had relatives among those Caughnawaga Mohawks who were living there.[2]

Growing up in the Ohio country would have involved Molly in a cultural mix even more promiscuous than that of the Mohawk villages. The Ohio River Indians were a conglomeration of Iroquois – who became known as Mingos – Delawares, Shawnees, Munsees and various fragments of French-allied groups. Both the British and the

French regarded these independent villages with some alarm as 'republics' beyond the control of the European Empires, the Indian confederations and indeed any individual nation. This suspicious contempt was bluntly expressed by Richard Peters of Pennsylvania who called them 'ye Scum of the Earth . . . this mixed dirty sort of people'.3

Early in the first French war the Mingos actually declared their independence of Onondaga, but Molly's parents clearly retained close ties with their Mohawk homelands. After her father's death Molly came back to Canajoharie with her mother, who married again but was quickly widowed a second time. Margaret then became the wife of Johnson's friend Brant Kanagaradunkwa, though not before she had conceived a child by him and been made to do penance by the Reverend Ogilvie at Fort Hunter. Brant and Margaret were formally married in September 1753 and Molly and her brother Joseph took their stepfather's name.

Johnson probably met Molly Brant through her stepfather, but by February 1755 he couldn't have helped noticing that she had another admirer: the twenty-seven-year-old nephew of Governor Morris of Pennsylvania, Captain Staats Long Morris, who held a commission as captain in Johnson's New York militia and was stationed at Albany. According to Daniel Claus, 'Capt StMs fell in love with Miss Mary Brant, who was then pretty likely not having had the smallpox.'4 Morris may well be the officer whose gallant attentions gave rise to the enduring story of how William Johnson fell in love with Molly Brant.

Molly may have had a relationship with Morris, and she would not have felt ill at ease, either culturally or socially, in such relatively elevated company. Culturally, Molly had grown up a Protestant and her stepfather Brant owned a substantial, colonial-style frame house and dressed in European clothes. She also spoke, and could read, English and seems to have been numerate, suggesting that she attended a mission school. Socially, Molly was a young woman of some status. In 1754 and early 1755 she accompanied a delegation of Mohawk elders to Philadelphia to discuss fraudulent land transactions which the nation wanted to rescind.5 Her presence in such an important delegation suggests that she was already marked out for a significant political role as a clan matron, a position whose powers included the choice of new sachems. Though her own parents were not part of the hereditary Mohawk leadership, her stepfather Brant Kanagaradunkwa was a sachem of the Turtle clan, and her connection with him raised Molly's status.

Johnson had had relationships with Mohawk women before, most notably with Elizabeth Brant. Whatever its origins, however, his connection with Molly was of a different order. The context was altered by events at both a private and a public level. In the first place, Catharine, the German mother of Johnson's white children, was fading out of his life. She and her children had been sent to Albany for their safety in the late 1740s, but she probably returned to live with Johnson at some stage in the 1750s. The young German Daniel Claus, who was courting their daughter Nancy, referred to her 'Love & Duty to her Parents', which suggests that Catharine had been very much involved in bringing her up.[6] By around 1758, however, she was ill, probably with tuberculosis.

Catharine died, almost certainly in April 1759. On 23 May, Peter Wraxall wrote to Johnson from New York: 'When I left you, I thought there appeared little hope of Miss Katy's life. I condole with you thereupon, and hope Miss Nancy's management of the house will supply the loss you have sustained.'[7] The unemotional and pragmatic tone of the condolences suggests that Catharine, for some time now, had served Johnson in the capacity more of a housekeeper than of a lover.

One undocumented account given by an old Schenectady resident in 1844 claims that Johnson married Catharine 'ten days before her death'.[8] This is certainly possible, but it is not likely. In his will, Johnson would refer to 'my beloved wife Catharine Johnson', but no record of a formal marriage exists. There was a strong incentive in drawing up his will to claim that Catharine was his wife and that their children were therefore legitimate, a concern that also argues against a legal marriage by her deathbed. To leave a record of a wedding almost twenty years after the birth of their first child would be to confirm that their offspring had been born out of wedlock. The vagueness of a general assumption that they had been man and wife was a great deal more useful. Probably, what happened in Catharine's dying days was some kind of personal ceremony marking the importance of their relationship and assuring Catty that their children would be the heirs to Johnson's mounting fortune.

What is certain, in any case, was that Molly Brant had begun a sexual relationship with Johnson before Catharine's death. In August 1759 Johnson wrote to Molly from Oswego, telling her 'not to come here', which suggests of course that she expected to do so and that they had previously discussed the possibility of her joining him.[9] He wrote to her again on 10 September, probably congratulating her on the event that explains his reluctance for her to travel to Oswego: the birth of their son. That the boy was named Peter Warren Johnson, after Johnson's distinguished uncle, suggests both that Johnson had forgiven his mentor for the slights he had suffered at his hands, and that Johnson was anxious, not simply to claim the child, but to place him in the official family lineage.

The likelihood is that Peter was conceived in Brant's house in Canajoharie in January 1759 when Johnson stayed there during a conference with the Mohawks. Molly had almost certainly moved into Fort Johnson by the time of Peter's birth. In his will, he would refer to her as 'my House Keeper Mary Brant', but the phrase is rather misleading.[10] It is not just that Molly was much more mistress than servant, having, for example, her own slaves within Johnson's household; it is also that Johnson's homes, after 1756, had a ritual significance for the Iroquois as places where the council fire burned, and Molly is more accurately regarded as a co-keeper of that fire. As Johnson's Indian wife and as a Turtle clan matron, she helped to validate his assumption of a place at the centre of the confederacy by tying him in to the traditional Iroquois lineages. Molly's political significance gave her a status at Fort Johnson far higher than Catharine's had been.

Through his association with Molly, Johnson could place his exercise of imperial authority within the framework of Iroquois culture. Johnson, unlike most Europeans, understood the important political role of the clan matrons. He told his brother Warren, who visited him from Ireland in 1760, that 'the Indian women have very great influence over the Indians, so that if the young Warriours are going to War they can almost hinder them, but when going all Sing the War song, & get a Charge from the Old Women, particularly to behave well & not be a Discredit to themselves, or their forefathers . . . Indian women assist at Councils . . .'[11] Johnson also understood that because Iroquois descent was matrilineal and chieftainship had a strong hereditary element, women could influence the choice of sachems. They could help to pick ambassadors and attend diplomatic gatherings.[12] As the keepers of the land, women also had a significant say in its disposal.

By identifying himself within Indian society as Molly's husband, Johnson could draw on these powers. He had been careful from the early days of the war to enhance his own appeal to the clan matrons and the wives of influential sachems, reminding himself in his 'Hints for a Commanding Officer' in 1755: 'When you make presents to the Indians let them be such as will be most acceptable to their Wives and Mistresses.' His account books show that he supplied jewellery, mirrors and patterned handkerchiefs for the wives of sachems and warriors, but also that he sometimes gave cash directly to these women: 'To a squaw to buy Leather for Mockasens . . . To a Mohawk Widdow for her sons gun who died lately . . . Cash to several squaws.'[13]

Molly's presence allowed him to go much further and to act as if he were an Iroquois matron himself. In naming sachems he took on the role of the clan matrons. In calling for the nations to go on the warpath he usurped their function of calling for the replacement of dead warriors with scalps or prisoners and of urging the men to bring honour to their forefathers. At the most basic level, his frequent provision of food for the warriors and sachems, either at the feasts that accompanied councils or in the form of provisions and presents sent to villages, put him in the position of the Iroquois women.[14]

Molly sanctioned this transference of her power to Johnson by acting as hostess at Indian conferences and, in effect, as his deputy. While her name is not recorded at the official sessions of conferences, it is clear that she played an important role in the behind-the-scenes negotiations. Daniel Claus later testified that Molly 'held a great sway' with the Six Nations as a whole.[15] One contemporary account mentions that 'she was of great use to Sir William in his Treaties with those people. He knew that women govern the politics of the Savages.' Another describes Molly as his 'faithful and useful friend in Indian affairs' and notes: 'When treaties or purchases were about to be made . . . she has often persuaded the obstinate chiefs into a compliance with the proposals for peace, or sale of lands.'[16]

Molly thus enjoyed a recognised status as Johnson's partner in both white and Indian societies. Merchants and innkeepers gave Indians hospitality on her orders: one trader's accounts record punch, rum and meals being ordered by Indians 'as per order of Miss Molly'.[17] Far beyond the Six Nations, it came to be assumed that she was due the courtesies of Johnson's wife. In a letter of 1770, the Oquaga chieftain Peter Ogwitontongwas writes: 'My Wife & her sister Salute Miss Molly,' a recognition far more important in a matrilineal culture than that of the chief himself. In 1768 the white trader Joseph Chew, who had been staying at Johnson Hall, declared himself 'greatly mortified over leaving the Hall without wishing miss Molly' goodbye.[18]

Molly also acted as a mediator between the European and Indian worlds. In 1771 Captain James Stevenson, who had commanded Fort Niagara, asked Johnson for confidential advice about his son by an Indian woman who had lived with him there for a year: 'I have a fine Boy amongst the Senecas & would be glad to get him from them . . . for I cannot think of leaving him amongst them.' Johnson evidently offered to help as Stevenson later thanked him 'for the pains you are willing to take to get my Boy from the Indians'. In fact, though, it was Molly who intervened with the Senecas on Stevenson's behalf, for in subsequent letters he expresses his 'thanks to Molly for the pains you have taken about my Young Warrior'.

That Molly should involve herself in Stevenson's attempts to get custody of his son is rather poignant. Stevenson acidly noted that in acknowledging his Indian son he had 'set a good example to own their offspring' to the inhabitants of Albany. 'When I have a little leisure I shall endeavour to compose a small History of the Dutch connection with the Indians, nameing the particular families who have the honour of savage blood circulating in their Veins.'[19] Molly had an interest in the acknowledgement by Europeans of their half-Indian children. She and Johnson had a total of eight children: Peter, Elizabeth, Magdalene, Margaret, George, Mary, Susanna and Anne.[20] Johnson certainly owned all of these children as his. In his will he left most of them a substantial farm and each of them thousands of acres of undeveloped land.[21]

Nor did he hide the fact that he had Mohawk children. When Peter was a teenager, Hugh Wallace wrote to Johnson from New York City: 'I saw your Son Peter at Philadelphia last Wednesday. He was verry well & I think a verry sober good Lad. He has a verry good Name from his Acquaintance –'[22] Peter, indeed, seems to have been raised to make a genteel impression in the world as the son of a baronet. He spoke and read English, French and Mohawk, asking his father in 1774 to send him 'some french & English Books to read at Leisure hours, & an Indian Book, for I am Afraid I'll lose my Indian Tongue If I dont practice it more than I do'. He also played the violin, 'as it is a great Deal of Pleasure to Play at Leasure Ours'.[23]

The daughters seem to have been raised with the same gentility. In later life, their appearance at a very proper fête given by the Governor of Canada in 1793 to mark King George's birthday created a stir, not because of their expected exoticism but because they were so little out of place: 'They appeared as well dressed as the company in general and intermixed with them in a manner which evinced at once the dignity of their own minds and the good sense of others. These ladies possessed great ingenuity and industry, and have great merit . . .'[24]

The acknowledgement of her children among both Johnson's Indian and his European acquaintances was just one aspect of Molly's status as his official consort. No effort was made to conceal her relationship with Johnson, even within the context of imperial wars. As his letter to her from Oswego in 1759 cancelling plans for her to join him shows, Johnson certainly considered taking Molly with him on military campaigns, as many of the Mohawks took their wives, at least to the camps. That her status was well understood within the army is also clear from his writing that, when he was encamped near Three Rivers on his way to Detroit in 1761, 'Captain Etherington told me Molly was delivered of a girl [Elizabeth], that all were well at my house, where they stayed two days.'[25]

Most important, Molly presided at Johnson's homes. She had her own suite of rooms at the second mansion he built, Johnson Hall, and the furnishings were considered to be hers.[26] Her taste seems to have mixed Indian and European cultures. She dressed in Mohawk costume and was an expert herbalist who retained the secrets of Indian medicine. At the same time, she seems to have enjoyed urban finery. Archaeological excavations at a house she occupied after Johnson's death discovered small beads used in traditional Mohawk ornamentation, but also hand-painted pearlware ceramic dishes, fine crystal glass, bone and ivory toothbrushes and combs and an amethyst finger ring.

These were possessions proper for the lady of the house, and so Molly certainly appeared to visitors. The Scottish writer Anne Grant, who visited Johnson when she was a little girl, remembered decades later that 'becoming a widower in the prime of life, he connected himself with an Indian maiden, daughter to a sachem, who possessed an uncommonly agreeable person, and good understanding; and whether ever formally married to him according to our usage, or not, contrived to live with him, in great union and affection all his life.'[27] She had gone to Johnson's house in the company of the eminently respectable Schuyler family, yet it is clear that no attempt was made to deny or understate Molly's status as the effective mistress of the household.

Molly's presence at Johnson's regular dinners for European guests seems to have been discreet, but it was slightly awkward for some. In a letter after he had stayed at Johnson Hall, Lord Adam Gordon sent his regards 'to the Ladies' and added in a postscript 'My Love to Molly' – a formula which at once acknowledged her intimate position in the family and yet managed not to concede her status as a lady. Gordon's own position, however, was invidious: his sister-in-law, the dowager Duchess of Gordon, married Molly's apparent former lover Staats Morris. The hint of embarrassment in his reference to Molly may have as much to do with this strange social entanglement as with Molly's status as a Mohawk.[28]

Another such visitor wrote of Molly: 'Her features are fine and beautiful; her complexion clear and olive tinted . . . She was quiet in demeanour, on occasion, and possessed of a calm dignity that bespoke a native pride and consciousness of power. She seldom imposed herself into the picture, but no one was in her presence without being aware of her.'[29]

This 'consciousness of power' could be fierce as well as dignified; she was a strong-willed woman. When Johnson sent her young brother Joseph, whom he was grooming as an important ally among the Mohawks, to a mission school in Connecticut, run by Eleaner Wheelock, Molly insisted that he be brought home after she discovered that he was required to do agricultural work. As an aggrieved Wheelock wrote to Johnson, he received 'a Paper with your Seal inclosing a Letter to Joseph from his Sister; wrote, I suppose in the Mohawk Language; and by which he informs me, he is ordered to come directly home; that the Indians are displeased with his being here at School, that they don't like the People &c'.[30] The woman who could defy Johnson's own wishes in such a haughty way was not to be taken lightly. Five years after Johnson's death, when she was at Fort Niagara, one of the white prisoners being held there offended her in some way and she terrified him and the others by demanding that she be given his head to kick around the fort.[31]

It was not just her strength of personality that made Molly a match for Johnson. She gained a great deal of status and material comfort from their relationship, but so did he. With Molly beside him, the Canajoharie Mohawks now thought of Johnson, not just as a part of their nation but as a part of their family. In December 1760, after an invitation to their 'Affectionate Brother and Friend' to come to the village, the council informed him of their intention to present him with a tract of land on the north shore of the Mohawk River 'as a token of their regard for him'. The deed, when it was drawn up and signed, was granted, 'Whilst it is in our power to give you this proof of our friend-ship, which we fear, will not be long as our White Brethren are getting all our Lands from us.' The gift consisted of 80,000 acres, virtually all the land bordering the river that the Canajoharie Mohawks still owned. They had decided that, since they would lose it to the White Brethren anyway, they might as well, 'before it should be out of their Power to have any Lands to bestow', give it to a white brother with Mohawk children.[32]

18

Rowing Against the Current

===

In August 1756 a colonial soldier guarding cattle near the Great Carrying Place by Lake Oneida heard a rustling in the bushes. He saw an Indian coming towards him and cocked his gun to shoot him. The man called out 'Johnson – Brother,' and made to shake hands with the soldier. He was subsequently recognised as Sam Norris, a Shawnee warrior who had been with George Washington on the Ohio River but had then been suspected of treachery. He was now claiming that he was on his way to Sir William Johnson with the news that 'he had heard great Cannonading at Oswego & that he imagined the French had beseiged it'.[1] Johnson, in fact, had already received intelligence to the effect that the French had surrounded this fort and trading post, and had sent messages to the military commanders.

For Johnson, the French assault on Oswego had a private significance beyond the evidence it provided that the British had almost entirely lost the initiative in the war. It was not just that he had supplied the garrison there for years and used it as the base for his trade with the western Indians; it was also that at least some of the 'French' attackers were people from his own Irish Jacobite background. Reports from a deserter contained the information that among the French troops were 'some cloathed in Red faced with Green which he imagines belongs to the Irish Brigade'. Not only were there fellow Irishmen among the enemy, but many of the Irishmen among the British and colonial defenders of Oswego – including, presumably, people whom Johnson knew as fellow countrymen – showed signs of wanting to desert to that same enemy. The French on Lake Ontario encountered 'a canoe full of men, women and children, and a deserter from Choueguen [Oswego], who represent themselves to be Irish and dissatisfied, and were coming to take refuge among us'.[2]

The news from Oswego was a reminder to Johnson of how far he had come and also how far he had to go if his grand plans for a new Iroquois confederacy were to be fulfilled. He knew that Indian allegiances would depend on the course of the war. The unified, pro-British league he was trying to create could not be forged by the sheer force of his personality. If Britain looked in danger of losing the war, the pro-French factions within the confederacy would maintain their allegiances and the neutralist centre ground would remain cautious. While Johnson could always attract dissident factions within each nation and act as a magnet for ambitious young warriors, a stable alliance needed military success.

In the summer and autumn of 1756, as Johnson was carrying out his strategy, long-standing Indian scepticism about the ability of the British to exert themselves for victory was proving justified. Shirley had been dismissed, but he remained in command until Major General James Abercromby arrived from Britain in June. He in turn did very little except wait for the new overall commander Lieutenant General John Campbell, Earl of Loudoun, who arrived in New York on 23 July. Loudoun, when he began to take control, was horrified to find that provincial militia objected to being under the command of regular officers. The ensuing row stalled the already haphazard progress of a force assembled for a repeat of Johnson's expedition against Crown Point in 1755.

While this bickering went on, Johnson received confirmation of his earlier intelligence that the French had attacked Oswego. An Onondaga Indian, who claimed to have run the 150 miles from the fort to Johnson, who was at Canajoharie, told him that Oswego had fallen and showed him the holes in his shirt through which bullets had passed as he escaped.

A French force of 3,000 regulars, militia and Indians, led by Dieskau's replacement the Marquis de Montcalm, had attacked the three parts of the fort which housed just 1,135 soldiers left there by Shirley. With Montcalm's disciplined regular troops, trained artillery men and eighty cannon, it had taken just three days for the fort to fall. The capture of the entire garrison with a huge amount of stores and the massacre of between thirty and a hundred Anglo-American soldiers and civilians by Montcalm's Indian auxiliaries represented a sickening blow to British prestige. English ships on Lake Ontario had no choice but to surrender.

Johnson, on receiving word of the defeat, immediately offered to raise a 'Considerable Number of Indians & if I find that the French are still there', go to Oswego and engage them.[3] It was by then too late, however. The French were well on the way back to Montreal, with the surviving members of the Anglo-American garrison. Johnson's intention to 'join Major General Webb & go with him to Oswego' was, in any case, wishful thinking. Webb, third-in-command after Loudoun and Abercromby, had arrived at the Great Carrying Place two days before Johnson sent his offer of assistance. He heard rumours that Montcalm was about to attack the Mohawk valley and panicked. He ordered that the recently rebuilt Fort Bull be burnt, Wood Creek be blocked with trees and that his troops retreat to German Flats, just seventy miles west of Albany. The entire western frontier had been abandoned. Loudoun almost immediately ordered plans for another attack on Crown Point to be cancelled. With British imperial power so openly humbled, Johnson faced renewed scepticism on the part of his putative Indian allies.

The collapse of Anglo-American prestige among the Indians was especially damaging because, with the cancellation of plans for formal military expeditions against the French, the contested terrain was again the forests and waterways around Lake George, where Indian support was crucial. To make matters worse, those Indian warriors whom Johnson could persuade to scout and raid on this frontier found themselves treated badly by the garrison at Fort William Henry, the base Johnson had established near the lake in the autumn of 1755. The British, for example, had 'but few Friends'[4] amongst the Cayugas, yet in late February 1757, some Cayuga warriors Johnson had sent out 'on a Scalping or Scouting Design' complained that 'the English at Lake George used them very ill, would not suffer them to go and speak to the Commanding Officer about Business but took them by the shoulders & turned them out like Dogs, this was the reason of their leaving said place & giving up their Design of going there upon any Service'.

Johnson tried to reassure them by reading a letter from William Eyre, now promoted to major and in charge of the defences of the fort he had designed, assuring Johnson that Indian allies would be well treated. The Cayugas interrupted him, 'being very warm about what he told them'. Even more damningly, the Mohawk sachem Abraham joined in and complained that, when he had returned from a scouting party with the scalps of two Frenchmen, General John Winslow, who was to command the expedition against Crown Point, would not see him or give him provisions. 'The french', he warned ominously, 'do not use their Indians so, by which means they must get all at last.'[5] Even Johnson's emollient assurances that these problems were the fault of 'some foolish Rash Soldier who did not perhaps know whether they were Friends or Foe' could not, as he admitted, 'thoroughly pacify them'.

Between the military humiliations of the British and the crass behaviour towards the Indians of some of their representatives, the effect even of Johnson's best efforts was limited. The old Oneida chief sachem Aguiotta, who came to live out the remainder of his days at Fort Johnson, told him in March 1757 that the Six Nations were now 'very much affraid of the French'. He believed that no more than half of their warriors would stand by the British.[6] Three months later, when delegates from all of the Six Nations came to Fort Johnson, they gave ritual assurances of friendship, but pleaded that 'they were in comparison with the Nations surrounding them (& who were in the French Interest) but as a small handful of People – that they were menaced from several Quarters' and that they therefore had to 'stay at home & be upon their Guard'. To reinforce these fears, the French agent Daniel-Marie Chabert de Joncaire, who was living with the Senecas, sent wampum belts to Onondaga warning the Six Nations warriors not to travel more than a day's walk from their villages, 'as Danger hangs over their heads'.[7]

Fear of the French and disillusionment with the British meant that Iroquois warriors were increasingly reluctant to risk their lives in the forests around and beyond Lake George. Johnson was forced to experiment with the relatively new idea of turning whites into Indian warriors. He had, in his Lake George campaign of 1755, discovered the talents of the New Hampshire scout Robert Rogers. 'Finding him an active man', as he subsequently wrote, 'I raised him to the rank of a Provincial Officer and employed him on scouting service, there being very few people then to be had fit for the purpose.'[8] In the winter of 1755–6, Johnson sent Rogers out about a dozen times to scout around Fort Carillon and Fort St Frederic. In early February 1756 Rogers burned a village about half a mile from Crown Point. In July, a raiding party of fifty members of what were now known as 'Rogers' Rangers' killed some French or Canadian sailors on the lake and sank some boats, destroying their cargoes, with the exception of some casks of brandy and wine, which they saved for themselves.

For the most part, though, these attempts to substitute white rangers for Indian warriors were ineffective. One fifty-man party abandoned a scouting expedition after three days when they 'heard or thought they heard some Party of the Enemy'. Another expedition was aborted when one of the sentries was found scalped and with a hatchet in his head. The rest preferred to be listed on a roll-call of named cowards rather than proceed. Another group of scouts heard musket shots and voted to return to Fort William Henry immediately.[9]

Johnson's private opinion of Rogers soon soured when the rugged ranger began to preen himself on the romantic reputation he was gathering. As he later wrote, Rogers 'soon became puffed up with pride and folly from the extravigant encomiums & notice of some of the Provinces, this spoiled a good Ranger, for he was fitt for nothing else, neither has Nature calculated him for a large Command in that Service, he has neither Understanding, education, or principles'.[10] French counter-measures, moreover, became steadily more effective. The failure of another of Rogers' expeditions in August, when his party was discovered on the west shore of Lake Champlain, was followed by a force of Canadian and Indian raiders killing or capturing near Fort William Henry all but six of a fifty-man scouting party. By the autumn it was obvious that the French were winning this guerrilla war too. They had 760 Indian raiders based at the French end of Lake George, including Abenakis, Hurons, Caughnawagas, Mississaugas, Nipissings, Ojibwas and Potawatomis.

Johnson, by contrast, was delighted at his achievement in recruiting 'near fifty River Indians'.[11] His hopes of being joined by a 'great Number of the Six Nations' were undermined by the crude behaviour of the regular troops he had sent to protect the Mohawk village of Canajoharie. The commanding officer seized a keg of rum from the house of a Mohawk man. When the man took the keg back, the sentry who had allowed him to do so was whipped and the Mohawks feared he would be shot. Soldiers also stole the corn that the Mohawk women were drying for their winter provisions and allowed their own cattle to trample the crops. To add insult to injury, the commanding officer told the Mohawks that the barracks in their village was 'a kings Garrison and Nott belonging to the Indians'. When the Mohawks threatened to complain to Johnson, the officer replied that 'the King was his Master [and] that [Johnson] had Nothing to Do in itt'. The Oneidas also complained of soldiers destroying their crops.[12]

The French, by contrast, were courting the Iroquois. In February 1757, for example, a priest based among the Catholic Iroquois on the St Lawrence River, in Canada, sent seven Indians with a message to the Oneidas congratulating them on their avoidance of the war. He added 'Four Bags of Powder to shoot Birds with. The reason I send you this is because I heard the English your Brothers gave you but a single handfull. I have it piled up here, you can have what you want for fetching.'[13]

This continuing combination of British weakness, British arrogance and French blandishments meant that a conference called by Johnson at his house in November 1756 was attended by too few sachems or leading men to have any proper status, and he had to send those who did arrive back to Onondaga.[14] To make matters worse, some of the Stockbridge Indians whom he had been using as scouts got involved in a row in Albany in which an Anglo-American was killed. When one of the Indians was arrested, his son threatened to burn the house of the Albany politician Robert Livingston. Adding to these tensions between the Indians and the Anglo-Americans, the destruction of Oswego had disrupted the trade on which the Indians depended. With Johnson also urging them not to hunt north of Albany for fear of enemy attacks, they were complaining: 'Our Children are almost naked.'[15]

Johnson, who had usually worked through the sachems of the various nations, now found himself having to work against some of them. In January 1757 a party of Onondagas whom he sent out to get scalps and prisoners reported back to him: 'As we were preparing to set off on that design our Sachem spoke to us . . . desiring we would not leave home nor persist in our Design as it was likely that a Peace between the English & French would soon take place. Then we should draw by this Step the French upon our backs.' Johnson found himself having to disparage the authority of the sachems, telling the warriors that he 'never expected you could be prevailed on to drop the Design at the request of the Sachems, and for such silly reasons as they gave you, it was very wrong for you to act in that manner.'[16]

The pressure on Johnson was fierce, not least because, with the French gaining control of the forests, Fort Johnson itself was now at risk. The threat to Johnson's own safety was, if anything, more acute than it had been a decade earlier. In September 1756 a delegation of Cayugas who had been in Montreal sent an urgent message to Johnson repeating what the French had told them: 'They would send out a considerable body of French and Indians to destroy Sir William Johnson's house.' The following June he received a message from Canajoharie in the wonderful Dutch English of Pieter Schuyler, whose grandfather had organised the visit of the Mohawk leaders to London in 1710: 'There is a leven franch Indeins in the woods about Your hous wich has a mind to take Your Honour or to Schulp your honour And there is one Indien with them wich Belonged once to this Castle and his Name is Antony hee has a Peace out of his nose hee is to take a walke with Your honour and soo to take or Schulp You and the Indiens Desire Your honour to bee upon Your geard Sir.'17

The very fact that the Indians had to warn Johnson of threats to his own safety undermined his stated position as their protector. The Marquis de Vaudreil in Montreal reported gleefully to his superiors in Paris what he had heard from Iroquois delegations: that Johnson 'had the weakness to tell them that it was very painful for him not to be able to go out of his house without exposing himself to the risk of having his skull cracked'. Vaudreil's informants told him that they had 'laughed at this speech; they sent word to Colonel Johnson that he was beginning to cry very early'.18

While these Indians may have been telling Vaudreil what they knew he wanted to hear, Johnson was certainly reduced to bluster: 'The English are now in earnest & determined to punish the French for their Villanous & Insolent Behaviour. They are resolved to bear it no longer & I would therefore as a friend advise all Indians to take care & consider & not be so ready to join the French, for they will not be able to protect & supply them with the necessaries of Life as the English can.'19

In truth, it was now the Six Nations who were protecting the English, and the Mohawk valley in particular. Loath as they were to take up the hatchet against the French, they could still exert some diplomatic power by issuing warnings that they would view an attack on the Mohawk valley as a provocation. An Iroquois deputation to Montreal in November 1756 saw a force of 200 French and 300 Indians preparing to attack the Mohawk settlements and specifically Fort Johnson.

They asked Vaudreil if he was determined to go ahead with this attack. When he said he was, they then approached the French-allied Indians and warned them that such an assault deep into the Iroquois homelands would 'absolutely breed a Quarrel . . . between them and the Six Nations'. This caused enough uneasiness for Vaudreil to suggest that these were Johnson's sentiments, not those of the Six Nations: 'He thought their Brother Warraghiyagey had put those Words into their Mouths – They assured him it was their own desire & Sentiments, adding that, as that was a Road of Peace which their Forefathers had always used when they came to speak with their Brethren the English, they would not have it stopped or covered with Blood. On this the Governor told them it should not be done, and that he would acquaint all his Children the Indians with it & forbid them going that way.'[20]

This assurance, when conveyed to Johnson, did little to ease his anxieties, since he regarded it as a ploy 'to lull us a sleep'. By February 1757 the intelligence he was receiving indicated that 'the Six Nations are greatly divided among themselves and . . . If we are not Active early in the Spring; they may all turn against us.' The Iroquois, 'seeing the French so successful against the English, and little or no Resistance made', were 'intimidated'. Indeed, the Six Nations increasingly regarded the British as indecisive and ineffectual, and the French as 'an active enterprizing People who never Sleep on these Occasions'.[21]

While Johnson still had Indians 'constantly coming and going all the Winter' of 1756–7, the task of recruiting them to fight or scout, hard enough in this climate, was made even more difficult by the practice that Governor Shirley had instituted the previous year, over Johnson's objections, of paying them wages and forming them into companies like European troops. This undermined Johnson's established system of using presents and elaborate networks of friendship and loyalty, and he complained to Loudoun: 'The many precedents Mr Shirley has sett of giveing Indians pay, & Commissions, has, I find run through the Six Nations, & River Indians, so that in short what goods etc I give them (altho it amounts to a great deal) is thought nothing of.'[22]

The problem was exacerbated when the Indians discovered that the white rangers were paid four shillings a day while they themselves, who were more adept at scouting in the forests, got two. While professing to believe that this new system of regimenting Indians might after all be 'productive of good consequences', Johnson effectively tried to scare Loudoun off these practices by drawing up an estimate of the cost of keeping a regiment of 500 Indians in the field for a year. The suspiciously precise figure of £33,602/10/-sterling was obviously meant to put him off the whole idea.[23]

In spite of these difficulties, Johnson did manage to gather a small force of about sixty Mohawks to join with around 1,200 militia that he led to the aid of Fort William Henry when the French, under the Governor's brother Rigaud de Vaudreil, attacked it in March 1757. He seems on this occasion to have reverted to the dress and style of a Mohawk war captain, as he was recorded as entering the room where the Mohawk warriors were dancing the war dance on the night before setting out and singing 'his War Song'. By the time they arrived at Fort Edward, however, they heard definite news that the French had abandoned their siege after four days.[24]

Any relief Johnson felt was short-lived. On hearing rumours that a French attack on German Flats was imminent, he rode all night to get back to Fort Johnson at five in the morning. Waiting for him he found Otawanie, a Cayuga, with intelligence that as soon as the ice was melted the French intended to attack Fort Johnson while another force would besiege Fort William Henry again. Before he could rest, he was then visited by a delegation from the Oneidas, who told him that, at a meeting with Vaudreil in Montreal, the Onondagas, Cayugas and Senecas had outlined a firmly neutral position, maintaining that the British and French – 'you white People together' – were 'the common Disturbers of this Country' and that any further involvement by the Six Nations would bring 'nothing but an entire ruin of us'.

This was not what Johnson needed to hear at this moment of crisis, but there was even worse news between the lines. It was evident that the delegation that had gone to Montreal representing the Iroquois had included each of the Six Nations except the Mohawks. Johnson's closest allies were being effectively excluded from collective diplomacy, evidently because they were thought too close to the British interest.[25]

Johnson now felt himself 'rowing against the Current' of Indian opinion, as he admitted to Loudoun, adding, ['This] requires much more application and Skill, than if I went with a smooth Stream.'[26] Even his energy and skill, however, could not disguise the obvious reality that his hopes of uniting a refurbished Iroquois confederacy under his leadership were in ruins. The French were increasingly confident that they could destroy him and completely neutralise the Six Nations. The Oneida sachem Tianogo told him in April that he had heard from a member of his nation who was working with the French that an attack on the Mohawks was imminent, and 'I heard the French Governor say that he would not stick at anything to catch the Fox in his Hole (meaning Sir William Johnson).'²⁷ Tianogo himself, though loyal to Johnson, was so sure of his friend's inability to defend the valley that he declared his intention to move his own family away to safety.

Nothing short of a spectacular British victory could now shift the balance of Iroquois inclinations away from the French side. The prospects of such a triumph, at least on the New York frontier, dimmed, however, when Loudoun sailed north in June for an abortive attack on the French bastion at Louisbourg that Peter Warren had captured in 1745 only to see it handed back in the peace settlement of 1748. Loudoun left the defence of the Lake George borderlands in the hands of Daniel Webb, the nervy general who had burnt Fort Bull the previous year on the mere rumour of a French advance. Webb, whom Loudoun himself called 'timid, melancholic and diffident', knew from the French attack in March that Fort William Henry was the likely first target of a French assault. He did little to prepare for such an attack, however, and even in early June the damage sustained in the earlier siege had not been repaired.²⁸

By the end of July, the French general Louis-Joseph, Marquis de Montcalm, had assembled an enormous auxiliary force of almost 2,000 Indian warriors from thirty-three nations at Fort Carillon (Ticonderoga) along with 6,000 French and Canadian regulars and militiamen, including members of the La Reine and Languedoc battalions with whom Johnson had tangled at Lake George two years earlier. There was an irony in the fact that Montcalm, a fastidiously professional European-style soldier, who disdained his Indian allies, had so many of them, while Sir William Johnson, the famous leader of Indian warriors, had so few. The unprecedented scale of Indian support for the French contrasted horribly with Johnson's difficulty in raising warriors for the British cause. Anglo-American ignorance was making it difficult even to keep the loyalty of his closest Mohawk friends. The stripping away of his authority was enacted before his eyes in a small but poignant drama played out for him just at the time when the French-allied Indians were gathering for the kill.

On 1 July an Oneida sachem named Nickus came to Fort Johnson with three other warriors and all were fitted out with clothes, arms, and gunpowder. Johnson gave them eight dollars for a feast, some corn and some sugar and they left the next day 'well pleased'. A week later Nickus returned in a rage because his brother and another of his fellow warriors had been murdered by an Albany trader at German Flats. As he spoke, Nickus 'stripped off a Scarlet Laced Coat, a Gorget, Laced hat & everything Sir William had given him together with a testimonial of his Brotherly regard for the English which he had from Sir William four years ago & threw them all down at his Feet & said he would not keep or wear them any longer as his regard for the English was now at an end'. Johnson, by performing the condolence ceremony and covering the graves of the dead men with ten black strouds, ten shirts and seven silk handkerchiefs, eventually persuaded Nickus to take his clothes and certificate back, but, as he privately admitted, 'It was the most difficult Jobb I ever had.'

He was now standing on the edge of a vicious circle. The more successful the French attack, the more likely it was that the Six Nations would decisively desert the British, leading to further French success. To assuage resentment at the murders in German Flats and to forestall further defections, he travelled to Canajoharie and distributed clothes for nearly 250 Mohawks 'great and small'. While he was away, Fort Johnson itself was fired on, presumably by a party of Indians acting for the French. After some shots were exchanged and the fort's cannon were fired at them, the attackers withdrew. The audacity of the attempt made its own point, however, not least to Johnson's remaining Indian allies.[29]

As the French and Indian force approached, Webb left Fort William Henry in the hands of Lieutenant Colonel George Munro, promising to send reinforcements for his 1,100 fit troops. He in fact sent Munro just 200 men from the 5,000 strong garrison at Fort Edward, and when the French assault on Fort William Henry began on 3 August, the result was all but inevitable.

Johnson had learned of the French approach at about midnight on 1 August in a message from Webb. He was at the time meeting a group of about seventy-five warriors at Fort Johnson, including some Mohawks, Tuscaroras, Cherokees and Nantichokes. He fitted out these men with arms and ammunition and sent wampum belts to Schoharie, Canajoharie and the Susquehanna, asking for more warriors to join him. In all, by the time he arrived at Fort Edward on the morning of 6 August he had 180 warriors and about 1,500 militia.[30] Munro, in the besieged Fort William Henry only sixteen miles away, received a garbled verbal message from Webb that morning conveying 'something about William Johnson and some Indians', presumably an attempt to use Johnson's name as a boost to the defenders' confidence.[31]

The French were by now so confident that Johnson had been entirely deserted by the Six Nations and their allies that they were inclined to disbelieve reports of his arrival at Fort Edward simply because the reports claimed he had Indians with him. Montcalm's Indian allies intercepted one letter from Webb to Munro containing news of Johnson's force but, as the French military records put it, 'As it was not possible that Colonel Johnson had any Indians with him, this letter was looked on with suspicion.'[32]

Webb wrongly believed that the French force consisted of 11,000 men and that even if he threw all of his forces at Fort Edward against them, he could not win. With Johnson's force and the rest of the British army held at Fort Edward, Munro's position was untenable and he surrendered on 9 August. When Montcalm forbade his Indian allies to plunder the fort or take prisoners, they were infuriated by his refusal to deliver the spoils of victory and killed perhaps 185 of the British soldiers and camp followers in the garrison, taking at least 300 as captives before withdrawing in disgust.

Although Johnson was helpless at Fort Edward, he was immediately woven into the emerging legends of this horrible event on both sides of the Anglo-French divide. On the British side, the story spread that Johnson had wanted to push on to Fort William Henry and attempt to save its garrison. It may have some basis in fact. Three weeks later, some of the Mohawks who went with Johnson said that it had been their 'Expectation not to stop until we arrived at that place [Fort William Henry] but when we came to Fort Edward a Stop was put to our Proceeding further which we understood was by orders of the Great Man commanding at that place [Webb]'.[33] This simple order, however, was quickly transformed into a colourful drama.

According to the tale told by Captain Eli Noble, who was at Fort Edward at the time, Johnson, his Indians and his militia, infuriated by Webb's refusal to rescue the defenders of Fort William Henry, had set out along the road but were ordered back by Webb. According to the ranger Israel Putnam, Johnson had led his men three miles up the road. He claimed that Montcalm, fearing his approach, had been preparing to retreat, but then Webb called Johnson back – a fanciful tale given Montcalm's scepticism about whether Johnson had arrived at all. As this myth was elaborated, the enraged Johnson was said to have then attempted to run Webb through with his sword and, when prevented from doing so, to have broken it in disgust.34

Oddly, on the French side, Montcalm's aide-de-camp Louis-Antoine de Bougainville, later to win fame as the pioneering explorer of the South Pacific, retailed an even more colourful story, which he said had come from the western Indians, who in turn had it from the Mohawks. In this version, Johnson arrived at Fort Edward 'at the head of his Indians, all in war paint, like his followers, tomahawk at his side and spear in his hand'. He proposed that they immediately march to the relief of Fort William Henry. Webb refused. Johnson then began to strip off his clothes: '"You won't do it?" (Tears off one legging.) "No." "You won't?" (Tears off the other legging.) "No." (Takes off his loincloth.) "You won't?" "No."' The question and the answer are repeated as Johnson takes off his shirt, throws down his tomahawk and discards his spear before storming off naked. 'Where oh where', wrote Bougainville, 'is there a Homer to depict such a heroic scene?'35

This outlandish story is almost certainly an accurate account, not of what happened, but of the tale told in the Mohawk villages at the time. In the metaphorical language of their political discourse, it is, moreover, easily comprehensible. It echoes the real incident a month earlier when Nickus the Oneida sachem had stripped off his clothes in front of Johnson as a gesture of disgust at the British. It is the Mohawks' way of saying that their friend William Johnson was now equally enraged at the behaviour of his British allies.

In fact, however, the bloody fall of the fort he had built two years earlier marked a turning point in Johnson's fortunes. The immediate consequence of Montcalm's dispute with his Indian allies that had led to the killings was the departure of those Indians. They had attacked the British garrison because Montcalm had denied them the opportunity to plunder the fort. And now Montcalm, in turn, was horrified and enraged by their actions. When the Indians deserted the French commander and headed back to their villages, it was impossible for Montcalm to press on towards Fort Johnson and the Mohawk valley. The French would never be able to gather such a large Indian army together again. At the same time, luridly exaggerated accounts of the massacre created a wave of enthusiasm for the war in the colonies.

While Johnson might have found himself being blamed for his failure to generate the Iroquois army he had long promised, he was instead, in the stories that circulated through North America, the brave, bold counterpoint to the miserable Webb. He was the man who would have saved Fort William Henry if only he had been given his head.

19

Sir William and His Myrmidons

═══

Events that become mythologised sometimes set history on a new and consistent course. The fall of Fort William Henry was not one of these events. Its long-term effects would contradict its immediate consequences. Over time, it would enter American mythology as a crystallisation of innate Indian savagery, the unrestrainable bloodlust of the Red Man for which European Christians bore no responsibility. Montcalm would become a tragic figure, a commander who tried, like Johnson after the battle of Lake George, to impose civilised limits on the violence of the savages but who, unlike Johnson, failed and was disgraced.

The cost of his disgrace was described in 1788 by the ranger Israel Putnam, who had in fact been with Johnson at Fort Edward and could not have witnessed the scenes he so grossly exaggerated: 'Dead bodies, weltering in blood were everywhere to be seen, violated with all the wanton mutilations of savage ingenuity. More than one hundred women, some with their brains still oozing from their battered heads, others with their whole hair wrenched collectively with the skin from the bloody skulls, and many (with their throats cut) most inhumanely stabbed and butchered; lay stripped entirely naked, with their bowels torn out, and afforded a spectacle too horrible for description.'[1]

This fantastical rhetoric affected American attitudes to Indians for well over a century, suggesting as it did an irredeemable evil that could be controlled only by violence. Yet the immediate consequences of the fall of Fort William Henry were very different. Johnson's failing strategy of creating an extensive alliance among the British, the Iroquois and the Indians of the Ohio valley was revived. The reverberations of the event shifted the pattern of the war in ways that made Johnson's ambitions far more realistic.

One almost instant effect was to galvanise the colonies. An appeal for volunteers to go to the aid of the besieged garrison had been astonishingly successful, if, in reality, pointless. Within three days Connecticut had drafted 5,000 militiamen, while Massachusetts sent 7,000 men to Fort Edward. Even though most turned back when it became clear that Montcalm was in fact unable to follow up his victory with a thrust into New York, the show of enthusiasm helped Johnson to persuade the Iroquois that the Anglo-Americans might, after all, be capable of winning the war.

The new mood in the colonies was underpinned by a larger shift in the British war strategy. William Pitt had come to power in London at the end of 1756, as the effective (though not titular) prime minister, but had been ousted in April 1757. Three months later he returned in a stronger position to impose his ideas. By the end of the year, helped, rather paradoxically, by the disaster at Fort William Henry, he gained a virtually free hand for a radical change of course. Whereas previously North America had been a sideshow in an essentially European war, now it would be the main event. The reduction of Canada became, for the first time, a serious and sustained aim of British imperial policy. Pitt, moreover, understood that the colonial response to the fall of Fort William Henry opened up the possibility of a more truly American war, in which the colonies themselves would be enlisted, not out of feudal duty, but out of patriotic enthusiasm. These policies finally allowed the British to exploit the overwhelming advantage in manpower that their colonies enjoyed over New France. In 1758 the colonial armies would number almost 50,000 men – a number equivalent to two-thirds of the entire French peacetime population of Canada.[2]

Gradually, this new strategy transformed the context for William Johnson's Indian diplomacy. Johnson's immediate task was to convince as many Indians as he could that the disaster at Fort William Henry was not a sign of British weakness. Back at Fort Johnson on 23 August 1757, he met a delegation of Oneidas, Oquagas and 'other Indians living on the Susquehanna River' and assured them that though 'the loss of that Fort affected me a good deal as I was the first beginner & founder of it, however these things being the effects of War must not discourage us but rather make us more alert & active . . . let us behave as our Forefathers have done & we will drive the French out of our Country & get rid of such troublesome Neighbours'.[3]

Though most Indians undoubtedly heard such assurances from Johnson with a degree of justified scepticism, circumstances were gradually making them more credible.

The debacle at Fort William Henry had exacerbated tensions between the French and their Indian allies. To make matters worse, the prisoners the Indians took from the fort brought with them the scourge of smallpox, which created a devastating epidemic in their villages. These disappointments added to the Indians' pre-existing resentment at Montcalm's attempts to treat them as soldiers bound to military discipline rather than as warriors, who came and went as they pleased, and 'consulted manitous and not French officers on the eve of battle'.4

By October 1757, moreover, the British navy had imposed effective blockades at Gibraltar, along the English Channel and in the Gulf of St Lawrence, making it very difficult for French supply ships to reach Canada. At the same time, the Canadian wheat harvest failed, for the second year in a row. The combined effect of these events was not merely a severe food shortage for the French-Canadian population, but also a dearth of the presents and trade goods that fuelled the French alliance with its Indian clients.

By March 1758 Johnson had heard, through the Iroquois, that several of the nations around Lake Erie were 'much distressed' because 'the French cannot supply them with the necessarys they want, So that their Familys are naked mostly.' Two months later he heard: 'The French are extreamely scarce of Provisions at Niagara, Cadaraghqui and Sweegachy, and . . . the latter Settlement is breaking up for Want of Provisions.'5 Johnson saw an opportunity for useful propaganda among the Iroquois through the display of goods intended for Canada that had been captured by British vessels. At one council, as Vaudreil heard from his spies, 'Johnson opened a large store to them, where they, indeed, saw nothing but French goods; he proved still more conclusively to them the reality of the fact, by a number of barrels of Cognac Brandy which he gave them.'6

Tensions between the French and their Indians came to a head in the winter of 1757–8, when the Menominees of Green Bay, in what is now northern Wisconsin, revolted and killed twenty-two Frenchmen. Even when pro-French sachems regained control of their warriors, the usual rituals of apology and forgiveness broke down. When seven of the killers were sent to Montreal to apologise, they were either shot or whipped in the town square. Such a willingness to provoke further resentment reflected a general French disillusionment with the Indians. An official memoire sent home to Paris from New France and entitled *Des Sauvages* complains that presents to the natives only encouraged indolence and drunkenness, that Indian fighters were ineffectual, and that Indians were cowardly, traitorous, cruel and lacking 'any sort of feeling'.7

Meanwhile, relations between the Ohio Indians and the British colonies were gradually improving. A grand conference in Easton, Pennsylvania, in July and August 1757, attempted to resolve the complex set of animosities that had created such ferocious violence on the Pennsylvania frontiers. The eastern Delawares were demanding the nullification of the so-called Walking Purchase of 1737, in which the Iroquois had connived with the Penn family to deprive the Delawares of huge tracts of land. Johnson's deputy, George Croghan, attended the conference as his representative, with an eye to protecting the interests both of his boss and of the Iroquois. This he did by helping to secure a tentative compromise: that the legitimacy of the Walking Purchase would be examined by a higher authority and that the authority in question would be Sir William Johnson. This temporary deal did not include the western Delawares, who were still allied to the French, but it did significantly alter the mood of British–Indian relations.

Some evidence of the 'alert & active' military response that Johnson had promised also began to emerge. After the 1757 campaign of the Earl of Loudon against Louisbourg in Nova Scotia petered out, Loudon was replaced, technically by his indolent deputy James Abercromby, but in effect by a team of young commanders, among them the forty-year-old Jeffery Amherst and the thirty-one-year-old James Wolfe.

Admittedly, the effects of this changed atmosphere were not immediately obvious on the ground. In early November 1757, while Johnson was lying ill in his house and most of the Mohawk men were out hunting, a French force operating with around 300 Indian warriors penetrated right down into the Mohawk valley and destroyed German Flats, the Palatine settlement just over ten miles west of Canajoharie, killing fifty settlers, taking 150 prisoners and gravely alarming the Mohawks, who heard rumours of French plans 'to destroy all the Settlements on the Mohawk River'.8

Nevertheless, by May 1758 Johnson was convinced that 'we may hope very favourable things from the Indians'.9 In the meantime, he used economic blackmail to apply pressure of his own. When two chief sachems and fifteen leading warriors of the Cayugas, who had maintained a strict policy of neutrality, came to Fort Johnson to seek assistance, he was unusually hard-hearted. The Cayugas pleaded that their warriors were 'quite destitute of everything necessary for them as Ammunition, Paint etc.' and that their womenfolk wanted 'three large Kettles to Boil their Victuals & some Petticoats to cover their Nakedness'. They presented him with two packs of skins, obviously expecting the specified goods in return.

Johnson did give the three kettles the women had requested, but coldly returned the skins and informed the sachems: 'All the Goods I have belong to the King my Master who has sent them to me & ordered me to give them to such Indians as will go with me to War against his Enemies.'10 The message of this insulting reply was clear. In the reciprocal gift-giving that structured Johnson's relations with the Indians, the only gift he was prepared to accept was a military alliance.11

These deliberate breaches of the ritual protocols that Johnson was usually so careful to observe were not accidental. He had clearly decided to shock the Iroquois into a breach of their policy of neutrality by throwing aside his accustomed courtesy and sensitivity. In late June 1758 Onondaga, Oneida and Tuscarora delegates joined the Mohawks at a conference in Fort Johnson called to gather warriors for yet another attempt to attack the French positions north of Lake George. The congress started, however, with Hans the Wildt, Mohawk chief sachem of the Bear clan, objecting to the lack of ceremony with which Johnson, who was under pressure from Abercromby, had informed the Indians that the expedition would set off in two days' time. He scolded Johnson that 'it was very contrary to our established Custom & Manners to be as it were thus drove out to War'. This time, he warned, the Mohawks would not be able to take Johnson's side in their discussions with the other nations, and this 'would occasion a fatal Confusion in our General Confederacy'.

Likewise, when Johnson welcomed the various delegations, he took four or five of their principal sachems upstairs with him and told them he was going to make a speech demanding immediate agreement to supply him with warriors for the expedition. Again, the sachems were shocked. They reminded him 'with great warmth' that he had gained his position as Indian Superintendent because 'he was the Person most agreeable to them and who best knew their Customs & manners', rightly pointing out that it was his skill with the ritual forms that was at the root of his power.

Yet Johnson had decided this time to break with the conventions. The speech he had previewed for the sachems was shorn of all the usual collective formulae: the condolence ceremony, the burnishing of the ancient Covenant Chain, the evocation of the great father beyond the seas who loved his Indian children. He made, instead, a purely personal appeal, speaking, not as the representative of the king, but as himself. Those who wished to be thought of as friends to the English must now, he said, 'tuck up their Blanketts & run with me'. He claimed: 'This is the day of Trial & I shall now see what Indians are my Friends, for such will go with me. You who are determined to fight with me, speak & you shall be immediately fitted out for War.'

In making this personal demand, he presented himself, not as an imperial officer, but as a sachem. He appealed for 'the Assistance of the Great Spirit above'. He promised that the French, after their defeat, would 'let us Smoak our Pipes in Peace'. And after this short, blunt speech, he 'threw down the War Belt & danced the War Dance, after which a principal Man of each Nation present also Danced'.[12]

This risky strategy was largely successful. Even though there was very little time, the war party that Johnson led to Lake George to join Abercromby for an attack on Fort Carillon at Ticonderoga was the largest and most representative that had yet followed him. A total of 395 warriors went with him, 172 of them Mohawks but with a fair smattering of Oneidas, Tuscaroras, Onondagas, Cayugas and a small but significant presence of fourteen Senecas. Over sixty Schoharie Indians and Mohicans joined in and another thirty Tuscarora and Onondaga warriors came close behind, informing Johnson that 'many more of several Nations were to follow them'.[13]

Unfortunately for Johnson, the attack was a grotesque farce. Abercromby had a huge army of 16,000 regulars and colonials, but when his most energetic commander, Lord Howe, was killed in a skirmish, he allowed himself to lose the initiative. When he did stir himself for an attack it was a madly reckless frontal assault on French barricades, a large-scale version of the battle of Lake George with Abercromby playing the role of Dieskau. Having hurled row after row of his disciplined regulars against a breastwork for eight hours, he finally retreated when 2,000 men had been killed or wounded. Johnson and his Indian warriors watched a British show of folly whose recklessness, as one regular officer put it, 'must have occur'd to any blockhead who was not absolutely so far sunk in Idiotism as to be oblig'd to wear a bib and bells'.[14]

Even this grisly spectacle, however, could not distract for long from the reality that the balance of power on the North American continent was shifting. Less than three weeks after the battle of Ticonderoga, Louisbourg had fallen to the British. The following month, a largely colonial force destroyed Fort Frontenac, the French post on Lake Ontario. These British victories weakened the negative impact of Abercomby's idiocy at Ticonderoga. When, in the aftermath of that defeat, Abercromby was replaced as commander-in-chief by the able and rigorously organised Jeffery Amherst, the feeling that Britain was finally about to assert its superiority in North America was unmistakable.

The continuing efforts to conclude a peace treaty with the Ohio Indians, especially with the western Delawares, who were still allied to the French, reminded Johnson and the Six Nations of their common political interests. The British commander for the Ohio campaign, the astute Brigadier General John Forbes, understood very well the importance of the Delawares to the French and the potential rewards of breaking the link between them. From the spring of 1758 onwards he was pushing for overtures to the western Delawares through the eastern Delaware leader Teedyuscung – a policy that made perfect sense from his own point of view but that threatened to disrupt Johnson's larger strategy. Direct negotiations between the Delawares and the British would infuriate the Iroquois, by effectively repudiating their claims to sovereignty in the Ohio. Forbes saw this as obstruction, and deeply resented 'the private interested views of Sir William Johnstone [sic] and his Myrmidons' (the Six Nations).[15]

When Abercromby gave Forbes permission to go ahead and convene another conference at Easton, it was a direct challenge to Johnson's authority as the sole intermediary between the British and the Indians. It was also, however, a reminder to the Iroquois that they needed Johnson's diplomatic skills if they were not to be outmanoeuvred. As George Croghan wrote to Johnson in his inimitable phonetic Irish-English: 'The Six Nations is Afread the Dalaways and Shannas wants to Settle A firm pace with the English Independent of them which I Blive from what I can Laurn is the Intenciens of the Later.'[16]

Johnson tried to undermine Forbes's intentions by reminding Abercromby that Teedyuscung, whom Forbes was treating as the man who could deliver the western Delawares and who was himself claiming to act for all the nations of the West was 'one of the Chiefs who headed & perpetrated the well known Desolations on the frontier of Maryland and Pensilvania'. He warned: 'It will not in my humble Opinion, be adviseable to give Tediuscung this exclusive Distinction in publick Treaties & Negotiations, as it will tend to give umbrage to the other indians & build our Fabric upon too narrow & precarious a Foundation.'[17] As for Teedyuscung's claims to be the king of the West: 'The Indian manner of speaking is indeed sometimes strongly figurative, but this is a Rant beyond what I have ever met with.'

He was, he insisted, 'not Jealous . . . of Incroachments upon my Department, whoever or whatever set of Men I think can advance the common good in Indian Affairs I would readily embrace & assist – but Matters stand upon a Delicate & ticklish Bottom & if the Indians find we pull different ways, we shall over-set what hopes are yet to be entertained'.[18]

At the same time, however, Johnson sent emissaries of his own to the western Delawares, urging them to go to the talks at Easton, but framing the invitation within the terms of a restatement of Iroquois overlordship: 'Your Uncles the Six Nations and your Brethren living on the Sasquehannah River are invited to a great meeting by the governor of Pennsylvania. I would have your chief men go thither, and they will hear Things for their good, and I hope they will open their Eyes to see what is in their true Interest.' Their true interest, he added, lay in listening to the advice that 'I and your Brethren of the Six Nations' would give to them.[19]

Johnson then used the coming conference to rally the Six Nations, confident that a threat to their claim of hegemony over the Ohio valley would rouse the confederacy. At the same time, he urged the Pennsylvania governor to appease all the Indian nations by 'giving them satisfaction with regard to their Land Complaints, and by a solemn public Treaty to agree upon clear and fixed Boundaries between our Settlements & their Hunting Grounds, so that each Party may know their own & be a mutual Protection to each other of their respective Possessions'.[20]

Through all this manoeuvring, Johnson engineered a diplomatic triumph for the Iroquois. Each of the Six Nations sent a powerful delegation to Easton, and also encouraged many of the small nations that lived under Iroquois protection – Nanticokes, Tuteloes, Chugnuts, Minisinks, Mahicans and Wappingers – to send observers. The delegation included three powerful sachems – the Oneida orator Thomas King, the Seneca Tagashta and the Mohawk chief Nickus, who was Croghan's father-in-law. With Croghan representing Johnson and looking out for Iroquois interests, Teedyuscung and his Delawares were isolated and forced to accept Iroquois authority. The treaty that Johnson wanted – with Pennsylvania ceding all lands that it claimed west of the Allegheny Mountains back to the Six Nations and promising to restrain settlements in Indian territory – was concluded. Forbes got the peace he wanted with the eastern Delawares, but, at the same time, Iroquois prestige was enhanced.

For the British war effort, the consequences were profound. Without the support of the Delawares, Fort Duquesne, the French post at the confluence of the Allegheny and Monongahela Rivers and the object of Braddock's doomed campaign in 1755, was indefensible. In November 1758 its commander, François-Marie Le Marchand de Lignery, evacuated the fort and blew it up.

For Johnson the consequences were almost as dramatic and positive. He had given the Iroquois what they wanted at Easton. The erosion of the French threat to their villages made an alliance of the full confederacy with the British a real possibility. By April 1759, after continuing diplomacy by Johnson, the possibility became a reality. At a conference with representatives of all Six Nations at Canajoharie, Johnson was told that the confederacy as a whole had decided to avenge English and Iroquois blood shed by the French. Claiming as a formal reason for the decision the ancient law that 'if any one of either of the Nations was killed by an enemy, the whole were to join in revenging it', they cited the killing of an Oneida sachem by the French as the *casus belli*. Johnson, in return and in fulfilment of the Easton treaty, handed over the deed to lands on the Ohio that Pennsylvania had acquired at the Albany conference of 1754.

20

Niagara Falls

═══

Though he had never seen it, William Johnson had long had his eye on Fort Niagara. It stood towards the western end of Lake Ontario, a defiant outpost of Europe in the New World. At its centre, a handsome grey granite castle, built on a bluff at the mouth of the Niagara River, overlooked the lake. Triangular in shape and bounded on two sides by the river and the lake, the citadel was the only fort in the American interior protected – on the third side – by extensive, European-style earthen outworks: a glacis, ditch and covered way.

The quality of these defences reflected what Johnson understood to be the strategic importance of the place. France's far-flung settlements in North America – Canada, the forts and trading posts in the Ohio valley, Louisiana – were connected by water. A traveller from the home country wishing to survey his King's American domain, would sail from the Atlantic up the St Lawrence River to Lake Ontario, over the Niagara River to Lake Erie and thence travel on foot to the Ohio or to the Mississippi, which would carry him onward to the Gulf of Mexico. Except, of course, that this watery network was broken, not just by gaps, but by falls and rapids. The portages across which goods had to be carried and people had to walk were critical points of vulnerability. The point where, seventeen miles from Lake Erie, the Niagara River drops down a series of rapids and takes its fearful plunge over Niagara Falls was a nerve centre without which movement between Canada and France's possessions in the rest of North America was unviable.

The French had long known this, of course. They had built outposts at Niagara from the late seventeenth century onwards, culminating in the construction of the castle in 1726. Also in the 1720s, Louis-

Thomas Chabert de Joncaire got permission from the Iroquois to establish a trading house on the Niagara portage, which gave the French a further hold over the local Senecas. From the time Johnson became involved in Indian diplomacy, he had regarded Joncaire and his sons by a Seneca woman, Daniel and Phillippe-Thomas, as his greatest rivals for influence over the Iroquois.

By the end of 1757 the French commander at Niagara, Captain Pierre Pouchot, had greatly enlarged the fort and constructed new earthwork defences. He had also expanded its interior and filled it with new buildings of wood and stone. Barracks, storehouses, a powder magazine and even a church had been added. In making all this effort, the French acknowledged the truth of William Johnson's contention that to take Niagara would be to cut off the whole system of French forts and settlements in the West.

Johnson had long tried to point this out to the British overlords in London. As far back as March 1755, he had urged, as an alternative to the ultimately doomed Ohio expedition of General Braddock, an assault on Niagara, which would, he wrote, 'be the speediest method to deprive [the French] of their Encroachments on the Ohio which they would find themselves under a Necessity even to abandon, if we take [and] keep Possession of that important Pass'.[1] Although Johnson's point was taken and Niagara featured heavily in British strategic plans, attempts to capture it had been so ineffectual that no actual assault had been made.

Early in 1759 Johnson again urged an attack on Niagara, confident now that he could assemble a very significant Iroquois force to take part. In February he wrote to Amherst: 'I flatter myself, and have some Reason to expect that (as Affairs are now Circumstanced) if an Expedition was designed against Niagara, or elsewhere, through the country of the Six Nations, I should be able to prevail upon the greater Part if not the whole of them, to join His Majesty's Arms.'[2]

Even before he went on the warpath, Johnson was crucial to Amherst's plans. He acted effectively as the head of intelligence for a planned attack, gathering, from the Senecas who were now sending delegations to Fort Johnson, details of the fort, the surrounding countryside and the best routes to take. These, together with Johnson's assurances of support from the Six Nations, convinced Amherst in mid-May 'to pursue the plan I had before formed for an Enterprize against Niagara'.[3] Johnson immediately sent messages asking the

Susquehanna nations to meet him at Fort Stanwix, which had been built at the furthest navigable point on the Mohawk River around seventy-five miles from Fort Johnson; the upper Iroquois to rendevous with him at Oswego, and the Mohawks, including Molly's sixteen-year-old brother Joseph Brant, to join him at Fort Johnson.

The expedition, in contrast to previous campaigns, moved quickly. By the end of May the main force of 5,000 men under General John Prideaux had set out along the Mohawk and Oneida Rivers to Oswego. By 27 June, when they arrived at this staging post, they found that Johnson's confidence that he could gather a larger force of Iroquois warriors than he ever put in the field before was well justified. Almost 1,000 fighters, representing each of the Six Nations, had answered his call, including a significant number of Senecas. Aside from the most westerly Senecas who remained loyal to the French, this was very close to a mobilisation of the confederacy's entire military strength.

Leaving 2,000 men to build and garrison forts along the way, Prideaux and Johnson set sail at the beginning of July for Niagara with about 2,000 regular troops, 1,000 provincial militia and 945 Iroquois. Johnson's impressive Iroquois mobilisation was not just a show of force. It had immediate and profound military significance. The firm adherence of the confederacy to Johnson had deprived the Niagara commander Pouchot of a vital resource: intelligence.

Previously, a neutral confederacy with a large pro-French faction would have ensured that a French commander in the West had ample notice of British troop movements through Iroquoia. This time Pouchot got no warning. As Johnson afterwards told Prime Minister William Pitt, the Iroquois 'kept our Designs so secret, that we had disembarked all our Artillery, and remained a Night at Niagara before the Enemy had any notice of our Arrival'.4 The secrecy had a crucial bearing on events because, by early June, Pouchot felt safe enough from attack for another year to send 2,500 of his 3,000 troops 180 miles away to Fort Machault on the Allegheny River (present-day Franklin, Pennsylvania) to prepare for engagements in the Ohio valley. When he finally learned of the British advance, he had to send urgent messages and hope that the relief columns would arrive in time.

A second major effect of the solid Iroquois backing for Johnson was to undermine the position of the hundred or so pro-French Senecas who were with Pouchot in the fort. When Johnson, Prideaux and their troops began to dig siege trenches half a mile from Fort Niagara on 10 July, Pouchot called a truce to allow his Seneca ally Kaendae to approach Johnson and his Iroquois allies. The French commander hoped that Kaendae could persuade his fellow warriors not to take part in the attack. The appeal had considerable force, since the historic purpose of the Great League was to ensure that its members never fought against each other. Yet the strength of the new consensus was such that the onus was really on the pro-French Senecas to avoid a breach. According to the French military report of the siege, 'Kaendae's council with the Iroquois had been held in the presence of Johnson, to whom that chief spoke boldly, reproaching him with having plunged his Nation into bad business. Johnson smiled, and took this reproach as a joke.'[5]

He could afford to laugh. He knew that Iroquois protocol dictated that the defeated minority in an internal dispute should withdraw into passivity. This is essentially what happened. After three days of discussions among the Iroquois, Kaendae's Senecas withdrew from the fort under a flag of truce. Pouchot, unwilling to have warriors of dubious loyalty within his embattled walls, did not object to their departure.[6]

While Johnson was overseeing these negotiations, General Prideaux's engineers were moving their siege trenches ever closer to the fort. Their highly technical job was not accomplished with conspicuous competence, but by 14 July the British cannons were in a position, just 250 yards from the fort's defensive glacis, to open fire. The carelessness that had marked much of the operation culminated, however, on the evening of 20 July, when Prideaux stepped in front of one of the mortars and the back of his head was blown off.

Immediately on Prideaux's death, Johnson took command and issued orders 'that as I am determined to persevere in the same just and vigorous manner, which was carried on by the Deceased General, that the troops will exert themselves to the utmost and act with the same laudable spirit which they have hitherto shown . . . The business we are on being nearly finished the completing of which will be easily effected by the continuance of the same measures . . .'[7]

In fact, his calm assurance of business as usual belied a degree of consternation in the British command structure. Lieutenant Colonel Frederick Haldimand, a Swiss soldier of fortune who had been left at Oswego to build a new fort, saw himself as the second-in-command for the expedition as a whole. The Scottish Highland officer Allan

MacLeane, writing to Haldimand on 21 July, expressed his worries that Johnson had taken command of a formal European-style siege with only the incompetent ensign George Demler to advise on the highly specialised task: 'Tho' Sir William is a very worthy man he knows little about Generalship and he has nobody can help for our Engineers – god damn them. Dembler has shown himself a fool & blockhead.' Amherst worried that the operations, 'which are of the greatest consequence to the general Plan of Reducing Canada . . . might fail on Sir William's and Colonel Haldimand's disputing the Command'.[8]

These concerns were justified in theory but irrelevant in practice. The fate of Fort Niagara would be decided, not by Johnson's ability to conclude a formal siege, but by his ability to prevent the rescue of the garrison by French support. He knew that there was neither the time nor the necessity to wait for Haldimand to make his way up from Oswego.

After the Senecas left, Pouchot's only real hope of withstanding the siege lay with the arrival of reinforcements from Fort Machault. Johnson discovered, presumably from the Iroquois, that a relief force consisting of about 1,200 French and Canadian troops and perhaps 400 Indians was approaching from the south along the river. In charge was Captain François-Marie Le Marchand de Lignery, an experienced officer who had commanded Fort Duquesne and who excelled in guerrilla warfare. To one observer, the mass of little boats carrying Lignery's troops seemed like 'a floating island, so black was the river with bateaux and canoes'.[9]

Johnson's Indian intelligence network, however, gave him time to prepare an effective reception for Lignery and his men. The situation – a French force approaching him through a forested landscape of trees, lakes and swamps – was familiar to him from the battle of Lake George four years earlier. He knew what to do. On the evening of 24 July, he sent out a detachment of light infantry to block the road. Early next morning he reinforced them with two companies of grenadiers and part of the 46th Regiment of Scottish Highland regulars. As at Lake George, he had a breastwork constructed across the road at a spot called La Belle Famille, about a mile and a half from Fort Niagara. Just as important, he sent Iroquois emissaries to warn the Indians in Lignery's force of what they faced ahead.

For a conventional military commander this was an unthinkable

act. To set up an ambush and then send ahead to warn part of the
enemy's force would be madness. It is notable that he made no mention of it in his report to Amherst on the engagement.[10] Johnson's confidence in his Iroquois allies, however, and his understanding of Indian
attitudes to warfare allowed him to win a significant part of the battle
without firing a shot. By the time Lignery came marching up the road
towards the British positions at eight o'clock on the morning of the
25th, his Indian allies had melted away.

Johnson, on the other hand, had 450 Iroquois warriors in the
woods on either side of the road. He had left one force to guard his
bateaux and another to protect the siege trenches in case the French in
the fort should make a desperate sortie, so he had about 350 regulars
and 100 New York militia facing Lignery's 600 regulars and militia.
With the French having to charge the breastwork under fire from three
sides, Johnson's forces had an overwhelming advantage. In the fighting which started about half past nine and ended within an hour,
Lignery's force was destroyed. Of the officers and cadets, three
escaped and twenty were captured, among them the commanders
Lignery and Charles Aubry, and one of New France's most capable
Indian diplomats, Joseph Marin de La Malgue. Most of the troops
who fled into the woods were hunted down and killed or captured by
the Iroquois warriors. The French reported at least 334 killed. Apart
from the twenty officers and cadets whom Johnson ransomed, the
Iroquois took 150 scalps and ninety-six prisoners. Johnson himself
seems to have been close to the line of fire – he told his brother that the
tree he stood beside 'had fourteen Balls Lodged in it' – but he was
unharmed.[11]

Pouchot, standing on a bastion at the fort, could see across the
cleared woods as the battle blazed and subsided. He was unsure of
the outcome, however, until two in the afternoon when a friendly
Onondaga came into the fort to tell him of the rout of the force that
was meant to relieve him. Even then, he had difficulty believing that
his hopes of relief were now gone. Two hours later, when Johnson sent
him an invitation to surrender and a list of captured French officers, he
insisted on sending one of his own officers to see the prisoners for himself. When the emissary returned, Pouchot was ready to surrender.

The final obstacle to the capture of Fort Niagara without further
bloodshed was fear. The French, like the Anglo-Americans, remembered what had happened at Fort William Henry, when the slaughter

of members of the British garrison by Montcalm's Indian allies had stained victory with shame and turned an ignominious British defeat into a rallying cry. Johnson, having been close to the scene of that debacle, was sensitive both to Pouchot's fears for his garrison and to the possibility of imminent glory being turned sour by the taint of barbarity. Yet no one was better placed than Johnson, with his understanding of Indian culture and his keen appreciation of the importance of propaganda, to satisfy honour on all sides.

The terms he offered Pouchot were that the French garrison would be given the honours of war, sent to New York as prisoners, but protected from reprisals by the Indians. The explicitness of this specific article – 'The General [Johnson] will recommend expressly to the Escort that they not allow the Savages to approach or insult any of the Garrison' – suggests his sensitivity to Pouchot's anxieties.[12] Just as important, though, were the terms he offered the Iroquois warriors fighting on his own side. Where Montcalm had inadvertently precipitated the murders at Fort William Henry by ignoring the expectations of his Indian allies, Johnson made sure that they would share in the victory and return home to their villages with the tangible spoils that would bear witness to their valour. In the first place, they could keep the scalps and most of the prisoners they had taken in the fight at La Belle Famille. ('The officers', as he noted in his diary, 'I with difficulty released from them, by ransom, good words etc.') Secondly, they could plunder all the booty they could carry from the fort and its associated trading storehouses, which were full of furs, skins and consumer goods.

The deal worked because Johnson's authority was credible to both Pouchot and the Iroquois. The fame of his chivalrous treatment of Dieskau in 1755 encouraged the French now to believe that he would, and could, protect them. The Iroquois, for their part, trusted his guarantee of access to the plunder. The prestige that Johnson had so carefully cultivated now allowed him to add to it by bringing the siege to a dignified conclusion. Pouchot surrendered at about seven in the evening, placing 607 men, eleven officers and an unknown but significant number of women and children under Johnson's protection. Among those who surrendered was Johnson's most formidable rival as an Indian diplomat on the French side, Daniel-Marie Chabert de Joncaire.

The only possible threat to the smooth completion of this delicate political manoeuvre was Haldimand's arrival to claim Johnson's command. As it happened, Haldimand did not reach Niagara until 28 July, the same day that 'the greatest part of all the nations set off in boats with a great deal of plunder for their several countries.' In any case Johnson refused to surrender his command, 'as my commission gave me rank of him'. Haldimand, who had little choice, 'gave up the point, until general Amherst's pleasure be known'. By then, too, the garrison had been sent off to Oswego, the women and children under escort to Canada.

Militarily, Johnson's victory was momentous. Of his forces, including the casualties sustained before he took command, sixty Anglo-Americans and three Indians had been killed, 180 Anglo-Americans and five Indians wounded.[13] In return for these light casualties, he had effectively ended French power in the West. The French frontier was rolled back north to Oswegatchie, just 115 miles upriver from Montreal. It was not just Niagara that had fallen. The survivors fleeing from the rout at La Belle Famille brought the news of defeat with them to Lake Erie, where they burned the forts of Presque Isle, Le Boeuf and Machault and withdrew along with their garrisons west to Detroit, leaving the whole Ohio valley to the British. Detroit itself, along with all the French settlements in the Illinois country, was now hopelessly cut off from Canada. When, almost immediately after the fall of Niagara Johnson sent a scouting party in three whaleboats to reconnoitre Fort Toronto, it returned with the news that this fort, too, had been 'burned and abandoned'.

More significantly, from Johnson's point of view, it also returned with Tequakareigh, a sachem of the French-allied Chippewa nation, who wanted to speak to him. After a short pleasure trip to see Niagara Falls, Johnson entered into cordial discussions with Tequakareigh, whose approach promised to give him a diplomatic foothold among the Indians of the so-called *pays d'en haut*, the vast area that stretched from north of Lake Superior down the eastern shores of the Mississippi and on into the Ohio valley. Having issued a formal invitation to 'his and all other nations living near them' to come to Niagara for talks in the spring, he took from around Tequakareigh's neck a large French medal and replaced it with an English one and a gorget of silver, 'desiring whenever he looked at them, he would remember the engagements he now made'.[14] The gorget, significantly, had two markings on it: the arms of the King, and a 'cypher' of Johnson's own, making it a mark of loyalty, not just to His Britannic Majesty, but to Sir William personally.[15]

For Johnson, this approach from the Chippewas opened up the possibility of a wide expansion of his authority. The Chippewas, and the related Mississaugas, had emerged in the seventeenth century as refugees from Iroquois attacks that had devastated their homelands around the Great Lakes. Intermarried with other nations, especially the Ottawas, they had villages around western Lake Superior and Michilimackinac, notably Sault St Marie.

As events continued to unfold through the rest of 1759, the prospect of extending his influence beyond even these horizons to the whole of Canada opened up more clearly. Johnson's victory in June was followed in July and August by the surrender of the French forts at Ticonderoga and Crown Point to General Amherst. Then, in September, General James Wolfe delivered the most stunning blow of all, taking Quebec with his daring night-time ascent of the bluff that had seemed to make the city impregnable.

For Johnson, the fall of Fort Niagara and of Quebec and the near certainty of final French defeat, opened up the question of whether he could bring the Indians of Canada and the West into his own sphere of influence. The one obstacle was that he himself was so closely identified with the Six Nations, against whom most of these Indians harboured long grudges. If Britain took control of vast new territories with a large variety of Algonquian-speaking nations hostile to the Iroquois, the argument for choosing someone other than Johnson as an intermediary with these peoples would be very strong. The speed and enthusiasm of Johnson's response to Tequakareigh, and his immediate proposal for a conference the following spring, came from a recognition of this threat and a determination to pre-empt it.

Just as he had done after the battle of Lake George, Johnson was already arranging his own laurels. In his diary, three days after the taking of Fort Niagara, he had written himself a reminder of the urgent need to 'write the secretary of state and send him a plan of Niagara; also give him an idea of the consequence of it to his majesty's Indian interest; the extention of the free trade, and, above all, its cutting off the communication between Canada and Louisiana', and to 'send Governor De Lancey a copy of the plan of the fort as soon as I can, in order to have it printed, or plates of it published, for the benefit of the public'.[16]

It is significant, though, that in the midst of these advertisements for himself, Johnson was anxious to emphasise the positive effect of the victory on relations with the Indian nations. Johnson's official order of thanks to the troops after the engagement at La Belle Famille told them that their victory 'ha[d] been of the greatest advantage to the English nation, and thoroughly Secured us the friendship of the Six nations'. That the effect on the Indians was so close to the top of his priorities is not surprising, but it does point to his hopes for a greater official emphasis on Indian relations and therefore, of course, on his own importance. Likewise, on 14 August, one of his main concerns as commander at Niagara was finding the thief who had stolen money from an Indian – again an issue which affected his own standing, not with the British but with his Iroquois allies.[17]

These priorities stemmed both from the lessons of the immediate past and anxieties about the future. The relatively easy but hugely significant success at Niagara confirmed what Johnson had always believed and argued: that Indian alliances were the key to control of the continent. Victory owed less to the rather bumbling efforts of the professional British soldiers and engineers than to the intelligence-gathering, diplomacy and skirmishing skills of the Iroquois which Johnson had been able, at last, to harness. But would a triumphant Britain, freed from the need to woo the Indians in competition with the French, understand their continuing importance? Would the booty Johnson had allowed the Iroquois to carry home from Niagara be the last reward for allies who, after victory was complete, might come to seem dispensable?

1. *Portrait of Hendrick* (Tee Yee Neen Ho Ga Row). Commissioned from John Verelst during the visit of the 'Indian Kings' to London in 1710, this image emphasises Hendrick's role as a genteel diplomat.

2. John Wollaston's portrait of Johnson was probably painted in 1751, and thus shows him at the age of 36. Johnson sent a copy to his father in Ireland but complained of 'the narrow hanging Shoulders' as 'Mine are very broad and square'.

3. *General Johnson Saving a Wounded French Officer from the Tomahawk of a North American* by Benjamin West. Painted in London in the mid-1760s, it shows Johnson's rescue of the French general Dieskau after the Battle of Lake George, and re-enforces his official image as a civilising influence on the Indians.

4. *Portrait of Sir Peter Warren* by Thomas Hudson, painted about a year before the admiral's death in 1752.

5. *Portrait of Johnson* by Benjamin West. Though variously catalogued as a portrait of Sir Joseph Banks and of Guy Johnson, it was almost certainly commissioned from West in the mid-1760s as an idealised portrait of Sir William. Niagara Falls, in the background, represents Johnson's most significant military victory and stakes his claim as a hero of the conquest of North America.

6. *The Death of General Wolfe* by Benjamin West (detail). Johnson's appearance, along with an idealised Iroquois warrior, in this iconic image of the Anglo-French War is remarkable because neither he nor Indians fought in the British victory at Quebec. Yet Johnson, dressed in the uniform of an American ranger, is explicitly identified by the engraving on the powder horn: 'Sr WM Johnson/ MOHAWK RIVER.'

7. *Johnson Hall Showing an Indian Conference in Progress* by Edward Lamson Henry (1903). Henry's depiction of the house is accurate, but the scene is far neater and less crowded than the usual reality.

8 & 9. Johnson's long-time assistant Daniel Claus and his wife, Johnson's daughter Anne (Nancy).

10. Johnson's nephew and later son-in-law, Colonel Guy Johnson, by Owen Staples.

11. Engraving of Sir John Johnson, probably from a portrait painted in London after the American Revolution.

12. Matthew Pratt's portrait of Sir William was probably painted in 1772 or 1773, when Johnson was around 57 years old.

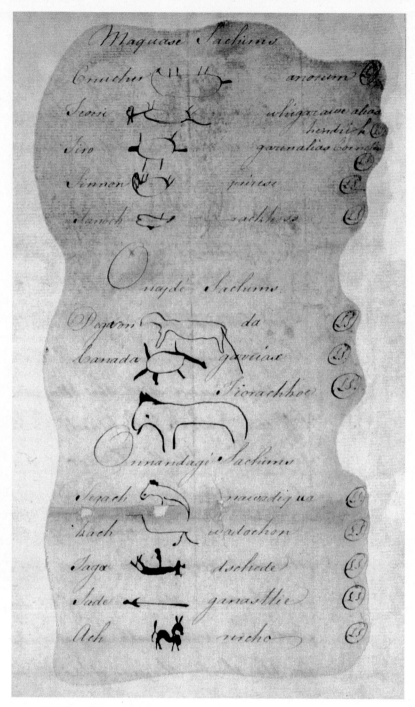

13. Signatures of the Mohawks of Canajoharie on the deed granting a vast tract of their land to Johnson in 1766.

21

Barbarians

═══

On 4 September 1760 the French commander at Montreal, François-Gaston, Chevalier de Levis, summoned the local Indian chiefs to a conference at La Prairie to ask for their help. The fall of Quebec had left New France with a single stronghold: Montreal. The Catholic Indians of the St Lawrence mission settlements, many of them exiled Mohawks, had been New France's most dependable Indian allies. Levis knew these warriors were crucial to his defence of the city and believed that he could, with their support, attack and possibly repel the expected invaders. He called the sachems together and began to appeal to their ancient bonds of religion and allegiance.

Even while Levis was making his entreaty, however, an envoy from one of the upriver villages arrived and announced that his people had concluded peace with the British. 'In a moment, [the chiefs] dispersed leaving M. le Chevalier de Levis with the [other] officers quite alone.'[1]

This was in effect the moment when Montreal, and with it all of Canada, was taken by the British. Without Indian support, Levis had no choice but to withdraw inside the flimsy fortifications of the city, which he knew he could not defend. His allies had deserted him because William Johnson, and the 600 Iroquois warriors he had brought with him into Canada, had persuaded them that they would get an amnesty for past attacks and the benefits of a renewed trade if they changed sides. It was one of Johnson's most effective contributions to the destruction of New France. His problem was that his commander, General Amherst, never understood why his final victory was so easy and so relatively bloodless.

From the autumn of 1759 Johnson had been engaged, through his Iroquois allies, in diplomatic contacts with the Indians in Canada. He had urged the Six Nations to 'make as many Friends as [they] Could' among the Canadian nations. Twenty-two 'Nations in the French Interest' had sent a delegation to Onondaga in response to a wampum belt sent by Johnson and the Six Nations. The Canadian delegates had reiterated their attachment to the French, citing in particular their mutual Catholic faith: 'We are thankfull for the Message Sent by You, and Warraghiyagey for Us to keep out of the way, when the English Army Approaches, but as the French have persuaded us to Stay, and Embrace their Religion, by which we are to be Saved; it would be hard Brothers for you to Expect We should leave them altogether, as We are taught by them to pray . . .'²

Johnson understood, from his own background, the reluctance of the Catholic Indians to abandon the French, but the very fact of the conference was encouraging. There was a backlog of bitterness between the Iroquois and their exiled brethren, and Johnson's allies claimed that Caughnawaga Indians had killed Mohawk prisoners in cold blood at the battle of Lake George. Even at Niagara, when the Six Nations had successfully persuaded the French-allied Indians to melt away, the Caughnawagas had been disinclined to parley.

Throughout the spring and summer of 1760 Johnson was sending Indian scouting parties up to Fort Levis (La Galette), the French base on an island in the St Lawrence River. Amherst was planning to assault Montreal from the west, by sailing from Oswego, through Lake Ontario and down the St Lawrence. The first obstacle to the progress of his flotilla would be Fort Levis, where Captain Pouchot, who had surrendered to Johnson at Niagara the previous year, had built strong defences. After that, Amherst's army would have to disembark and make its way on foot around a dangerous stretch of rapids. At that point the British force would be at its most vulnerable – unless, that is, William Johnson's Indian diplomacy could deprive the French of the Indian allies they would need for an assault on Amherst's men as they struggled ashore.

As he prepared to join Amherst's army, Johnson was getting an encouraging response to the feelers he had sent out to the Indians of Canada. After Johnson sent three Iroquois emissaries to talk to them, the Indians at Oswegatchie (La Presentation), the mission settlement just three miles downriver from Fort Levis, declared that they 'had quitted the french Interest and would no more act against the English'. In May a Canassadaga Indian arrived at Fort Johnson with his wife and son, bringing a New England ranger who had been captured a year earlier. By urging the newly re-established British post at Oswego to trade with Canadian Indians, Johnson continued to encourage a realignment that would make the defence of New France impossible.[3] The French were so alarmed at Johnson's success that they told their Indian allies that they had intercepted letters showing that the 'English intended their entire exterpation, which was to be put in execution immediately after the reduction of Canada'.[4]

Johnson set off to join Amherst at Oswego at the beginning of August 1760, with a huge contingent of 1,368 Indian warriors, women and children from the Six Nations and allied tribes. From there, he sent messages to the Canadian Indian villages, urging their headmen to meet him near Fort Levis. When he arrived there, he in effect disarmed 800 warriors who could have caused Amherst serious difficulty as his exposed army made its way awkwardly through the rapids between the fort and Montreal. Representatives of nine different nations came to negotiate with Johnson. They agreed a treaty, whereby they would remain neutral in return for a guarantee of future friendship. The result, as Johnson put it, was that Amherst's army 'passed all the dangerous Rapids, and the whole way without the least opposition'.[5] It was the result of this conference that interrupted the Chevalier de Levis's appeal for help from the Indians at La Prairie, and that caused his last allies to abandon him.

Some of the Canadian Indians, indeed, went beyond neutrality and actively assisted Johnson and the British, taking French and Canadian prisoners to provide intelligence. To display this remarkable turnaround, and to spread dismay among the French, Johnson surrounded himself with a guard of Caughnawagas, the exiled Catholic Mohawks who had been among the most loyal French allies. According to Johnson's younger bother Warren, who was with him shortly after the campaign, 'Five French Caughnawags rowed Sir William's whale Boat, up to Montreal.' If this was intended to infuriate the French, it seems to have worked: 'The Enemy knowing my Brother's Boat fired at it in particular from a Fort going up to Montreal.' After the fall of Montreal, a delegation of Caughnawagas – perhaps these same warriors – accompanied Johnson all the way back home and 'behaved extremely well all the time'.[6]

Johnson needed these extra warriors in part because Amherst's arrogant and dismissive attitude to the Indians in his own army was beginning to cause friction. Johnson had taken 585 Iroquois fighters with him to Fort Levis, and more than a hundred recruits from the Canadian tribes had joined him. From their experience with Johnson at Niagara, they clearly expected to share in the booty when Pouchot surrendered Fort Levis after a week-long siege; but Amherst regarded them as savages, and seems not to have understood their importance in clearing his passage towards Montreal. Johnson later described the scene to his brother, who wrote in his diary:

The Indians were greatly disgusted at not being admitted into fort Levi on Isle Royal after the Surrender; Some however got in & seen the Grenadiers, who took possession of it, plundering & pillageing, & themselves not allowed; but Such as got in, ordered out by the General, they were universally dissatisfied, & many returned home upon that Account. There were some plundered Goods given to them but in all not worth 30 pounds nor had they Liberty to see the prisonners, Sir William had a great Deal of Trouble to Satisfie them.7

This confrontation with Amherst, ominous for the future, also had the immediate effect of causing most of Johnson's Iroquois warriors to withdraw from the campaign in disgust. Of the 691 Indians Johnson had at Fort Levis, only 185 proceeded with him to Montreal. The potential cost of this arrogance was averted by Johnson's success in neutralising the French-allied Indians, but it might have been considerable. In the event, when Amherst's flotilla passed, on its approach to Montreal, the potentially dangerous point of Caughnawaga itself, '500 french Indians, but Neuter by Sir Williams good Management, were assembled on the Shore Side, as our Army rowed up the river . . . & behaved very well.'8

Once Amherst's army had safely passed the rapids, with Johnson and the Iroquois sachems ensuring a peaceful transit past all the Indian settlements, the game was up. On 6 September, the army rowed onto the west end of the island of Montreal and landed at Lachine, where they camped for the night. Johnson and his Indians seem to have been left in an exposed and uncomfortable position. As he told his brother, he 'and the Indians were in a Dangerous Situation at Montreal the Night before the Capitulation, if the french would have fought . . . there were Neither Tents nor Provisions, particularly with the Indians & it rained very hard'. Their misery was brief, however. By the morning of the 9th, Levis and Vaudreil had surrendered, not just Montreal, but New France. Except for Louisiana, and some scattered outposts in the west, North America was now a British domain.

Whatever joy Johnson felt at the end of a conflict in which he had been embroiled, on and off, for most of his time in America was tempered by his realisation that his world had changed profoundly. His dominion – the exercise of influence among Indians who held the balance of power between rival European empires – had disappeared. One side of the scales, the French, had been lopped off and the delicate operation of shifting the equilibrium through Indian influence was now a redundant skill.

He himself was partly responsible for this change, of course. He had kept the Mohawks loyal, and through them limited the capacity of the French and their Indian allies to sweep away the frontier settlements of New York. At Lake George in 1755 he had delivered a victory, however equivocal, that for a long time stood out as an island in a sea of French success. He had educated the British and colonials in the virtues of Indian woodland warfare and, with his creation of the rangers, he had sowed the seeds of a new American military style. Through skilful diplomacy and cool command, he had taken Niagara and caused the collapse of French power in the west. And, though Amherst seemed not to know it, Johnson's neutralising of the Canadian Indians had not just turned the fall of Montreal into a relatively bloodless affair, but had made Britain's new territories far more governable than they otherwise would have been.

The problem for Johnson, though, was that his own position depended on the British continuing to recognise the importance of a dignified relationship with the Indians. Yet Amherst had shown, by his treatment of Johnson's warriors at Fort Levis, that he regarded the Indian role in his victory as, at best, a minor and regrettable necessity. Amherst's official report on the campaign to Pitt entirely ignored the contribution of Indian diplomacy, and gave Johnson merely the backhanded compliment of having 'taken unwearied pains in keeping the Indians in humane bounds, and I have the pleasure to assure you that not a peasant, woman, or child has been hurt by them, or a house burned, since I entered what was the enemy's country'.9 In other words, Johnson's achievement, as Amherst saw it, was to restrain the savages from their expected savagery. The reality of the Iroquois' sophisticated and successful effort in tandem with Johnson to achieve victory with minimal bloodshed and to save the lives of hundreds of Amherst's troops was replaced in Amherst's mind by the minor miracle that the Iroquois instinct for massacring women and children had been checked.

This ignorance might not have mattered had it not been a symptom of a deeper antipathy. Amherst's attitude to Indians was shaped in part by the emerging legend of the fall of Fort William Henry. In his campaign on the Lake George–Lake Champlain frontier, he ordered a raid by Rogers's rangers on the Abenaki village of St François, seventy miles north-east of Montreal. In his instructions to Rogers, Amherst tried at once to return to the Indians the violence they had inflicted at Fort William Henry and at the same time to claim a higher moral ground: 'Remember the barbarities . . . committed by the enemy's Indian scoundrels on every occasion, where they had an opportunity . . . Take your revenge, but don't forget that tho' those villains have dastardly and promiscuously murdered the women and children of all ages, it is my orders that no women or children are killed or hurt . . .'[10] Not surprisingly, Rogers and his men had trouble understanding how they could reply in kind to the dastardly murderers of women and children without hurting women and children. They torched the village and slaughtered Indians of both sexes and all ages. This event did not enter the official British and American annals of barbarity.

Amherst's attitude was again apparent at Montreal. In the negotiations for the surrender, he blankly refused to allow the French regulars the honours of war, citing 'the infamous part the troops of France had acted in exciting the savages to perpetrate the most horrid and unheard of barbarities'.[11] Whereas Johnson had encouraged and supported Indian military practices like scalping and the taking of prisoners to replace the dead, Amherst saw Indian violence as occupying a moral space outside the boundaries of European, and therefore honourable, brutality.

This dismissal of Indians to an exterior darkness had a direct and immediate political purpose. The little drama at Fort Levis, with British grenadiers allowed to loot the fort but the Indians 'ordered out by the General', was a small-scale version of the larger British image of victory in North America. The Indians were to understand that they were not allies who shared in a triumph and its attendant spoils; they were savages to be kept 'in humane bounds', by force if necessary.

As early in the war as 1755, when General Braddock was seeking the help of the Delawares, Shawnees and Mingo Indians of Ohio in his campaign against the French, they asked him what would happen to the land if the French were driven away. He replied 'that the English should Inhabit and Inherit the Land . . . No Savage Should Inherit the

Land.'¹² In the minds of the victors, it was now a relief to know that the savages could be put in their proper place. Colonel Hugh Mercer was pleased that the British 'can now speak to the Indians in proper style since services are not necessary'. General Thomas Gage summed up the position of the Indians with admirable brevity: 'All North America in the hands of a single power robs them of their Consequence, presents & pay.'¹³

Johnson had sensed the emergence of this narrow, triumphalist mood ever since the fall of Fort Niagara. His deputy George Croghan had reported to him from Pittsburg:

It is generally thought by the Gentlemen of the Army, that the Indians must from their Necessitys come into our Measures, and Every Body thinks that any thing given to the Indians [is] thrown away . . . The Success of his Majesty's Arms, this Campaign, in Different Parts, gives rise to an Opinion generally received in the Army, that We have conquered the Continent, it is true We have beat the French; but we have nothing to boast from the War with the Natives, yet it is thought every Penny, thrown away, that is given to them, which Obliges me to think the [Indian] Service very disagreeable.¹⁴

For Johnson, the thought that the Indian service was indeed very disagreeable soured the taste of victory. It cannot have helped his mood that he returned home to a bleak scene at Fort Johnson, where sickness was sweeping through the garrison and importunate Indian families, whose livelihoods had been disrupted by the absence of most of the menfolk in the war, clamoured for help.

In November 1760 the visiting Warren Johnson described a place that was more like an overcrowded medieval town in time of plague than a baronet's estate:

More Custom at Fort Johnson than any Inn in England from the Number of Regular & Provincial officers passing by every Day . . . The Provincial Troops are soe Sickly, particularly the New England ones, that they bury 40 of a Day, chiefly oweing to their dirtiness which gives them fevers and fluxes, they throw them on the Beech, as they die, & some they bury Just by the House, and Scarecely below the Surface . . . There are here vast Numbers of Indians, who are troublesome beyond thought to my brother; they often kill one another in drunken fits, there is noe Law to punish them, but some of the Deceas'd's friends, very often, nay, almost always kills the Killer at an other drunken Bout: The Indian Skwas pick the Lice of one another and eat them . . . the Indians are very Sickly.¹⁵

Sitting in his study with these scenes unfolding outside, Johnson wrote a long letter to Prime Minister William Pitt. In it he outlined the services he had performed since 1755 as a major general and as Indian

Superintendent, for neither of which posts, as he pointed out, he had yet been paid a penny. He reminded Pitt that he had brought the entire Iroquois confederacy over to the British side, that he had taken Fort Niagara, that he had played a large part in the taking of Montreal and that 'Thus Sir we became Masters of the last place in the Enemys possession in these parts and made those Indians our friends by a peace, who might otherwise have given us much trouble.' Almost as an afterthought, he added his resignation: 'Permit me to add that having now discharged my Duty during the War to the utmost of my Ability, I should be glad to be freed from the discharge of an Office so fatigueing, in which I have greatly impaired my constitution, & neglected my concerns in this Country, which I would willingly apply the rest of my life to retrieve.'

Now that he was returning to private life, he added a final piece of advice. If, he warned, Britain were to take the Indians for granted and 'totally neglect that Interest which we have hitherto been at so much pains & expense in improving', there would be trouble. He saw it coming and, exhausted, disillusioned and entering middle age, he wanted no part of it.[16]

22

Seeds Worth Sowing

===

William Pitt never read his letter. He was, as Johnson was informed, 'a Gentleman who is not to be seen even about the most Urgent business, nor ever Answers any Letters but what his Office obliges him'.[1] Now that victory had been achieved, the affairs of the Indians of North America were no longer urgent enough to oblige him to pay attention to Johnson's warnings. And, as it happened, Johnson effectively ignored his own letter. He allowed his resignation to lie unnoticed in some dusty pile in London, and pretended that he had not sent it. He did continue to threaten that, if he were not paid for the years of service, which had made him 'a verry considerable Sufferer both in Interest and Constitution', he would 'endeavour for the time to come to repair both in another way'.[2] But he also came to realise that there was too much at stake for him to walk away from the management of Indian affairs.

Part of Johnson's mind was indeed still drawn to the notion of a retirement in which he would, literally, cultivate his garden. 'I am going to Commence a Husband man,' he announced to Daniel Claus, asking at the same time for 'Seeds of every kind worth Sowing'.[3] To escape from the fetid and crowded Fort Johnson, he built a summer house, which he called Castle Cumberland, on a low hill overlooking a swampy tract called the Vlaie, full of the ducks he loved to hunt, and took refuge there for a significant period. In March 1761 he noted: 'I keep mostly here since I came home.' After the human carnage of the wars, he loved the purer violence of the hunt. Later in the year he recorded the pleasure of a kill: 'At a river within fifteen miles of Sandusky Lake, I saw three wolves on shore who had driven a fine buck into the lake, which I shot through the head; and in the evening,

I divided it among the party and Indians; it was enough for them all. The horns, skin and sinews I took with me as a trophy.'4 He also built a fishing lodge, known simply as 'the Fish House', on the south side of the Sacondaga River, about seventeen miles from Fort Johnson. Between shooting, fishing and talking to his younger brother Warren, who had served as a captain in the invasion of Canada and who stayed with him until late April 1761, he was able to distract himself from the frustrations of the new dispensation.

The seriousness of his intention to give himself over to the life of a leisured landlord, developing his properties in between bouts of gardening, fishing and shooting, cannot be doubted. In January 1761 he received a letter from his old co-conspirator Thomas Pownall, the man who had done so much to promote Johnson's interests, and his own, in the struggle against William Shirley. Pownall had succeeded Shirley as Governor of Massachusetts in 1756, and had then returned to London in the summer of 1760. Now, this supreme fixer had a proposal for Johnson. James De Lancey, who had been Acting Governor of New York, had died. How would Johnson like to be the new governor?

Coming from the well-connected Pownall, this was a serious proposition. It offered Johnson the prospect of significant power, great prestige and opportunities for substantial self-enrichment. Back in 1755, when he had been given the command of the expedition against Crown Point and before his falling-out with Shirley, he had declared quite frankly to the latter: 'I am ambitious.'5 For the child of a middling Irish family of Catholic tenant farmers, the governorship of a huge colony growing by the year in population and wealth should have been a dream come true. For a man complaining that his health had been undermined and his fortune depleted by his hard service in an often sordid war, it was surely the perfect reward. Yet he spurned Pownall's offer with no apparent trace of hesitation or regret. After the usual expressions of gratitude and a falsely modest protestation that he was 'sensible of [his] inability for the execution of so important a Trust', he came to the point: 'As I have hitherto had the most fatiguing and disagreeable Service I now propose to retire and spend the rem[ain]der of my Days more tranquile.'6

The rejection of Pownall's proposal suggests that he was entirely serious in his determination to luxuriate in tranquillity. Yet just over six months later he set out on a long and dangerous expedition to

Detroit, the small, walled French town on the western shore of Lake Erie, to ratify peace with the western Indians. Beginning on 5 July 1761, and accompanied only by his son John and his nephew Guy Johnson, who had joined him from Ireland in June 1756, he undertook a gruelling round trip of over a thousand miles that kept him from home for four months. His journey started with warnings of danger, the Mohawks telling him that 'they were very uneasy for my safety, there being several nations of Indians, through whose country I must pass, very much attached to the French interest'. On his third night out from Fort Johnson, as he waited for the boatloads of supplies he was to take with him, he 'was obliged to lie out in the open air without any manner of covering or conveniency'. Two nights after that, after painfully slow progress because the level of water in the Mohawk River was so low, he was obliged to sleep 'in a burying ground' east of Oneida Lake.7 This was hardly the tranquillity he had promised himself.

At one level, the trip to Detroit was the completion of unfinished business. He had promised the Iroquois and the western nations that British victory would help them get rid of the French garrisons whose presence they had always resented. What many of them had not expected was that these posts would instead be occupied by the British themselves, meaning that they had merely exchanged one bunch of occupying soldiers for another. The British move to garrison Niagara, Pittsburgh and Detroit had caused serious unease and threatened the tentative peace that had been arranged the previous year. Johnson travelled west, to head off disaffection and conclude a treaty.

Six days after he left, he was overtaken by his old comrade from the Lake George campaign, William Eyre, now a colonel. Eyre brought news from Detroit 'concerning some design of the Indians rising against the English'. The British occupation of the former French forts had so alarmed the Geneseo Senecas around Niagara that they had attempted to form a new western confederacy to attack the forts. While Johnson was travelling to Detroit, a grand council of Indian nations – Iroquois, Delawares, Shawnees, Mohicans, Mingos, Wyandots, Kickapoos, Miamis, Chippewas, Ottawas, Potawatomis and Huron-Petuns – was meeting around the same place to create a new anti-British confederation. Messengers arrived from the sachems in Canajoharie, warning Johnson of the same plot and expressing renewed fears for his safety. 'They begged that I would not proceed, as it must be very dangerous to pass through the country of nations, who would not now be our friends.' Yet this news merely brought out Johnson's self-confidence: 'If they had any such wild wicked design in view, I did not doubt but my presence among them might put a stop to it.'[8] He pushed on, camping out in the fields at night and navigating the rivers by day. Meeting the Seneca sachem Saquerisen, he warned him that the plot to attack the British forts had been discovered and tried to persuade him that such an attempt would be 'madness'.

When a group of Onondagas who had fought with him at Niagara came to see him at Oswego on 21 July, however, the depth of disgruntlement, even among the Six Nations, became all too clear. The Onondaga speaker produced a wampum belt that Johnson had sent to their nation when he was looking for warriors to take part in that campaign. He went through the promises listed on the belt: good trade and 'good usage for them forever after'. Now, the speaker said, those promises had been reneged on. As Johnson wrote: 'They were very ill used and treated . . . in point of trade, and at the several posts, where they are roughly handled, very often without any cause. As this is so contrary to what they expected in case we conquered the French, they all entreated that they might be better used, or else they must think that what the French told them was true.' What the French had told them was that a British victory would be followed by the Indians being crushed. They were also disturbed that Johnson was going to Detroit to treat with the western Indians, since, as they told him, 'you know that the chief and only council fire burns at your house and Onondaga'. The implication was not just that Johnson had broken his promises to the warriors, but that he was now dispensing with the protocol and ritual which had bound him to them.[9]

The complaints about the behaviour of the British garrisons at the forts were specific and entirely justified in the light of repeated incidents of rape, theft and even murder. The soldiers and traders, the Onondagas told Johnson, 'seem not to have any liking for us and use us very ill at times without any cause, taking our women from us by violence, using them and us ill besides, and hindering us from fishing and hunting on our own grounds near the posts, and often taking what we catch and kill from us'.

Johnson's position was weak and awkward. He knew very well that the Onondagas' complaints were justified. Yet he could neither acknowledge their truth – and thereby admit that the promises he had made had been broken – nor reject them, thereby losing the trust he had built up over so many years. He responded instead with a few anaemic arguments: that the Onondgas had deserted him at Fort Levis and broken the deal, and that rows at the forts were caused by the Indians getting drunk. Other than an invitation to a future conference with the Six Nations and a promise to try to get them some gunpowder, he had little to offer. It must have occurred to him again that his earlier decision to retire had been the right one.

After he had crossed a sometimes turbulent Lake Ontario on a schooner and arrived at Niagara, his journey continued as a trail of tears and anger. Some Senecas complained of soldiers stealing their horses and killing a man 'without cause'. At the fort itself, two Onondagas complained of being cheated by two different traders. A Seneca explained to him why messages announcing the plan to attack the forts had been sent to Detroit: 'The Indians about Ohio . . . had one of their men killed at or near Fort Pitt last spring . . . others were abused much by the English, and, lately, five Delawares were killed near Shamokin, and a Seneca killed by the garrison at Venanago . . . he believed that to be the reason of their sending such a message to Detroit, imagining the English intended their destruction from their unfriendly and rough behaviour to the Indians who came to see them.'[10]

Johnson did his best to assuage these fears and put on a small show of justice, having 'four men whipped, for robbing a Seneca Indian of a keg of rum, in their presence'. He issued regulations for fair trade with the Indians and urged the Geneseo Senecas, who had organised the plot for a rebellion, to send a delegation to the conference he was going to hold at Detroit. Yet he knew that his own stock was falling so sharply that he was now in real danger from at least some factions within the Six Nations. When he met the Onondagas, their speaker had urged the mutual honouring of the promises made when the Iroquois agreed to join him in the war in 1759, so that 'we may both live to be grey'. The implicit threat that he might not live to old age if things did not get better was made explicit a few days later at Niagara. His friend the Mohawk Nickus of Canajoharie, who had travelled to the fort, told him that on his journey 'he had heard, by the way, from several Indians, that I was to be destroyed or murdered on my way to Detroit, and that the Indians were certainly determined to rise and fall on the English, as several thousand of the Ottawas and other nations had agreed to join the Five Nations in this scheme or plot'.[11]

Yet Johnson seems hardly to have thought of these embarrassments and dangers. His mind was still taken up with daydreams of a genteel retirement. On the journey, he was collecting seeds from flowers that caught his eye ('Have picked some seed like Piony') and medicinal herbs for Molly's range of traditional cures ('seed of a weed good for a flux'), and was reminding himself in his notebook that among his priorities on his return home should be 'To sow the several seeds I pick up in my way to Detroit'. He was picturing in his head 'Little summer houses to build in my gardens when I get home'. He was planning: 'To have my books and all my accounts properly settled; and all my tenants' accounts adjusted regularly and put into one book.' He was thinking about what he would do when he got to Detroit, not, as might be imagined, of the delicate and critical negotiations he had to conduct with an array of Indian nations on the verge of bloody rebellion, but of how 'To give diversions at Detroit to the Indians, and also to the French, of the best sort, balls etc.'. He was reminding himself to 'get my ten black beavers dressed and made up into a large blanket for a bed'.[12]

These are odd thoughts for a man who has just been told repeatedly that there are serious plans to murder him on the road ahead and that the people whom it is his job to pacify are close to open revolt. There is indeed a dazed, dreamy air about the rough journal Johnson kept in a small, leather-bound notebook on his trip to Detroit. In it we get a glimpse of a man who knows that he is the middle of a grave personal and public crisis, but who keeps trying to tell himself that he is a veteran in repose, an ancient general who has retired from the wars to tend his own estates and his own pleasures. We can picture him on shore picking peonies and on the water softly humming the music of the grand ball he is going to throw for the best sort of French ladies as he moves through a landscape rank with dark conspiracies and pitted with the raw wounds of betrayal. He takes his son and nephew to view Niagara Falls. He notes the 'fine meadows' and the 'very remarkable' islands where the Grand River meets the northern shore of Lake Erie near present-day Port Maitland, even while news is reaching him that a Cherokee uprising to the south has been put down by 'burning fifteen of their towns'. He stays up late with a Frenchman, a Captain Gamelin, whom he had captured at the battle of Belle Famille two years earlier, and, as if all wars were over for ever, Gamelin 'got very drunk . . . and told me several things very openly'. He sees a swamp and thinks that, like his own summer house, it would be 'a fine place for ducks, geese, etc.' Camping near the mouth of the Detroit River on 2 September, he looks across to the east shore and sees some cleared ground where the Hurons had lived with their Catholic priests before they were displaced by the war, and all he can think of is that 'There might be now mowed a vast quantity of hay' from it.[13]

Early on the cold but bright morning of the next day, he sailed up the river, past 'several fine islands and drowned meadows', and disembarked a mile from Detroit at the house of a former French captain, who treated him to some melons. He mounted the horse that had been sent out for him and rode towards Detroit to the sound of cannon and small-arms fire that greeted his approach. Arriving at the walls, he was hailed in grand style by the artillery of the fort and given the finest house in the town, vacated by the last French commander, the Sieur de Bellestre. Yet, his princely reception soon lulled him back into his wistfully ethereal mood. Fifty Huron women 'old and young' came to pay homage and offer him some of their finest corn. He gave them wine and biscuits, drank their several healths, and presented them with a side of beef. The leading French townspeople arrived with their priest 'to pay their respects and desire protection' and he graciously offered assurance of his good auspices 'while they continued to behave as good subjects'.

It was in this intoxicating atmosphere of power and glory that he went, on the Sunday evening after his arrival, to a ball arranged 'that I may see' the ladies. He saw one in particular, 'a fine girl', whom he picked out as the one to take his arm and to open the ball with him. She was Angélique Cuillerier, the twenty-six-year-old daughter of Antoine, a French fur trader who had been heavily engaged in Indian diplomacy. Angélique herself spoke some of the Indian languages and had been involved in diplomatic councils. This, as well as her beauty, captivated Johnson. They danced until five o'clock on Monday morning. That he was greatly taken with Angélique is clear. A week later, on his second last night in Detroit, he threw a ball at his house and this time danced with her until seven o'clock the next morning. The bleary, euphoric note he scribbled in his little pocketbook hints both at the rapture of the evening and at a proposal, perhaps ambiguous, of marriage: 'All parted very much pleased and happy. Promised to write Mademoiselle Curie [sic] as soon as possible my sentiments; there never was so brilliant an assembly here before.'[14]

Johnson's 'sentiments' belonged to his reverie of ease. The idea of bringing a young French wife to the Mohawk valley was part of a broader pattern of desires: the fine mansion he was thinking of building, the summer houses in his abundant gardens, the fishing lodge, the plans to spend his time settling tenants on his now vast estates. It was wrapped up in his dream of tranquillity and civility. He was a forty-six-year-old man with a bullet in his thigh that sometimes kept him awake at night ('I was very full of pain all night with my old wound') and a chronic bowel complaint, and he was still sometimes sleeping on the ground 'with all my baggage wet'. He had now lived as long in America as he had in Ireland and he must have known that there was no going back. He had handled bloody scalps and paid bounties for the murders of children. Was a life of European-style civility now too much to ask?

At both a private and a public level, those dreamy desires were pinched awake by pressing realities. By his side, he had his – and Catharine's – son John. How would his heir presumptive, born out of wedlock, feel about a new stepmother whose legitimate children might claim his inheritance? While he was dancing deliriously with Angélique, Molly Brant was giving birth to Johnson's daughter Elizabeth. On 21 October, when he was at Three Rivers on his way back, 'Captain Etherington told me Molly was delivered of a girl; that all were well at my house.'[15] What would Molly think of a new mistress arriving at that house, and what would a separation from her do to his relationship with the Mohawks?

At the public level, he had to remember the purpose of his journey to Detroit: to stave off the threatened rebellion. In this he succeeded with his usual conspiratorial and diplomatic skill, but in a way that must have left his mind uneasy with the knowledge that the causes of the Indians' discontent had not been addressed. He arranged the conference outdoors on a fine morning, with each nation allocated seats and their presents divided up in neat parcels. He performed the condolence ceremonies to wipe away their tears for those who died fighting the British. He opened the passages to their hearts so 'that you may at this Meeting speak honestly & brotherlike, & not from the Lips as some unthinking and evil minded Nations have lately done'. He took out of their heads 'the Hatchet with which were obliged to strike you', and applied 'a healing salve to the Wound'. He gathered up the bones of the dead so as to 'bury them deep, & level the graves with the ground so that they may no more be seen'. He took a burning brand which he said was from the council fire at Fort Johnson and lit a new council fire with it, making Detroit a symbolic extension of his own domain. And he presented a huge wampum belt of twenty rows of beads, representing the renewed and extended covenant chain of friendship.

These solemn and impressive ceremonials, of which Johnson was now a high priest, were, however, the prelude to an old-fashioned drama in which the classic imperial strategy of divide-and-rule was carried through to perfection. Johnson demanded from the assembled sachems the names of those who had sent a war belt to Detroit urging a rising against the British forts. As an inducement, he made a tempting offer to the western nations. He had, over the previous five years, evolved a policy of playing the Iroquois and the Ohio nations off against each other, now making men of the Delawares, now reasserting the territorial claims of the Six Nations. This time he offered straightforwardly to recognise the independence of the western nations from the Iroquois, promising to 'treat with you independent of any other Nation, or Nations of Indians whatsoever'. Through this, he said, they were 'now furnished with the means of becoming a great and flourishing people'.[16] He added assurances that the Indians' lands would be respected and that a fair trade would be instituted.

Johnson's offer was simply put, but its significance was well understood. James Kenny, a Quaker who ran the Pennsylvania trading post at Pittsburgh, understood it as soon as he heard of it: 'The Conclusion of Colonel Johnson's Treaty is said to be that he has cast off ye Onandago Yoke (of ye Six Nations) from ye Delawares, Shawanas, Wyondots, Picks or Tweetwees, & others to ye Westward which makes those Nations a Seperate Power Independt of the Six Nations.'[17]

The offer was accepted. The Huron chief sachem Anáiása, in a carefully staged piece of theatre, told the assembly that though he didn't know the motives of those who had sent the war belt, there was a man who did. He pointed at Kayashota, the Seneca sachem who had brought the belt. The Ottawa speaker Macátepilesis then referred to 'certain . . . bad Birds' who had been among them, and told Johnson: 'If you would know who this bird is, Cast your Eyes to Kayashota & you will see him.' In what was clearly a pre-arranged performance, the Chippewa sachem Wabbicommicott then presented Johnson with a belt of green wampum, and praised 'our Brother Warraghiyagey who has now brought peace to our Country which was in a treamor, & has fixed our hearts in their proper places which before his arrival were fluttering & knew not where to settle'.[18]

Kayashota was immediately on the defensive. He rose and declared 'with vehemence' that he had innocently accompanied another Seneca messenger Tahiadoris (a son of Johnson's old antagonist, the French Indian diplomat Phillipe-Thomas Chabert de Joncaire), and was 'greatly astonished' when the latter had begun to urge war. Once this blame game started, Johnson knew he had shattered any immediate hope of a united front of western Indians against the British. To finish it off, he privately met with three chiefs of the Huron-Petuns, whose village outside Detroit was just one component of the diverse array of Indians in a putative western alliance, and told them 'he looked upon them as the head of the Ottawa Confederacy for which reason he had lighted up a Council fire at Detroit'.[19] He spent a night at the Huron village as a mark of special favour, and apparent mutual love. Both sides, however, knew that there was a degree of disingenuousness in the whole performance. The Hurons themselves had sent out belts trying to organise resistance against the British. But since Johnson had effectively broken that resistance for the time being, declarations of loyalty and affection suited everybody.

Johnson had to know that his success at Detroit was rather hollow. The British triumphalism and arrogance that had sparked the conspiracy were not about to disappear. All the reasons for his letter of resignation after Montreal – Amherst's hubris and Johnson's own weariness – were still valid. The dreams of a quiet life still clung to his thoughts. Why, then, did he go on, plunging himself ever deeper into the treacherous currents of Anglo-Indian relations? Because in spite of his exhaustion, the conflict that was unfolding between himself and Jeffrey Amherst touched William Johnson to the core.

23

'Intoxicated with Providential Success'

═══

Sir Jeffery Amherst did not, at first glance, look like a man who could contemplate genocide with equanimity. He took pride in his own humane civility. When he was besieging the French bastion of Louisbourg in 1758, he offered to allow the sick and wounded to take refuge outside the town. When he refused the garrison at Montreal the honours of war, he wanted his severity to be understood as an international condemnation of French tolerance for cruelty and barbarism and to 'manifest to all the world by this capitulation [his] detestation of such practices'.[1] His inability to acknowledge, perhaps even to perceive, the importance of his Indian allies in his world-shaping victory was rooted in a genuine disgust at what he believed was their inherent tendency to anarchic violence.

Amherst was a consummate professional soldier for whom the organisation and deployment of violence was an honourable calling. His style of war was slow but intensely rational. He worked out what was necessary and carried it through with resolution and tenacity. He had served the British Empire and its ruling class from his early childhood in Kent, when he had been a page to the Duke of Dorset. He had joined the army at sixteen and learned his trade in the large-scale formal warfare of Europe. He had served at Fontenoy against Dieskau and Johnson's Warren kinsmen. He knew, or thought he knew, where the borders of acceptable conduct lay, where valour ended and bloodlust began.

He enjoyed a touch of American wildness and was not immune to its colourful and exotic allure. When Johnson was at Detroit, Amherst took the trouble to write to him with a special request: 'to buy me some black Fox, or any curious Furrs which may be found there, to make presents to two Ladys in England'. Johnson, still anxious to be on good terms with Amherst who, since the fall of Montreal, had been both commander-in-chief and Governor of British North America, had to send all the way to Lake Michigan for exotic furs, which cost him 150 silver ear bobs, 200 silver brooches, and ninety large silver crosses.[2]

Nor was Amherst entirely impervious to the romantic European view of the Indians. He had named the armed sloops on which he had taken his troops down the St Lawrence to attack Montreal the *Onondaga* and the *Mohawk*, inaugurating an American tradition of drawing on Indian imagery to enhance the allure of advanced military technology. Yet curious furs and resonant names were about as far as Amherst's interest in Indian cultures ever went.

Johnson had made an effort to deepen Amherst's awareness of the complex situation of the native peoples. In 1760, when Indian allies were still needed for the Montreal campaign, Amherst stayed at Fort Johnson and then accompanied its master on the route to Oswego. Johnson had shown him the Oneida village at Oneida Lake and took him to visit an Onondaga family at a fishing site on the far shore. Johnson pointed out Indians praying, gardening, weaving, preparing dried eel and salmon, hoping, evidently, to convince the general that these were civilised human beings. Amherst gave some salt pork to an infant, who guzzled it down and then suckled its mother's breast. Amherst was struck, half in admiration and half in anxiety, by the way the child was fondled and adored by its parents. This image, though, was cancelled in his mind by another, when some Indians got drunk and carved up a horse. 'They are devils when drunk', wrote Amherst, '– when sober, quiet enough.'[3] This thought stuck in Amherst's mind. Indians, to him, either were quiet or were devils. This was a perfectly rational distinction and he would apply it with calm rationality. Quiet Indians could be regarded as humans and beneficiaries of a well-organised Empire. Devils, on the other hand, were fit only for extermination.

For Johnson, Amherst's post-war attitudes first manifested themselves through an economy drive. Amherst was upset at the cost of Johnson's Indian diplomacy, which, between November 1758 and December 1759, came to just over £17,000. Some of the expenses Johnson listed were easy enough for a military professional to understand: £50 to a party of Geneseo Senecas and Onondagas for 'taking a french Officer, killing another, and burning a Magazine near Niagara', or £40 for capturing a prisoner from whom to extract valuable intelligence. But Johnson also spent a lot of money greasing the wheels of cultural exchange, flattering sachems and satisfying Indian honour. Presents to seal diplomatic agreements, wampum belts to send messages and attest to the truth of assurances given, marks of distinction for chiefs, tobacco for ritual smoking at conferences, money paid 'in lieu of a laced Coat and Hatt' – these appeared to a man like Amherst merely as ridiculous indulgences.

Even worse from his point of view was the expense of preventing the Indians at Niagara from taking French prisoners home to their villages to replace their dead. After the battle of Belle Famille, for example, Johnson paid the Indians £160 for 'giving up their Claim to the french Officers taken in the Battle'. For Amherst, though, they had no such claim in the first place.[4] It was clear to him that Johnson had been indulging his Indian friends and that such indulgence would lead merely to more demands. The cycle had to be broken.

Thus, within three months of the fall of Canada, Amherst ordered Johnson to disband the small core of officers he had assembled to assist him in the organisation of Indian war parties: John Butler, Jelles Fonda, William Hare and Hendrick Nellus. These men had built up valuable experience in working with Johnson, but Amherst insisted: 'The Severall Sallaries of the Indian Officers, are a heavy charge to the Publick, and . . . from the present Circumstances of affairs, their Services can be dispensed with, and Occasion a great Saving.'[5] His real concern, however, was with the Indian warriors themselves, whom, in the aftermath of victory, he redefined as an expensive luxury.

In objective terms, there were no grounds for Amherst's feeling that Iroquois warriors were inordinately expensive. Johnson's expenditure bought much more than military muscle, but even if all of it had been counted as wages, it would have come to around £24 in New York currency per man. This was, in fact, a little cheaper than the colonial militia. The Connecticut provincials cost almost £25 a man; the Massachusetts men just over £26. Given that the average Iroquois warrior was a far more effective woodland fighter than the average New England farm boy, and that the Iroquois were investing virtually their entire manpower, which could not then hunt for furs and skins, Amherst had got a terrific bargain.[6]

Such rational calculations, however, were beside the point. Amherst was beginning to apply a new set of standards for imperial governance and a new ideology of human behaviour. Fifteen years later, in his book *The Wealth of Nations*, Adam Smith would write: 'To found a great empire for the sole purpose of raising up a people of customers, may at first sight appear a project fit only for a nation of shopkeepers. It is, however, a project altogether unfit for a nation of shopkeepers; but extremely fit for a nation that is governed by shopkeepers.' Amherst was determined to govern his great empire as a shopkeeper. He was set on applying the logic of the free market in a way that would pose a ferocious challenge to William Johnson's sense of empire, of the Indians, and, indirectly, of his own Irish identity.

Johnson's Indian department was intimate, familial and above all Irish. By the early 1760s it was run by four people. At the top, in New York and dealing primarily with the Iroquois, there was Johnson himself. Working alongside him was his nephew Guy, the son of his Catholic brother John. Short and fussy, with powdered hair, a stern face, an occasionally haughty demeanour and a strong harsh Irish accent, Guy had come over from Warrenstown around June 1756 and operated as a ranger and Indian captain in Johnson's campaigns against the French.7

Johnson's principal deputy, operating in Pennsylvania and dealing with the western Indians of the Ohio, was another Irishman, George Croghan. His exact origins in Ireland are unclear, but he had strong Jacobite sympathies, suggesting that he was originally Catholic, and his sometimes bizarre, idiosyncratic and phonetic use of English suggests that he may well have been brought up speaking Gaelic as his first language. He was the same age as Johnson, and left Ireland during the severe famine of 1741, again suggesting that he came from a background in which loose talk about the total extirpation of a people would not be taken lightly. As Johnson's first appointment after his confirmation as Sole Superintendent in 1756, he was a critical part of Johnson's construction of that office as an Irish fiefdom.

The third member of Johnson's triumvirate of deputies, Daniel Claus, had the immeasurable bad taste not to be Irish, but he did his best to acquire that high status. Claus was, like the rest of the Indian Superintendency's staff, a marginal man. He had arrived in Philadelphia in 1749 from his native Germany intending to make his fortune. Having failed to do so, he had fallen in with his fellow countryman, the Pennsylvania Indian agent Conrad Weiser. He had travelled with him into the Mohawk area in 1750, stayed briefly at Mount Johnson, and been encouraged by Weiser and Johnson to learn Mohawk so that he could work as an interpreter. He had then lived with Johnson's closest Mohawk friend Brant Kanagaradunkwa and learned the language from him and his son. In 1751 Johnson had hired him to work in his trading store, and invited him 'to stay at his house where he could improve as much in the Indian Language as at Brant's there being always 6 Nations Indians about the house'.[8]

Claus became an honorary Irishman by marrying Johnson's daughter Nancy. In an even more incestuous overlapping of official duties and familial ties, Guy Johnson married his own first cousin Mary (Johnson's other daughter by Catharine Weisenberg), and doted on their 'pretty little Sheelah Grah, who is ye lovely and lively picture of them both'.[9] Even Croghan ultimately became a kind of kin to Johnson when his daughter by a Mohawk woman married Molly Brant's brother Joseph.

This tight little network, with its deeply Irish character, operated in a way that was beyond Amherst's comprehension. It was, at one level, a group of imperial servants made up of white Europeans. These were people who worked for and identified with the Empire in their official capacities, but whose private hinterlands could not easily be mapped by a straightforward Englishman like Amherst. He came from the centre. They were liminal creatures whose natural habitat was ambiguity. If Amherst's world-view was black and white, Johnson's was full of merging shades and dappled hues. If Amherst's voice was monophonic, Johnson's broadcast simultaneously on many channels, sending out signals resonant with undertones.

At its most basic level, the conflict between them was about the humanity of the Indians. Johnson and his deputies could not think of obliterating a race without thinking about the annihilation of people they loved. Johnson and Croghan had befriended Indian men, made love to Indian women; they had Indian children. Claus had lived in Brant's house. Guy Johnson had shared the dangers of the forest with small groups of Indian scouts and known moments when his life depended on them. Even at the nub of Amherst's solution to the Indian problem – the free market – where the trading experience of men like Johnson and Croghan might have been expected to create agreement, there were quite fundamental differences of understanding.

In one sense, the Indians were already, in Adam Smith's phrase, 'a people of customers'. They were tied in to a global system of trade and they were at the forefront of the consumer revolution. Yet, as Johnson understood and Amherst did not, the meaning of trade was not, for them, the same as it was for an English merchant. Even after centuries of European influence, they did not have a European notion of individual wealth. A great sachem might have access to more material goods than an ordinary member of the nation, but the sachem's role was to procure those goods and share them with the village. His status depended on his success in doing so. A war chief brought resources to the village by capturing prisoners and booty. A diplomatic chief of the kind that Johnson cultivated made alliances and received presents to distribute.

Around these collective notions of exchange there were systems of courtesy, protocol and ritual that Johnson had thoroughly mastered. The fifty Huron women who came to greet him after his arrival at Detroit, for example, gave him corn and received beef in return. This exchange could be understood in crude economic terms as an act of barter, but it had ritual, political and cultural dimensions. What passed back and forth in the transaction was not just different goods of equal value, but a heavy freight of trust and alliance, of mutual recognition and obligation, of friendship and protection, of common humanity.

To dispense with these other dimensions of trade was to call forth mutual incomprehension. Amherst could not understand the political and cultural meanings implicit in Indian trade. Indians, especially the more westerly nations who had less experience of European culture, could not understand the notion of profit regulated by laws of supply and demand. The Minisink religious leader Papoonhoal explained in 1760 his objections to European-style trade, even of the regulated kind that Johnson tried to impose to prevent the Indians from being cheated:

Brother, It comes to my mind to mention something to you that I think wrong in your Dealings with the Indians. You make it publick that you will give a certain price for our Skins, and that they are to be weighed and Paid for at that set price according to their weight. Brother there are two bad things in this way of dealing. You alter the price that you say you will give for our Skins, which can never be right. God cannot be pleased to see the price of one and the same thing so often altered and changed. Our young men finding that they are to receive for their Skins according to their weight play tricks with them . . . to make them weigh more . . . Brother you see that there is no love or honesty on either Side . . . Now Brothers, I desire you will not raise your goods to too high a price, but to lower them so as you can afford it, that we may live and walk together in one Brotherly Love and Friendship as brothers ought to live.[10]

The notion that brotherly love was a hard currency did not appeal to Jeffery Amherst. Now that military alliances were no longer necessary, he saw the marketplace as the proper arena for British-Indian relations. It was this belief, and Johnson's resistance to it, that lifted the conflict between the two men above the level of a political manoeuvre. Theirs was a clash of ideas and values, and it prefigured disputes that would rage for centuries as the whole world became a marketplace.

Once he started to scrutinise Johnson's accounts of expenditure on Indian relations, Amherst identified the whole idea of giving presents as both a fiscal and a political mistake. His attitude was laid out to Johnson in August 1761 with admirable clarity:

You are sensible how averse I am, to purchasing the good behaviour of Indians, by presents, the more they get the more they ask, and yet are never satisfied; where-fore as a Trade is now opened for them . . . I think it much better to avoid all presents in future, since that will oblige them to Supply themselves by Barter, & of course keep them more constantly Employed by means of which they will have less time to concert, or Carry into Execution any Schemes prejudicial to His Majesty's Interests; and to abolish entirely every kind of apprehension on that account, the keeping them scarce of Ammunition, is not less to be Recommended; since nothing can be so impolitick as to furnish them with the means of accomplishing the Evil which is so much Dreaded.[11]

This decision Amherst followed through with the patience and tenacity he had applied to the taking of Canada. In November 1761 he was asking Johnson for accounts and adding, 'I am hopefull all the occonomy that could be used has been observed tho' I must own, even these Expences I have seen appear to be high.' He stressed '[his] Desires that You'll be pleased to be as sparing in these presents as possible'. When he got Johnson's accounts for the costs of the Detroit conference, Amherst complained of the 'prodigious Expence'. Johnson tried patiently to explain: 'In case I did not appear there with a present adequate to the importance of the Embassy, matters would not be so smoothly carried on, & amicably accommodated.' He pointed out that presents were divided among a whole village, and that 'each persons share was but a trifling recompense'.[12]

These protestations were useless, however. Amherst had begun to see the whole business of presents and alliances as essentially a system of blackmail. He felt that His Britannic Majesty was being held to ransom by the implicit threat of a revolt by the savages. As the conqueror of North America, he was not prepared to countenance such threats.

He was happy for Indians who behaved themselves to be treated by the officers who commanded the frontier posts in 'a Steady, Uniform, and Friendly' manner. He was, however, determined that 'Services must be rewarded; it has ever been a maxim with me; but as to purchasing the good behaviour either of Indians, or any Others, is what I do not understand; when men of what race soever behave ill, they must be punished but not bribed.'[13]

The effects of Amherst's policies were quickly felt among an Indian population that had little accumulated fat to live off. His order to keep the Indians 'scarce of Ammunition' was particularly disastrous and self-defeating, since without gunpowder they could not hunt and without the fruits of the hunt they could not trade as he proposed. Johnson warned him:

I am to observe to You Sir, and you may depend upon it, that unless all our Old as well as New Indian Allies are allowed Ammunition for their Livelyhood, or hunting, all Treaties held with, or Presents made to them will never secure their friendship, for they will in such case ever be Jealous of Us, as I find they are a good deal so already, by reason of their not being able to get, or purchase any from Us. – I therefore think it will be absolutely necessary to have it in my power to give them, what I may see requisite.

He added that Indians suspected that the main reason for depriving them of ammunition was that the British were planning to attack them.[14]

These warnings were not abstract. At a council at Fort Johnson in March 1761, the Six Nations, he wrote, 'complain greatly of our breach of promise to them, having told them, before Canada was taken, That, if they would join us against it, we would doe fine things & find that now we want to shake them off'. A Cayuga sachem called 'the Englishman', whose nickname summed up his loyalty to the British, told Johnson that his people, too, were deeply unhappy: 'Their being debarred the use of powder, or the liberty of purchasing it by General Amherst, is the chief cause of their discontent, as they are perishing for the want of it.' The Mohawks, who had always been the keystone of Britain's Indian alliances, were further enraged by a fraudulent land purchase, and Johnson had 'never known the Indians of both Mohawk Castles so uneasy in their Minds'. The Oneidas told Johnson they were 'in a very wretched situation at present, for the want of provisions; that although they were starving . . . their brethren would not give them any provisions.'[15]

Even the Indians who did have enough gunpowder to go hunting were being treated with insolence. The Caughnawagas, whose shift of allegiance to the British had been so useful to Amherst in his campaign against Montreal, complained to Johnson in June 1761 that soldiers fired on their canoes and 'ha[d] taken our meat & what they fancied from us without pay & beat any of our people severely who grumbled'. Johnson's representative in Montreal, Daniel Claus, told him at the end of 1761 of the 'indifferent and dispiteful Eye [the Indians] are looked upon here by the People in Power' and of the 'many ill Usages and Robberies they meet with from the Soldiery etc.' Any time the subject of the Indians arose in conversation among the British officials and soldiers in Canada, he wrote, the attitude was that 'they may be dealt with as we please'. As Claus put it, casting his sceptical Germanic eye on the swaggering British in Montreal, 'We are so intoxicated with providential Success that we will presently stumple over the whole Universe, if no Block should happen to lay in our way.'[16]

The stumbling block was the Indians themselves, of course. Insults and privations were pushing them into revolt and Johnson's diplomacy could avert war only for so long. Even while he was admonishing the western nations for their conspiracies, Johnson privately blamed the British authorities for the growing disaffection among the Six Nations: 'I am sorry to say their late ill behaviour is occasioned in a great measure by our Ill treatment of them in severall respects.' He was concerned 'to have the Management Settled on some one Certain Plan, or footing, as the precarious manner it now Stands will never answer the End Designed, which is the Good of His Majesty's Service, & Extension of his Indian Alliance'.[17]

He was deeply contemptuous of the 'oppression and Ill usage' of the Indians and of the new arrogance that gave rise to it: 'I am surprised to hear that gentlemen of any rank or sense should give themselves Airs now in talking so Slightly of Indians who before would fly before a handfull of them, nay perhaps would do the same now if put to the trial. Those are the kind of people whom the Indians would have least to dread from if they ever were to engage, for brave men would not talk so idly or inconsistently.' His problem was that one of the gentlemen who talked most nonchalantly of the contemptible state of Indian power was his commander-in-chief Amherst.

Johnson's diplomatic system had enhanced and sustained the prestige of older sachems. By giving them presents to distribute and conducting negotiations with them, he had restored some of their traditional authority, which had eroded over time. This system had created a mutual dependency: the sachems needed Johnson to uphold their position; he needed them to exercise influence on his behalf. Now, by cutting off the supply of presents, Amherst undermined this nexus of mutuality. As the older sachems lost influence, the young warriors came to the fore.

A delegation that came to Johnson's house in April 1762 from the Geneseo Senecas was made up entirely of younger warriors. Seeing Johnson's surprise, their speaker declared: 'We the Warriors, were made Choice of to Attend you, & transact business; and I beg you will Consider that we are in fact the People of Consequence for Managing Affairs, Our Sachems being generally a parcell of Old People who say Much, but who Mean or Act very little, So that we have both the power & Ability to Settle Matters.'[18] This was a profound shift in the internal politics of the Indian nations, and it made a violent backlash against British arrogance more likely.

Yet Amherst was confident of the ability of British military force to crush any Indian rebellions. As he assured Johnson, '[Indian] Machinations never gave me a moment's Concern, as I know their Incapacity of attempting anything serious, and that if they were rash enough to venture upon any ill Designs, I had it in my power not only to frustrate them, but to punish the delinquents with Entire Destruction, which I am firmly resolved on, whenever any of them give me Cause.'[19] Johnson couldn't help noticing that his civil, rational commander was growing fond of that phrase 'Entire Destruction'. Amherst used it three times in different letters to Johnson within a week in August 1761. He also liked 'Extirpate them Root & branch'.[20] William Johnson was thus the first person to perceive that in the imagination of Jeffery Amherst rationality and genocide were being linked together as two aspects of the same thing. He wrote of 'cruel necessity'. He even used, in one of these letters, the phrase 'Reduce them to Reason' as a polite euphemism for 'their Entire Destruction'. Johnson now had to realise that the propaganda claims of the French emissaries who had told the Indians that the British would wipe them out after they had won the war were not grotesque lies but genuine possibilities.

24

A Stop to Their Very Being

When it went on display in the Royal Academy Exhibition Gallery on Pall Mall, in London, in April 1771, the crowds who queued excitedly on the street watched as the great personages – Lord Temple, William Pitt, the Duchess of Devonshire – arrived in their carriages and went in to see Benjamin West's epic painting *The Death of General Wolfe*. It was the sensation of the hour, a heart-stopping emblem of the conquest of America. Wolfe was a secular martyr for a Protestant country, a hero who had given his life in the capture of Quebec. In West's colossal canvas, Wolfe dies at the very moment when a messenger is spied on the edge of the picture, coming to announce victory. For public consumption at the heart of the Empire, West's painting *was* the fall of Canada.[1]

Like all such images, it is largely a fiction. The gathering of officers around the dying general, whose body is arranged like the Christ of a *piéta*, is a purely rhetorical gesture. The chaos, confusion and horror of war are transformed into a glorious tableau of sacrifice and triumph.

Yet two elements of West's scenario are especially unreal. While the figures arranged around the dying Wolfe do mostly represent officers who fought with him at Quebec, a place of particular prominence is given to a pair of men who were nowhere near the battle. One is an anonymous, half-naked Mohawk warrior, who hunkers on the ground and contemplates the general's death with the inscrutable expression of a Stoic philosopher. The other, immediately beside the Mohawk, his arm pointing off to the left to announce the arrival of the messenger with the news of victory is an American ranger, dressed half in European and half in Indian costume, his green jacket hung with a belt of wampum, his feet covered with moccasins, his legs wrapped in Indian leggings. For those who came to see the painting and wondered who this half-savage, half-civilised American was, West went out his way to provide a definite identification. On the powder horn that hangs from the wampum belt around the man's shoulder, he inscribed the clearly legible words 'Sr. Wm. Johnson/MOHAWK RIVER'.

West's insertion of Johnson and the Mohawk warrior into his self-consciously mythic painting was not accidental. The elements he used in this part of the canvas were drawn from a set of elements he used in two other paintings of Johnson, also done in the late 1760s. The first, *General Johnson Saving a Wounded Officer from the Tomahawk of a North American Indian*, depicts the by then famous incident of Johnson's rescue of the wounded Dieskau at the battle of Lake George. It turned the story into an allegory of an ideal America. The Mohawk warrior is beautiful, noble and roused by righteous anger, but Johnson's restraining arm – the same arm that points to victory in *The Death of General Wolfe* – calms and controls him. Indian nobility and vigour are fused with the benevolent restraint of European civility to create the perfect temperament for a new continent.

In West's other painting of Johnson, an idealised version of the real man sits serenely in a beautifully stylish costume that combines European and Indian dress. A Mohawk beside him points to the scene of a happy Indian family with, in the background, the great American spectacle of Niagara Falls, alluding to Johnson's victory at Niagara. Johnson's mixed European and Indian outfit in this picture is strikingly similar to that in the Wolfe painting, except that his coat is red rather than green. In his original sketch for the Wolfe painting, however, the coat is also red, showing that West intended to create a visual continuity between the three images.[2]

These paintings are significant, not just as aspects of Johnson's fame, but as evidence of the image he wished to project. The two portraits of Johnson, and perhaps his presence in *The Death of General Wolfe*, are most likely to have resulted from commissions by Johnson himself. His son John was in London, where West was working, from 1765 to 1767. He carried a letter of introduction to General Monckton, whose portrait West also painted. There are references in Johnson's correspondence to the shipping of 'your picture' in 1767.[3] The circumstances point to Johnson's creation of his own visual epic, in which the management of Indian affairs by a wise and benevolent hero of the war against the French creates an ideal America. Not only are the Indians painted back into the picture of British triumph in Canada, but the civilising touch of Johnson's arm guides their energies towards a peaceful future. Like most great propaganda, this imagery arose from terrible evidence that it was not true.

In 1764, in a camp on the Maumee River, west of Detroit in the Ohio country, a sick, cold and half-naked English girl approached the fire at which the Ottawa chief Pontiac was warming himself. Betty Fisher was one of the prisoners in Pontiac's camp. She was just seven years old. She had been sick for some time and the rags she had on were fouled with diarrhoea. She brushed against the Indian leader and soiled his clothes. Pontiac, drunk and bitter, boiled up into a scalding rage. He picked up the child and hurled her into the river. He then ordered two Frenchmen, one of them still very young, to drown Betty Fisher. The two, 'Muchet & young Cuillerie, went in after her and keept her under the water till she was quite Dead and afterwards brought her out and Buried her, or helpt to bury her.'[4] Jeffery Amherst's policies had created the savage Indians of his imagination.

This atrocity had, for William Johnson, a special poignancy. 'Young Cuillerie', who was later charged with Betty Fisher's murder and escaped from prison, was a brother of the beautiful young Angélique with whom Johnson had danced four years before in Detroit. Though he never let her know his 'intentions' towards her, as he had promised, they had stayed on each other's minds. In June 1762 Captain Donald Campbell, who was at the fort, had written to tell him: 'I gave a Ball on the Kings Birthday where a certain acquaintance of yours appeared to great advantage. She never neglects an opportunity of asking about the General, what says she, is there noe Indian Councils to be held here this Summer – I think by her talk Sir William had promised to return to Detroit.'

A year later, after the new commander at Detroit, Henry Gladwin, had evidently passed on some further message from Angélique, Johnson wrote to him: 'I have not forgot the powerfull Effect of the Charms of the Lady who honours me with a place in her remembrance, & should be very happy in any opportunity which might offer of paying her my Devoirs.'[5]

These sweet nothings had given way to violent realities. Angélique's father Antoine Cuillerier, a veteran French trader and Indian diplomat, had been spreading letters claiming to be from the King of France telling the western Indians: 'I only left you for a little while, I am now come again, I have already taken Quebec and the Three rivers, and with Thirty large Ships, have drove Forty English up to Montreal.' At the end of June or the beginning of July 1763, he had been among a group of Detroit's principal French inhabitants who had secretly met with Pontiac and told him: 'They could not fight with him against the English, as they would thereby expose their Wives, and Children to inevitable Ruin, should they not succeed, but that there were above 300 Young men in the [French] Settlement [outside the fort], who had neither parents, or much Property to lose that might and ought to join him.' It was agreed at this meeting that 'The Garrison was to be attacked without by the Savages, and French, and within by the French Inhabitants residing in the Fort.'6

The shattering of Johnson's erotic daydreams about Angélique did show, rather paradoxically, that his grasp on reality had been much firmer than Amherst's. Pontiac's rebellion was, above all, an expression of Indian rage at the breaking of British promises. Before the fall of Canada, Pontiac, with other Ottawa and Delaware chiefs around Detroit, had visited the English forts in the west to ask what treatment they would receive if the French were gone. They had been told 'that all the Rivers were to flow with Rum, – that presents from the Great King were to be unlimited – that all Sorts of Goods were to be in the utmost Plenty, and so cheap, as a Blanket for two Beavers . . . which they told in the Settlement on their return with much Joy'. When British generosity did not match these promises, Pontiac was heard to complain 'and say the English were Liars, which opinion became general . . . so that on the whole they say that all the Promises the English made, were only to blindfold & delude them, for which they had been heard to Say, they would kill all the Liars'. That Gladwin, the commander at Detroit, had a tendency to call the Indians 'Dogs, Hogs, and bid them go out of his house' did not help to quell the rising anger.7

Johnson and Croghan knew from late 1762 that the peace Johnson had made at Detroit the previous year was falling apart. Croghan, at Fort Pitt (previously Fort Duquesne and later the city of Pittsburgh), wrote to Johnson in December: 'The Sinecas, Dellaways & Shawnas has been ploting against his Majesty's Subjects since this Sumer . . . Undoubtedly the Gineral [Amherst] has his own Rason for Nott allowing any presents or ammunision to be given them . . . Butt I take this opertunity to acquaint you that I Dread the Event as I know Indians cant long persevere.'[8] Johnson later received reports of a message from the Senecas and the Cayugas calling on the Indians of Detroit to revolt in the spring. Yet in the midst of all of this, Amherst was ever more obsessive in his efforts to cut back the 'Unnecessary Expenses' of Johnson's Indian department, denying a request for Johnson's friend Richard Shuckburgh to be hired as a secretary, closing a storehouse for Indian goods in Albany, questioning why Johnson employed two interpreters when one would do. Amherst's spite even extended to demanding to know where Johnson got the brass cannon at Fort Johnson that Sir Peter Warren had given him during the frontier guerrilla war of the 1740s.[9]

Johnson himself was distracted for much of 1762 by the unfinished business of a previous Indian revolt. Attacks of the Delawares on the Pennsylvania frontiers had been halted by the Easton treaties of 1757 and 1758 in which the Delaware leader Teedyuscung was promised that Johnson would adjudicate on the legality of the so-called Walking Purchase. Johnson himself now had to go to Easton, Pennsylvania, in the early summer of 1762 to make his decision on whether, as Teedyuscung claimed, the Penn family and the Iroquois had jointly defrauded the eastern Delawares of their lands with the Walking Purchase.

Johnson's position as a judge was in fact rather invidious. Teedyuscung himself acknowledged Johnson's authority, not as a representative of the British, but as 'one of the Chief Counsellors of their Nations, as He was of the Six Nations' – in other words as an Iroquois chief. He declared: 'When I do speak to you I shall put the largest Buck-Horns on your Head, that all the world may know I have spoken to you.'[10] The buck-horns were the sign of a great sachem, and Teedyuscung was cleverly implying that it was in the guise of an Iroquois leader that Johnson came to Easton. As the Iroquois themselves were a party to the dispute, lining up with the Penn family interests against Teedyuscung and the pro-Indian Quakers who advised him, this was a subtle way of questioning his impartiality. Teedyuscung had a point. Knowing that trouble was brewing, Johnson was anxious to keep the Iroquois happy and was never likely to find in Teedyuscung's favour.

The conference was a mess and Johnson's irascible behaviour at it showed the pressure he was under. Teedyuscung was drunk for days on end and his often wild ramblings prompted the Quaker Israel Pemberton to intervene on his behalf. Johnson asked Pemberton 'what right he had to interpose in this matter' and pointed out that even the Governor of Pennsylvania did not presume to interfere. Pemberton replied: 'He was a Freeman, and had as much Right to speak as the Governor.' Johnson, it was later alleged, drew his sword and threatened to run the Quaker through.[11]

The stress of the dispute and of the journey, added to the frustrations of Amherst's disastrous policies, brought on a return of the intestinal complaint that increasingly undermined Johnson's health. The Easton conference was, in any event, essentially irrelevant. In spite of Teedyuscung's pleas, Johnson's assurances and a clear British policy statement to the contrary, white settlers poured into Indian territories, adding to the tensions that continued to rise steadily across the western frontiers. The Delaware prophet Neolin was preaching a new vision of a heaven in which there were Indians but no whites, and his message was heard with increasing eagerness.

The last straw seems to have been the conclusion of a peace treaty between Britain and France in February 1763. The western Indians were quickly aware that the treaty had been signed and that it ceded control of North America to the British. Just a month after the treaty's conclusion, Croghan told Johnson that the Indians around Fort Pitt 'apeard very Jelous of our Growing power Butt Sence I acquainted them of the paice [peace] & Lett them know that all North America was Ceaded to greatt Britian they Seem Much More So'.[12]

The uprising finally began on 27 April 1763 when Pontiac held a council of war with a band of Ottawas, Hurons and Potawatomies ten miles from Detroit. Two days later Amherst was writing to the commander of the fort, Gladwin, that the Indians 'Never can Hurt Us', and to Johnson: 'I cannot think the Indians have it in their Power to Execute any thing against Us, While We Continue to be on our Guard . . . it certainly is not in their Power to Effect any thing of Consequence against Us.'[13] On 9 May, Pontiac's warriors laid siege to Detroit. In the first week, they killed or wounded twenty British soldiers or refugees and took another fifty captive. They then intercepted supply parties, killing or capturing around seventy soldiers, *bateau*-men and civilians. The rising spread fast. Wyandot warriors seized Fort Sandusky on the western side of Lake Erie, fifty miles south of Detroit, while Potawatomies captured Fort St Joseph on the south-eastern shores of Lake Michigan. By the end of the first week in June, Fort Miami (now Fort Wayne, Indiana) Fort Ouiatenon (near Lafayette, Indiana) and Fort Michilimackinac on the strait between Lake Huron and Lake Michigan had all fallen. Fort Edward Augustus at Green Bay, Wisconsin, and the former French forts on the Ohio – Fort Venango, Fort LeBoeuf and Fort Presque Isle – were soon in Indian hands. By the beginning of July, every British post west of Detroit had been taken. Fort Pitt was cut off from its supply bases on the Great Lakes and in Canada.

Amherst, having ignored Johnson's warnings for three years, found it 'difficult . . . to account [for] any causes that can have induced these barbarians to this perfidious attempt'.[14] He responded to the rising by giving vent to the genocidal feelings he had previously intimated to Johnson. Colonel Henry Bouquet, whom Amherst ordered to relieve Fort Pitt, wrote to the commander-in-chief of his hopes to 'extirpate that Vermine from a Country they have forfeited, and with it all Claim to the Rights of Humanity'. To Amherst, the behaviour of these sub-human pests now proved that he had been right all along and that Johnson was wrong. As he wrote to Johnson, 'They can never be considered by us as a people to whom we owe *rewards*; and it would be madness to the highest degree, ever to bestow favors on a race who have so treacherously, and without any provocation on our side, attacked our Posts, and butchered our Garrison. Presents should be given only to those who remain our firm friends.'[15] He did not choose to remember that he had denied them presents even when they were his firm friends.

Bouquet and Amherst concocted the idea of sending the Indians blankets and handkerchiefs impregnated with smallpox. Proposing this biological warfare, Bouquet wrote to the commander-in-chief: 'I will try to inocculate the Indians by means of Blankets that may fall in their hands, taking care however not to get the disease myself. As it is pity to oppose good men against them, I wish we could make use of the Spaniard's Method, and hunt them with English Dogs Supported by Rangers, and some Light Horse, who would I think effectively extirpate or remove that Vermine.' Amherst replied: 'You will Do well to try to Innoculate the Indians by means of Blankets, as well as to try Every other method that can serve to Extirpate this Execrable Race. I should be very glad your Scheme for Hunting them Down by Dogs could take Effect, but England is at too great a Distance [for the importation of dogs] to think of that at present.'[16] Bouquet, implicitly mocking Johnson's approach as Superintendent of Indian Affairs, informed Amherst: 'I have no pretention to be a judge of Indian Affairs, but . . . I would rather chuse the liberty to Kill any Savage that may come in our way, than to be perpetualy doubtful whether they are Friends or Foes.'[17]

Amherst wanted Johnson to understand that the same annihilationist policy would apply to his friends the Six Nations if they were foolish enough to join the rebellion: 'Tis as much their own Interest as Ours to Remain Quiet & Peaceable; Indeed it is more so, for their Commencing Hostilities against Us & Persisting therein might be Attended with the Loss of our Inferior Posts & a few of our People at *first*, but must Inevitably Occasion such Measures to be taken as would Bring about the Total Extirpation of those Indian Nations.' He added a month later that the threat of extermination applied to all Indians: 'I shall only Say, that it Behooves the Whole Race of Indians to Beware (for I Fear the best of them have in some measure been privy to, & Concerned in, the Late Mischief) of Carrying Matters much farther against the English, or Daring to form Conspiracies, as the Consequence will most certainly occasion measures to be taken, that, in the End will put a most Effectual Stop to their very Being.'[18]

The cruelty was not all on the British side. When Indian emissaries to Detroit suggested peace negotiations, Captain Donald Campbell, who had been Johnson's closest friend in the town (he threw the ball at which Johnson met Angélique) and who was the most respected of the officers, left the fort under a flag of truce to treat with Pontiac. He was, instead, taken prisoner. A month later, when the nephew of Wasson, a Chippewa war chief from Saginaw, was killed in a skirmish, Wasson had Campbell tortured to death, and his heart eaten.[19]

There was, indeed, an element of the Indian uprising that mirrored the genocidal fantasies of Amherst and Bouquet. Pontiac and many other Indian leaders were animated by Neolin's vision of a world free of whites. Johnson heard from his spies that the Hurons of Sandusky were saying 'that their Gods tell them they must make War . . . for seven Years, at the end of which by force [or] treachery during that time all the English would be drove away, and that then they would have Peace and not till then'.[20] Johnson's middle ground of cultural, diplomatic and economic exchange was under threat from both sides.

Indian atrocities spurred on Amherst's drive to wipe out his Indian enemies. His underestimation of Indian power and overestimation of his own, however, led to a military stalemate. As Johnson tartly reminded Amherst on the eve of the rebellion, 'I have not represented [the Indians] more formidable than they may appear to be.'[21] Detroit, Fort Pitt and Niagara held out. Bouquet, marching to relieve Fort Pitt, defeated a party of Delawares, Shawnees and Mingos at Bushy Run Creek but lost a quarter of his own force in the process. This was soon followed, moreover, by a stinging defeat of the British at Niagara by the Geneseo Senecas and the Chippewas, who inflicted heavy casualties and gained control of the crucial portage road, blocking attempts to resupply Detroit. By the end of the summer, more than 400 redcoats had been killed, hundreds more were in captivity and perhaps 2,000 civilians had died in Indian attacks along the frontiers from New York to North Carolina.[22]

Johnson reminded Amherst that the uprising was 'what I have often been induced to expect, knowing that [the Indians] will consider friendship as verry trifleing when unattended with Gifts which might bind them by Motives of Interest to preserve peace'. He nevertheless moved to head off the very real possibility of the Six Nations as a whole joining the revolt. Anti-British feeling was running so high even among the Iroquois that one of Johnson's closest Indian friends, Nickus of Oneida, was threatened in his own village, 'as they knew his attachment to me', and came to Johnson's house to seek refuge.[23]

At conferences with Iroquois delegations in July and September 1763 Johnson laid out a simple but powerful appeal to their self-interest. Given the revolt of the western Indians and the troubles of the British, he suggested, the Six Nations had the opportunity to reassert their position as the most favoured of nations. 'You have therefore a happy opportunity now before you (if you will Embrace it) of becoming a greater People, than ever you were, of having all your wrongs redressed, and of attaining to all the priviledges, and Advantages which the British Nation can bestow.' The implication of a more whole-hearted support for Iroquois claims to sovereignty over the western nations was as unmistakable as it was welcome. While Amherst wanted to have no dealings with the Senecas, except 'Shewing them that We Considered them as Infamous Scoundrels', Johnson managed to keep lines of communication open to at least two of the Seneca villages.[24]

Even in the midst of this crisis, however, Amherst was still ordering

Johnson to 'Pay the Strictest Regard to . . . Oeconomy' in his dealings with the Six Nations. Most ludicrously, he even saw a bright side to the bloody revolt he had created: 'The Late defection of so many Tribes, in my opinion, ought to Lessen the Expences in your Department.'[25] It was more obvious than ever, not just that Amherst had learned nothing from his mistakes, but that he didn't even know he had made them.

This final idiocy drew a cutting rebuke. Johnson wrote to Amherst in October denouncing his policy of attempting a military solution to the crisis and puncturing his illusions of success. He reminded him that if Johnson had not succeeded in detaching their Indian allies from the French 'without derogating from the known bravery of our Troops, we might not as yet be in possession of their Country'. He pointed out the difficulty of inflicting a real defeat on the Indians: 'None of their Castles lye open to Surprise, & Should a large body of Men reach one of them, they will most probably find it abandoned, & can only burn a few bark Hutts of small consequence to the Indians, who are everry where at home.' He warned that, if the Six Nations were now antagonised enough to join the rising, 'Nothing that I can at present See, can prevent the destruction of all these Frontiers, & perhaps many places down the Country might share the same fate.' This, he added with bitter sarcasm, 'would be a loss much greater to the public than the expence of conciliateing the affections of all the Northern Indians would amount to'. The cost of Amherst's false economies, he said, 'will amount to such a Sum as will certainly engage Your Excellencys most serious Attention'.

In dealing with the Indians, he went on, 'Friendship and Benevolence cannot be idly disposed of.' Peace would have to be restored through diplomacy and generosity sooner or later so why not now? 'If these advantages can be effected on cheaper terms (and not less honourable) than that arising from a War, & without the loss of Men so severely felt by a Young Country, I flatter myself it will be judged the best Oeconnomy.' As for Amherst's fantasy of genocide, it was not a real alternative to peaceful diplomacy. 'Can we destroy them all? This certainly none will suppose; we may indeed after much expence and loss drive those who are nearest to take Shelter with the Westeren & Northeren Indians, which will but increase their power and hatred, and which our Colonies will frequently feel the effects of.'

Amherst, in reply, continued to rant obtusely about his hopes that 'we shall be able Early in the Spring to put into Execution a proper Plan for reducing the Barbarians as they Deserve'.[26] But Johnson was determined that Amherst would not be around in the spring, and he moved against him in the same way as he had undermined Shirley – by going over the head of the commander-in-chief and appealing to the Board of Trade in London. Pleading 'the disagreeable necessity of pointing out the causes' of the revolt, he sent them a long memorandum arguing that the Indians were an independent, unconquered and formidable people and pointing out the futility of Amherst's policies. They in turn recognised that Johnson was all that stood between Anglo-America and a general Indian revolt which, if it spread through the Six Nations, could virtually undo the British conquest of North America. Essentially, Johnson put his own prestige up against that of the great hero of that conquest.

Johnson won. With George Croghan in London, primarily to seek recompense for his personal losses in the war against France but also to carry Johnson's campaign against Amherst to the heart of power, and Johnson using his connections to Thomas Pownall's brother John, who was secretary to the Board of Trade, the outcome of the conflict was quickly sealed. On 29 September 1763 the Board of Trade wrote to inform Sir William Johnson 'we have little other immediate hope of comfort than what arises from our reliance upon your ability and activity, and the influence you have so deservedly obtained amongst the confederate Nations; and which you at all times exerted with so much zeal and success'. They added, in what amounted to a terse but damning condemnation of Amherst, 'We do entirely agree with you in opinion as to the causes of this unhappy defection of the Indians.'[27]

Amherst was spared the immediate embarrassment of dismissal by being informed politely that his presence was required in London for consultations on military affairs in North America. He left New York in mid-November. Only when he arrived in London did he realise that he had been summoned, not to a celebration of his great achievements in America, but to take the blame for a disaster he still did not understand. Though his formal dismissal would take the best part of a year, Johnson's friends were by then already doing mocking imitations of his grand manner and rejoicing that 'the late, great Commander in Chief ha[d] done for himself'.[28]

25

What the Great Turtle Said

═══

First they built the house of bark and wood, large enough for the whole village to stand inside. Then they drew a circle within it, about four feet in diameter. Here, for the reception of the spirit, they erected the tent of moose-skins hung over a framework of wood and supported by five ten-foot poles, each cut from a different kind of tree. The skins were tied down tightly, but a small part was left unfastened for the shaman to enter. Then, as night fell, fires were kindled around the tent and the whole village assembled inside to wait and listen.

That morning some stranger Indians had arrived at the Chippewa village of Sault Sainte Marie. The Chippewas had joined the Indian revolt in 1763, killing traders and taking part in the capture of Fort Michilimackinac. The strangers had come by canoe from Niagara, and when word of their arrival reached the village, they were invited to a council. After a long silence, one of the strangers produced a belt of wampum and spoke:

My friends and brothers, I am come with this belt from our great father Sir William Johnson. He desired me to come to you, as his ambassador, and tell you that he is making a great feast at Fort Niagara; that his kettles are ready, and his fires lit. He invites you to partake of the feast, in common with your friends the Six Nations, which have all made peace with the English. He advises you to seize the opportunity of doing the same as you cannot otherwise fail to be destroyed; for the English are on the march, with a great army, which will be joined by different nations of Indians. In a word, before the fall of the leaf, they will be at Michilimackinac and the Six Nations with them.

The Chippewas were uneasy at the news and told the ambassadors that they would send deputies to Johnson's feast; but after the strangers had gone, they were unsure what to do, and decided to ask the Great Turtle. So, when night had fallen, when the fires were lit and the village had assembled, the shaman, almost naked, appeared. As he approached the moose-skin tent, the flaps were lifted up so that he could creep in on his hands and knees. As soon as he was inside, the tent began to shake violently and a horrible cacophony of noises began to emerge. Dogs barked; wolves howled; something almost human yelled and roared. There were screams of pain, sobs of anguish, moans of despair. 'Articulate speech was also uttered as if from human lips, but in a tongue unknown to any of the audience.' One of the members of that audience whispered to Alexander Henry, a trader who had been captured in the rising, that these were the voices of 'evil and lying spirits, which deceive mankind'.

There was a sudden and perfect silence. Out of it came a new voice – not loud or harsh, but low and feeble, like the whimpering growl of a young puppy. As soon as they heard it the villagers clapped their hands for joy, because they knew that the Great Turtle, 'the spirit that never lied', had come. Then new sounds came from inside the tent, song after song carried by a range of different voices, none of them that of the shaman. After half an hour of these songs, the shaman's own voice emerged, declaring that the Great Turtle was present and was willing to answer questions.

The headman of the village went silently to the aperture through which the shaman had crawled and gently pushed a large piece of tobacco into the tent as an offering to the spirit. Then he asked the shaman to request from the Great Turtle the answers to two important questions: were the English preparing to make war on the Indians? Were there many troops at Fort Niagara? The tent began to shake so violently that Alexander Henry thought it would collapse. Then a great shout announced that the Turtle had left.

For fifteen minutes, nobody spoke. The villagers waited calmly until the quiet voice of the Great Turtle was heard again, speaking in a language that no one but the shaman could understand. The spirit, the shaman explained, had just crossed Lake Huron and gone to Fort Niagara, then swooped over to Montreal and returned. His answer to the chief's questions was that there was no great number of soldiers at Fort Niagara, but that on his journey up the St Lawrence to Montreal he had seen the river covered with boats and the boats filled with soldiers whose number was like the leaves of the trees.

The chief was troubled and asked a third question: 'If the Indians visit Sir William Johnson will they be received as friends?' The Great Turtle answered: 'Sir William Johnson will fill their canoes with presents; with blankets, kettles, guns, gun-powder and shot, and large barrels of rum, such as the stoutest of the Indians will not be able to lift; and every man will return in safety to his family.' A wave of joy washed over the house outside the tent and dozens of voices cried out: 'I will go too! I will go too!' The English prisoner crawled up to the opening in the tent, placed an offering of tobacco inside and asked the Turtle whether he would ever see his own country again. The Turtle told him to take courage, not to fear any danger, for nothing now would hurt him.

On 10 June 1764 a delegation of sixteen Chippewas left Sault Sainte Marie with their captive and began the journey to Niagara. When they reached Missisaki, they were given a feast and several speeches were addressed to them asking 'that we should recommend the village to Sir William Johnson'. When they got to La Cloche, they found that most of the villagers had already left for Johnson's council, and the travellers from Sault Saint Marie were relieved that they were not 'the first to run into danger'.

On 15 June they reached the village of Point aux Grondines. Their prisoner, Alexander Henry, was cutting some firewood there when he spotted a rattlesnake, four to five feet long, just beside his naked legs, coiled and with its head raised to strike. He ran to his *bateau* to get his gun, but when he returned the Chippewas had surrounded the snake. They knew it was a manito-kinibie – a rattlesnake-spirit sent to meet them. They lay down beside it and gently blew tobacco smoke towards it, calling it 'Grandfather' and apologising for the ignorant Englishman – whom they protested was no relation of theirs – and his wicked intention to kill it. Henry was astonished to see that the snake 'stretched itself along the ground in visible good humour' while they talked to it. It stayed like that for quite a while, then slowly began to move away. The Indians followed it, still calling it 'Grandfather', and pleading with it 'to take care of their families during their absence and to open the heart of Sir William Johnson so that he might show them charity and fill their canoe with rum'. A week later they disembarked near Fort Niagara, painted themselves in their brightest colours to show their peaceable intent, and paddled on in hope and anxiety towards Johnson's council, singing the song they sang in times of danger.[1]

As soon as Amherst's ship had sailed for London, in November 1763, Johnson dispensed with the general's orders that no peace talks were to take place until the barbarians had been made to suffer. Amherst's departure had placed Johnson back in effective control of Indian policy. The acting commander-in-chief, General Thomas Gage, was stolid and relatively unimaginative, but he was sharp enough to know that Johnson had helped to bring down his predecessor and was seen by London as the man who could resolve the crisis. There was a general understanding that Amherst's dismissal meant official approval of Johnson's approach. As the Acting Governor of New York, Cadwallader Colden, put it to Johnson in January 1764: 'It gives me great pleasure to find that your measures have received an approbation so very honourable to you. It is a misfortune that Sir Jeffery Amherst when he went from this place did not seem to agree in the same Sentiments with you.'[2]

Gage, catching the drift, acknowledged to Johnson around the same time: 'The Indian Nations . . . have acted upon principles of policy which would have excited more enlightened Nations, to have taken Measures, tho perhaps better concocted, of the same nature.'[3] More important, he agreed to Johnson's plan to kindle a council fire at Fort Niagara in July. As soon as the spring thaw set in, Johnson sent ambassadors all over the *pays d'en haut* with messages and wampum belts like the ones that reached the Chippewas of Sault Sainte Marie in early June.

The unsettled state of things made the journey to Niagara dangerous, and Johnson, who had previously brushed aside warnings of peril, this time took two dozen soldiers, partly 'to make some appearance with the Indians, but more so for my own Security, as many of the Straggling Delawares, Mississagaes etc. who all know of my intended Journey, and are greatly Irritated against me, might be induced to way lay me'.[4] His apprehensions were undoubtedly increased when some delegates from the rebellious Geneseo Senecas came to his house to put out feelers for a peace. While they were there, the pro-British Seneca sachem Onoghsoghte arrived to warn Johnson that the Geneseos 'had declared that they would murder Sir William at the present Meeting, and had pitched upon two Men for that purpose whom he then named'.[5] The Geneseos in question then fled, and though Johnson sent constables after them, they do not seem to have been caught.

On his progress to Niagara for the conference, the Mohawk sachems took him aside and warned him that the Geneseos 'were still ill disposed and determined to make use of treachery, if possible at Niagara, and begged he wou'd be on his guard'. He also heard from Detroit that the Hurons of Sandusky had stated mockingly that 'they were very sorry that Sir William was coming here, as they imagined by that he wanted to leave his Bones there'.[6]

The risk was worth taking, however. Johnson needed a big set-piece event to demonstrate that his peace policy could work and to re-establish himself as the master of Indian diplomacy across the whole vast stretch of the northern colonies. A council at Fort Johnson, now established as the meeting place of the Six Nations, would not have this effect. By showing his pulling power beyond his own familiar domain, Johnson could re-establish, for both the British and the Indians, that he was indispensable.

The response was enormous. Johnson reckoned that the assembly at Fort Niagara, numbering more than 2,000 people, was 'the largest Number of Indians perhaps ever Assembled on any occasion'. There was even a delegation from the Shekonijkamynanee from the far north near Hudson's Bay, who travelled for 150 days to get there. Some of the more distant nations, for whom Warraghiyagey was a mythic, unseen figure, came to see him as they would a king or a god. One brought him a blanket – 'to serve you for a Bed; – You see how white it is: – My Heart is as white – and quite free from any evil Thought' – and presented him with an Indian slave.[7]

The gathering of such disparate and far-flung nations, many of whom had taken no part in the great revolt of 1763, showed the effect of Johnson's name within Indian societies around and beyond the Great Lakes. He now had two utterly different webs of fame. As Sir William, he cut a figure in polite and educated conversation in Europe, known to readers of the *Gentleman's Magazine* in London, and discussed by the *philosophes* of the Enlightenment in Paris. In 1760, for example, the Baron de Dieskau, back in Paris after his release from captivity, had given Denis Diderot a long account of the incident after the battle of Lake George in which Johnson had rescued him from the Iroquois. The story, in turn, influenced Diderot's reflections on civilisation and savagery in his *Histoire des Deux Indes* and *Supplement aux Voyage de Bougainville*.[8]

At the same time, as Warraghiyagey, Johnson had become, as

Alexander Henry's account of the reception of his messages in Sault Sainte Marie suggests, a strange and uncertain presence, a liminal being somewhere between the real and the imagined, capable of either harm or benevolence, analogous to the spirits and manitous who could curse or bless the Indians.

This feeling was no more irrational or naive than the versions of Johnson that circulated in the great cities of England and France. Distance, for the sophisticates in the coffeehouses, lent enchantment, and Johnson acquired for them an exotic allure. Distance, for the exposed and fragile village societies of the *pays d'en haut*, lent anxiety. The unknown was sometimes a source of rare benevolence that would magically fill their canoes with presents, but more often a source of malign energy. Promises of canoes filled to overflowing often turned out to be cruel lies. Their plea to the rattlesnake manitou to open the heart of Sir William Johnson was a prayer to the forces of inscrutable fortune that they might, for once in a while, act kindly.

Johnson had this power, not by magic, but because his house was a crossroads where different kinds of knowledge met and conversed. Just as his image was radiating outwards in radically different directions, so echoes of information came back to him from many points on the compass. He got books, newspapers and letters from London and New York, so he knew, as the Indians could not, how their story might fit with the larger pattern of European power, whether they were a footnote to the great narrative or a central and suspenseful chapter read with great intensity; but he also knew things about them that they thought were secret. With his ever-flowing stream of informants, tapping into the internal divisions and manoeuvres of the Indian villages, he could watch the tides and currents of opinion from a vantage point that no isolated village sachem, however acute, could ever reach. He could put their behaviour in context and tell it back to them with an eerie ring of truth.

The texture of this relationship was captured a year after the Niagara conference by Daniel Claus, writing from Montreal, a place where Johnson had not been since he had helped to capture it five years before. Picking up the sentiments of some Caughnawagas who had been to Johnson's house, where he had admonished them for some apparent breach of faith, Claus wrote: 'They are notwithstanding convinced within themselves that you have hit their real Sentiments, and told them truth, as I was since informed they were all amazed how you could know the things you reproached them with, thinking you must have a supernatural insight of their Sentiments.'9

The Great Turtle, who had conversed with this fellow denizens of the supernatural world, had not lied to the Chippewas. Johnson brought with him to Niagara a vast quantity of presents, worth the then phenomenal sum of £38,000 sterling. He also spent £25,000, in New York currency, feasting and maintaining the vast crowd for over a month.10 The atmosphere was cordial, with rum flowing freely, and the terms Johnson offered were not especially onerous: the return of white captives, severing relations with those Indians who remained hostile, compensating traders whose stocks had been destroyed in the uprising, guaranteeing the future safety of traders, and submitting future disputes to the ultimate wisdom of Sir William Johnson. Pushed forward in 'private Meetings with the several Northern, and Western Indians at which more was done than at the publick ones' and at which Johnson's personal charm could be at its warmest, this set of demands proved broadly acceptable.

One Chippewa chief announced that on Sir William's arrival 'the Lakes became placid, the Storms ceased and the Whole face of Nature was changed'. The Hurons of Detroit declared: 'Our Children yet unborn, will Remember, and be thankful for this good Work.' Johnson for his part promised: 'No Ill Disposed People will ever be suffered into your Country, nor any lies told you to blind your Eyes, whilst they Stole your Furrs – the English will deal fairly with you – they will treat you kindly, and trade with you honestly. You will grow Rich, and happy, and your Brothers Contented, so that our Union cannot be shaken.'11

The most significant achievement was the formal submission of the Francophile Geneseo Senecas, the very ones who had earlier planned to assassinate him. They delivered ten prisoners to Johnson. Johnson was notably harder on them than on the other nations, probably because the revolt of a part of the Iroquois confederacy had been more damaging to his personal prestige than that of Indians who had not previously been under his influence. Johnson made them agree to give up land on both sides of the Niagara portage, thus securing for the British control of a vital transportation corridor. With the conclusion of a deal, however, their speaker declared that he had now taken up a Pine Tree 'and under its Roots, we bury the Bones of your People that were killed, so that they may never more appear either in your Sight, or ours . . . I now take up a large Smooth Stone with which I cover the Crack made by the taking up the Tree, so that it can no more appear.'[12]

Perhaps as a gesture of apology for the plan to assassinate him, the Geneseos then offered him a remarkable personal present: 'all the Islands in the Streight from the Great Falls to Lake Erie, as a return for the great trouble they had repeatedly given me'. Johnson declined to accept the gift on the grounds that 'those Islands [were] within the District secured by the Treaties in 1701 and 1726 to the Indians, and their posterity'.[13] The offer nevertheless suggested that the hole in which the dead were buried had indeed been covered by a large smooth stone.

The success of the Niagara council did not mean that the war was over, however. Gage had ordered Colonel John Bradstreet to lead a force down from Niagara to Detroit, chastising, along the way, those Indians still in arms. In the Ohio country, Colonel Henry Bouquet had orders to march westwards from Fort Pitt and attack the centres of resistance in the valleys of the Muskingum and Scioto Rivers. There was a crucial difference, however, between these expeditions – especially Bradstreet's – and those planned the previous year by Amherst before his departure. Johnson had successfully insisted that the armies should have large Indian contingents with them.

Johnson's aims in organising Indian war parties to accompany the expeditions against the still-recalcitrant nations were twofold. One was to demonstrate in a tangible way the restoration of the British–Indian alliance, and thus, paradoxically, to encourage a general peace. The campaign against Montreal in 1760 had shown how effectively an Indian war party could act, in fact, as a diplomatic mission. At the very least the presence of large numbers of Indians alongside the Anglo-American armies would discourage attacks. As Johnson told Gage, 'The Sight of an Army accompanied by a body of Indians at a time when [Pontiac's] Gang are probably in want of Supplys, will I hope check any hostile designs they may have conceived.' He expected the Shawnees and the Delawares to be likewise 'Staggered at the Indians Joining our Troops, & probably [to] make all necessary Submissions'.

The other, subtler aim was finally to defuse Amherst's attempt at a race war in which civilised whites would destroy Indian barbarians. He reminded Gage, using Amherst's favourite phrase, that 'A Total

Extirpation appears to be neither in our power nor for our Interest' and that therefore the western Indians, 'who have tasted the French favours can [n]ever be hearty friends until by a like treatment we establish ourselves in their Esteem'. There could not therefore be a merely imposed solution. By making the conflict one in which Indians would fight on both sides, he would make its eventual settlement one in which Indians would have a stake.

In this regard, it is significant that when he declared this war among the Indians in April 1764, he did so in an ostentatiously Indian manner. At the culmination of a large conference with the Six Nations, including some still-wavering Senecas, he 'invited all the Nations to the War Feast prepared on the present Occasion, at which he Sung his *War Song*, declaring War in a Solemn Manner against the Shawanese, and Delawares, and any other Nation who might join them, which was followed by the Senecas, and all the Nations present in the most solemn Manner, and Continued the whole night'. Later, when he was bringing the Caughnawagas into his Indian forces, he also adopted this ritual: 'After recommending it to them in the most strong manner to exert themselves as men on the present Occasion, Sir William then threw them the bloody *Belt*, stood up, and sung his *War Song* with Hans Croyne,' the latter a 'whiteish Indian living at the Mohoks'.[14]

These explicitly Indian rituals were matched by an attempt to educate the British in the protocols of Indian culture. Whereas Amherst and Bouquet had imagined the Indians as beasts and devils, Johnson took the opportunity of the expeditions to teach his colleagues some manners.

When Bradstreet called at Fort Johnson as he passed up the Mohawk with his army in mid-June 1764, Johnson instructed him in the etiquette of dealing with his Indian allies:

It will be necessary on Seeing the Indians to address them with affability & make a short speech to them, expressing [your] satisfaction at seeing so many of them assembled . . . To See that they are properly cloathed, & armed, also victualled plentifully, with a Dram likewise Morning & Evening . . . That as the Indians have their own particular customs, & have been used to frequent councils etc. from the beginning, they may frequently express a desire to speak to the Commanding officer, on which occasion, if they are some times indulged with a patient hearing they will act with greater ardour & spirit . . . That whenever any unexpected or sudden movement is made, they may be always told of it in form, & some reasons assigned for so doing, this is of the highest importance & cannot be safely neglected.[15]

While Amherst had seen the expeditions as a tool for hammering the savages, Johnson also saw them as a chance to civilise the whites.

In Bradstreet's case, however, Johnson failed. Because of the success of the Niagara council and the presence in his ranks of 500 Iroquois, Caughnawaga and Chippewa warriors recruited by Johnson, Bradstreet's march was something of a triumphal progress, with offers of peace coming from every direction. All this submission went to his head, however, and he made an appalling mistake.

The most glaring absentee from Johnson's Niagara conference had been Pontiac. Shortly before it, Johnson noted: 'Pondiacs Spirit Seems only to have been Stifled for a time, but not fully Subdued,' yet during it he was optimistic that the Ottawa leader was both isolated and ready to come to terms. 'Pontiac is now with about 300 Men some distance up the Miamis [Maumee] River, but has expressed his desire of makeing peace, finding himself deserted by so many of his People, but he has not as yet Attempted to come in, apprehensive probably that he might be ill treated.' Bradstreet was likewise confident by the end of August that Pontiac '[was] to be given up to be sent down to the Seacoast & maintain'd at His Majesty's Expence the Remainder of his days'.[16]

Pontiac was indeed a waning force after the collapse of his siege of Detroit in October 1763 and the drunken despair in which he had murdered Betty Fisher. He therefore sent a wampum belt to Bradstreet at Detroit, offering peace. Bradstreet, utterly underestimating the power of symbolism and protocol in Indian culture, took up a hatchet, smashed the belt and ordered the pieces to be thrown into the river. To do this in public and with such evident relish was a stunning insult, not just to Pontiac, but to the Indians in general.

As a furious Johnson noted when he heard of the incident, 'His cutting to peices with a Tommohawk at a public meeting a Belt of Wampum which he was spoke to with, greatly incensed all the Indians and made them look upon him in a verry strange light.' The Seneca sachem Sough'na'egy, who described himself as Pontiac's 'intimate friend', confirmed the disastrous impact of Bradstreet's gesture. Pontiac, he told Johnson shortly afterwards , was a 'man of the greatest Influence amongst all the Nations to the Westward, and Southward' and was now 'greatly incensed against Col Bradstreet for cutting his Belt of Wampum to pieces with an Ax, which he

Pondiac look'd upon as a Threat, or Challenge, though he meant well by sending it. – as are also all the Nations who heard of the rash Action.'As Johnson also remarked, Bradstreet's insult might have made some sense if he had then gone and *attacked* the Ottawa leader, but since Bradstreet had nothing to offer but a crude insult, Pontiac 'must think little of us'.[17]

Johnson found, moreover, that Bradstreet had ignored his instructions for the courteous treatment of the Indian warriors who accompanied him. As the warriors returned 'half Starved & all naked' and complained to him, he drew up a detailed indictment of Bradstreet. It is a photographic negative of Johnson's own careful conduct in the campaigns against the French, and as such an unconscious description of the reasons for his own success as a leader of Indian warriors.

The vainglorious Bradstreet had treated the Indians with contempt. He set off from camp without telling them in advance. He left behind warriors who had gone to hunt, so that they arrived at Detroit 'half Starved'. Asked by some of the Indian leaders how they were going to get onto crowded boats, he replied, 'Swim and be damned.' He stated in front of them that he wondered 'what they were brought here for & whether it was to make a Parade'. He failed to have proceedings with the Ottawas translated for the Six Nations warriors so that when he ordered the two sets of Indians to shake hands because they were now friends, the latter replied that 'that was more than they knew, as they did not understand a word passed between him & them'. Some of the Iroquois were so enraged that when they finally got back to Niagara, having been forced to walk for days without provisions, they attacked the British guards on the Niagara portage.

This attitude to the Indians outraged Johnson sufficiently for Bradstreet to succeed Shirley and Amherst to the dangerous title of his number one enemy, and he denounced his 'flighty and unsettled disposition', 'ill natured' behaviour, 'rash and bad Policy', 'odd and fickle' conduct, 'obstinacy', and 'Ridiculous Orders' to his commanding officer, Gage.[18]

Above all, Johnson was furious that the chance of a general peace had again been thrown away by arrogance and ignorance. Johnson was sure that Pontiac 'might certainly have been brought to terms' but for Bradstreet's insult. Instead, Pontiac's campaign was revitalised and his standing among the Indians was restored. He moved into the villages of the Wabash and Illinois country and the effect of his charismatic presence was profound. George Croghan told Johnson that Pontiac commanded more respect among the Wabash Indians 'than any Indian I ever saw could do among his own Tribe'. Gage reported to Johnson: 'The Savages there were well dispos'd 'till Pondiac arrived . . . [and] undid in one night' the work of pacification that had been going on 'for Eight Months'.

Gage then summed up for Johnson the dilemma they both faced. On the one hand, Pontiac's intelligence and reputation would make his submission the signal for a general peace. On the other, Pontiac's known crimes, like the murder of Betty Fisher and the betrayal of Donald Campbell – both of which touched Johnson in a personal way – made it difficult to embrace him without looking weak. As Gage put it, 'This fellow shou'd be gained to our Interest, or knocked in the head. He has great Abilities, but his Savage Cruelty destroys the regard we should otherwise have for him . . . He would be glad of peace, if he could hope to be forgiven, but He thinks he has been guilty of too many Cruelties.'[19]

Though he did not yet realise it, Pontiac's great achievement had been the restoration of Sir William Johnson. The Indian revolt had not been powerful enough to destroy British America, but the Anglo-Americans were not powerful enough to defeat the wider rebellion. The need for compromise and mediation was gradually becoming clear to both sides. This was Johnson's territory, and he was now a more pivotal figure than ever. Both the Indians and the British needed him to make peace.

Yet, less obviously, Johnson also needed Pontiac. It was not just that the revolt which Pontiac symbolised had given Johnson back the power and prestige that had been ebbing from him after the fall of Canada. Amherst's policies had destroyed the structures of authority through which Johnson had always worked. Without presents and diplomacy, the prestige of the old sachems had been shattered. As Donald Campbell's killer, Wasson, put it in September 1764: 'Now the Young people have the direction of Affairs.'[20] The young warriors, however, lacked the diplomatic skills and the wider authority to create or sustain a durable peace. Even when they appointed older men to speak for them, those they chose were not necessarily veteran negotiators. At the Niagara council, the man who spoke for the Ottawas apologised to Johnson for his awkwardness in the presentation of their case: 'I hope you will Excuse my Ignorance, being an Old Man chosen by the Young People.' The war leaders were so internally divided that, at a conference held by George Croghan in Fort Pitt in the spring of 1765, two Delaware warriors quarrelled openly and 'stabb'd each other, in such a manner that their Lives [were] despaired of.'[21]

Johnson would have to find, or if necessary invent, a figure to represent Indian power. The more strongly the diverse Indian revolt came to be identified as Pontiac's rebellion, the more inevitable it was that this figure would have to be the man who murdered Betty Fisher and betrayed Donald Campbell.

26

Many Civil Things

═══

Early in 1765 Johnson sent George Croghan into Illinois country to reopen trade and send peace feelers out to Pontiac. After a successful conference with the Shawnees, ten of their sachems accompanied Croghan down the Ohio River. While Pontiac waited to receive Johnson's emissary, Croghan's party was attacked by eighty Kickapoo and Mascouten warriors. Johnson received word from Detroit: 'We have two very plausible accounts of Col. Croghan's being assasinated on the Ohio.' One French informant even reported seeing Croghan's detached scalp being shown around.

In fact, though three of the Shawnees and two of Croghan's porters were killed, Croghan took a hatchet wound to the head but survived. He was captured and taken 250 miles upriver, where his captors, having second thoughts about the wisdom of starting a new war against both the Shawnees and the British, asked him to arrange peace talks. Croghan, recovering from his wounds, made light of his horrible experience, telling Johnson: 'I got the Stroke of a Hatchet on the Head, but my Scull being pretty thick, the hatchet would not enter, so You may see a thick Skull is of Service on some Occasions.' His near-death experience had in fact been a catalyst, for a settlement. As he wrote to Johnson, with his unique orthography temporarily improved by the blow to his head, 'I am perswaded this unluckey affair has been of More Service then any presents or Speechess I Could have Made to them.'[1]

Pontiac, who had been losing prestige to the Shawnee war chief Charlot Kaské, took the opportunity of this turn towards peace to make his own overtures and place himself back in a position of leadership. Realising that his best hope of retaining his status now lay in his ability to project himself as a suitable partner for Johnson in peace negotiations, he transformed himself from cruel, irascible and violent war leader to calm, civilised sachem. Alexander Fraser, who fell into his hands in the Illinois country, wrote to Johnson that Pontiac was 'the most sensible Man among all the Nations, and the most humane Indian I ever saw, he was as careful of me, and my men, as if we were his own Children, and has twice saved my life since I came here'.

This new disposition was all about making himself a middleman, a conciliator and negotiator who could deal with his white counterpart on equal terms. Johnson heard from Croghan: 'Pondiac has Greatt Sway Amoungst those Nations and is on his Way hear. He Sent Me a Mesidge . . . that he wold be Glad to See Me and that if he Licked what i had to Say he wold Do Every thing in his power to Reconcile all Nations to the English as he is an old Acquaintance of Mine I hope I shall be able to Setle Matters with him on a Good footing.' When Pontiac eventually met Croghan, he gave the Irishman a pipe, which he asked him to send 'to Sir William Johnson that he may know I have made peace'.[2]

In the spring of 1766 Johnson, in return, offered to meet Pontiac at Fort Ontario, beside Oswego, along with delegations from the Twightwees, Chippewas, Ottawas, Hurons and Potawatomies. His hopes for a final peace were threatened, however, by a spate of murders of Indians by white settlers. Johnson complained to Gage, for example, that '2 Soldiers having straggled from a party at Riviere Rouge near Detriot ravished a Squaw for which they were both put to Death by the Womans Husband & the rest, that Lieutenant Colonel Campbell had Sent out a party who seized two Indians, & that in the scuffle an Indian Child was killed'.

Johnson protested, as he had done many times before, that the unwillingness of the colonial authorities to punish crimes against Indians in the way 'they so Justly deserve[d], as well in a legal as political sense', made it impossible for him to 'counteract such proceedings, or preserve Tranquillity'. His immediate fear was that the crimes and subsequent reprisals 'may prevent Pondiac from coming down', but he was, as he put it to Benjamin Franklin, in 'daily dread [of] a Rupture with the Indians occasioned by the Licentious Conduct of the frontier Inhabitants who continue to Rob, and Murder them'. When he heard that Pontiac was nevertheless making his way to Fort Ontario, he sent ahead with orders 'to receive & treat them kindly 'till my arrival, as from the Accounts of Murders daily committed by our people they cannot be in a very good humour'.3

Johnson's apprehensions about Pontiac's nervousness were justified. When he and the other chiefs arrived at Fort Erie on their way to Oswego, they heard shots which were being fired at pigeons and thought they were to be 'massacred'. Johnson's instructions were obeyed, however, and Pontiac soon declared that the British were his brothers '& that they did not intend to kill him'. Pontiac, indeed, was as much a danger to his fellow chiefs as the British were. At Detroit, on the journey, he stabbed one of his party, an Illinois principal chief.4

Johnson made his way wearily to Oswego 'in a very indifferent Condition for a Journey, having had an attack of my disorder Just before setting out'. He had, indeed, been reluctant to travel at all because of his ill health, but Pontiac was insistent that his final peace be made with Johnson.5

At the conference, held during the last week of July 1766, Pontiac and Johnson enacted an elaborate version of the Catholic ritual of Confession. Johnson, as the confessor, offered 'the great lenity and kindness of your English father who does not delight in punishing those who repent sincerely of their faults'. Pontiac, as the penitent, 'candidly declared what Steps he had taken in the late rupture' and told Johnson that he would deliver his war belt to him. Johnson urged that Pontiac and the others would trust him to send them interpreters, smiths and a regulated trade, and to ensure that whites who committed crimes against Indians would be punished.

He asked them to turn their eyes to the east, towards Johnson Hall, 'where you will always find me your sincere friend'. Pontiac took Johnson by the hand, addressed him as Father, and declared it 'the will of the Great Spirit that we should meet here today'. With detailed agreements on the conduct of trade and distribution of ample presents, the two men parted with a satisfactory peace concluded and a formal end put to a six-year insurgency.6

For Johnson and Pontiac, though, the treaty had very different meanings. With the securing of peace Johnson's reputation as the ultimate Indian diplomat was secure and his prestige was higher than ever. For Pontiac, however, the outcome was tragic. The threat of violence, and Johnson's eagerness to avert it, had been Pontiac's last card. Without it, he had no real power. His achievement had been very real, but it was Johnson who gained most. Pontiac, and the wider insurgency of which he had become the symbol, had forced the British to take the Indians seriously as a living force on the continent. The uprising had brought down Amherst and nullified, for the time being, his notion of complete submission or complete destruction as the only viable alternatives for Indians. It had restored Johnson and his careful, respectful and culturally sensitive approach, to the centre of colonial policy. Once that was done, Pontiac could do no more.

He himself fell into the trap of playing up to Johnson's need for a single dominant chief whose assent to a treaty would mark the end of the war. Pontiac had been so flattered by Johnson's anxiety to deal with him that, at the Fort Ontario conference, he declared himself virtual king of the West, claiming that he 'spoke in the name of all the Nations to the Westward whom I command'.7 This was both untrue and dangerous. Pontiac was a famous and charismatic figure, but his prestige was fluctuating and continually contested, and the western Indians who had fought on and off for the previous decade to assert their independence did not take kindly to claims of command. After the conference, Normand MacLeod at Fort Ontario heard rumours already afloat that Pontiac was being paid ten shillings a day by the British and that this was creating a resentment among the Indians 'that will end in his ruin'. A Frenchman offered MacLeod a bet that Pontiac 'would be killed in less than a year, if the English took so much notice of him'.8

The Frenchman would have lost his bet, but only because his timing of Pontiac's downfall was somewhat askew. Pontiac wanted to build on his relationship with Johnson, seeing it as his best hope for acceptance as a powerful figure in the politics of the British alliance. In January 1767 Pontiac sent a message to Johnson to say that he would visit him at Johnson Hall in the spring, but the visit never happened.9 The fragmentary communications Johnson had from him chart a rapid decline into penury and fractiousness.

In early August 1767 Pontiac was sending messages to say that 'he had no corn & that he was going a hunting to try get wherewith to purchase his necessarys' but still promising that 'in the Spring he would go down [to Sir William] Johnson'. Later that month Pontiac was denouncing one of his own nephews as a 'lying treacherous Villain' and promising that when he visited Johnson he would 'beg pardon for him'. He was also apparently haunted by the murder of Betty Fisher, asking that Angélique's young brother, whom he had involved in the killing, 'be pardon[ed] in case caught'.10

By 1768 he had fallen out with the Ottawas and gone to the Illinois country, whose inhabitants had probably not forgotten that he had stabbed one of their chiefs at Detroit on the way to meet Johnson. In April 1769 he accompanied the nephew of an Illinois chief to a trading post in the French settlement of Cahokia. As they left the store, his companion clubbed Pontiac from behind, stabbed him and left him to die on the road.

The irony was that, even as Pontiac was spinning downwards towards irrelevance and an ignominious death, Johnson was being acclaimed for his achievement in bringing the apparently all-powerful war chief to an accommodation. Johnson's prestige was now such that by January 1767 he was being congratulated by his friends on his elevation to the peerage. The rumours were unfounded, but Johnson had hopes that they were merely 'premature'. Other false rumours were that Johnson was to be made a Knight of the Garter, that he was to be a member of the Order of the Bath and that his son John was to be made governor of one or other of the American colonies. The one actual honour that did descend on the family was bestowed on John. Johnson had sent his son to London in 1765 'to acquire some knowledge of the World, and wear off that Rusticity which must accompany the Actions of a Young Man, whose Life has been chiefly spent on the frontiers of *America*'.[11] John was personally received by King George III, who engaged him in a long conversation about his father, the Indians and America, and then 'knighted him immediately on the spot'.[12]

With his prestige at its zenith, Johnson was sure that 'there never [would] again be so favourable an opertunity' to establish his Indian department on a permanent footing according to his own ideas. This would involve a strict regulation of trade to ensure a fair deal for the Indians, the appointment of commissaries and smiths at all the main forts and trading posts to serve the Indians' interests, and the use of 'Upright Dealings & Pacific Conduct' to persuade the Indians that 'we do not intend to disturb their Libertys, or possessions'.[13] Above all, though, his plan involved an ambitious attempt to define, once and for all, the grounds on which whites and Indians would meet.

27

An Imaginary Line

In 1760, when Warren Johnson had visited his brother William, one of
the things he noticed on the frontier settlements was that 'Some People
have an Indian's Skin for a Tobacco Pouch.'[1] The lurking contempt
many back-country settlers felt for Indians was brought to the surface
during the subsequent decade by the Indian rebellions, which seemed
to confirm the ineradicable savagery of the natives. Ironically, the
gradual establishment of peace allowed these feelings to be expressed
anew in vengeful assaults. For Johnson, the settlers who were pushing
ever further into Indian territory took on the characteristics that the
settlers themselves attributed to the Indians. He saw them as wild,
lawless, savage people who failed to fight when there was a war but
who now took out their resentments in unprovoked attacks on
defenceless Indians.

Johnson understood that honour and revenge were powerful forces
in Indian life. While most whites tended to see Indian lives as cheap,
he believed that in their small and intimate societies, each death was
felt even more strongly than it would be in a European community. He
wrote to General Gage in April 1767: 'As the Life of an Individual is
of much more consequence to them than those of Ten in our
Estimation, their thirst for Revenge is without bounds.'[2] His great fear
was that the need within Indian culture for murders to be avenged
would create a vicious circle of vengeance and retaliation that could
spiral into another general uprising. The murder of a Mohawk by a
settler in January 1766, for instance, prompted him to express his anxiety that 'this Spirit, which has so often shown itself of late amongst
the Inhabitants, will not stop here, and that this ill-timed rage of theirs
must doubtless rouse the resentments of a People prone to Revenge'.

His own efforts to bring peace would come to nothing if settlers confirmed the worst fears of the Indians, who had long suspected that the Europeans were plotting to destroy them: 'Had this been the first or second Instance, I might have pacifyed the Injured, but at present I am somewhat at a Loss how to speak to, or take upon me to promise them a Redress.' His own credibility with the Indians was being continually undermined, as his promises of protection and redress were 'daily contradicted by these Unjustifiable Actions'. He felt it 'almost unsafe for me to continue my assurances of redress, for where will this redress come from, or will it come at all?'3

He knew these questions were rhetorical. Johnson's sympathies in these disputes lay with the Indians. The Mohawk in this incident, he wrote, was 'causelessly and treacherously murdered by a White man'. He was depressed by the failure of the colonial legal system to bring to justice the perpetrators of crimes against Indians. 'Neither our Laws, nor our People are much Calculated for redressing Indians and we are in the utmost want of some method for doing them effectual Justice without leaving it to the decision of those whose prejudices will not permit them to see the necessity there is for relieving them in these cases.'4

Johnson saw the back-country settlers, many of them so-called 'Scotch-Irish' Presbyterians from Ulster, in much the same way as Gaelic landowners and their bards in Ireland had traditionally seen these incomers. He painted them as wild, crude and uneducated. He called them 'these Ignorant People', 'banditti', 'Country People, who think they do good Service when they Knock an Indian in the Head', 'the very dregs', 'low', 'Idle Persons' who were not 'under Landlord or Law', 'persons worse than savages'. He accused them of 'Anarchy', 'riotous Conduct', and 'turbulency'.5

These complaints were rational enough, but their edge was sharpened by inherited Irish prejudices. The Catholic Jacobite poets of Johnson's youth and his parents' prime railed against lower-class Presbyterian settlers in exactly the same terms, calling them 'the crafty, thieving, false set of Calvin', 'the contemptuous brood', 'churls', 'stupid people', a 'blind ignorant crew'. Like Johnson, those poets characterised the newcomers as an anarchic threat to the old-established hierarchical social order. It is especially striking that Johnson linked his distaste for the Scotch-Irish settlers who were streaming into the backlands of Pennsylvania and Ohio with a lament for the loss of

the Jesuit missionaries, who had a complex and sophisticated understanding of Indian culture. The Jesuits, he told the Board of Trade,
were 'men of spirit, Abilities and a knowledge of the World'. The
British Protestant missionaries who had taken their place were, on the
other hand, 'well meaning but Gloomy people' who had no sympathy
for Indian culture and wished to 'abolish at once their most innocent
Customs, Dances, Rojoycings'.6 It is not hard to see in these views significant if unconscious vestiges of a world-view imported from
Ireland.

The depth of feeling was such that Johnson and the commander-in-
chief Thomas Gage, to whom Johnson frequently aired his views on
the subject, both came to feel privately that Indians were quite justified
in killing settlers who perpetrated serious crimes against them. Johnson felt that 'Englishmen who so wantonly Continue to Violate public
Treatys, regardless of the Consequences to their Neighbours, scarcely
deserve pity'. Gage, reflecting on an incident near Fort Pitt in which
two white men were rescued from distress by an Indian hunting party,
which they then robbed and murdered, confessed to Johnson: 'I most
Sincerely Wish, that the Indians had killed them that we might Shew
them our approbation in the Punishment of Such Execrable Villains.'7

Yet Gage also acknowledged to Johnson the hopelessness of enforcing the law against those who killed and robbed Indians. He himself
was 'realy vexed at the Behaviour of the Lawless Banditti upon the
Frontiers, and what aggravates the more, is, the Difficulty to bring
them to Punishment. The true Cause of which, is not the Excuses
we get when Complaints are made . . . [but] the Weakness of the
Governments to enforce obedience to the Laws, and in some, their
Provincial Factions run so high, that every villain finds some powerfull
Protector.'8

Things were made much worse by the almost immediate collapse of
a key part of Johnson's strategy for putting Indian-colonial relations
on a sound footing. He had argued long and hard for Indian trade to
be heavily and centrally regulated, on the grounds that if anyone who
chose to do so was 'permitted to trade without inspection, all our Skill
will not be able to overcome the indiscretion of some, & the Villainy
of Others together with the licentiousness of the Frontier Inhabitants'.

He wanted trade confined to official posts where official commissaries would enforce a system of fixed prices and ensure fair treatment
for the Indians. He had even been confident enough to insist that he,

not the Board of Trade in London, appoint these commissaries to conduct trade at the posts. 'I think I have spent my time to little purpose unless I am the best Judge who to appoint, for any persons sent from England, or even any American Strangers to the Indians, must certainly be of little use for some Years, & before they acquired that knowledge, might thro Error or indiscretion, overset everry thing.'[9]

Johnson's system was adopted, and the appointment of commissaries was left largely to his discretion. This attempt to create a controlled market quickly failed, however. French traders operating in the villages of the upper Mississippi, Ohio, and Wabash Rivers and in the Illinois country, often with the collusion of British merchants, continued to bring goods up and down the Mississippi from New Orleans and were able to evade Johnson's restrictions. The governor of Quebec, Guy Carleton, issued his own trading passports, and insisted that Johnson had no control over Canadian traders, who naturally proceeded to operate far beyond the boundaries specified in their passports. The Indians themselves often resented the official insistence that they travel to the posts and forts for trade. By mid-1766 Johnson was already despairing of his own reforms: 'I see plainly how it is now throughout the Continent. People expect to do now as they please . . . I have wrote home so often on all these Subjects that I am heartily tired of it.'[10]

His constant letters of complaint to the Lords of Trade probably made them weary of the subject too, and in March 1768 they recommended the abandonment of Johnson's system and the return of the management of the Indian trade to the colonial governments. They recognised, in an echo of Johnson's arguments, that when these same colonies had previously mismanaged the trade, 'Many abuses were committed by the Traders, little care was taken to subject them to proper regulations and the misconduct of the Colonies in this particular contributed not a little to involve us in the enormous expences of an Indian War.' Attracted, however, by the prospect of 'saving much expence both at present and in future' by abandoning Johnson's scheme, they managed to convince themselves that the colonies had learned their lessons and that the abuses of the past would not be repeated.[11]

The failure of his schemes for regulating trade and the continuing drift of European settlement into Indian territory led Johnson to push for an ultimate solution in which the rights of Indians and settlers would be justly balanced. As early as July 1758, when the outcome of the war for the control of North America was still very much in doubt, Johnson had begun to envisage a final act of definition, freezing the white colonial territories within clearly drawn limits and effectively ceding the rest of the continent to the Indians. He wrote then to William Denny, Governor of Pennsylvania, suggesting the need for a 'solemn public treaty to agree upon clear & fixed Boundaries between our Settlements & their Hunting Grounds, so that each Party may know their own & be a mutual Protection to each other of their respective Possessions'.[12]

This radical idea challenged the vague but powerful assumption that the Indians in general were British subjects and their territories, in principle at least, British protectorates. Yet the Indian risings of the 1760s showed that the lands beyond the settled colonial boundaries were essentially ungovernable and the Board of Trade became increasingly receptive to Johnson's arguments. The growing difficulty of governing even the fractious colonies themselves made the notion of a fixed boundary between Indian land and British possessions seem attractive to the harassed potentates in London.

Johnson's idea began to take shape in 1763. He urged 'that a certain line should be run at the back of the Northern Colonies, beyond which no settlement should be made, until the whole Six Nations should think proper of selling part thereof'. His advice resulted in a royal proclamation of October 1763 forbidding the colonies to grant new land holdings 'for the present . . . beyond the heads or sources of any of the rivers which fall into the Atlantic Ocean from the west or northwest'.[13] This was at first put forward by the Board of Trade as a temporary expedient – 'mere provisional arrangements' – in the face of the rebellion. By the following year, however, after further consultations with Johnson, the idea had hardened into a definite proposal from the Lords of Trade for 'the fixing a Boundary between the Settlements of your Majesty's Subjects and the Indian Country . . . by compact with the Indians'.[14]

The proposal was left in the air, however, and Johnson decided to push it forward on his own initiative. In the spring of 1765 he raised the plan directly with the Iroquois, agreed with them a proposed boundary, and promised to 'lay the same before the great King'. Johnson managed to present this deal to the Lords of Trade as a response by him to an initiative of the Six Nations. As their lordships recorded it, 'a line of separation was in 1765 suggested by them, in which Sir William Johnson acquiesced'.[15] At the same time, Johnson's counterpart as Commissioner for Indian Affairs in the South, John Stuart, agreed a boundary with the Indians there.

Not until March 1768, however, was Johnson given formal permission to go ahead and negotiate a boundary. He called together a huge conference at Fort Stanwix in September 1768. Accompanied by twenty boat-loads of presents, the Governor of New Jersey, and Commissioners for Virginia and Pennsylvania, he met with 2,200 Indians from the Six Nations, the Delawares and the Shawnees.

Johnson conducted the conference very much as an Indian council. He opened it with the condolence ceremony and announced that the forms and rituals of the different nations would be observed: 'As I would deal with all people in their own way, and that your Ancestors have from the earliest time directed and recommended the observation of a Sett of Rules which they laid down for you to follow, I do now, agreeable to that custom, take of the clearest water and therewith cleanse your inside from all Filth and every thing which has given you concern.' The Oneida speaker, Canaghquieson, then repeated Johnson's ritual utterances almost word for word. His only addition, marking the Indian nature of the event, was to point out that the New Jersey Governor, Benjamin Franklin's son William, had no Indian name. In a significant gesture, Franklin was then given a name – Sagorighweyoghsta: Doer of Justice – which honoured the fact that he had given orders for the execution of murderers of Indians.[16]

Johnson's courtesies, which extended to his clothing of the old chiefs of each nation, 'the weather being cold', were matched by a frank admission of white wrongdoing: 'Several of our people ignorant of Indian Affairs have advanced too far into your country.' Efforts to obtain redress for the Indians had been 'generally unsuccessful'. These admissions somewhat softened Indian scepticism. The speaker for the combined nations stated: 'Daily experience teaches us that we cannot have any great dependance on the white People, and that they will forget their agreements for the sake of our Lands.' He reminded Johnson: 'We were formerly generous & gave the white people in many places Lands when they were too poor to buy them. We have often had bad Returns.' He did, however, politely add: 'We are willing to believe more favorably in this case.'

Much of the negotiation took place at private councils between the

Indian nations from which Johnson was excluded, though individual sachems continued to meet him at night and hear his remonstrations on particular points. These private, unrecorded night-time meetings were undoubtedly of great importance, giving Johnson the chance to play on the conflicts within the Indian delegations. The Indians were 'much divided in opinion', not least because the Six Nations were prepared to cede lands to which they had a theoretical claim but on which the western Indians actually lived. And the process was further complicated by the continuing influx of more Indians eager to witness or take part in the proceedings. The 2,200 Indians who were present at the start of the council on 24 October had become 3,100 by the time it ended on 6 November.[17] Johnson, whose health was 'in a verry low state', was worn out by having to 'set whole nights generally in the open woods in private conferences with the leading men'.[18]

Making his life more difficult and complicating things still further, Johnson also had to deal with pressure from the Anglican Church. Eleazar Wheelock, the missionary whom Johnson had originally supported and then came to dislike, had a plan to propose. In collusion with the colony of Connecticut, which had ambitions of its own, Wheelock demanded that Johnson 'not Suffer the boundary to go far North or West but to reserve those lands for the purposes of Religion'. A huge tract of the Susquehanna country would be reserved effectively for the Church. Wheelock sent his own delegation, headed by a wild preacher, the Reverend Jacob Johnson, to Fort Stanwix to urge the Oneidas, who claimed the Susquehanna country as their territory, not to cede it in the negotiations but to keep it free for the missionary cause.

The Reverend Jacob Johnson wore a hair shirt in imitation of John the Baptist and conversed with angels. Wheelock assured William Johnson that the preacher was, 'whatever his appearance and address may at first suggest . . . an honest upright-hearted Minister of Christ'. Johnson was at first tolerant and pleasant towards the Reverend Jacob and his visions, but when he and a fellow missionary were 'publickly avowing before Several Gentlemen that they had given all the obstruction they could' to Johnson's plans, he became so enraged that he declared: 'Had anyone perhaps but myself presided at the late Treaty those Missionaries would have been bound over . . . or sent down as prisiners.' Even Wheelock had to apologise to Johnson for this 'Wild, distracted, stupid, head long Conduct'. Johnson in turn complained of

Wheelock's shifting inconstant support of a man he 'first represented to me as a Man of great Piety & Worth and afterwards represented a Lunatic Enthusiast'.[19]

The interference of lunatic enthusiasts gave Johnson headaches, but the essential problems he had to deal with were far more fundamental. The key question for the council was Johnson's insistence, supported by the Six Nations, that the boundary line should be drawn significantly farther to the west than the temporary limit established in 1763, leaving significant new areas of the Ohio country open to official settlement. This position both revealed and attempted to obviate a fundamental weakness in the positions at the talks of both the Iroquois and Johnson. Both were pretending to make a deal on behalf of people who were in fact beyond their control. The Iroquois claimed that the Ohio lands were theirs by right of ancient conquest, a pretence that Johnson had supported when it suited his purposes. Yet, as Johnson had also recognised at various times, the Delawares and Shawnees were effectively independent peoples, and the Iroquois could not force them to abandon land they regarded as theirs.

Johnson's own weakness was that he had no control over the back-country settlers he was committing to honour the new boundary he was attempting to establish. He knew that whites were already pushing into western territories beyond the limits that London had had in mind when it agreed to his proposal for a boundary. This reality convinced him to press the Indians to agree a boundary farther to the west, so that the land that had already been grabbed would be on the British side. As he subsequently explained:

These frontier People were daily pushing into that fertile country and would continue to do so without any title whatsoever (a circumstance they little regard) & . . . [since the] Colonies would not, or could not, prevent them, this would have been such a disgrace to Government, [so] that I judged it most politick to purchase it for His Majesty, [rather] than to further discover our weakness to the Indians by admitting their Title to Lands which were dayly settling without any title at all.[20]

It was better, in other words, to gain a quasi-legal title to lands in the Ohio over the heads of its Indian inhabitants than to allow those lands to be stolen anyway and make the government look weak. Since the frontier settlers could not be held back '& as they were guilty of great abuses towards the Indians & others . . . it was better to have some Government (if such can be properly supported) than none, in that Quarter'.[21]

This was not an entirely dishonourable position. The chances of making a final boundary stick depended on the credibility of the boundary itself. If there were British settlements already on the Indian side, the whole idea would be discredited from the start. The manoeuvre did, nevertheless, involve a large dose of cynicism. The legal fiction that the Iroquois owned the Ohio valley would allow Johnson to purchase it from them. The British would gain territory, the Iroquois would be paid for property they did not really own, and the illegal back-country settlements would be legalised. Everyone would gain except, of course, the Ohio Indians.

There was, though, another, rather startling aspect of Johnson's plan. It was in direct contravention of his orders from London. His instructions were quite explicit: to 'induce the fixing the Boundary Line at the Kanawha River', that being the supposed limit of Iroquois territory. The boundary of colonial settlement was thus supposed to be the junction of the Ohio and Kanawha Rivers, where Johnson's boundary would meet that extending up from the south and already agreed by John Stuart. The Iroquois, however, claimed that their territory extended farther west and south to the Tennessee River. On the back of this claim, Johnson drew the boundary almost 400 miles further inland, at the junction of the Ohio and the Tennessee Rivers and, at the conclusion of negotiations, purchased these lands for the Crown from the Six Nations for $10,000.[22] Effectively, Johnson's boundary meant that all lands south-west of Fort Stanwix down to the mouth of the Tennessee River belonged to the Indians and the land east of the fort belonged to the English. Bisecting present-day New York and Pennsylvania from north-east to south-west, and following the Ohio River almost to its junction with the Mississippi, Johnson's boundary thus ceded to the British most of present-day West Virginia and Kentucky.

Johnson's pushing back of the boundary line was splendid news for some of his friends, who thereby gained or strengthened their claims to vast tracts of land. The excuse for doing this was the agreement he had reached with the western nations after Pontiac's rebellion that traders who had suffered severe losses in the conflict would be compensated with land. Thus, in the treaty, Johnson formalised an Indian deed to his own deputy George Croghan of 100,000 acres between Lake Otsego and the Unadilla River. He also secured for a syndicate of Philadelphia traders, led by the Quaker Samuel Wharton, an astonishing two and a half million acres in what would become West Virginia.

Johnson later admitted that he had allowed the interests of the traders and land-hunters to exercise an excessive influence over his dealings at Fort Stanwix. He told William Franklin: 'My Friendship, and good wishes towards the sufferers may have led me to espouse their Cause, & perhaps to Serve them with more warmth than others would have done.' He nevertheless declared that he was 'only fulfilling an Engagement the Indians previously entered into' and that he had acted 'on the most equitable as well as disinterested principles'. He denied 'clogging the Treaty with an Affair in which I was Interested' and claimed that he did not have 'any Interest at all' in the land cessions. He protested to the Lords of Trade: 'Private interest governs none of my representations.'[23]

This last claim was, however, a lie. He clearly had a private arrangement with the leader of the Philadelphia traders Samuel Wharton, giving Johnson himself a slice of the land that he had opened up to settlement. He referred in correspondence to his London agent in 1771 to 'my proportion of the Ohio Tract', and the following year to 'my Share in it'. Wharton applied to this agent, indeed, for the payment of £200 'for Your Share in the Grant of Lands upon the Ohio River'.[24] His claims to be entirely disinterested in the outcome of the council merely show that he knew how disreputably he had behaved.

At first, Johnson's stark disobedience to his instructions from London threatened for the first time in his career to earn him the wrath of his imperial masters. The Earl of Hillsborough, at the head of the Board of Trade, admonished Johnson for being 'induced to depart from the Boundary line, directed by the Report of the Lords Commissioners for Trade & Plantations, which upon the whole, after much consideration, had been determined upon political and commercial principles to be the most desireable one, and to which by His Majesty's commands you was instructed to adhere'.[25]

On the other hand, however, the opening up of the Ohio valley was an enticing prospect for many rich and powerful people. The land cessions on the Ohio attracted the support of significant political and commercial interests, among them Benjamin Franklin, who kept Wharton, and through him Johnson, informed of the political manoeuvres in London. Wharton himself went to London to bolster the case for the treaty. He heard that 'there was not one member of the cabinet Council but what thought Lord Hillsborough mad in his

Objections to the Boundary'. The Lord Chancellor, the Earl of Camden, was 'afraid Sir William would not understand the true meaning and design of the Cabinet Council', which was to support Johnson's decisions.[26] Hillsborough, isolated as he was, was forced to accept the treaty and informed Johnson in May 1769: 'His Majesty, rather than risk the defeating [of] the important object of establishing a final Boundary Line will, upon your report of this matter, give the necessary directions for the confirmation of it as agreed upon at Fort Stanwix.'

It was a hollow victory, however. The problem with Johnson's whole scheme for a boundary line was the ample evidence that land-hungry settlers could ignore the laws with impunity. Thomas Gage had pointed out to Johnson long before the Fort Stanwix council that the line 'might doubtless preserve Tranquillity for some time; but it appears to me to be only a Temporary Expedient, for some people upon the Frontiers are not be kept in by any Bounds. If the Governments are too feeble to enforce obedience to Laws Proclamations etc. at present, they can't obtain more strength by being extended.' He predicted that 'in less than three years, The People would go beyond the limits, tho' they are fixed at the Ohio'.[27]

Moreover, Johnson's own behaviour in securing a tract of the newly opened lands for himself was, at worst, flagrantly corrupt. Entrusted with critical negotiations for a treaty to shape the future development of North America, he allowed private interests, including his own and Croghan's, to influence the agenda. At best, he could be accused of exploiting for private advantage an opportunity opened up by the rivalry of the Iroquois and the western Indians.

It would be wrong, however, to reduce the treaty of Fort Stanwix to a cynical carve-up. Johnson was utterly sincere in his belief that his boundary line would map the full extent of European settlement in North America. For all the lands ceded by the Iroquois, his boundary, if it had been respected, would have confined the future expansion of white America to a relatively small stretch of the continent's eastern reaches. Illusory as such a notion undoubtedly was, it sprang from a deep-rooted desire to defeat the designs of time. It was an ageing man's way of bringing a halt to the gallop of history, of conceiving a once-and-for-all world in which change itself could be confined within narrow and predictable bounds. Feeling old now and increasingly ill, he was trying to return to a time outside history, to place the astonishing unpredictability of his life back inside a firm and familiar frame. For even as America was gathering itself for another earthquake of change, Johnson was thinking himself back into an old, lost Ireland.

28

The Patriarch

Eggshells, dark-green wine bottles, an iron knife blade, Jew's harps, one of them so tiny it can only have been made for a child, straight pins, a stone marble, twisted metal threads of the kind used to braid officers' uniforms or on the edges of Native American coats and blankets, white and purple wampum beads, a mirror fragment, a gunflint chip, forty white-clay tobacco-pipe fragments of a kind made in England especially for Indians. Seventy-two mammal bones, burned white from cooking fires. A few scraps of pewter used to wrap flint for flintlock guns and some droplets of lead left over from the manufacture of musket balls.

These were the buried remains from the grounds around Johnson Hall, the new mansion William Johnson had built for himself in 1763 about ten miles from Fort Johnson, which he gave to his son John. They were dug up by archaeologists 250 years later. They form the detritus of Indian councils and the preparations of war. Yet nearer the house they found the vestiges of a more genteel life. Alongside the bones of wild duck, grouse, passenger pigeon, turkey and wood turtle, all of which had been cooked here, there were the remnants of domestic feasts more familiar to the old gentry of Ireland: the bones of cattle, pigs, sheep and chicken. Many of the bones showed chew-marks, probably from William Johnson's many dogs. There were also large numbers of oyster shells, brought in barrels up the Hudson and the Mohawk Rivers all the way from Long Island.

The food was served on plates of hand-painted Delft. Tea was sipped from Chinese porcelain cups. The saucers had hand-painted blue-and-white designs, and the very best ware was of Chinese origin, imported to Europe and then overglazed and enamelled. Fine wines were drunk from exquisitely fashionable opaque white Bristol glasses.[1]

When Johnson invited high-class guests from the cities to visit him on the frontier, he asked them to come to 'This Wild place'.[2] He knew that when people came from far away, part of the attraction of his homes was their exotic location, on the edge of the forest, among the Indians, out at the borders of civilisation. Yet he himself wanted something very different. He craved the life of an Irish country gentleman, part tribal chief and part bucolic patriarch, perfectly balanced between upper-class opulence and indulgent conviviality.

By the late 1760s Johnson had become one of the largest landowners in America. He had on different occasions turned down offers of land from Indian nations with whom he dwelt, including vast tracts near Detroit and the Senecas' proposed gift around Niagara. He could afford this apparent selflessness, however. The most famous story about Johnson, originally recorded by the Indian trader John Long, was about his cunning acquisition of Indian land. He was, the story went, sitting in council with a group of Mohawks when 'the head chief [usually identified in other versions of the story as Hendrick] told him, he had dreamed last night, that [Johnson] had given him a fine laced coat, and he believed it was the same he then wore'. Johnson smiled and asked Hendrick if he had really dreamed it. The Mohawk assured him he had. 'Well then', said Sir William, 'you must have it.' He pulled off his coat and gave it to Hendrick, who left the council well pleased.

The next time they met, Johnson told Hendrick 'that he was not accustomed to dream, but since he had met him at the council, he had dreamed a very surprising dream'. Hendrick asked what it was. 'Sir William, with some hesitation, told him he dreamed that he had given him a tract of land on the Mohawk River to build a house on, and make a settlement, extending about nine miles in length along the banks.' The sachem smiled and told Johnson that if he really had dreamed it he must have it, 'but that he would never dream with him again, for he had only got a laced coat, whereas Sir William was now entitled to a large bed, on which his ancestors had frequently slept'.[3]

The story is surely apocryphal – a similar tale was told about Conrad Weiser and Hendrick was dead by the time of the Mohawks' cession of their Canajoharie lands to Johnson in 1760. But it encapsulates the deeper truth of Johnson's ability to turn his sympathetic understanding of the Indians to his own advantage. By the time of his death he had accumulated about 170,000 acres of land, most of it virgin forest. As well as his part in the purchase on the Ohio (which was not sanctioned by London in his lifetime), he accumulated large parcels of land in New York. The Canajoharie grant of 1760 was not confirmed by the Board of Trade, and Johnson began to lobby for it as a reward for his services. In June 1769 he received the news that his request had been approved, and that a Royal Grant of 99,000 acres had received the King's seal. He had also promoted the purchase from the Oneidas of more than 120,000 acres west of German Flats by a consortium in which he had a quarter share along with the then Governor of New York Sir Henry Moore, Lord Holland and Thomas Gage. With a 27,000-acre share in two other patents on Schoharie Creek and further tracts to the south-west and north-east of Johnson Hall, he was a landlord on the scale of the greatest British magnates.

This gave him, in his own mind at least, a kind of feudal Irish lordship in the Mohawk valley, and he wanted to live up to the best Irish style. In the earlier years of his American life, he had given his friends back home 'many promises of Seeing poor Ireland'.4 The exigencies of war and public office had made it impossible to fulfil those promises, and he gradually abandoned all hopes of a trip across the Atlantic. Towards the end of his life, Johnson wrote to a correspondent in Dublin: 'My health has been for several years past so much impaired that I cannot have the least prospect (was it otherwise Convenient) of Visiting Ireland, and therefore one great satisfaction of my Life is to hear of the happiness of my friends there, since I cannot be a Witness of it.'5

His inability to return to Ireland, though, did not mean that he was ever really cut off from the country where he had spent the first twenty years of his life. His sister Catherine came to live with him in the early 1750s. His son John visited Ireland in 1766. His brother Warren visited him in 1760 and 1761. His daughter Anne went to Ireland in 1776. His nephews Guy Johnson and his sister Anne's son John Dease came to live with him in New York. Johnson even imported from Ireland, in a spectacular case of bringing coals to Newcastle, 'a Barrell of good Munster Potatoes' in the hopes of planting and growing his own Irish spuds.6

More important, though, Johnson consciously created an Irish world for himself both at Johnson Hall and in the nearby village of Johnstown, which he founded. He surrounded himself with Irish retainers and friends. Almost all the people outside his own family to whom he was closest were Irish: his doctor Patrick Daly 'for whom I have a particular regard'; his assistant and 'faithful friend' Robert Adams, originally a merchant's clerk from Dublin; Robert's brother William, also a doctor; Johnson's farm manager Thomas Flood; his accountant Thomas Shipboy; his crony Mick Byrne, whose brother 'was married to a near relation of ours' and whose high voice made him the butt of affectionate jokes; Mick's brother John; and Johnson's live-in lawyer Bryan Lefferty.[7]

Beyond this inner circle, there was a much larger pool of Irish servants and tenants. He was constantly on the look-out for hired help from home. In 1769, for example, he hired a gardener and his wife from Dublin, and in 1772 he was inquiring for more Irish servants.[8] Also, from the beginning of his time in New York, a large proportion of his tenants was Irish. (Even now, 17 per cent of the population of Johnstown claims Irish ancestry.)

When Johnson established a free school in Johnstown, attended by both European and Indian children, he hired a schoolmaster from Ireland to run it, Edward Wall, 'who received a liberal education in Europe' – suggesting that he had at one time been trained for the Catholic priesthood at Louvain or one of the other Irish seminaries on the continent.[9]

Wall's style of pedagogy gives a glimpse of the genteel aspirations that were as much a part of Johnson's world as the wilder elements of frontier existence:

He observed the most rigid formality in teaching his scholars *manners*; If a child wished to go out, it must go before him with a complaisant *please master may I go out?* accompanied with a bow, a backward motion of the right hand, and drawing back upon the floor the right foot. On returning to the schoolroom, the pupil had again to parade before the master, with another three-motioned bow, and a very *grateful thank-you, sir!*

The lad Jacob Shew, on becoming initiated into the out-and-in ceremony, accompanied his first bow with a scrape of the left foot. '*Take the other fut, you rascal!*' was roared with such a brogue and emphasis by the old Pedagogue, as to confuse him, and he flourished the left foot again. '*Take the other fut, I tell ye*' came louder than before, attended with a stamp that carried terror to the boy's heart. Comprehending the requirement, he shifted his balance, scraped with *the right fut*, heard a surly '*that'll doh!*' and went on his way rejoicing though trembling.[10]

Wall's attitude is also indicative of the patriarchal quality of life in Johnstown. Wall 'was very severe with most of his pupils, but the

Baronet's children were made an exception to his inclemency – they ever being treated with kind partiality and pointed indulgence'.

Johnson was a benign dictator, but unmistakably the master of his own realm. In an almost feudal exchange, he received gratitude and returned a convivial, playful bonhomie and a generous concern for the welfare of his subjects. In his case, to the general obligations of the position of patriarch was added a specific national duty to look out for his Irish retainers. In 1770, for example, an old woman, Mary Grace, wrote to him from Dublin wondering about her son (probably Walter Grace employed by Johnson in trade), 'is he liveing or dead', and relying on 'yor genaral caracter of relive in the distress of Every endevedel'.[11]

The atmosphere Johnson generated around him was that of the classic Irish middleman, neither peasant nor aristocrat, but accommodating to both. Upper-class visitors like Lord Adam Gordon, or Lady Susan O'Brien, the daughter of an earl who scandalised English society by marrying an impecunious Irish actor and ran away to Johnson Hall with him to seek refuge, would have found much that was recognisably respectable, even cosmopolitan.

While visitors may have expected to be close to nature in Johnson's domain, they would not have expected to find, as well as the numerous dogs he kept, a monkey and a parrot.[12] Nor can they have expected the artificiality of a large house whose outside walls were of wood painted to look like stone. Along the inside walls were prints of Poussin paintings, Titian's *Loves of the Gods*, Watteau's scenes of camp life, Le Brun's paintings of the battles of Alexander the Great, and portraits of the champion racehorses at Newmarket.[13] There were backgammon and billiard tables.

Johnson was regularly supplied with literature from London and New York. His orders include 'Sundry New polite pamphlets and a play', 'sundry books and pamphlets', the *Court Register*, the *Gentleman's Magazine*, the *London Magazine*, Smollet's *Roderick Random*, pamphlets on the Stamp Acts, Langhorne's *Letters*, *Biographia Britannica*, *The History of Louisiana*, *An Historical Review of the Transactions of Europe from the Commencement of the War with Spain* and a 'Collection of Scots Caracatures Pictures etc in 2 vols'. Johnson's own taste in books seems to have been more for scientific and historical material than for fiction. One of his suppliers heard from William O'Brien that Johnson was 'disgusted with my sending too many of the literary publications from England'.[14] But for 'the ladies' there were books like *The Cheval Pierrepoint, Millennium Hall,* and *The Polite Lady.*[15]

Nor, for all Johnson's immense sexual appetite, were polite ladies likely to feel out of place. Johnson's daughters had been raised to be European ladies. Anne Grant recorded that, as young women before their marriages, they led highly regulated lives:

In the morning they rose early, read their prayer-book, I believe, but certainly their bible, fed their birds, tended their flowers, and breakfasted; then were employed for some hours with unwearied perseverance, at fine needle-work . . . they then read, as long as they chose the voluminous romances of the [eighteenth] century . . . after dinner they regularly in summer took a long walk; or an excursion in the sledge, in winter . . . and then returned and resumed their wonted occupations . . . they wore wrappers of the finest chintz, and green silk petticoats.[16]

This demure atmosphere for his daughters contrasted with Johnson's own continuing sexual adventures. In his later years, he went reasonably regularly to the seaside for a rest cure. These holidays in New London, Connecticut, also seem to have involved some sexual recreation. His presence attracted interest from local women. Hugh Wallace wrote, in August 1773, replying to some lost references of Johnson's: 'I observe the Curiosity of your Country Islanders – but I am realy not in the greatest pain about your Virtue – tho the Females are so handsome. I should fear more for theirs, tho I fancy they dont fear what Man can do unto them.'[17] The Biblical joke on Christ's injunction that 'as you would that men should do to you, do unto them in like manner', suggests that Johnson had intimated that this female interest went beyond curiosity.

Sexual banter was woven into the conversation of Johnson's male circle and sometimes even surfaced in writing. Captain Normand McLeod wrote to him from New York in 1770:

I'm glad to hear that Mr Roberts is a live and knocking the Balls about but sorry to hear he could not knock his balls about as he would choose to do at Michilimackinac, but he is not the first that the fair sex have disappointed. I wish My Lord Mayor would find some agreeable place to roll his balls on as to Lord Mansfield he has enough of it. Mr Daily's balls, I'm afraid are wore out in the Service and ought to be sent to Chelsea. Mr Byrns I'm afraid by the Melody of his voice has been cut out like your Italians for singing so that his balls are left in Italy or perhaps as he was so long in the East he was fitted for taking care of the Ladys in the Seraglio.

He signed off with his compliments to 'the Ball drivers' at Johnson Hall.[18]

Johnson's sexual entanglements seem from time to time to have created some embarrassment. His liaison with Mary McGrath in the 1740s resurfaced in the late 1760s through such enigmatic but suggestive phrases as 'that unaccountable Man Magra'; 'the mysterious behaviour of Mr Magra'; 'there was no method of doing [him a] Service without running the risque of affronting him'; and 'behav'd so unbecoming the Character of a Gentleman'.[19] The circumstances suggest that this man was either Mary McGrath's husband or one of her relatives who was able to exert an unusual hold over Johnson by virtue of some shared secret.

The fragmentary nature of these references makes it impossible to be certain what was going on, but they do strongly suggest that this McGrath's hold over Johnson allowed him to behave with an arrogant abandon. In April 1768 McGrath, who had been with the army in Niagara, turned up at Johnson Hall 'in a very distressed condition' and Johnson claimed to be 'a Stranger to his Affairs and . . . not [to] know what to do with him'.[20] Yet he was not in fact a stranger to McGrath's affairs – which had been mentioned in at least three previous letters from Johnson's informants at Niagara in a tone that suggests that Johnson already knew about him.

According to Johnson, McGrath had turned up at his house and told him that 'he had been obliged to leave [New] York with the greatest Expedition to avoid being arrested for Debt, and that he did not know where to go out of the Way of Danger, unless to get to some of the Posts, upon which I told him there were then Indians at my House who would for a Small Matter conduct him to Oswego, or Niagra'.[21]

This seems odd and it is hard to understand why Johnson would send a man on the run from the law to a sensitive frontier post. In his drunken ramblings at Niagara in February 1768, moreover, McGrath was claiming that he was going to be in Johnson's 'Employment in spring' and that 'if there's no Vacancy' Johnson was going to 'get him the Command' of one of the forts. He also complained: 'At present you [Johnson] only allow him 50 pounds sterling.'[22]

This might be regarded as nothing more than the wild boasting of a drunk, were it not for the extreme discomfort which McGrath evidently caused Johnson. In late April, when Johnson was going to New

London to rest and recover his health, he informed General Gage: 'Magra is gone to Canada. I wish he had left this Continent entirely. – A principal cause of my going the Rout I mention is to avoid too much Company which in my present verry low State would exhaust my Spirits.'[23] The suggestion that McGrath had brought Johnson to the verge of nervous exhaustion indicates that the man was more than just an annoying drunk, and McGrath's claim that the powerful baronet was paying him money and promising him promotion points, perhaps, to a degree of fear. Even for a man famed for his promiscuity, the fathering of a child in wartime with a woman whose husband was a prisoner of the enemy had to be something of an embarrassment. Assuming that this McGrath is indeed connected to Mary and Christopher, Johnson's earlier affair with the captive's wife may well have continued to haunt him.

Awkward secrets like these were in sharp contrast to Johnson's intensely respectable behaviour as a father to his daughters. He adopted towards them all the haughty propriety an eighteenth-century gentleman could hope to muster. When, in 1761, Daniel Claus gently broached the fact that he 'always had and ever shall have a Sincere Regard and Esteem for Miss Nancy your elder Daughter, who likewise was kind enough as not to discourage me therin', Johnson was outraged that his deputy had not sought his permission before disclosing his sentiments to Nancy. 'It seems verry extraordinary, and precipitate, besides it is giving me a bad impression of my Daughters regard & duty towards me, whom she should consult in a case, which concerns her happiness so nearly. It shall ever be a Maxim with me, to give a Child great liberty in the choice of a Husband, or Wife, as is consistent with the Duty they owe to a Parent . . .'[24] Nancy, whose reading of contemporary novels obviously stood her in good stead, got her way, presumably without pointing out the absurdity of her father's discovery of puritan morals.

These contradictory attitudes were emblematic of a wider ambiguity. Johnson's life as patriarch of the Mohawk valley combined the respectability of a powerful landlord with a wild, occasionally riotous style of living that was unlike most British baronial halls. Visitors were entertained, not just by imported Irish musicians, but by a dwarfish fiddle player known only as 'Billy'. They were served by the Bartholomew brothers, 'dwarfish-looking white men', by a tall German called Frank, by various Irish people and by Johnson's personal slave, a half-African, half-Indian whom he called Pontiac. With the constant presence of Indians of different nations and the babble of English, German, Dutch, Mohawk, Gaelic and even Latin that filled the air, Johnson Hall had a rich, frantic flavour unknown in Wiltshire or Warrenstown.

The daily routine, or rather lack of routine, at Johnson Hall was described by one visitor, Judge Thomas Jones. It was 'a kind of open house' always full of Indians and travellers 'from all parts of America, from Europe, and from the West Indies':

The gentlemen and ladies breakfasted in their respective rooms, and, at their option, had either tea, coffee, or chocolate, or if an old rugged veteran wanted a beef-steak, a mug of ale, a glass of brandy, or some grog, he called for it, and it always was at his service. The freer people made, the more happy was Sir William. After breakfast, while Sir William was about his business, his guests entertained themselves as they pleased. Some rode out, some went out with guns, some with fishing-tackle, some sauntered about the town, some played cards, some backgammon, some billiards, some pennies, and some even at nine-pins. Thus was each day spent until the hour of four, when the bell punctually rang for dinner, and all assembled.

He had besides his own family, seldom less than ten, sometimes thirty. All were welcome. All sat down together. All was good cheer, mirth, and festivity. Sometimes seven, eight, or ten, of the Indian Sachems joined the festive board. His dinners were plentiful. They consisted, however, of the produce of his estate, or what was procured from the woods and rivers, such as venison, bear, and fish of every kind, with wild turkeys, partridges, grouse, and quails in abundance. No jellies, creams, ragouts, or sillibubs graced his table. His liquors were Madeira, ale, strong beer, cider, and punch. Each guest chose what he liked, and drank as he pleased. The company, or at least a part of them, seldom broke up before three in the morning. Every one, however, Sir William included, retired when he pleased. There was no restraint.[25]

This lack of restraint extended from the high table at Johnson Hall to the almost medieval festivities that Johnson organised for the villagers and tenants. St Patrick's Day was, of course, a great occasion for revelry. At the hall, there would be, as a bleary-eyed Warren Johnson noted in 1761, 'a great Meeting at my Brother's House to drink Saint Patrick, & most got vastly drunk'.[26] Outside, there were games and competitions. In one of the earliest references to the sport in America, the Johnstown innkeeper marked down in Johnson's account '2 Gallons of beer for the foot Ball players' on St Patrick's Day 1773.[27]

Johnson encouraged and delighted in all sorts of games. On festivals like St Patrick's Day, 'not only young Indians and squaws, but whites, both male and female, were often seen running foot races, or wrestling for some gaudy trinket, or fancy article of wearing apparel. Men were sometimes seen running foot races for a prize, with a meal-bag drawn over their legs and tied under the arms.'

Often a greased hog was let loose with the stipulation that whoever caught it could keep it, leading to some ingenious forethought. 'An old woman is said to have seized on one, amid the jeers of the laughing multitude, after it had escaped the grasp of many strong hands, and firmly held it. The secret was, she had prepared herself with a handful of sand.'

Johnson would offer half a pound of tea to the winner of a gurning contest. He erected greased poles with tempting prizes on top, usually won by naked Mohawk boys. He hid money in muddy puddles so the children could compete to find it. He arranged a boxing match between an Irishman in his service and a Dutch champion which, to his undoubted chagrin, the Irishman lost – a small defeat that did little to dent Johnson's Irish pride.

Up to a point, Johnson succeeded in creating at Johnson Hall and in Johnstown a remarkable polyglot community in which Irish, Mohawk, German, Dutch, French, Scottish and English people lived side by side. The names of some the children enrolled at the free school run by Johnson's schoolmaster Edward Wall tell their own story: Richard Cotter, Hendrick Rynnion, Randel M'Donald, John Foilyard, David Doran, Abraham Boice, Caleb McCarty, Simeon Scouten, Sarah Connor, Leny Rynnion, Betsey Garlick, Mary McIntyre, Peggy Potman, Eve Waldroff, Catharine Servos. Though Indian names are not listed, it is clear that Mohawk children also attended, making for a cultural and ethnic mix that would become, over the following centuries, quintessentially American, but that was, in the mid-eighteenth century, still part of a new world. Children from almost anywhere might end up in Johnson's domain – except, of course, the children of many of those who lived with him on the most intimate terms.

29

Negroes' Handcuffs

In 1754, in the midst of a grand Irish family row over Sir Peter Warren's will, William Johnson drew up a detailed and pedantic account of monies he believed were owed to him by the admiral's estate for his work on Warren's New York lands. The list is almost comical in its bloody-minded insistence on the smallest expenditures for padlocks and keys, candlesticks and snuffers, dishes and plates. It ceases to be funny when the eye catches one item listed in the same blithe, banal reckoning:

Negroes Handcuffs charg'd Boston Money 18/- is York Currency . . . 6/-[1]

Sparely eloquent in its own way, the entry speaks from a great silence. The frontier where European encountered Indian was also a zone where both encountered Africans. William Johnson, friend of the Mohawk and protector of the Iroquois, was also an enthusiastic slave-holder.

The black presence on the Mohawk River and elsewhere on the New York frontier was not confined to slaves. When Johnson arrived, he found black farmers already among his neighbours. In 1738 Peter Warren referred to 'the land the Negroes possess' and the following year, Johnson mentioned 'the Willigee Negroes' (the Willigee being one of the streams that watered the terrain) conducting a survey of 'their lands'[2], which, they claimed, included some of the property that Johnson had cleared. In 1761 Warren Johnson, on a visit to Johnson Hall, noted: 'There are many free Negroes here who have good Estates.'

There were also blacks in the upper New York towns, some of them slaves but others free. In 1771 the Church of England congregation in

Albany included fifty black adults and children, close to a quarter of the total, though their pastor did not think their names worth recording.3 Black people from northern New York were seized as prisoners by raiding parties of Indians and French soldiers in 1745. In the raid of Saratoga, as Robert Sanders reported to Johnson, the local blacks '[are] most all prisoners & the Number of them Exceeds the Number of the white'.4

Johnson's interaction with African America was, however, first and foremost as the master of men, women and children whom he believed himself to own, body and soul. From his first days at Warrensburgh in 1738, he had slaves helping to clear the land and hired an overseer to keep them in order.5 For the rest of his life, the slaves he accumulated in larger numbers as he got richer were the silent partners, unwilling and unrewarded, in his energetic enterprise.

That most of the back-breaking work on Johnson's estate was done by the slaves is clear from the instructions he left for the running of the place when he was expecting to be away for a while in early 1754:

To let the Negroes take Good Care of all the Cattle & feed them well also to ride Home all the Hay from the Old Farm, the Oats of the Isleand & the Wheat as fast as possible. Rest of the Negroes to keep Cutting & Clearing the Side of the Road at the End of the Stone Wall quite to the next Bridge. When it is good rideing after they have done bringing home the Hay, Wheat, & Oats, then let them ride Home the Stones from below round the Wall here, and also the Stones out of the feild, beyond the Bridge for a fence, to be laid Streight.6

Slaves also worked in his kitchens, served his food, hauled his trade goods, and carried the *bateaux* that were the essential mode of transport in this watery world across the portages between rivers. 'As the Battoes are Some returned from Oswego, which I had of You,' he informed Jacob Glen in 1747, 'I have ordered the Negroe to deliver them to You with that poles & paddles are yours.' They probably also suckled his infant children: Warren Johnson noted: 'Negroe Women Suckle white Children in the West Indies, & a great many here.'7

This vast contribution to his wealth was never met with any sense of gratitude or attachment. In his papers, the slaves usually come with a monetary value attached. 'Cash paid for a Negroe Wench . . . 65 pounds'; two black men Abraham and December, both of whom were about twenty-four and imported from St Croix through New York City, £90; a young man of nineteen, £50; 'a Negro Wench and two children', £70.8

An obvious question is whether, like so many white masters, he slept with any of his female slaves and fathered black, as well as Indian, children. Documentary records tend not to answer such questions, and there is no direct evidence one way or the other. One suggestive trace, however, is an entry in Johnson's account with the New York City merchant John Wetherhead, for 10 March 1769: 'To Cash paid Doctor Bard his Bill & sundry other Expences attending the lying in and nursing of the Negro Wench: 7. 10.'9

Bard was a noted New York City physician of the kind whose services would not normally be afforded to slave women in labour. The relative luxury of 'lying in and nursing' with medical assistance seems unusual for a slave. The circumstances are therefore suggestive – though no more – of the woman giving birth to Johnson's child at the safe remove of New York City.

If Johnson did have a sexual relationship with a slave woman and formed any kind of attachment, it would have been a rare flaw in a pattern of indifference. In general, he treated slaves as commodities to be bought, sold and exchanged. In 1744 Johnson swapped with an Albany blacksmith one slave, a boy called Stepney, for another called Quack.10 In 1766 he instructed Thomas Flood, who was travelling, presumably to New York City: 'If you can meet any who want a healthy young Wench You can agree to send them Jenny on your return, and as to Harry take him with you, & dispose of him in the best manner you can.'11 The casual willingness to dispose of Jenny suggests an indifference to family ties: Jenny was the personal slave of Johnson's Mohawk wife Molly Brant, and her sister Juba also worked in the house.12

This notion of slaves as a disposable asset was probably absorbed from his Warren and De Lancey relations during his earliest days in America. In 1741 Susan Warren peremptorily ordered the delivery of a slave: 'Mr Warren desires you'll make one of your best negroes drive your wagon to make him fit for a Coach man for me.' Johnson in fact decided to train two, 'and the one I find that does best I will send him down when you think proper'.13

Johnson does seem to have been at least mildly concerned for the welfare of his slaves even though they lived 'on Salt provisions all Winter'.14 When Governor George Clinton sent one of his slaves to Johnson with a message, he was assured that as to 'the Negroe fellow . . . I shall have as great Care taken of as if my own'.15 John Lydius reported to him from Albany on the state of one of his slaves who had presumably taken ill there: 'Your Neger is Quit Recoverd and is well.'[16] When another slave, Charles, travelled on Johnson's business, he was boarded in the same conditions, and at the same expense, as Johnson's white servant.[17]

At Johnson Hall, Johnson's slaves 'dressed much as did their Indian neighbors, except that a kind of coat was made of their blankets by the Hall tailor'.[18] Large amounts of duffel, flannel, serge and even leather breeches were bought for the slaves, and significant amounts were spent on shoes and shoe repair, and on expensive medicine for sick slaves.[19] The 'Negroe room' in the stone blockhouse beside Johnson Hall, where the slaves lived, had a pine table, pewter plates, a brass kettle and some dishes. There was also a wash-house for the slaves which had tubs and kettles for their ablutions.[20]

These basic provisions, however, amount to little more the acts of a prudent owner investing in the maintenance of his property. Slavery was a system enforced by fear and implicit threats of violence that were sometimes brought home by explicit demonstrations of raw domineering power. The 'Negroes Handcuffs' Johnson bought were not idle trinkets. Captivity, in Johnson's domain as in the rest of slave-holding society, was sustained, when necessary, by brutality. In 1760, in a letter since destroyed, Johnson's steward at his holiday home, Castle Cumberland, informed him of his activities, which included, along with harvesting crops, building barns and sawing wood, another routine exertion: 'flogging slaves'.[21]

Whether Johnson was better or worse than the average slave-master is unclear. On the scale of infamy, the north-eastern colonies were in general a better environment for slaves than the southern states or the West Indies. The best measure of relative cruelty is probably the frequency with which slaves fled their masters, and in this regard the surviving evidence is ambivalent. Some of Johnson's slaves certainly sought their freedom by running away to Connecticut. One escaped in 1761 but was captured and returned. Another, known as Master Johnny, ran away in 1764 or 1765, was captured and sold in Connecticut and eventually returned to Johnson. On the other hand, however, in 1773 Mister Dick, another of Johnson's slaves, ran away while on a trip to New York City when he heard a false rumour that he was to be sold, and was apprehended and imprisoned in Westchester. At the time, he was making his way back to Johnson

Hall, suggesting that he was more anxious to stay in Johnson's service than to be sold.[22]

Johnson was probably no worse than the general run of white colonial landowners, but the real question is why he was no better. His sensitive and sympathetic attitude to the Indians and their culture showed that he was exceptionally free of run-of-the-mill European assumptions about the inherent superiority of the white race. His complex appreciation of cultural differences and human similarities ought, on the face of it, to have extended to the black people whose lives were interwoven with his own. He came, moreover, from a culture that continued to suffer from being on the wrong side of a supremacist divide. Though the oppression of Irish Catholics did not compare in scale to the horror of the mass enslavement of Africans in America, it did give Johnson a tangible experience of what it felt like to be in the wrong when might makes right.

In truth, however, the wounded pride of the Irish dispossessed often found a salve in the joy of dominating others. Irish experiences of oppression did not necessarily lead to any particular sympathy with the plight of Africans abducted into slavery. Irish slave-owners dominated the West Indian island of Montserrat, and one of Johnson's acquaintances from home, Silvester Ferrall, boasted to him: 'There is two Gentlemen of my Name that Lives at Montserrat, they have great Plantations, and are vastly rich and Keep a great Number of Negroes.'[23] Keeping a great number of Negroes was proof of the resurrection of Irish fortunes.

Instead of making men like Johnson more sympathetic to the sufferings of slaves, Irish conditions tended to create a degree of callousness. Poor European whites who went to America as bonded servants were also bought and sold during the period of their indenture, just as Johnson had bought Catty from her master. Very many of these people were Irish: in the pre-Revolutionary period of the eighteenth century, more than half and perhaps as many as two-thirds of Irish immigrants came to America as bonded servants, contractually bound to serve a colonial master for an average of four or five years in return for their passage. In the early 1740s more than 90 per cent of the indentured servants in some of the colonies were Irish.[24]

Since many of these servants worked in the fields alongside African slaves, this situation might be expected to create some kind of fellow feeling, even though the servants enjoyed the immense advantage over the slaves that their bondage was temporary. Instead, however, for Irish masters like Johnson, it made the whole idea of buying and selling people seem normal and familiar. Rather than an act of horrific racial oppression, it was simply one of the things that rich people could do.

That Johnson saw black slaves and bonded white servants in the same light, as goods to be purchased, is clear from a letter he wrote to a New York City merchant in 1749: 'As I understand there are a parcel of Negroes Expected Soon into [New] York, If they are reasonable, I would have you buy me one, or two likely boys about 14 or 16 years of age, and in such Case Send them up as Soon as you Can, also a good Cliver lad of a white man, if any Such to be had there I should be glad you would buy one for me, if such Comes.'25

He was perfectly capable of treating Irish bondsmen effectively as slaves. In 1765, for example, he purchased the four-year bond of Connor O'Rourke, evidently an Irish servant. When O'Rourke absconded, he reacted as he would to a runaway slave, having advertisements posted on the roads towards Connecticut offering a reward for his capture and return.26

The individual humanity of black slaves was, to be sure, given even less recognition than that of white indentured servants. A man like Connor O'Rourke was at least permitted a full name, whereas the slaves were invariably known merely as 'Kitchener' or 'Juba', 'Jenney' or 'Jethro', 'Vulcan' or 'Punch'. In Johnson's will, his white indentured servants were all freed from their bonds and given ten pounds each. The slaves feature repeatedly in the phrase 'my Slaves and stock of cattle'.27 Only Molly's own slave Jenny and her sister Juba are given even the minimal dignity of a name. The image of slaves as livestock occurred to him, also in 1761, when he was telling Daniel Claus of an outbreak of illness among them: 'I fear it will thin my Flock.'28 Johnson would never have thought of his impoverished fellow countrymen in this way, but the experience of buying their bonded service probably inured him to the habit of possessing other people.

His relationship with the Iroquois and his growing public importance as an Indian diplomat did not help to inspire any horror of slavery either. Some of the Indians with whom he dealt practised slavery, employing or selling subject Indians whom they called 'Panis'. Johnson bought some of these Panis in late 1755 to give to Iroquois families in the place of members lost in battle against the French.29 At a peace conference over which Johnson presided in 1762, the Abenaki

Indians arrived with a slave they had purchased to make restitution to the Stockbridge Indians for a man they had killed. Johnson accepted delivery of the slave and sent him on to Stockbridge.[30]

These Indian slaves were sometimes bought by whites. In 1762 Johnson had to deal with the murder of a white trader in Detroit by two Panis whom he had purchased. The two slaves, a man and a woman, had cut off their master's head and thrown his body into a river. The man escaped, but the woman was publicly hanged, in order, as Jeffery Amherst informed Johnson, to provide 'a Terror to others from being Guilty of Such Crimes for the future'.[31]

In 1761 Johnson's Indian Affairs department was heavily involved in the capture and return of a Pani enslaved by the Mohawks, who had fled to Canada. The man had run off when his Mohawk masters were so drunk that he feared they might kill him. Johnson was utterly unsympathetic to the slave's plight and told Daniel Claus, then in Montreal: 'I am resolved to have the fellow at any rate.'[32]

Even though there were slaves within Indian society, Indian villages were also refuges for runaway blacks. In 1764, for example, there was a 'Large Lusty Negro at Chenussio' (Genesseo) and a mulatto blacksmith who himself had bought a captured white girl as a servant for five pounds.[33] These men were runaway slaves 'who came several years ago from the Southward' and whom their adopted tribe 'look[ed] upon as Indians'.[34] Some free blacks also lived in Indian communities. In the late 1760s Johnson employed a 'Free Mullatto' named Sun Fish to take messages and gather intelligence in the Niagara area.[35] Sun Fish had lived among the Senecas for more than a decade, was fully integrated into local society, and was sufficiently well informed about Seneca politics to be a valuable informant.[36]

In his official capacity, Johnson actively demanded the return to slavery of black people who had fled to or been taken prisoner by Indian tribes. While these demands could be regarded as matters of public policy, it is clear that Johnson had no private compunction about catching and returning slaves who had fled to live among the Indians. In the negotiations of 1764 he secured the agreement of the Genesseo Senecas to 'deliver up all our people who are among them whether Prisoners, Deserters Negroes etc.'[37] The separate listing of prisoners and blacks suggest that the latter in this case were runaway slaves rather than captives. Around the same time, his instructions to Henry Montour, whom he sent to conclude peace with some western tribes, included a demand that they must 'immediately deliver up all Whites, Negro's & French Amongst them'.[38] His treaty with the Hurons of Detroit in the same year also called for the return of 'prisoners, or Deserters, Negro's'.[39]

In 1767 he was asked privately by the Connecticut clergyman Samuel Johnson to help find a black man – 'a short, thick, sensible fellow, & speaks English well, & can read & write, & is said to forge passes in which he calls himself Sam' – who was thought to be living among the Indians at Fort Augusta. He replied: 'If I can yet hear of him, I shall do all in my power to have him apprehended.'[40]

Johnson also encountered a runaway slave called Sam Tony, who had fled from a plantation in Maryland, and taken refuge with the Indians on the Susquehanna, 'where he acquired much influence'.[41] Sam Tony was taken to Johnson in 1764 by some of the Indians who alleged that he was spreading 'dangerous and Treasonable reports amongst these Indians, tending to alienate their Affections from the English by assuring them that we design shortly to fall upon and destroy all the Indians in alliance with us.' Johnson had him sent into military custody in Albany and urged that he be charged. He feared that if he were released he would 'return to the Indians with the Strongest prejudices against Us'. Sam Tony's fate was almost certainly brutal. General Gage informed Johnson that 'the Negro you have sent down may easily be disposed of in the West Indies', and this is presumably what happened.[42]

Johnson was part of a power structure in which blacks were at the bottom. The colonial authorities needed Indians as allies and therefore had to give them, at least collectively, some respect. Slaves, on the other hand, were required, not to co-operate but to obey. For the Indians themselves, the sight of black slaves was a constant reminder of the condition to which they might be reduced. French agents exploited this fear by telling the Iroquois in 1749 that the English 'looked upon them as our Slaves, or Negroes'.[43] To counteract this reasonable anxiety, it had to be made clear that the Indians were more highly respected than the blacks. If it came to a conflict between Indians and black slaves, Johnson and the imperial power he represented were always more likely to favour the former.

The white authorities, often so reluctant to punish crimes against Indians by Europeans, were happy to make an example of black criminals.

Johnson received a report on an incident at Detroit in 1766 in which two Indian women were raped and murdered by 'an English Negro' belonging to a local merchant. The man was caught, and as the Detroit commander, Lieutenant Colonel Campbell informed his superiors, 'I wish with all my heart he could be tried here & if condemned to suffer death, his being made an example of in the presence of the Indians, I believe wou'd have a very good effect, and convince them that we never skreen bad people from Justice.'44 In this case, General Gage even regretted the bother of a trial, and suggested to Johnson that 'the Indians Should not have been withheld from doing themselves Justice on such a Villain'.45

This willingness to appease Indians at the expense of blacks extended to the endorsement, where they arose, of Indian prejudices. Johnson received a copy of a formal edict from the Narragansett tribe deposing one of their sachems, Thomas Ninegrett, for crimes including 'Marrying a Molatto Woman without the approbation of the tribe'.46 And, shortly after Johnson's death, his nephew, son-in-law and successor Guy Johnson completed a deal which had been initiated by Sir William, granting some Oneida land to remnants of the Mohegan, Narragansett, Montauk and Pequod tribes. The land was gifted 'with this particular Clause, or Reservation that Same shall not be possessed by any persons, deemed of the said tribes, who are descended from, or have intermixed with Negroes, or Mulattoes'.47

The absence of any evidence that Johnson was ever troubled by being a slave-holder or by the subjection of the black people he lived with, throws some light on his very different relationship with the Iroquois. It is a reminder that he was not acting out of enlightened benevolence. His subtle and sympathetic view of the Iroquois in general and individual Indians in particular was born of a mutual dependence that required a respectful relationship. He was in America not to protect the Iroquois, but to restore and advance his family name and his personal status. In that sense, casual cruelty to his African neighbours was part of his Irish pride.

30

Irish Dreamtime

═══

The Quaker trader James Kenny believed that 'dreams often come from the ideas and thoughts that are prevalent in the mind'. In March 1762, when he was at Fort Pitt, he had a terrible dream. He was sitting in a strange house with some people and he instantly sensed, though he did not know why, that the Devil was in the company. He felt 'great abhorrence and resentment of mind' and stood up to leave. As he did so he looked straight at Satan and saw that he was wearing the face of the Moravian preacher Frederick Post and was dressed in Post's clothes. He left the room and woke up.

Wondering what ideas and thoughts could have been so prevalent in his mind as to create such a nightmare, he remembered that he had had an argument the night before with Frederick Post. They had been discussing the abominations of Catholics and Post had made the mistake of defending some of their practices. He had told Kenny that 'the papists did not Worship Idols & endeavour'd to Excuse their making such things as if useful, but I shamed him so that he was Struck Silent'. Continuing to trace the source of his dream to its roots, Kenny then remembered that Post, just to reassure Kenny that he was not a lover of papists, had let him in on the secret source of Kenny's nocturnal disturbance.

This secret was about a dinner that had been held at Fort Pitt on the evening of St Patrick's Day. William Johnson's deputy George Croghan had been at the fort and had been chosen to preside at the dinner and be toasted as if he were Saint Patrick himself. As the drink had flowed and the exuberance risen, Croghan had allowed the hard crust of conformity and orthodoxy that surrounded Johnson's Indian superintendency to be washed away by a surge of sentimental emotion.

He had stood up and proposed a toast to 'King James's Health'. King James was the Old Pretender, James Francis Edward Stuart, son of the deposed James II, and, to the Jacobites, King James III of Great Britain and Ireland. He was, at the time, still alive and residing at the heart of papist idolatry in Rome.

Not only had Croghan proposed a toast to the Pretender but the rest of the company had taken it up. When one drunken officer had objected, calling Croghan a 'damned rascal', he had been shouted down and forced to 'drink a Bumper for refusing'. Kenny, when he had heard of this abomination, had 'told Post in some parts this would be looked upon like Treason & the Man that had that so near his heart was not very fit to be Trusted as an Indian Agent for the Crown of England, considering what Interest & Influence he has amongst so many Nations of Indians, & the Effect that French or Spanish Money might have on him'.[1]

Croghan's moment of madness, and James Kenny's horrified reaction to it, provide a unique glimpse of the hidden layers of William Johnson's world. Had he got to hear of it, Johnson would have been enraged and appalled by his deputy's wild indiscretion. He had spent much of his life guarding his reputation and controlling his image. He had marked the map of America with declarations of his loyalty to the Hanoverian dynasty that James III fantasised about replacing. He and his son had been honoured by the real king, George III. The taciturn, watchful Johnson whom Anne Grant remembered was a man who had learned from his earliest days in Ireland to govern his tongue. Croghan's recklessness would have struck him as an outrage. Yet, long before any biography of him had appeared, the Dutch New York novelist James Kirke Paulding, who had only the vaguest notions of Johnson's career, could write with confidence that his background was Jacobite. Without revealing his private self as crudely as Croghan had done, he had left traces of his mentality somewhere in the atmosphere.

Johnson never betrayed the emotions buried beneath the calm surface of his official attitudes quite as crudely as Croghan did that night in Fort Pitt. He did, however, leave on the official record one highly suggestive trace of what those inner feelings might have been. In September 1764 Colonel John Bradstreet concluded peace deals with some Ottawas, Shawnees, Chippewas and Wyandots, details of which outraged both General Gage and Johnson, though largely for different reasons. Gage criticised this 'most Astonishing Treaty of Peace' because it 'contain[ed] no one Article whereby the Least Satisfaction [was] given for the many horrid Murders committed by those Barbarians', and also because Johnson had not been consulted.[2] Johnson naturally agreed with the latter criticism, but his main concern was, on the face of it, puzzling: that Bradstreet had asserted, and the sachems had apparently accepted, British sovereignty over the Indians.

In Bradstreet's record of the talks, Johnson found some startling passages that threatened to undermine his whole approach as a mediator between two independent peoples. The document quoted the Mississauga sachem Wapacomagat as saying that 'it gave him infinite pleasure to find the Indians had put themselves into the Arms of the Great King of England and that they were now his Subjects and Children'. Bradstreet seized on this phrase and objected that in general the Indians described the British as brothers. 'Colonel Bradstreet observing they [the Indians] made use of the word Brother[s] instead of Subjects and Children of the King of England, told them nobody were to be admitted into the aforementioned Submission and Articles of Peace, but such as acknowledge themselves Subjects and Children of the King of England.' Wapacomagat replied that 'it was very proper and they now throw aside the name of Brother and should ever after Acknowledge themselves Subjects and Children of the King of England which they should in future call themselves'.[3]

To Johnson, as a royal official and a baronet, this ought to have been pleasing. It was his job to uphold and extend His Majesty's power and the clear expression by these troublesome Indians of their acceptance of the royal yoke should have met with his approval. There was no evidence that Wapacomagat's submission had caused any problems or had been experienced as a humiliation. Yet it stirred something so deep within William Johnson that it erupted in a passionate objection.

Johnson immediately protested to both Gage and the Board of Trade in London that Indians were not, and would never accept themselves as, subjects of the King. He suggested that the Indians' recorded acceptance of Bradstreet's demand that they be described in this way was either a linguistic misinterpretation – 'neither have they any word which can convey the most distant idea of subjection' – or the result of coercion.

The best clue to what was going on in his mind is that he expressed this latter possibility in terms poignantly redolent of his own Irish Catholic background: 'When a Nation find themselves pushed, their Alliances broken, and themselves tired of War, they are verry apt to say many civil things, and make any Submissions which are not agreable to their intentions, but are said merely to please those with whom they transact Affairs.'4

The emotional palimpsest beneath the surface texts of Johnson's letters on this subject makes them a revealing expression of the resonance in his own mind of the words 'subject' and 'subjection'. There is a sense in them that an act of ventriloquism is being performed, that a hidden voice from Johnson's own history is sounding out through the words he puts in the mouths of the Indians:

None of the Six Nations, Western Indians etc ever declared themselves to be Subjects, or ever will consider themselves in that light whilst they have any Men, or an open Country to retire to, the very idea of Subjection would fill them with horror . . . it may prove a dangerous consequence to persuade [the British government] that the Indians that have agreed to things which (had they even assented to) is so repugnant to their Principles that the attempting to enforce it, must lay the foundation of greater Calamities than has yet been experienced in this Country – It is necessary to observe that no Nation of Indians have any word which can express, or convey the Idea of Subjection, they often say 'we acknowledge the great King to be our Father, we hold him fast by the hand, and we shall do what he desires' many such like words of course, for which our People too readily adopt & insert a Word verry different in signification, and never intended by the Indians, without explaining to them what is meant by Subjection. – Imagine to yourself Sir, how impossible it is to reduce a People to Subjection, who consider themselves independant thereof both by nature & Scitiation, who can be governed by no Laws, and have no other Tyes amongst themselves but inclination, and suppose that it's explained to them that they shall be governed by the Laws, Liable to the punishments for high Treason, Murder, Robbery and the pains and penaltys on Actions for property of Debt, then see how it will be relished, and whether they will agree to it . . .

As soon as he had finished this letter, which is much more emotional than the sober one he sent to the Board of Trade on the same subject, he wondered if he had revealed too much of himself. He added a note to Gage: 'For my part I have . . . only given You my private Sentiments on the Subjection mentioned in the Treaty, as to a Freind in whom I can thoroughly confide.' He marked the letter, almost uniquely in his official correspondence, 'Private' – as, indeed, it was. His rage at seeing the rebel Mississaugas, supposedly his enemies, acknowledge themselves to be subjects, in the words of Bradstreet's treaty, of 'our

Sovereign Lord George the third, King of England France & Ireland'
had for a moment disrupted his controlled and official self.

The images he conjures in his letter to Gage are as much ancestral
and personal memories as comments on the Indians – a last stand in
which there are no men left to fight and no open country to hide in; a
nation tired of war pushed into submission; people who grow up
learning that they have to 'say many civil things, and make any
Submissions which are not agreable to their intentions'; the art of
uttering the phrases necessary 'to please those with whom they transact Affairs'; punishments for high treason, and the pains and penalties
of lost property and accumulated debt. The litany is as much a romantic summary of the private myths of the Warrens and Johnsons as it is
a delineation of Indian principles.

This train of thought was linked to intimations of his own mortality.
He was then approaching fifty, and the rigours of his life had taken a
toll in pain and increasingly frequent bouts of ill health. He was rather
gloomy about his chances of ever being able to enjoy the grand retirement he had dreamed of after the war. With the politics of Indian
diplomacy as demanding and frustrating as ever, he doubted that he
would ever live to be a man of leisure. 'Altho I am not far advanced in
years,' he confided to Cadwallader Colden, 'yet I am so involved in
cares & business that I can have little prospect of ease or Retirement.'5
The weary feeling of being unable to enjoy the rewards of all the energy he had expended seems to have prompted an introspective admiration for Indians, 'who can be governed by no Laws'.

This fusion in Johnson's mind of private history and public policy, of
Irish memories and the contemporary rebellion, suggests a well of sympathy for the Indians who were asserting the very independence he claimed
for them. His anger in the letter to Gage is directed, not at Bradstreet
for making the Indians say they are subjects – 'probably', he writes,
'his motive might be well intended' – but at Wapacamagat for submitting. One reason why Johnson never railed against Indian rebels was
that diehard defiance held some allure for a man like himself whose fame,
fortune and career had been built on an ability to submit to the realities of his times and accommodate himself to the prevailing climate.
As he got older, he allowed himself a little more harmless defiance.

When they came to see him, visitors to Johnson Hall saw two prints
hanging in the lobby. One was a map of Ireland. The other was one

of the many versions of the last parting of Hector and Andromache.[6] The images were not as distant from each other as they might have appeared to the casual eye. Hector is Troy's last champion, and the last loved one his wife Andromache has left. He is going out to be killed too, and he finds his wife at the top of the tower. She begs him not to go. He foresees his own death, the deaths of his parents and his people, the fall of his city and his world. He prays that he will be dead by the time Andromache is hauled away screaming into slavery, to work at someone else's loom and draw water for foreigners.[7]

These two images in the hallway were not a bad introduction to the house and the man who had built it. One of them touched on the melancholy pride of a dying world, the tragic dignity of its fast-fading glories. The other image, the map of Ireland, hinted at Johnson's desire to re-create the defunct cosmos of his ancestors. Even while the British America he had helped to create was crumbling from the inside, while his body was reminding him of his own mortality, he was imagining himself as a Gaelic lord, an idealised feudal chieftain from a time before the city fell and his class was dispossessed. He gathered around him broken shards of the old Irish order: harp music and the Gaelic language, Catholicism and the ancient sacred spring of his Warrenstown childhood.

Music was a constant interest of Johnson's, and he accumulated in his houses a flute, oboes, a French horn, a trumpet, a guitar, and three violins. He sent all the way to New Jersey for an organ for the church he built near the Hall.[8] His correspondents sent him topical songs on contemporary New York politics and even a cantata of satirical ballads. Johnson Hall, and the settlement of Johnstown which Johnson established beside it, were, in this respect, a cultural crossroads, one of the places where an American music began to harmonise itself from the strains of Irish airs and ballads, Scottish jigs, African chants, Iroquois ritual songs and European art music. Richard Shuckburgh, Johnson's friend and secretary, who spent a great deal of time at the Hall, wrote 'Yankee Doodle' as an affectionate satire on the colonial militia in Johnson's Lake George army of 1755, using a tune from John Gay's *The Beggar's Opera*. Mohawks, meanwhile, learned baroque melodies at the Hall. Warren Johnson in 1761 'heard an Indian playing many European Tunes, & pretty well on the Fidle'.[9] Peter, Johnson's half-Mohawk son with Molly, was also an enthusiastic violinist.

Within this swirl of sound, Johnson became obsessed with hearing one remembered note. At least from the mid-1760s Johnson was trying to get a harper and a piper to come from Ireland to Johnson Hall. In now-destroyed letters, his Irish friend Hugh Wallace reported to him on his efforts to fulfil Johnson's wishes, and warned him that finding a harper in Ireland was now difficult, as they were 'verry scarce in and out of Ireland'. The search seems to have gone as far as Wales.[10] Eventually, in the summer of 1766, a 'blind musician with an Irish Harp who seemed an honest man' was persuaded to come.[11] John Cain travelled from Ireland with his wife as an indentured servant to Johnson.[12] Cain seems to have been reasonably intimate with Johnson, who was able to report on his health in some detail.

Why did Johnson go to so much trouble to find a blind harper for the Hall? The dispossession of Johnson's ancestors, the O'Neills of the Fews, was a major theme for two of the most important blind harper-poets of his childhood and adolescence. One, Patrick McAlindon, was born and raised in the Fews. The other, Seamus Dall MacCuarta, came from Omeath, just across the county border in north Louth. Both were fervent Catholics and Jacobites, and MacCuarta's family, like Johnson's Warren relatives, had deep-rooted traditional associations with the Franciscans. The complaints of these bards centre on 'deceiving English law', 'heretic' religion, the advance of the English language and the decline in hospitality for men like themselves in the houses of their traditional patrons.

All of this might seem, on the face of it, to make them anathema to the Johnsons and Warrens, who had compromised with the new political, religious and cultural order. Yet poems like MacCuarta's were also deeply flattering to their sense of self-importance. While MacCuarta praises many of the old Gaelic families, the O'Neills of the Fews take pride of place in his work as representatives of the old nobility. This has been taken by scholars as evidence that he was patronised in particular by the descendants of that sept, and the fact that MacCuarta spent much of his career in Meath strongly suggests that the Johnsons were among them.

This is not as odd as it might appear. Lineage and descent were intensely important to the self-image of the dispossessed Gaelic families, and the harper-poets extravagantly proclaimed the superiority of their breeding to that of the 'puffed-up New English'. At the same time, however, the work of bards like MacCuarta, while it contained ritual visions of a messianic future in which the exiled Jacobites would return to sweep the English back into the sea, was essentially fatalistic. It was haunted by the scale and finality of the Jacobite defeat at the battle of the Boyne in 1690 and the battle of Aughrim in 1691, by the notion that the true nobility lay buried under battlefields and ruined castles, and that nothing short of an unlikely apocalypse would call it forth again. For all the self-pitying rhetoric, their underlying realism was not so deeply at odds with the mentality of Johnson's family.

By the time Johnson was becoming an imperial hero in America, the note of fatalistic nostalgia in the bardic poems and songs in praise of his ancestors was dominant. The Gaelic songs of Art MacCooey, who was from Creggan in the Fews and who was active from the late 1750s until shortly before Johnson's death, also centre on the destruction of the Fews O'Neills. But the lamentation is for a dead past. In one of MacCooey's poems, the ruined walls of Glassdrumman Castle, the seat of Johnson's paternal ancestors, speak to the poet:

> I shall not be restored in future, I will be swept away
> With all the loyal noble sons who won renown in me,
> They are under the slabs in Creggan and I'll not see them
> Till death there.

In another of MacCooey's poems, Ireland appears as an imaginary woman who is linked both to Troy and to Tara, who praises 'the heirs of the Fews' and who 'wakens music' in the 'true homes of the learned'.[13] It is not hard to see why this kind of dreamy, proud but politically safe nostalgia for a lost Gaelic past, with its assertions of past nobility and flattery of the cultured landowner, would be music to Johnson's ears.

That Johnson was entertaining notions of his O'Neill ancestry and Gaelic past is clear from his wonderfully odd design for a coat of arms which he used as a bookplate and as a seal for his letters, and seems to have conceived at some time in 1762. The design has some of the usual heraldic clichés of fleurs-de-lis and scallop shells. The shield is held up, however, by two archaic semi-naked Indians with bows and arrows. At its apex is the red hand of Ulster, the traditional symbol of the O'Neills, which alludes to the founder of the tribe, who, in a race to be the first to lay claim to Ireland, cut off his hand and threw it onto shore from the deck of his ship. The conjunction of Indians, O'Neills and pseudo-aristocratic trappings makes the coat of arms a curiously authentic representation of Johnson's mindset.

This kind of yearning prompted Johnson's search for a blind harper to sing him the old praise songs of his ancestors and the eventual arrival of John Cain at Johnson Hall. Nostalgic hankerings seldom sit easily with mundane realities, however. The noble bards that Johnson remembered from his childhood had become a shattered remnant, deprived of patronage and drifting into something like vagrancy. John Cain turned out to be a wild and unstable character. The surviving glimpses of him suggest a presence far from the courtly subservience that Johnson might have imagined. Cain ordered three gallons of rum on Johnson's account in Schenectady in June 1769. He wandered off at various times to Connecticut, to New Jersey and then to Philadelphia, where he was arrested on suspicion of the murder of a fourteen-year-old boy. Johnson released him from his indenture and his friend Francis Wade helped to get Cain out of jail. His ultimate fate is unclear, but he does not seem to have returned to Johnson Hall.[14]

Johnson's search for a harper was, however, just one aspect of his quest for a restoration of his Gaelic past in the Mohawk valley. In the war against the French, Johnson had co-operated with Colonel Simon Fraser, the remarkable leader of Highland Scottish troops who is placed next to Johnson in Benjamin West's epic painting *The Death of General Wolfe*.[15] In placing the two men together, West was making a subtle statement, for they shared a hinterland in the treacherous terrain of Jacobitism. Fraser's shift from opposition to the Hanoverians to imperial warrior was even more dramatic and recent than Johnson's, for Fraser had been an active Jacobite rebel in 1745 and had been found guilty of high treason for bringing reinforcements to Bonnie Prince Charlie's beleaguered forces in their doomed last stand at Culloden. His own father, Lord Lovat, the seventy-nine-year-old chief of Clan Fraser, had been hunted down by the Hanoverian authorities and beheaded.

Fraser had trimmed his sails to the prevailing winds with an icy ruthlessness that made the subtler, more ambiguous pragmatism of the Warrens and Johnsons look ethereal and absent-minded. Even in prison and within a few month's of his father's execution, he helped the Hanoverians to win a Scottish election. Having thus secured his release he became a lawyer and helped to prosecute and hang an old Jacobite comrade. The government, having then figured out that the remnants of the Highland clans could at once be defused and deployed by sending them to the colonies, gave him his own regiment, the 78th, or Fraser's Highlanders, and sent him with them to the American frontier. They were regarded by the English as the equivalent of Indians – in Wolfe's words: 'hardy, intrepid, accustomed to rough country, and no great mischief if they fall'.[16]

These Highlanders, Gaelic-speaking and Jacobite and therefore part of the cultural and political nexus from which he himself had emerged, could not fail to interest Johnson. It was not just that he could understand better than most colonists the tragedy and irony of their fate as servants of those who had recently shattered their own civilisation. It was also that they offered him, in a peculiarly archaic yet safe form, the possibility of re-creating a kind of nostalgic Gaelic chieftaincy in the Mohawk valley. Having demonstrated their loyalty by fighting fiercely and effectively against the French, they had been politically neutralised. Yet they retained their sense of a communal identity embodied in the figure of the clan chief – a role in which Johnson could easily imagine himself.

After the Seven Years War, therefore, he set about establishing a Highland community on his lands. In 1764 he brought Hugh Fraser, who had been a lieutenant in the 78th Regiment, to the Mohawk valley 'under his protection'.[17] Fraser returned to Scotland, married, and came back with his wife, her younger brother and a number of Highland tenants. Fraser's father-in-law, Lieutenant John McTavish (also from the 78th) and his son; Murdoch McPherson, John Cameron and Alexander McDonnell also became involved in Johnson's schemes for a Highland colony that came to fruition in September 1773 when a party of 425 men, women and children set sail from the west Highland town of Fort William.[18] As they explained in a letter published on their arrival in New York, 'the hardships and oppressions of different kinds imposed . . . by the landlords' in Scotland had 'obliged them to abandon their native country' and seek a better life under Johnson's patronage.[19] Some were 'genteel people of considerable property', others had fewer resources.

Almost all were both Gaelic-speaking and Catholic, however. The leaders of the exodus were MacDonnells: John MacDonnell of Leek, Allan MacDonnell of Collachie, Alexander MacDonnell of Aberchalder, John MacDonnell of Scotus. Their clan had suffered some of the heaviest losses at Culloden. It was, moreover, strongly linked with

Ireland. The MacDonnells were frontier people, with a branch in the Glens of Antrim, where they had become a kind of hybrid Scottish-Irish population. In the songs of Seamus Dall MacCuarta, the MacDonnells joined Johnson's O'Neill ancestors as exemplars of the old nobility.

Allan MacDonnell expressed to Johnson 'a great desire of Settling under your Wing'.[20] It must be assumed that at least some of that desire was motivated by an expectation that their religious freedom would not be interfered with. This, indeed, is the most intriguing aspect of Johnson's creation of a Gaelic community on his lands. Outwardly and officially an enthusiastic upholder of the established Anglican Church, he was nevertheless forming an unofficial Catholic colony under his personal protection.

Religious orthodoxy, it must be remembered, was still a prerequisite for power. Vigilance was still an official duty. In September 1763 Johnson was informed of the 'oath required of persons qualifying as commissioners: disavowing the doctrine of transubstantiation and condemning the invocation or adoration of the Virgin Mary or any other saint. Oath of allegiance to King George III; abjuring the doctrine that excommunicated princes "may be Deposed or Murthered by their Subjects"; and denying the claims of the [Jacobite] Pretender'.[21] A slightly later but very similar version of this same oath was in Johnson's papers, signed by, amongst others, Guy Johnson, John Johnson, John Butler, Robert Adams and Daniel Claus. It includes, as well as the disavowals of Jacobite claims, of the Virgin Mary and of the adoration of saints, an explicit statement that 'the Sacrifices of the Mass as they are now used in The Church of Rome, are supersticious and Idolatrous'.[22]

Formed as he was by the experience of converting from one Church to another as a career move, Johnson had evidently lost any personal interest in religion. He does not seem to have attended church. It is notable that the Reverend Harry Munro of the Society for the Propagation of the Gospel in Foreign Parts, whom Johnson accompanied to Canajahorie in 1770, subsequently praised the religiosity of Daniel Claus – 'a true friend to religion' who set a good example by 'attending divine Service & partaking the holy Communion' – but confined himself to mentioning merely 'Sir William's friendship & Patronage'.[23] Johnson never invoked God in his letters. He was perfectly comfortable with Iroquois religious practices. He didn't marry his long-term lovers in church or worry much about sin. Yet he built Anglican churches, encouraged Protestant missions to the Indians and sent his Mohawk brother-in-law Joseph Brant to be educated by Eleazar Wheelock.

Johnson, deeply sceptical of the whole ideology of conquest in which the right of Europeans to invade America was founded on the moral duty to propagate the gospel, understood the latter as a facade for the subjugation of Indians. European claims to as yet unexplored territories on the continent were, he wrote, founded in 'the practice of the Popes who took upon them to give away all Countrys not Christian in favour of Some Sons of the Church whose Clergy & Subjects were to Convert them, but in reality to deprive them of their Possessions, Libertys, & Lives'.[24] He did not even believe in the religious motives of the first Puritan settlers in New England, holding that 'all Understanding people who have read at all must very well know' that faith 'had very little to do with the Settlement of the Country. Some few discontented people did at first come on that head, but the rest came on principles at present more interesting than Religion, whatever pretences they Make to it.'[25]

Johnson understood religion as a cultural force that determined political loyalties. The intertwining of sectarian and imperial struggles in the America of the 1740s and 1750s meant that Catholic Indians would be anti-British and Protestant Indians pro-British. Abstract goals like the saving of souls were meaningless in this context. As he put it in 1761: 'I am sensible of the great effect Religion has on all Indians, and think it should be encouraged as much as possible, as well out of christian Principle as good Policy, but then it should not be the Roman Catholic Religion for their Priests will always infuse such principles into them, as must be prejudicial to the English interest in spight of all threats or rewards.' Whatever lip service he might pay to 'christian Principle', there was no doubt that 'good policy' had an infinitely higher place in his thinking.[26] His political antipathy to the Jesuit missionaries who had been so powerful a force in bringing Indians into the French fold was evidently reciprocated. In 1762 General Henry Gladwin reported, in a letter that was copied to Johnson, that some Jesuits had sent two belts of wampum to the Catholic Iroquois of Caughnawaga, the message of one of which was that 'they were to murder Sir William Johnson if they did not approve of his Council'.[27]

Yet his essentially pragmatic, sceptical view of religion, along with the knowledge that much of his own family was still Catholic, also encouraged tolerance. He was quick to reassure the Catholic Indians of Canada after the British conquest that their religious liberties would be protected. In March 1762, when a delegation of Abenakis arrived at Fort Johnson to ask that a Jesuit priest who had left them be returned 'so that we may not forget, or Neglect our prayers', he promised 'the free use of their Religion' and told them that the supply of Jesuit missionaries would be 'left entirely to the determination of the Clergy who have always managed these affairs'.[28]

In the late 1760s, with the influx of the Highland Scots adding to the existing Irish Catholic population of about sixty tenant families in Johnstown, Johnson extended this toleration in a quiet but highly significant way. The Anglican Church regarded him as a bulwark against popery. The Reverend Richard Mosley of the Society for the Propagation of the Gospel in Foreign Parts wrote just after Johnson's death: 'The Church will want a good friend in Johnstown now he is gone. – It is doubtfull to me whether many will not follow their own Religion Roman Catholick – An number of the Inhabitants are Irish and all of that opinion, But Sir William would not permitt them –'[29]

In fact, however, Johnson did permit his Catholic tenants to practise their faith. He defied the penal laws prohibiting Catholic worship and allowed the Irish-born Catholic priest Peter McKenna, who accompanied the MacDonnells, to settle in Johnstown and say Mass for the Irish and Scots Highland tenants.[30] This quiet rebellion can be seen as a part of Johnson's return to his own past and as a final revenge for the silences and humiliations of conversion and conformity that had been forced on his family in Ireland. With his blind harper and his Catholic Gaelic-speaking tenants, Johnson was engaged in a process of cultural recapitulation. To complete that process and to close the circle of memory and desire, he conjured in his own way the water spirits that drew the great gatherings to the holy well at Warrenstown for the first hours of St John's Day when he was a child. Appropriately, he did so through a combination of Indian and European forms.

From the mid-1760s onwards Johnson was a Freemason, and he took the whole business of Masonry seriously enough to be raised to the Sublime Degree of Perfection in April 1769. He first joined a lodge established in Albany in the late 1750s by Irish soldiers in the British army. After this lodge lost its Irish character when the soldiers departed, he founded, in May 1766, his own Masonic unit at Johnson

Hall, and called it St Patrick's Lodge after his home country's patron saint. It met every fortnight with Johnson as Master, Guy Johnson as Senior Warden and Daniel Claus as Junior Warden.[31]

The attractions of Freemasonry for Johnson are obvious enough. It combined the ritual practice that had become so much a part of his Indian life with a European form of clannish conviviality. The lodge meetings, indeed, seem to have been Johnson's way of re-creating in a white, largely Irish setting the combination of prescriptive protocol and enthusiastic feasting that he had discovered at Indian councils. The local innkeeper Gilbert Tice recorded some hefty bills, amounting at times to eight or nine pounds, for drink and food at meetings of the 'Club at Lodge'.[32]

Masonry also had for Johnson a nostalgic content. The movement had been popular in County Meath in his youth, especially among the crypto-Jacobite Catholic gentry. The Grand Master of the Grand Lodge of Ireland in the years before Johnson left Ireland was Viscount Netterville, a local Anglo-Norman aristocrat and a Catholic. His successor was a scion of another of the classic Old English Jacobite Catholic families, Henry, Viscount Barnewall. Somone growing up in Johnson's social nexus would have regarded Freemasonry as a mark both of high status and of quietly Jacobite affiliations. The latter assumption was so general that some hostile witnesses went so far as to describe Freemasonry as a 'gigantic Catholic conspiracy'.[33]

The greatest attraction of Freemasonry for Johnson, though, was a private one. The primary Masonic festival, like the biggest festival of Johnson's youth, was St John's Day. Johnson had huge enthusiasm for marking the day with a combination of revelry and ritual reminiscent of the wild yet sanctified scenes at St John's Well. He invited the Reverend Abraham Rosencrantz (in Latin) to attend his lodge 'to observe Saint John's Day with sacred ceremonies'.[34] He seems in fact to have been able to celebrate St John's Day twice a year, once when St Patrick's Lodge went to Albany to join the Masons there in the ceremonies and a second time when the Albany men returned the compliment.[35]

To complete this imagined voyage back to the holy well, he took a trip that itself became a part of the folklore of the New York forests. In the story, as it came to be elaborated, he set out in August 1767 with a party of Mohawks who had promised him a magical relief from his bouts of dysentery and the pain from the bullet in his thigh. They went by canoe on the Mohawk River as far as Schenectady, then by litter to the rude cabin of Michael McDonald, an Irishman who had recently began to clear some land beside Lake Balston. From there, Johnson was carried along the Indian hunters' paths skirting the shore of Lake Saratoga until the Indians found the secret spring.

As the party emerged from the glade, it slowed to a reverent pace and paused a few yards from the spring. Johnson pushed himself off the litter; and approached the spring. He knelt, with uncovered head, and solemnly placed upon the rock a roll of tobacco as a propitiatory offering to the manitou of the spring. Still kneeling, he filled and lit a great calumet, and passed it to each Mohawk in turn. Then, amid the profound silence of the warriors, he, for the first time, touched a white man's lips to the water and drank the holy, life-giving fluid.[36]

This is the foundation myth of Saratoga Springs, which subsequently became a popular resort. Those who would drink its restorative waters would never know that, when Johnson did so that first time, he was a sick man dwindling towards the end of life and remembering how, in his far-off childhood, the waters of another spring, in the first hour of St John's Day, the feast of the Baptist, between midnight and one in the morning, would bubble and roil and whoever drank them in that state would be blessed and healed.

31

A Death Foretold

===

Long after his death, the idea that William Johnson took his own life lingered in both folklore and history. The founding father of American history, Francis Parkman, wrote in his *The Conspiracy of Pontiac* in 1851 that he was 'hurried to his grave by mental distress, or, as many believed, by the act of his own hand'.[1] Challenged by a correspondent about his evidence for this suggestion shortly after publication, Parkman admitted that he had little, yet he remained curiously insistent: 'With regard to his death, there must always be some doubt on the subject and it is proper that this doubt must not be passed without notice. On reverting to the passage in *Pontiac*, it seems to me that it is dealt with there in the manner which the case demands . . .'[2]

The belief that William Johnson, deranged by distress, committed suicide was not a mere invention of the scrupulous Parkman. He took it from local Mohawk valley traditions, where it seems to have taken root shortly after Johnson's death in 1774 and to have persisted well into the 1840s. It sprang up, not because it was true, but because it answered deep needs. There was a need to know how such a man should die, to find an appropriately epic ending to his story; and since his world was swept away by a violent revolution within a year of his death, the end was shaped as the demise of a tragic hero, caught between opposing and ineluctable loyalties, embracing the only decent destiny left open to him and delivering to himself the death he had long foretold.

Jeptha Simms, who interviewed old acquaintances of Johnson's in the Mohawk valley in the early nineteenth century, reported: 'It was supposed by many of his neighbours at that time, that he found means to shorten his days by the use of poison . . . several old people still living,

314

who resided at that time, and have ever since, but a few miles from Johnson Hall, believe to this day that he took the suicidal draught.'

The story, like most folktales, had multiple versions, but all agreed in understanding the self-administered poison as Johnson's response to the coming times. In one, he received, on the day of his death, despatches from London urging him to use his influence with the Indians to get them to attack the rebellious Americans in the event of an attempted revolution. In another, the letters came, not from London, but from Boston, informing him that a war between the colonists and the Crown was now inevitable and seeking his support for the Sons of Liberty.

In the folk memory recorded by the earliest writers on Johnson's life, Jeptha Simms and William L. Stone, the pressures of the coming revolutionary war pushed him towards oblivion. The conflict of loyalties was unbearable. 'He had been taken from comparative obscurity, and promoted by the government of England, to honors and wealth. [But] many wealthy and influential friends around him, were already numbered among the advocates of civil liberty. Should he raise his arm against that power which had thus signally honored him? Should he take sides with the oppressor against many of his tried friends in a thousand perilous adventures?' He 'must either prove recreant to his principles, or take part against the crown'. Johnson himself had sensed the approaching storm and declared his determination to seek shelter from it in death. 'The Baronet declared to several of his valued friends, as the storm of civil discord was gathering, that "England and her colonies were approaching a terrible war, but that he should never live to witness it."' When he died, these valued friends 'being together after the event, and speaking of the Baronet's death, agreed in their opinion that his former declarations were prophetic, and that he was a man sufficiently determined to execute such design if once conceived'.[3]

The belief in this grand, tragic gesture is all the more striking because it is so patently ill-founded. Johnson's actual death was a public and entirely predictable event. He foresaw it, not from some dark resolve to escape an unbearable future, but because he had been plagued by illness. Those who knew him were expecting him to die. One acquaintance reported sadly to another in November 1769: 'Yr friend Sr Wm Johnson is sore fail'd he is every now & then in a bad way, wherefore is thot not to last many years more, which will be a

great loss to mankind in general, but particularly to this neighbourhood & I don't see that any one of the Family is capable of keeping up
the genl applause when he is gone.'4

Johnson did everything he could to delay the inevitable, using
European and Indian medicines, bathing in the sea, drinking from
sacred springs. By the time he died, in July 1774, he was nearly sixty –
not a bad age for an eighteenth-century man who had lived both a
rough life in disease-ridden surroundings and a high life of pleasant
indulgence. He had known by then that he was not long for the world
and he had taken rational steps to prepare for a future that threatened,
so far as he knew, a turbulence no more violent than the tumult that
had been the familiar weather of his life. For a man whose family had
survived the loss of their world, who had himself helped to shape a
continent's destiny and the collapse of France's American empire,
there were no special terrors in the prospect of another upheaval.

What is true is that in the last years of his life, events on the continent were drifting gradually beyond Johnson's reach. In Indian affairs,
he remained the paramount figure, but his achievements were largely
negative, consisting as they did in a series of brilliant manoeuvres to
prevent the emergence of an alliance among all the Indian nations of
the North-East. In the broader context of the relationship between the
colonies and the Crown, he was but dimly aware of the great irony of
the British victory over France. Just as Johnson's role in that victory
had helped inadvertently to weaken his Indian allies by depriving them
of the balance of power, so it had also weakened his own imperial
masters. Freed from the threat of an assertive – and assertively
Catholic – French presence in North America, the colonial population
had been given the opportunity to assert itself as a political force in its
own right. The emerging struggle was conducted in terms alien to
Johnson's semi-feudal, paternalistic mindset.

His attitude to the disputes between the colonial assemblies and
popular movements on the one hand and the British government on
the other was, in general, mildly ambivalent but essentially loyalist. It
was shaped by both his inheritance and his experience. The Jacobite
culture from which he emerged was a kind of archaic radicalism, mil-
lennial and even apocalyptic in its dreams of a restored golden age, but
pre-modern in its ideal of a good king who would make all things
right. Johnson's own experiences in America were broadly of support
and sympathy from the Crown and its officials in London and of

obstruction from the New York colonial assembly, which he tended to see, not without reason, as an arena for factional disputes among different commercial interests. Neither of these influences predisposed him towards sympathy for republican or democratic ideals. The only one of the subsequent leaders of the revolution with whom he had any sustained contact was Benjamin Franklin, and Franklin himself was, until late in the day, horrified by the gradual drift towards American independence.

In the battles over the Stamp Act of 1765 and import duties, Johnson was not entirely unsympathetic to colonial demands, but he objected to the radical methods of the protestors: 'Whatever reason or Justice there may be in some of the late Steps . . . there is a probability of their being carried farther than a Good Man can wish for.'[5] He was used to seeing politics as a game played between members of an elite and could not see the Stamp Act agitation as anything more than the result of machinations by a self-interested minority. He wrote to a correspondent in London in 1765, of 'the Violent & unaccountable Conduct of the Americans, occasioned by the Stamp Act, all which has been Excited by a few pretended patriots & Lawyers in these parts'.[6] Even if he sympathised to some degree with the opposition to the Stamp Acts, his own background, which had taught him to value pragmatism over principle, gave him a cynical view of patriotic rhetoric.

Thus, on the one hand, he condemned, during the anti–Stamp Act agitation, 'the clamourous conduct of a few pretended Patriots, who have been always remarkable for opposing Government in everry Article, & its Officers in everry Character, & have propagated their Republican principles amongst an Ignorant People, whose Religious & Civil tenets incline then to embrace that Doctrine'. During the anti-government riots in Boston in 1768, when Thomas Gage wrote to him describing the radicals as 'a most turbulent seditious People', Johnson replied: 'I believe you know my Sentiments of these people,' implying that he shared Gage's disapproval. The following year, he wrote to Cadwallader Colden, who, as Lieutenant Governor of New York, was under fire in the renewed conflict between radicals and loyalists, that 'Tho' Patriotism is the pretext on most such occasions I look upon it as you do that the late Contest was really of another nature, but in this Patriotic Age, no point can be carried under any other Colours, it is a Charm with which the populace have been often led to Measures highly dangerous & Injurious to their true Interests & it will always be the Case in free Governments.'[7]

On the other hand, in the same letter in which he deprecated the republicanism of the anti–Stamp Act agitators, he also worried that the attempts to impose the act would create serious trouble: 'Having a property to lose, I cannot be supposed to think differently from the real Interests of America, Yet as a lover of the British Constitution I shall retain Sentiments agreeable to it, altho I should be almost singular in my opinion, and I have great reason to think that the late transactions, & what is daily expected in other Colonies will be productive of dangerous Consequences . . .'[8]

Johnson's correspondents were sceptical of the motives of the colonial radicals when the Sons of Liberty imposed a virtual boycott of British goods in 1768. Johnson's New York agent John Wetherhead took the cynical view that the merchants who were prominent in the movement were hoping to sell off their surplus stocks: 'God knows when the Sons of Liberty will permitt us to have any more Goods, I Suppose not till they have sold all their Old & refuse Goods, which they are doing at an exorbitant Rate.'[9] On the other hand, however, the Sons of Liberty were not especially antagonistic to Johnson. They allowed him to import goods for the Indian trade, recognising the importance of his diplomatic work. Aside from one occasion when bad feeling was created by an attempt, made without Johnson's knowledge, to import other goods by claiming they were his, the relationship between the Superintendent and the agitators was businesslike.[10]

Johnson seems to have imagined the unfolding conflict as a dispute between Britain and America in which the Irish like himself could act as mediators. In a now-destroyed letter to his Irish friend in New York Hugh Wallace, in 1765, he complained that the agitation had been carried too far and stated his willingness to encourage the formation of a 'Hibernian Concert', meaning presumably a faction of Irish property-owners in the colonies who could help to bring about a resolution.[11] The notion that his Irish skills of negotiation and compromise could make much of a difference in the circumstances of the times suggests a failure to grasp the fundamental nature of the divide, and it is not surprising that nothing came of it.

Johnson was, in any case, still preoccupied with the fractious business of the Indian Superintendency. His dream of a final settlement between the white colonies and the Indian nations, made incarnate with the boundary line, proved predictably illusory. He had pleased the Iroquois, the traders and the land speculators, but his opening up of the Ohio valley had merely outraged the western Indians without putting an effective stop to illegal white settlements. As the rumblings of revolution and the financial constraints imposed by the crisis convinced Gage to abandon many of the army's western outposts, the Shawnees tried to create a new league to oppose the Fort Stanwix treaty. Denying the right of the Iroquois to cede their lands, they conspired to undo Johnson's work by force. He, in turn, was doomed to spend his last years in a brilliant but rather inglorious campaign to thwart them. To the Earl of Hillsborough, who had opposed Johnson's extension of the boundary line, he was now the victim of his own 'fatal policy'.[12]

After the treaty of Fort Stanwix, Johnson had adopted an open policy of preventing the Indian nations as a whole from forming a coherent alliance among themselves. He would have been happy to have the resources necessary to propitiate all the nations with presents and diplomacy, but the increasingly sharp divisions between the colonies and the Crown meant that he had to operate on a minimal budget. This left him, as he put it to Thomas Gage, with no choice but to keep the Indians divided: 'We cannot expect to keep them in Temper but at an Expence too great (at least in the opinion of Government) for the Object, Consequently all that can be Expected from the present Establishment is to keep some of them in our Interest, and endeavour to divide the rest, and I am hopefull that the Constant pains I take and Influence I have over many of them will at least have these Effects.'[13]

On behalf of a dying empire, a dying man orchestrated the tensions, jealousies and resentments among the different Indian nations, successfully preventing the formation of a hostile alliance by the Shawnees. The Shawnees in turn tried to subvert Johnson's authority by seeking to open direct negotiations with Pennsylvania, to send a delegation of their own to London, and even to treat directly with the back-country settlers.[14] Johnson thwarted all these efforts, and retaliated by seducing allies from the Shawnees and by encouraging internal disputes.

Johnson managed all of these manoeuvres with undiminished skill, and continued to wear out his diminishing health in the maintenance of the British–Iroquois alliance. William Tryon, who became Governor of New York in 1771, visited him at Johnson Hall in early August 1772 and observed the 'credit and confidence Sir William was held in by the Indian Tribes'. Johnson evidently tried to disabuse Tryon of the usual prejudices, and evidently succeeded. The Governor reported to London that the Mohawks 'appear to be actuated as a community by principles of rectitude, that would do honour to the most civilised nations. Indeed they are in a civilised state, and many of them good Farmers.' He was struck, nevertheless, by the continuing burdens of Johnson's office: 'It is impossible any man can have more uniform zeal and attention than Sir William has in his Department, so much so, that it would be no great impropriety to style him the Slave of the Savages.'15

All this effort was expended, however, on behalf of an empire whose hollowness was becoming ever more apparent. Johnson had become almost resigned to the incapacity of the British and the colonies to conduct a sustained Indian policy with the sensitivity, generosity and foresight to place relations on a sound footing for the future. The diminution of presents, the unchecked eruptions of new settlers and the continuing crimes against Indians, had created conditions for another general revolt. 'Thro' the imprudence of our own people', Johnson warned the Earl of Hillsborough in 1771, '& [the Indians'] natural suspicions, [they] have become more and more alarmed for themselves, tho they still believe that it is in their power to give us such a check as may prevent us from attempting what they apprehend we have in view. Many will talk, some will think, and a lesser number will act otherwise, but this is nevertheless the true political state of their sentiments in general at present.'16

While atrocities against the Indians continued to be committed through what Johnson called 'wantonness and cruelty' and 'sentiments of barbarity superior to the most cruel savage', there was little prospect of justice for the victims or the perpetrators. The murders in the spring of 1772 of a party of Mississaugas, including a woman and an infant, by a trader on Lake Erie provided yet further proof of the inability of the colonial system to deliver justice to Indians. The killer, a trader called Ramsay, was apprehended, but Johnson, from long experience, had 'little expectation of its final issue in any manner satisfactory to the Indians'.17

These problems were by-products of the vacuum of authority created by the struggle between the colonies and the Crown. The Covenant Chain linking the Great King in England to his Indian children, so often evoked and refurbished by Johnson, was close to breaking. For all Johnson's efforts to keep up the Indian side of the alliance, the British side was becoming incapable of meeting its commitments. When, in late 1772, Johnson pushed the new Secretary of State in London, the Earl of Dartmouth, for a new system of trade regulation to prevent frauds against the Indians, Dartmouth's reply was as frank as it was, from Johnson's point of view, depressing. He acknowledged the force of Johnson's arguments and lamented the absence of the necessary policies, but then confessed the essential powerlessness of the imperial government: 'There is not sufficient authority in the Crown for the execution of such a Plan; and as the Colonies do not seem disposed to concur in any general Regulations for that purpose, I am at a loss to suggest any mode by which this important service can be otherwise provided for . . .'[18]

If there was any epic dimension to Johnson's descent towards death, it was simply that his morbidity paralleled that of the empire he had served so well. Dartmouth's admission that the Crown itself was 'at a loss' came at a time when Johnson's illness, previously spasmodic, was becoming chronic. In September 1772 his 'Disorder attacked [him] with much Violence' and he was laid up for a fortnight. In October, he was complaining of 'a very severe Indisposition'.[19] He was becoming 'sensible of his approaching end' and, by the end of the year, so were the Indians. 'The declining state of my health', as he wrote to Gage, had 'alarmed the Indians' to such an extent that they had begun to openly discuss what would happen after his death: 'The Indians who have of late years frequently been Witnesses of the Suddenness and Violence of the Attacks of my Disorders, have latterly Addressed me very Seriously upon it.' Although they broached the subject as tactfully as possible, the concern of these Indians – presumably Mohawk sachems – was that Johnson might die without having arranged a successor who would carry on his work in a manner acceptable to them.[20]

Johnson knew that it was merely a matter of which one of his frequent attacks would prove to be the last. He drew up his will on 27 January 1774, months before his death, and had it witnessed by four Johnstown residents, including a cabinetmaker and an innkeeper. He arranged to leave substantial sums of money and huge tracts of land to his family, friends and retainers, with most of the estate going, as a matter of course, to his son Sir John. The most revealing parts of the will, however, are the passages that show the care he took to provide for his unofficial children by Molly Brant. Not only did he leave them substantial legacies of land and money, but he made arrangements to try to ensure that they would not be cheated after his death. He established a trust to protect their interests, and it may be significant that its members did not include his more conventional heirs, his son John and sons-in-law Daniel Claus and Guy Johnson.

The language of his charge to the six friends whom he appointed to the trust suggests both an anxiety that his Mohawk children might be defrauded and a deep concern for their future. He enjoined the trustees to remember his 'close connection' to Molly's children and 'the long uninterrupted friendship subsisting' between him and Molly. He called on them to 'strictly and as *Brothers* inviolably observe and Execute *this* my last charge to them. The Strong dependence on, & expectation of which unburthens my mind, allays my cares, & makes a change the less alarming.'[21]

The change took a little time to come. In early April, when he had a moment alone, he called Daniel Claus to his study, locked the door behind him and told him he had a serious matter to discuss. He told Claus, in effect, that he was dying and that Guy Johnson would succeed him. He promised Claus, however, that he would get half the superintendent's salary and that he would be treated as being of equal rank to Guy.[22] Around the same time, Johnson wrote to Lord Dartmouth: 'The several duties & fatigues I formerly experienced for many years both in a Military and a Civil capacity, [have] within these few years drawn upon me a train of Infirmities which have often threatened my life, & at best renders it verry precarious.'[23]

In July, 'His Health visibly declined.' Even so, he chose to die as an active man, doing what he had done for thirty years. A spate of unprovoked but organised attacks on the Ohio Indians in the spring of 1774, led by a failed farmer and merchant Michael Cresap, had marked a further stage in the disintegration of the negotiated frontier that Johnson had established. Johnson yet again denounced this violence, warned of a general revolt on the western frontiers and complained of the 'disorderly measures of the inhabitants, & the present imbecility of the American Governments, who are I fear as unable to procure as their people are unwilling to afford justice to the Indians'.[24]

The Iroquois confederacy requested an immediate council with Johnson to discuss this new crisis. A party of Onondagas arrived on

19 June and by 8 July around 600 sachems and warriors from all of the Six Nations were encamped around Johnson Hall. That morning, in his last direct exercise of authority, Johnson released a Seneca man who had been charged with the murder of a trader, on the grounds that punishing Indians for crimes against whites was unjust while white killers of Indians went free. The following day Johnson listened as the Seneca chief Serihowane pointed out to him: 'We are sorry to observe to you that your People are as ungovernable, or rather more so, than ours.' That evening, Johnson dined with the sachems, urging them to restrain the desire for revenge.

The following day, a Sunday, Johnson rested. On the Monday morning, 11 July 1774, he made his last speech, apologising for the 'encroachments made by some of our people' and the tendency of 'some of our ignorant frontier Inhabitants to commit irregularities'. Even though he knew that the chances were slim, he promised: 'These men will be sought after & punished.' After a complaint from the Mohawks of Conojahorie about a particularly egregious fraudster who was trying to cheat them out of land, he proclaimed, in his last formal words in the council of the Iroquois, that such conduct was 'disagreeable to the King'. Having spoken for the final time on behalf of a King whose power in America was ebbing away, he ordered pipes, tobacco and some liquor for the Indians.

At this stage, he was already ill and had to be carried to his bedroom. Two hours later he was dead. The official record of the conference reports that, 'having been very weak from his former Indisposition, the fatigue brought on him a Relapse which in about two hours threw him into a fit in which he suddenly, and most unfortunately, died'. Guy Johnson reported that he was 'seized of a suffocation'.[25]

As soon as they heard of his death about 500 Indians clamoured around the house in 'the utmost confusion and doubt', and sent belts of wampum through the forest to inform the nations that Warraghiyagey was no more.

On the afternoon of Wednesday, 13 July, his body was carried from Johnson Hall to the church he had founded in Johnstown. The pall-bearers included Governor William Franklin of New Jersey and the judges of the New York Supreme Court as well as his son and sons-in-law. A crowd of more than 2,000 people followed the cortège, among them large numbers of Indians, 'who all behaved with the greatest Decorum and exhibited the most lively marks of real Sorrow'. They announced that they would perform their own condolence ceremony the next morning.[26]

Early on Thursday, the sachems of the Six Nations gathered for the ritual. Conoqhquieson, the Oneida chief, wiped a string of wampum beads over Guy Johnson's face to clear the tears from his eyes so that he might look cheerfully and with friendship on his brothers again. He placed another string of wampum on his throat to clear the obstructions which might otherwise prevent him from speaking freely and in the tones of a brother. A third string stripped William Johnson's death bed and brushed the blood from the dead man's eyes so that his spirit would rest and cause them no harm. With a double belt of white beads, he covered Johnson's grave so that he would cause his loved ones no more grief. With a belt of six rows, he collected all the bones of William Johnson and buried them deep in the earth so that they would be out of sight for ever. Then he symbolically poured the clearest water into Guy Johnson's body to cleanse his breast and remove the disturbance from his mind. 'The heavy clouds which have hung over you, and us, have prevented us from seeing the Sun,' he said. 'It is therefore our business with this string to clear the sky which was overcast. And we likewise with this string put the Sun in its proper Course, that it may perform the same as before, so that you may be enabled to see what is doing & pursue the good works of peace.'

These rituals, Conoqhquieson said, would 'keep our young men within reasonable bounds, who otherwise would have lost their senses' at the news of Johnson's death. They also anointed Guy Johnson, who had not as yet been appointed by London, as his uncle's successor, thus reclaiming the Superintendency as an office of the Iroquois league. Conoqhquieson banished grief but also evoked a deep desire for continuity. He buried Johnson but also ritually resurrected him. He handed Guy Johnson a wampum belt of six rows and solemnly charged him:

Brother. Since it hath pleased the Great Spirit to take from us our great Brother Warraghiyagey, who has long desired at our Request to put you in his place, we very much rejoice to find you ready to take this charge upon you, without which we should be in Darkness and great confusion. We are now once more happy, and with this Belt we exhort you to take care of our Affairs, to follow his footsteps, and as you very well know his ways, and transactions with us, that you will continue to imitate them . . .

The sun would move through the sky as it had always done, the council fire would 'burn clear as usual at this Place, and at Onondaga, which are our proper Fire Places', and Guy Johnson would take care of the affairs of the Six Nations 'as that great man did who promised you to us'. Nothing would change.[27]

And yet, of course, everything changed. The world that Johnson had sustained for so long was dying with him. A new sun was rising in the sky. The great council fire of Johnson Hall was soon extinguished and new fires would burn across the colonies. The last promise of the great man – that another Johnson would take his place and follow in his footsteps – could not be kept, because the world in which it had been made was imploding.

32

The End of the World

═══

On 19 August 1777 John Adams, revolutionary leader and subsequently the second president of the United States of America, wrote from Philadelphia to his wife Abigail: 'In the Northern Department they begin to fight. The Family of Johnson, the black part of it as well as the white, are pretty well thinned. Rascals! they deserve Extermination.'[1] By the black and white parts of the Johnson family, the founding father meant the wider network of William Johnson's relatives and descendants, Mohawk and Irish. The glee with which Adams could contemplate their collective extermination is especially eloquent. There was no place for the Johnsons in the emerging American story. They would fall through the gaps in the official narrative into the subterranean sump of myth and oblivion, to be glimpsed now and then as exotic shards of forgotten history.

On the night of Sunday, 21 May 1780, 500 men – regular troops, rangers and Indians – penetrated through the borderlands between Canada and New York along the routes that William Johnson had fought over in the 1750s. They moved by way of Lake Champlain to Crown Point, and thence through the woods to the Sacondaga River. From there they managed what no force had done while William Johnson was alive, and crept right into the heart of his little empire. Before they reached Johnson Hall they divided into two groups. One went through the village of Johnstown to the Hall; the other was sent east to strike at the Mohawk river settlements whose inhabitants were sleeping unawares.

Before it reached the river, the second platoon attacked the house of one Lodowick Putnam. He and his son were killed and scalped. The next house assailed was that of a Mr Stevens, which was burnt, and its owner killed. Arriving at Tripe's Hill, they murdered three men by the names of Hansen, Platts, and Aldridge. They proceeded toward Caughnawaga, the Mohawk village now occupied mostly by Dutch settlers, and about daylight arrived at the house of one Visscher, a colonel in the New York militia and an ardent supporter of the revolution. Visscher was scalped but survived, as did his wounded mother. His two brothers, however, were killed.

Meanwhile, the other platoon of the invading force passed through the village of Johnstown, unnoticed by the small garrison in the little stockade that had been erected to guard it. Making its way to the confluence of the Cayadutta River with the Mohawk, it arrived at the home of Sampson Sammons, a revolutionary of German extraction. The eldest of Sammons' sons was then leasing the Johnson farm at the Hall. It and all of Johnson's lands and properties had been seized six months earlier under an Act of Attainder passed by the rebel New York legislature allowing the 'Forfeiture and Sale of the Estates of Persons who have adhered to the enemies of this State'. Sir John Johnson was on the list of individuals 'convicted and attainted' as Tory traitors.[2] The revolutionary Committee of Sequestrations had seized the Hall and the farm. William Johnson's ancestors had had their property seized for being disloyal to Britain. His heirs had their American property seized for being loyal to Britain.

Sampson Sammons had taken a lease on the farm and bought one of William Johnson's favourite personal slaves, who had been sold as part of the property. The raiders who came to his house that morning wished to punish the Sammons family for their effrontery in occupying the lands that William Johnson had carved out of the forest. They took Sammons and his three sons prisoner. When the youngest insisted on leaving the room to get his shoes, he was almost stabbed by a bayonet, but one of his sisters threw herself in the way and saved him. The prisoners were led away to Caughnawaga, where the two halves of the little army joined up. They then moved off westwards, several miles along the Mohawk valley, burning every building not owned by a Loyalist, killing sheep and cattle. Returning again to Caughnawaga, they torched every building except the church, took more prisoners and killed more people, among them nine old men.

Finally, the army moved back to Johnson Hall. The soldiers dug up the Johnson family silver, which had been buried when Sir John

Johnson had fled in the spring of 1776, after he had been placed under house arrest as a Loyalist. The plate, which filled two barrels, was divided up and placed in the knapsacks of forty soldiers, who carried it all the way back to Montreal.3

This punitive and vindictive expedition was led by Sir John Johnson and Molly's brother, Joseph Brant. In its ranks were men who would leave a permanent mark on Iroquois history and culture, such as the Seneca chief Cornplanter and his half-brother Handsome Lake, to whom, in later life, the spirits would communicate their demands for a great religious revival. Their incursion was devastating. Along with other raids into the Cherry and Mohawk valleys led by John Johnson and Joseph Brant, it was part of a cycle of atrocity and counter-atrocity in which the Johnsons, the Mohawks and the Highland Scottish and Irish tenantry were ranged against the revolutionary Patriots. These raids wiped out virtually all white settlement in the Mohawk valley west of Schenectady. Ultimately, 1,000 Iroquois warriors and 500 Tory rangers were able to lay waste almost 50,000 square miles of colonial territory between the Mohawk and Ohio Rivers. William Johnson's belief that the Iroquois could be a formidable enemy was vindicated: of the 2,500 men enrolled in the revolutionary militia in this part of New York at the start of the war, just 800 remained by 1781. The rest had been killed, captured, or had chosen to flee or desert in the face of the Johnson/Brant onslaught.4

Even as they proved the truth of William Johnson's contention that the Six Nations were a force to be reckoned with, these events also altered the meaning of his legacy. In the firestorm of violence, the reputation of William Johnson as protector of the Mohawk valley was turned on its head. The invasions from Canada which he had so long held at bay were now led by his son, his brother-in-law, his Mohawk friends and his tenants, and the 'Family of Johnson' became, in the minds of men like John Adams, a pestilential breed of white and red savages. In 1779 Johnson's rangers and Brant's Iroquois raided the Cherry valley and killed around thirty civilians. The Cherry valley massacre joined the massacre at Fort William Henry in the evolving legend of Indian atrocity. Lurid rumours that the Iroquois had ripped open and dismembered the bodies of women and knocked out the brains of infants transformed the colonies' old allies into monsters.5

The Iroquois, and the Johnsons, had been pulled into the revolutionary war largely against their will. Initially, the Six Nations had been determined to remain neutral between the British and the Americans, and Guy Johnson, Sir William's successor as Indian Superintendent, had supported this resolution. The revolutionary Continental Congress, too, seemed anxious to leave the Iroquois to their own devices. At a meeting between Congressional delegates and the Six Nations in Albany in August 1775, the latter had made known their decision 'not to take any part, but as it is a family affair, to sit still and see you fight it out. We beg you will receive this as infallible, it being our full resolution; for we bear as much affection for the King of England's subjects on the other side the water, as we do for you, born upon this island.'

They had, however, added a warning that the Johnsons were to be left alone: 'As for your quarrels to the eastward, along the seacoasts, do as you please. But it would hurt us to see those brought up in our own bosoms ill used. In particular, we would mention the son of Sir William Johnson. He is born among us, and is of Dutch extraction by his mother. He minds his own affairs, and does not intermeddle in public disputes.'[6] It was this determination to preserve the Johnsons as the link between themselves and the whites that ultimately dragged them into the conflict and destroyed the confederacy itself.

The Patriot commander George Washington was alert to the danger that any move against Sir John might undermine Iroquois neutrality. As he wrote to Major General Philip Schuyler in May 1776:

Our situation respecting the Indians is delicate and embarassing. They are attached to Johnson, who is our Enemy. Policy and Prudence on the one Hand, suggest the Necessity of seizing him and every Friend of Government; on the other, if he is apprehended, their will be Danger of incurring their Resentment. I hope the Committee will conduct the Matter in the least exceptionable Manner . . .'[7]

The Patriots of the Mohawk valley, however, regarded the Johnsons as a dangerous presence. Their obvious connections to the Crown combined with their influence over the Iroquois created a fear that they might weigh in on the Tory side. In January 1776, on foot of false rumours that Sir John Johnson was accumulating a secret arsenal at Johnson Hall to arm the local Loyalists, Schuyler marched on the Hall with 4,000 men. Johnson gathered a force of around 600 of his tenants, mostly Scottish Highlanders, but they were overwhelmed and disarmed by Schuyler. The search for the supposed arsenal proved fruitless, but, as well as taking 360 guineas from Sir John's desk, the Patriots also ordered him to enter a bond of £1,600 sterling not to 'aid the King's service or to remove within a limited district from his house'.[8]

The specific allegations against Sir John seem to have been false, but the fear that the extended Johnson family might take the British side was not unreasonable. Guy Johnson had gone to Canada on orders from General Gage in May 1775, taking his family, his retainers and a party of Mohawks, including Joseph Brant, with him – about 120 whites and ninety Indians in all. Though Molly Brant stayed behind, Peter Johnson, her son by Sir William, went with Guy. Daniel Claus also left, taking his wife – Johnson's daughter Nancy – with him. It was a tragic journey for the Johnson family, and not just because some of them were leaving the Mohawk valley for the last time. Mary Johnson, Guy's wife and Sir William's daughter, was heavily pregnant. At Oswego, she died in childbirth.[9]

These exiles fought for the British in the defence of Canada against a Patriot incursion in 1775. Young Peter Johnson in particular became a Loyalist hero. The Vermont revolutionary Ethan Allen, having taken Ticonderoga in the first colonial victory of the war, pushed on to Montreal in August 1775. After the assault on Montreal was repulsed, the 'intrepid and active' Peter, as the New York Governor William Tryon reported to London, 'took with his own hand Eathan Allen in a barn'. For this exploit, Peter was later given a commission as an ensign. He was also, according to Tryon, chosen by the Indians 'to be their Chief'.[10]

Most of this Johnson party left Canada for England in November 1775, however. Daniel Claus with Nancy and their daughter, Peter Johnson, Guy Johnson and his three young daughters, Sir William's nephew John Dease, Joseph Brant and a few others, went to England partly to find safety for the women and children and partly to have Guy's temporary appointment as Indian superintendent made permanent, as indeed it soon was. They brought Ethan Allen with them as a prisoner and a token of their prowess, though Joseph's gentle demeanour and good manners disappointed James Boswell, who had hoped for the 'ferocious dignity of a savage leader'.[11]

Although Guy, Joseph Brant and Daniel Claus had left, however, the suspicion among New York's Patriots was that Sir John Johnson and the remaining Mohawks must be in secret correspondence with their departed allies and the Crown. In May 1776 further rumours that John Johnson was organising the Iroquois to massacre the revolutionaries led Schuyler to send a force to seize and imprison him. Johnson, getting word of their approach, fled through the forests to Canada. The Patriots declared that he had broken his bond and seized his wife and children as hostages to be held in Albany. This in turn created panic among the Mohawks and the wider Iroquois confederacy. The Six Nations, with the exception of the Oneidas, who were under the influence of a pro-Patriot dissenting missionary, saw John Johnson's forced flight as a breach of the understanding they had forged with the Continental Congress at Albany in 1775. At a council with the British at Oswego in the early summer of 1777, the Six Nations agreed to take up the hatchet against the Americans.

The Iroquois thus became enemies of the nascent United States. The Mohawks were attacked by the Americans and forced into exile, the upper village under Joseph Brant (who had returned to America with Guy Johnson in July 1776) moving ultimately to the Grand River on the north shore of Lake Erie in Canada. Molly Brant, who was living in Canajoharie with some of her and Johnson's children, was attacked by a party of pro-American Oneidas, robbed of her cash, clothes and cattle and driven to take refuge at the British base at Niagara.[12] The villages at Onondaga, the ritual centre of the confederacy, were burned to the ground by the American Major General John Sullivan in 1779. The great Iroquois confederacy, which had lasted for at least 300 years, tore itself apart as pro-British Mohawks attacked pro-American Oneidas. Its two council fires were extinguished: first at Johnson Hall in 1776, then at Onondaga in 1777. The great long-house was permanently broken into two, with one new league at Grand River and the other at Buffalo Creek.[13] The interests of the Six Nations were ignored in the eventual treaty of peace between the British and the Americans signed in Paris in 1783. The United States declared itself sovereign over Iroquois lands. The Mohawks had been driven out of the Mohawk valley during the war. By 1787 New York State had purchased, under duress, all Oneida, Onondaga and Cayuga lands except for a few small reservations. Johnson's boundary line of 1768 was abolished, and by the end of the century all of the Iroquois territory in New York, outside the reservations, had been sold. The largest of the Six Nations, the Senecas, retained just 200,000 acres of New York.[14]

The private empire of 170,000 acres of upper New York that had been carved out by Sir William Johnson was confiscated by the victorious Americans. His heir, Sir John, estimated his loss at £103,182 sterling and was ultimately awarded £38,995 in compensation by the British government.[15] He received a commission as a brigadier general in 1782 and in the same year was appointed Indian superintendent in succession to his cousin Guy. He held the post until his death at his home, Mount Johnson, near Montreal, in January 1830. Guy left the position because he was accused of padding the accounts of the Indian department to his own advantage. He went to London to try to clear his name and to plead for compensation for the loss of £22,140 sterling incurred when the lands that Sir William had left him were seized by the Patriots. He died there in March 1788.

After the defeat of the Loyalists, Joseph Brant attempted to establish a new confederacy of all the nations of the lower Great Lakes around his base on the Grand River. He managed to establish a community of around 1,850 people, mostly Six Nations and Delawares, that played a vital role in the slow recovery of the Iroquois from the suicidal depression that gripped them after their defeat and removal from New York. In 1802 or 1803 Brant left the Grand River settlement for Burlington Bay on Lake Ontario, where he lived comfortably in the European style. He talked of learning ancient Greek so he could translate the Bible into Mohawk from the original scriptures.[16] He continued to exert a profound influence over Iroquois affairs until his death in 1807. Peter Johnson, Sir William's son with Molly Brant, was killed fighting for the British at Mud Island on the Delaware River near Philadelphia in late 1777. Molly herself, having remained loyal to the British during the war, was given a pension of £100 sterling a year and settled in Kingston, Ontario, where she remained a recognised Iroquois leader and go-between with the Canadian authorities until her death in April 1796.

From the *Guardian* newspaper (London), 30 June 2003, obituary of Sir Peter Johnson:

Peter Colpoys Paley Johnson was born in London and inherited the title of 7th baronet of New York from his father in 1976. The baronetcy was conferred in 1755 on his ancestor General William Johnson, who had large estates in the then British colonial territory of New York state. The title was conferred when he defeated the French at the Battle of Crown Point (sic) . . . After education at Wellington College and the Royal Military College of Science, Johnson served in the Royal Artillery between 1949 and 1961. He turned from the army to a maritime life and was for some years a director of a yacht-fittings manufacturing company before joining the Nautical Publishing Company as a director. He published *Sailing*, which has sold 360,000 copies in 13 languages . . . His son Colpoys becomes the 8th baronet of New York.

In the summer of 1838, a small party of visitors came to Johnstown and took rooms at the Fonda Hotel. They signed in as Mrs Farley, her niece Mrs Kerr, her son-in-law Captain W. J. Kerr and some of her grandsons. They were a respectable, even impressive, family group. Mrs Farley, a large, squat woman, looked about seventy years old. Her daughter Elizabeth had a fine, elegant face, and, as one admirer wrote of her, 'in her speech and manner she has a softness approaching to oriental languor'. Captain Kerr had the noble military bearing of a man who had fought bravely in battle, taken wounds, and survived dangers. One grandson was especially handsome, and notably, if pleasantly, flirtatious.

Mrs Farley visited a local lawyer, Daniel Cady, known for his expertise in the real-estate laws of the state of New York. She had a question about a piece of property. If a minor had been left some land – say 2,000 acres of a royal grant – by a man who died before the Revolution, and that land had been confiscated in the upheavals of the 1770s and 1780s, could it be claimed back? The answer was that it might indeed have been possible to challenge the confiscation of land from a minor, but that, alas, the statute of limitations made it too late for such an action now.

Mrs Farley took the news calmly and spent some days walking around Johnstown with her family. She went several times to Johnson Hall and chatted amiably to the ladies then in residence. She remembered so well, she said, the games she had played as a little girl around the house and fields. What she remembered most of all, though, was the great gala days when hundreds of Indians from different nations would gather around the house and when her father would distribute presents from the King. Though she was only about ten when she left, she had spent many years boasting of the magnificence of her childhood. She laughed now at the relative modesty of the place that memory had exaggerated into a vast palace. Scanning the dimensions of the house, she was heard to exclaim: 'And is this – can this be Johnson Hall? O how I have lied about this building! I have always told my friends in Montreal, that there was no house in all that town as large as Johnson Hall. Why there are houses there as large as three or four of it.'[17]

Mrs Farley was Mary, the daughter of William Johnson and Molly Brant. Her niece, Mrs Kerr, was Elizabeth, youngest daughter of Joseph Brant. When James Buchanan, the British consul at New York, went to visit them at Burlington Bay in 1819, he and his wife were amazed by the house, with carpets and mirrors, stylish chairs, well-stocked bookcase and guitar, and even more so by Elizabeth:

To our astonishment, in walked a charming, noble-looking Indian girl, dressed partly in native and partly in English costume. Her hair was confined on the head with a silk net, but the lower tresses escaping from thence, flowed down on her shoulders. Under a tunic or morning dress of black silk was a petticoat of the same material and colour, which reached very little below the knees. Her silk stockings and kid shoes were like the rest of her dress, black. The grace and dignity of her movement – the style of her dress and manners – charmed us. All was so unexpected. With great ease, she welcomed us and maintained conversation until an Indian woman, wearing a man's hat, brought in a tray with preparations for breakfast, with tea, coffee, hot rolls, butter in ice coolers, eggs, smoked beef, ham . . . Having inquired . . . about her mother, she told us she generally remained with her other sons and daughters, who were living at the Grand River; that her mother preferred being in the wigwams and disapproved to a certain degree of her and her brother John's conforming so much to the habits and customs of the English.[18]

They had stumbled on a re-creation of Johnson Hall and its hybrid Indian-European world.

The full name of Elizabeth's husband, Captain Kerr, was William Johnson Kerr. He was a grandson of Johnson and Molly Brant. After the death of Joseph Brant's son John, the venerable Catherine, widow of Joseph Brant, daughter of George Croghan and Turtle clan mother, conferred the hereditary Mohawk chief sachemship on her grandson, and William Johnson's great-grandson, Walter. The title 'Dekarihokenh' (or Tekarihoke) was the first in the roll-call of the mythical founders and first chiefs of the Iroquois confederacy. William Johnson's descendant became the reincarnation of the original chiefs brought together by the Peacemaker Deganawidah. The name Dekarihokenh means 'Double Word' or 'Double Life', and the ritual function of its bearer was that of Firekeeper. In a strange way, the two council fires of Onondaga and Johnson Hall had again become one.

A visit of His Excellency the Right Honourable Frederick Temple, Earl of Dufferin and Governor General of Canada to the Mohawk and Tuscarora reservations, August 1859: In the church, their excellencies looked at the Communion plate and the Holy Bible presented to Hendrick by Queen Anne in London in 1710. As they passed under the third ceremonial arch the band of the Ojibwas played 'God Save the Queen'. Further on, the Mohawk band played 'Rule Britannia'. The pathway to the council house was lined with Indian chiefs and warriors, and in its rear was a public hall decorated with flags, in which was erected a carpeted dais, having in its rear the British ensigns, a royal crown, and an illuminated ribbon or scroll with the motto: Welcome Lord and Lady Dufferin. As their excellencies were conducted to the dais, their path was strewn with flowers by Indian maidens and the children sang the national anthem. The governor general said it was exceedingly interesting to himself and Lady Dufferin to find themselves in a locality surrounded by so many historical associations. On the walls of the Council House were portraits of Queen Victoria, the late lamented Prince Consort and Sir William Johnson. On the dais beside the governor general was the Speaker of the Great Council, Sir William's descendant Chief John Smoke Johnson.[19]

From the children's book *Pictures from Canadian History for Boys and Girls*, 1899:

Before the Revolution, Sir William Johnson was agent for Indian affairs in the colonies. Brave in battle and just in all his dealings with them, no other white man ever gained such power over the savages as he. At his fine colonial mansion in Maine is still shown the place where the Mohawks used to come and sit on the lawn for hours, waiting patiently to speak to him. In 1742, while the English and French were still at daggers drawn, a little Indian baby was born to the Chief of the Mohawks. The child had a pretty native name of his own, but the colonists called him, like his father, Brant . . . Sir William Johnson, seeing how clever the boy was, sent him to a Christian Indian school. With what he learned there, Brant became very anxious to teach the heathen races about our Lord Jesus . . . He meant to have written an account of his people, and it is a great pity he did not do so, for very little is known of the early history of the Indian tribes.[20]

The 'Smoke' in Chief John Smoke Johnson's name was a corruption of 'Sakayengwaraton', which means 'the mist that rises from the ground in the autumn and disappears with the advancing day'. Smoke Johnson contradicted the evanescence of his name, however. He was born in 1783 and was William Johnson's grandson.[21] His father was almost certainly either Brant Johnson or William of Canajahorie, both of whom fled to Canada in the Mohawk exodus of 1779. With Joseph Brant, he led the Mohawks in the British forces in the war of 1812 against the United States.

Smoke Johnson was a great orator. Even in 1879, when the linguist and ethnographer Horatio Hale went to meet him at the Iroquois reserve at Brantford, he was struck by the old man's eloquence: 'When an occasion has for a moment aroused his spirit, I have not known whether most to admire the nobleness and force of his sentiments and reasoning, or the grace and flowing ease with which he delivered the stately periods of his sonorous language.' Like the great old sachems of the original Iroquois league, he was also the keeper of memory and tradition, and was 'considered to have a better knowledge of the traditions and ancient usages of the Six Nations, than any other member of the tribes'.

Smoke Johnson had a surprise for Horatio Hale and a story to tell him. He described how, in 1832, cholera had swept through the reserve. Smoke had been helping to tend to the sick, when he was called to visit one of the oldest of the sachems. The old man had told him he was afraid he might die and his most precious possession be mislaid. He had taken out a book and asked Smoke to make a copy of it, lest it be lost for ever. The younger man had transcribed it in a school copybook. The book was a description of the traditional Iroquois rituals, with the list of the hereditary league titles and, in particular, a detailed description of the condolence ceremony.

The original book was probably the one made for William Johnson in the 1750s, when he was setting out to become the primary master of Iroquois protocol. He mentioned at a council in 1773: 'I do well know all your ancient customs, that I cannot be mistaken in them, having committed them all to writing an age ago . . .'[22] By 1879 that original was, just as the old sachem had feared, lost, and Smoke Johnson's copybook had become the crucial storehouse of a people's cultural memory.

And so, in the autumn of 1879, the ethnographer sat patiently with Smoke Johnson and his son Chief George Johnson. William Johnson's grandson read out the ceremonial forms and explained their obscurities, as only he now could. William Johnson's great-grandson translated his father's words into English. Four years later Hale published *The Iroquois Book of Rites*, making indestructible the fragile, half-forgotten memory that had barely survived the calamities of the previous century.[23]

33

The Afterlife

In James Kirke Paulding's novel of 1831, *The Dutchman's Fireside*, Sir William Johnson is made to reflect on the extinction of an Indian tribe and the stories that leak away through holes in the fabric of history:

History [he remarks of the death of a people] says nothing of this; but if a bedrid king or a superannuated queen had died that day, it would have been carefully recorded. The causes which change the destinies of men and the face of the earth lie unseen and unnoticed, while little things and little men are carefully handed down to future times as mighty agents in the vast business of the universe. Such is history, and in fact tradition is no better. One conceals or overlooks the truth; the other tattles falsehoods.[1]

In his own lifetime William Johnson knew that he was already becoming a fictional character. When his countryman Charles Johnstone brought out a third volume of his epic satire on globalisation *Chrysal: or, The Adventures of a Guinea*, in 1767, Johnson probably read it. His bookseller had previously sent him a copy of another Johnstone novel noting merely that the book was 'a continuation of the Authors first work, *The Adventures of a Guinea*; in which the same acrimonious Vein is highly preserved & a great variety of leading Characters are delineated in the most animated Stile'.[2]

Chrysal was the first novel to take as its subject the way money was making the world a smaller place. It is narrated by a guinea coin who crisscrosses the world in the pockets of his different owners. He ends up in the possession of a British general in America. The indolent soldier is thinking about the joys of money when William Johnson enters his tent. The guinea is immediately enthralled: 'There was something in the whole appearance of this person that struck me with the strongest curiosity the moment I saw him. His stature, above the common size of man, was formed with the justest proportion and denoted ability to execute the most difficult attempts, which the determined and enterprising spirit that animated his looks could urge him to.'³

Johnson is, in contrast to the venal general, the model of a new sensibility that would come to be called American: plain-spoken, honest, open, energetic. He has 'the unaffected ease of natural liberty'. He is 'above the hypocritical formality of studied rules of behaviour'. He applies intuitive good sense rather than conventional wisdom, declaring openly that he knows nothing of the art of war other than what 'Heaven and common sense have taught me'. He has learned from the Indians who 'see by the light of natural reason'. He treats them 'as rational creatures and they behave as such to me'. When the guinea ends up in Johnson's pocket and returns to Johnson Hall, he finds that his new master exercises an extraordinary sway based, not on force, but on truth – 'power in its most rational sense'. He gratifies his sexual passions openly and lovingly.

The Johnson of *Chrysal* is thus the archetypal republican hero, the ideal man of the Enlightenment. He thinks rationally and behaves honestly. He has broken free from the tyranny of calcified institutions and dogma. He embodies a new political state that has yet to come into existence because he founds his authority on 'the justest of all principles, voluntary consent'. He is a harbinger of the democratic revolutions that are to come. In this strange way, as an icon of the new sensibility, Johnson's image played its part in the creation of the American republic his family tried to strangle at birth.

The all-too-evident fact that Johnson's immediate legacy was Tory and anti-revolutionary made it necessary to suppress this aspect of his influence in the immediate aftermath of the creation of the United States. Yet he was too deeply entwined with the roots of America, and too usefully potent as a memory, not to re-emerge. Buried in official history, he rose again in fiction.

Johnson became significant in the early nineteenth century because he solved a problem for the emerging national culture. On the one hand, the revolutionary origins of the United States owed much to the Enlightenment imagery of natural man. The Indians were important to that imagery, both as a distinctively American culture and as the people around whom ideas of natural virtue had cohered. On the other hand, however, the destiny of America lay in the complete conquest and utter subjugation of that very culture. The expansion of

America to the west would mean the annihilation of the Indians. Notions of racial and religious purity also required the relegation of the Indians to the realms of a savagery that, in the face of the advance of civilisation, must disappear.

Within this ambiguous framework, contradictory impulses were at play. The imagined freedom of the Indian – physical, political and sexual – carried an erotic charge, but freedom was also a rank and swampy wilderness, where energy and righteousness could get lost. The nobility of a doomed people gave a heroic, tragic cast to the grubby business of extermination. The existence of a third race, neither black nor white, complicated and threatened to undermine the racial determinism that justified slavery. The rapid clearing of the great forests was hailed as progress but also induced an immediate nostalgia for the once pristine landscape. This was a psychic terrain pockmarked with pitfalls and mapped only with the most convoluted contours.

The way through this confusing cultural landscape lay in the figure of the White Savage, the virile, racially pure embodiment of American values who is yet at home in the wilderness because he had adopted the best of Indian culture. An American with white skin but Indian dress, Christian decency but Indian simplicity, European accomplishments but Indian skills, would have the right to take the West. In the lead-up to the passage of the Indian Removal Act in 1830 and the expulsion over the next decade of Indians from huge tracts of land east of the Mississippi, the cultural and political attractiveness of such a figure became overwhelming. With his awkward Tory politics sheared off, and the sexual libertinism of Johnstone's portrait in *Chrysal* suppressed, Sir William Johnson was an ideal anvil on which to shape this necessary myth.

Johnson began to be woven into the nascent national myth of the triumph of civilisation over savagery in James Fenimore Cooper's Leatherstocking novels of the 1820s. If he is not a more explicit presence there, it may simply be because Cooper took his aura for granted. Cooper's family lands were part of a tract granted to Johnson's deputy George Croghan. Cooper's wife was a De Lancey. It was perhaps inevitable that in the testing of sexual, political and racial boundaries in his most influential novels the landscape is Johnson's forest and Johnson himself is its silently presiding spirit.

When Johnson is first referred to in *The Last of the Mohicans*, it is in a chapter whose epigraph is taken from *A Midsummer Night's Dream*, linking the forest of upper New York with Shakespeare's magical woodland where reverie and madness are given free rein. Cooper stresses its exotic, dream-like texture, calling it 'a region that is, even to this day, less known to the inhabitants of the states, than the deserts of Arabia or the steppes of Tartary'. Within this otherworld, Johnson's name is introduced as a focus of supreme ambivalence. On the one hand, it promises safety and civility; on the other it threatens to lure the upright Major Duncan Heyward away from familiar certainties.

Heyward persuades the Indian Magua to take the two captured daughters of Colonel Munro to the British with the promise of rewards, including a medal of the kind that Johnson used to bestow on loyal Indians. They travel 'through the boundless woods' and Heyward wonders whether they are being led

towards a well known border settlement, where a distinguished officer of the crown, and a favoured friend of the Six Nations, held his large possessions, as well as his usual residence. To be delivered into the hands of Sir William Johnson, was far preferable to being led into the wilds of Canada; but in order to effect even the former, it would be necessary to traverse the forest for many weary leagues, each step of which was carrying him further from the scene of the war, and, consequently, from the post, not only of honour, but of duty.[4]

Throughout the first sequence of Leatherstocking novels, Johnson's ambiguous ambience hovers around Cooper's archetype of American heroism. Johnson lies behind the figure who came to embody a specifically American style of manly virtue, Natty Bumppo, also called Leatherstocking and Hawk-eye. Cooper's white Indian is a protégé of Johnson, who followed him to the battle of Lake George. In the first of the Leatherstocking Tales, *The Pioneers*, published in 1823, and set in the early 1790s, Natty is introduced in the opening pages as a wild, romantic creature, a white man who dresses and looks like an Indian. His attire would have brought to mind the Johnson figure from Benjamin West's celebrated painting *The Death of Wolfe*:

His gray eyes were glancing under a pair of shaggy brows, that overhung them in long hairs of gray mingled with their natural hue; his scraggy neck was bare, and burnt to the same tint with his face; though a small part of a shirt collar, made of the country check, was to be seen above the over-dress he wore. A kind of coat, made of dressed deer-skin, with the hair on, was belted close to his lank body, by a girdle of coloured worsted. On his feet were deer-skin moccasins, ornamented with porcupines' quills, after the manner of the Indians, and his limbs were guarded with long leggings of the same material as the moccasins, which, gartering over the knees of his tarnished buck-skin breeches, had obtained for him, among the settlers, the nick-name of Leatherstocking . . . Over his left shoulder was slung a belt of deer-skin, from which depended an enormous ox horn, so thinly scraped, as to discover the dark powder that it contained.

Almost immediately after he is introduced, Natty recalls: 'Some thirty years agone, in the old war, when I was out under Sir William, I travelled seventy miles alone in the howling wilderness, with a rifle bullet in my thigh, and then cut it out with my own jack-knife.' This fierce stoicism, in which American endurance outfaces the howling wilderness is, we are to understand, enacted under Johnson's orders, and Natty has learned it in emulation of the great man himself.[5]

It becomes clear later in the novel that the ageing Natty is forever recalling the days when he was 'out under Sir William' even at moments of danger: '"The Iroquois had none of the best powder when I went ag'in the Canada tribes, under Sir William. Did I ever tell you the story, lad, consarning the skrimmage with–" "For God's sake, tell me nothing now, Natty, until we are entirely safe. Where shall we go next?"'[6] Yet Sir William is never fully named in *The Pioneers*. He is not a character in the story but a landmark in Natty's imaginative terrain. Johnson is the frame within which his stories – and, by implication, the Leatherstocking Tales as a whole – unfold.

This appearance of Johnson as the story that Natty never quite gets to tell, the name so often quoted by the white Indian that his listeners impatiently interrupt its completion is repeated in *The Prairie*. When the young Paul Hover is boasting to Natty of a ludicrous feat, he almost gives Hawk-eye the opportunity to tell a story of Sir William:

'This has been a regular knock-down and drag-out,' he cried, 'and no bones broke! How now, old trapper, you have been one of your training, platoon, rank and file soldiers in your day, and have seen forts taken and batteries stormed before this – am I right?' 'Ay, ay, that have I,' answered the old man, who still maintained his post at the foot of the rock, so little disturbed by what he had just witnessed, as to return the grin of Paul, with a hearty indulgence in his own silent and peculiar laughter; 'you have gone through the exploit like men!' 'Now tell me, is it not in rule, to call over the names of the living, and to bury the dead, after every bloody battle?' 'Some did and other some didn't. When Sir William push'd the German, Dieskau, thro' the defiles at the foot of the Hori–"Your Sir William was a drone to Sir Paul, and knew nothing of regularity.' So here begins the roll-call . . .[7]

The only time in the Leatherstocking series that Natty gets to talk at any length about his hero is in *The Last of the Mohicans*, in a passage where Johnson is a kind of ghost. Natty, attempting to lead Heyward and the Munro girls to safety, comes into the ravine where Dieskau ambushed the force that Johnson had sent out from Lake George in 1755. It is in this terrain that Leatherstocking is 'at home, for he held on his way, with the certainty and diligence of a man, who moved in the security of his own knowledge'. Cooper links this sense of Natty being on home ground with the feeling that this place is holy, haunted by the spectres of Johnson, Dieskau and the dead of Lake George:

Suddenly, Hawk-eye made a pause, and waiting until he was joined by the whole party, he spoke; though in tones so low and cautious, that they added to the solemnity of his words, in the quiet and darkness of the place. 'It is easy to know the path-ways, and to find the licks and water-courses of the wilderness,' he said; 'but who that saw this spot, could venture to say, that a mighty army was at rest among yonder silent trees and barren mountains! . . . See,' he said, pointing through the trees towards a spot where a little basin of water reflected the bright stars from its still and placid bosom, 'here is the "bloody pond"; and I am on ground that I have not only often travelled, but over which I have fou't the enemy, from the rising to the setting sun!' 'Ha! that sheet of dull and dreary water, then, is the sepulchre of the brave men who fell in the contest! I have heard it named, but never have I stood on its banks before!' 'Three battles did we make with the Dutch Frenchman [Dieskau] in a day!' continued Hawk-eye, pursuing the train of his own thoughts, rather than replying to the remark of Duncan. 'He met us hard by, in our outward march to ambush his advance, and scattered us, like driven deer, through the defile, to the shores of Horican [Cooper's invented alternative name, 'instead of going back to the House of Hanover for the appelation of our finest sheet of water']. Then we rallied behind our fallen trees, and made head against him, under Sir William – who was made Sir William for that very deed; and well did we pay him for the disgrace of the morning! Hundreds of Frenchmen saw the sun that day for the last time; and even their leader, Dieskau himself, fell into our hands, so cut and torn with the lead, that he has gone back to his own country, unfit for further acts in war.'[8]

'Twas a noble repulse!' exclaimed Heyward in the heat of his youthful ardour; 'the fame of it reached us early in our southern army.' 'Ay! but it did not end there. I was sent by Major Effingham, at Sir William's own bidding, to out-flank the French, and carry the tidings of their disaster across the portage, to the fort on the Hudson. Just hereaway, where you see the trees rise into a mountain swell, I met a party coming down to our aid, and I led them where the enemy were taking their meal, little dreaming that they had not finished the bloody work of the day . . .'

When all was over, the dead, and some say the dying, were cast into that little pond. These eyes have seen its waters coloured with blood, as natural water never yet flowed from the bowels of the 'arth.' 'It was a convenient, and, I trust, will prove a peaceful grave for a soldier!' . . . 'As for the grave there, being as quiet as you mention, it is another matter. There are them in the camp, who say and think, man to lie still, should not be buried while the breath is in the body; and certain it is, that in the hurry of that evening, the doctors had but little time to say who was living, and who was dead.'

In these passages, in three of the Leatherstocking Tales, Johnson figures as a potent absence: the wellspring of the stories Natty tells, as it were, offstage, or the commander at the battle whose uneasy casualties lie in the Bloody Pond, not properly buried, somewhere between life and death. Leatherstocking never refers to him as 'Sir William Johnson', but always, without explanation, as 'Sir William', making him an intimate, familiar figure for Natty but a somewhat puzzling one for the reader. Yet he is to be understood as Natty's progenitor, the creator of the context in which the latter has emerged. His new American values of guileless honesty, hardy earnestness and stoical prudence, combining white racial purity with raw Indian toughness, have grown in Johnson's forest. Yet those values, in Cooper's anxious critique of emerging America, are threatened in *The Pioneers* by the new world of property rights, civil law and a market economy, and the aged Natty is both a survival and a rebuke. He and Johnson are heroic but uncomfortable exemplars of an American virtue that is struggling to exist in the expanding America.

Cooper's rival in the attempt to create an American national myth through fiction, James Kirke Paulding, followed logically on from the first sequence of Leatherstocking novels and wrote a story in which Johnson moves from spectral absence to overwhelming, heroic presence. Paulding was an important ideologist of Jacksonian expansionism, who served as navy agent in New York and then as Navy Secretary in the cabinet of Martin Van Buren. As a staunch anti-British nationalist and a believer in American destiny, he argued in his 1820 essay 'National Literature' that vigorous fictions for the emerging United States could be founded on the eighteenth-century pioneers and 'the motives which produced the resolution to emigrate to the wilderness; in the courage and perseverance with which they consummated this gallant enterprise; and in . . . their adventures and their contests with the savages'.[9] Picking up on the hints in Cooper and on Anne Grant's *Memoirs of an American Lady*, he decided to use Johnson as the literary fulfilment of these possibilities.

Paulding's major novel *The Dutchman's Fireside*, published in 1831, a year after the passage of the Indian Removal Act, went through six editions in a year, was republished in London and was translated into French and Dutch. Through the book, Johnson became a prototype for the ideal American, a forest superman who could teach the young men of the continent to throw off the enervated, feminised culture of old Europe and stride forth in their natural manly glory. In Johnson's magical forest, America could find its native virility, its blunt, refreshing honesty, its dauntless energy, and its modest, self-effacing courage. When, as Paulding confidently expects, 'The red man is gone, and the white man is in his place,'[10] nothing will be lost because all that was worth saving from the annihilation of the Indians will be incorporated into the good white American.

The Dutchman's Fireside self-consciously enacts the transformation by William Johnson of an overwrought, overeducated, shy and brooding young New Yorker into a proper man. The hero, Sybrant Westbrook, is an orphan, and Johnson becomes his surrogate father. His real father, a corrupt British officer, abandoned his mother, who subsequently died. Sybrant has been raised in upper New York by his kindly Dutch relatives, and educated at home by a stuffy Dutch pastor. Though he is handsome, honourable and quietly courageous, his sheltered upbringing has made him exquisitely sensitive. Tormented by self-doubt, especially in the presence of his beautiful cousin Catalina, Sybrant appears sheepish and ungainly and is unable to declare his love. His natural virtues thus spoiled by excessive fastidiousness, he is in despair. Rebuffed, as he believes, by Catalina, he sets off to prove himself by going on a trading expedition among the Mohawks of the forest.

Before he enters the story, Johnson is introduced as a beacon of civility in the wilderness. As Sybrant passes through the 'wild, solitary region' beyond Fort Edward, Paulding informs readers that 'the nearest settlement was at Johnstown, towards the south, where Sir William Johnson resided, and exercised that sway over the tribes of Indians far and near which still remains, and will remain forever, a subject of admiration and wonder'. Almost immediately in the narrative, Sybrant comes to another mark of Johnson's presence in this depopulated forest: the fishing lodge where the baronet sometimes came to hunt and fish.

These intimations of admiration and wonder are strengthened by Paulding's hostile portrayal of the Indians. The sophisticated Hendrick is excised and replaced by the monstrous, one-eyed cyclopean Paskingoe, who lures Sybrant to the empty fish-house in order to steal his goods and murder him. The familiar folktale of Hendrick dreaming a coat from Johnson who in turn dreams a piece of land from Hendrick is now retailed by Paskingoe: 'He dreamed away my best hunting-grounds but I only dreamed away his red coat.'[11] A story that presented both Johnson and Hendrick as witty sophisticates in friendly competition is turned by Paulding into evidence of Johnson's wonderful ability to control a corrupt, murderous savage. In the same passage, Paulding refers to the 'uncontrolled and uncontrollable animal spirits' of Paskingoe and his accompanying warriors.[12] Johnson is thus envisaged, even before he enters the action, as a Prospero whose magical powers can somehow restrain the brute Caliban.

He enters, naturally enough, just at the point when Paskingoe's warriors, deranged by drink and yelling 'like tortured fiends', are about to kill Sybrant: 'The door of the fishing house was violently burst open, and a tall, majestic white man in a hunting dress rushed into the room, followed by half a dozen people. The arms of the Indians, the moment they saw him, were arrested, and their weapons remain suspended above their heads.'[13] Paulding's Johnson thus enters American fiction as a named character in his own right, a mythic creature, both mighty mage and emperor of the forest. The power which can cause the tomahawks of frenzied fiends to freeze in mid-air is mysterious. Twice within two pages Paulding describes him as 'indescribable': he enters the room, speaking Mohawk, 'with an air of indescribable authority'; his face 'united those indescribable yet indelible characteristics which seem inseparable from a cultivated intellect'. He is so hard to describe in republican America, perhaps, because he is a king. Paulding calls him 'majestic'. When the wounded Sybrant is taken to Johnson Hall to recover, Paulding has Johnson refer to the house as 'the capital of my kingdom, it is a wide empire, not very populous'. Shortly afterwards, he refers to 'a meeting of Mohawks at my court'.[14] Yet precisely because his subjects are Indians, Johnson's status as an emperor is not at all offensive. Democracy is for whites, but Johnson's imperial sway is evidently regarded by Paulding as the proper system for the governance of Indians.

While Johnson is immediately introduced as a 'white man', and Paulding is careful to emphasise his status as a 'gentleman', his mythic power derives from his ability to marry whiteness with the best aspects of Indian culture. Paulding sums him up in the phrase 'careless superiority': he is superior as a charismatic white man but carries his authority with a natural carelessness that roots it, not in force of arms, but in force of personality. His combination of cultures is not a promiscuous miscegenation but an accumulation of graces:

345

His manner and mode of expressing himself sufficiently indicated that he had sat at good men's feasts and been where bells had tolled to church, at the same time that they were totally distinct from those of the gentlemen Sybrant had seen at the house of his uncle. His motions exhibited the ease, facility, and unembarrassed vigor of an Indian, and there was a singular force, brevity, and richness in his phraseology that partook somewhat of the Indian manner of expression. He wore a hunting dress equally partaking in the modes of savage and civilised man, and indeed altogether exhibited a singular confusion of the peculiarities of the two races.[15]

This fusion in William Johnson, it turns out, has created the American superman. Johnson has super-powers. Out hunting, his companions play a game in which they try to knock a squirrel out of a tree without drawing blood by striking the bark just next to it with a bullet. All fail. Johnson succeeds every time. This and other exhibitions of extraordinary powers convince Sybrant that he has encountered in Johnson the perfect man: 'It was by frequent instances of this sort that the mystery of his unbounded sway over his people was explained to Sybrant. The human character can only be perfected and consummated by the union of superior knowledge and superior strength, directed and animated by a courage that dares all dangers, defies all obstacles.' Johnson, writes the rapturous Paulding later in the novel, 'combined as much mental and physical power as was ever concentrated in one individual'.[16]

This portrait of a superhero may be gauche, but it is not naive. Paulding has a political purpose. His Johnson is white America. The ecstatic praise of Sir William is a nationalist's hymn to his nation. For Johnson's qualities as they are eulogised in *The Dutchman's Fireside* pertain essentially to the right to rule. Since white hegemony over the Indians cannot be rooted in the democratic theory of the Enlightenment, it must be legitimised by a notion of natural superiority. To serve as the image of white America in relation to the continent's indigenous population, the real Johnson has to be transformed into a monarch who has the right to rule absolutely because even the savages recognise his innate magnificence.

'He had', Paulding writes of Johnson, 'by the exercise of courage, talents, energy, and perseverance, conquered the stubborn minds of the proudest, the most daring and impracticable race that ever trod the earth, either in the Old or the New World. In short, among savage and civilized men, he exercised the only divine right ever conferred on man – the right of leading and being obeyed on the ground of superior physical and mental energies.' The magic of Paulding's Johnson lies in his ability to make the brute facts of American expansion – violence, dispossession, fraud – disappear and to put in their place a God-given right to command, rooted in the just recognition of a higher, more advanced humanity.

In this sense, Johnson is imagined not so much as an aspect of America's past as of its future. At the end of the book, when Sybrant and Catalina are getting married and Johnson is the guest of honour, the young Dutch-American describes his surrogate father: 'You are a prophet, as well as a warrior and legislator.'[17] And what Johnson prophesies is that 'the great frame of social life' (white civilisation) 'will one day, I believe, comprehend the whole of this vast continent'. In this inevitable process, the Indians must either conform 'to the laws, customs, and occupations of the whites' or 'they must perish'. Even in building Johnson up to astonishing heights of superiority and praising his efforts to effect the former transformation, however, Paulding hints that the latter option may be a not altogether regrettable necessity. If it takes a mythic ruler like Johnson to keep them in check, he seems to suggest, they will, in banal reality, have to die. The Indians' 'instinctive insurmountable wildness of character . . . renders the labour of winning this race into the fold of civilisation, so dear to humanity, an almost hopeless task'.

Yet the good qualities of this doomed people must not be lost. In this sense, Johnson's superiority in *The Dutchman's Fireside* faces both ways. This superman is, as he says, 'half a savage myself', and that other half has made him great. His task in the novel is to pass that other half on to the future America represented by Sybrant, to make the pale intellectual enough of a redskin to be a real man. 'Young man,' he tells Sybrant, 'you are a scholar; I have found that out already. But your education, I doubt, is not quite finished. I shall put you through an entire new course and make a man of you, as well as a scholar.'[18] Sybrant's course of studies is an education in removing the gloss of overbred European introspection and allowing the inner, vigorously virile American to emerge. Johnson's influence over Sybrant parallels his influence over the Mohawks. Just as he seeks to civilise the wildness of the Indians, so he adds wild energy to Sybrant's enervated mind. Sybrant learns that Johnson is a Gulliver who was once tied down by the 'little peevish trammels of civilised life', but who, in the forest, has cut those bonds and emerged as a giant among

Lilliputians. Sybrant, as infant America, is gradually instructed by his new Irish Mohawk father in the breaking of such unnecessary ties. 'He caught from the stranger [Johnson] something of his fearless, independent carriage, lofty bearing and impatience of idleness or inaction. In short, he acquired a confidence in himself, a self-possession, and self-respect, such as he had never felt before, and which freed him from the leaden fetters of that awkward restraint which had hitherto been the bane of his life.'[19]

Within this careful and self-consciously didactic structure, there is space for a brief rhapsodic episode in which the older white dream of an Indian idyll of sexual and racial freedom is revisited. Paulding was a champion of slavery and *The Dutchman's Fireside* includes an idealised old black slave who is utterly devoted to Sybrant. Included, too, is a chapter on an evil Europeanised Indian called Hans Pipe, who tries to murder Catalina, and who exemplifies the dangers of mixing an Indian into white society and creating a monster of miscegenation, 'the worst, the most mischievous of mongrels; a compound of the ferocity of the savage, and the cunning, deceit, and sensuality of the civilised scoundrel'. Yet, for Paulding's moral lesson to make sense, the reverse must not hold true. The Indian who becomes half-white may be a mischievous mongrel, but the white who becomes part-Indian must be a classic breed.

Johnson, in the novel as in reality, has an Indian wife, and their children are not monsters but 'an evident mixture of the wild and the tame, the perfect images of nature in her finest proportions'. The household, moreover, is a domestic Utopia, filled with simple ease and unblemished happiness. There is an 'air of happy freedom from restraint'. The Indian wife has 'always a smile on her face; the children, freed from the soul-harrowing, soul-subduing surveillance of eternal nursing and restraint, gamboled about, the happiest of all God's creatures'.[20] Sterilised as it is by the presiding presence of a dominant white man, the scene nevertheless reveals the vestigial power of the Noble Savage, the uncomfortable persistence of the Indian dream that was the other side of the Indian nightmare.

This freedom from restraint, though, is quickly reeled back into the structure of Sybrant's course of study. At the climax of the novel, when Sybrant becomes a man by enlisting as one of Johnson's rangers and going off to spy on the French, Johnson paints his face 'so as to resemble that of an Indian'. To his white skin and Christian manners, he adds the necessary layer of Indian wildness that will make him a model American: intrepid, bold, energetic, free at last from the peevish introspection that has hobbled him. He is fit now to go off and conquer, not just Catalina, but the immeasurable wild continent that lies around him and that, as the imaginary son of its natural ruler Johnson, he has a right to inherit.

The Dutchman's Fireside, published fifty-seven years after Johnson was buried, was his second death. It killed off his richly ambiguous existence as a man who moved deftly on the borders between empires and cultures, and reinvented him as an icon of American nationalism and the growing American empire. Though he would feature in dozens of other historical novels, Paulding had fixed him as a harbinger of Manifest Destiny and the model for a specifically American mode of masculinity: frank, energetic, distrustful of introspection, and able to prove itself, when necessary through violence.

Yet there was one last fictional role for Johnson in a very different kind of drama. When the useful part of him had been appropriated for a budding American identity, there was something left over. A part of his story, the Irish Jacobite part, had no place in American myth and hovered in the forests of New York until a great Scottish writer came to Sarnac near the Canadian border and on a very dark winter night when the air was 'extraordinary clear and cold, and sweet with the purity of forests', imagined a 'story of many years and countries, of the sea and the land, savagery and civilisation'.[21] He wanted a story that would somehow bring together the intimate tragedies of the Jacobite wars with a global epic, and that would end with death and resurrection 'in the icy American wilderness.' It somehow came into his mind that this ghostly gothic tale would culminate in the domain of Sir William Johnson.

Paulding, in *The Dutchman's Fireside*, had evidently thought of making something of Johnson's Irish and Jacobite hinterland. He has Johnson announce: 'My family was Jacobite'; but a Johnson rooted in Irish history did not suit his purpose of creating an American prophet. He invented instead, another character to carry this strain of Johnson's story, an Irish officer, Barry Gilfillan, whose family has suffered 'divers forfeitures for its loyalty to the Stuarts'.[22] Gilfillan is full of the self-importance of a deposed aristocracy. When he is wounded in a fight alongside Johnson and Sybrant, he dies gallantly as 'a true son of my father and of old Ireland'. Before he is buried in the wild woods of New York, with the Gaelic lament 'Eileen A Roon' played at his graveside, he gives Sybrant 'my crest – the crest of the ancient Connaught kings', and asks the young man to wear it proudly in America's future.[23]

It may have been a reading of this scene that prompted Robert Louis Stevenson to reconnect this odd, displaced fragment of European history with Johnson and to make him the essential witness to the final winding-up of the tragedy and romance of Jacobitism. *The Master of Ballantrae*, which Stevenson wrote in the Adirondacks in 1887 and 1888, is partly narrated by an Irish Jacobite officer, the Chevalier Francis Burke. The story dramatises the painful choices that families like Johnson's had to make between pragmatic submission and loyalty to the old cause. The Durie family in Scotland hedges its bets when the Young Pretender, Bonnie Prince Charlie, invades. A coin is flipped. James, the heir, goes with the Pretender. His younger, duller brother Henry stays at home and, when the heir is reported dead, inherits both the land and his brother's sweetheart. The supposedly dead James repeatedly returns, however, full of evil intent and sexual allure. He is the undead spirit of Jacobitism, repellent but seductive, violent but infinitely more compelling than the boringly decent Henry, that refuses to be excised from history.

Strangely, Stevenson has this story reach its gruesome climax in the forests of New York, where James is buried, literally undead, waiting to rise and frighten his hated brother to death. When Henry goes into the forest in search of his brother, he is accompanied by Sir William Johnson, who 'had a diplomatic errand in these parts'.[24] Johnson at first seems rather puzzled about what he is doing in this story. The half-deranged Henry tells Johnson repeatedly that he has 'a brother somewhere in the woods'. When he realises that Henry is mad, Johnson replies: 'It is none of my affairs. But if I had understood you I would never have been here.'[25] It is as if Stevenson's gnarled narrative has wandered into Johnson's world by mistake.

Yet Johnson's importance to the working out of this epic does become clear. In the novel's theme, the rash, vivid romanticism of the Jacobite rebel and the dull stability of the compromiser both become deathly. Johnson is the idealised alternative to both, a rational romantic whose glamour lies in his ability, not to wage war, but to bring peace. Stevenson describes him as 'not any more bold than prudent', but also links him explicitly with the magnetic last stand of the

Jacobite and Gaelic cause at Culloden, where the Highland Scottish armies, and the Stuart cause, were defeated once and for all: 'His standing with the painted braves may be compared with that of my Lord President Culloden among the chiefs of our own Highlanders at the 'Forty-five; that is as much as to say, he was, to these men, reason's only speaking-trumpet, and counsels of peace and moderation, if they were to prevail at all, must prevail singly through his influence.'

Johnson is travelling into the forests in an attempt to stop a threatened Indian uprising. In the event of his failure, 'The province must lie open to all the abominable tragedies of Indian war – the houses blaze, the wayfarer be cut off, and the men of the woods collect their usual disgusting spoil of human scalps.'[26] In linking this description of frontier war in New York with the civil wars of Ireland and Britain, Stevenson also conjures up a historical fantasy in which a man like Johnson could, with his 'counsels of peace and moderation', have prevented the tragic violence from happening.

This evocative dream, however, is immediately interrupted by a discussion of the apparent death in the forest of the wicked Jacobite James. When James's brother Henry insists on going on into the forest to confirm James's death, Johnson objects: 'But, God damn me, the man's buried.' 'I will never believe that,' replies Henry. The tragic past may be buried, but it is not dead. When Johnson dismisses these fears as ravings, Henry catches him by the lapels and raves at him: 'He's not of this world . . . I have struck my sword throughout his vitals . . . I have felt . . . the hot blood spirt [sic] in my very face, time and again, time and again! But he was never dead for that . . . Why should I think he was dead now? No, not till I see him rotting.'

Johnson wants to shrug off this mad history, to escape from the unfolding nightmare of a past that will not lie down even when it is buried. He tries to send Henry back to Albany and civilisation: 'I desire simply to be quit of you.' But he cannot shake off either Henry or his strange story. Johnson is the necessary witness to its grotesque end. He sees James's servant digging up his master's grave and demands to know: 'What do you here among the graves of the dead and the remains of the unburied?'[27]

Johnson must experience this madness for himself. Stevenson makes his dialogue more fragmentary and exclamatory as he struggles to comprehend what he is seeing: 'Buried and not dead? What kind of rant is this? . . . My head goes round . . . My lot seems to be cast with the insane.' When James is taken from the grave uncorrupted, his smooth face now covered in a beard, Johnson gropes for a rational explanation: '"They say hair grows upon the dead," observed Sir William; but his voice was thick and weak.' James's week-old corpse flutters briefly back to life and the fright kills Henry. Johnson leaves the two corpses and moves on to complete his mission of pacifying the frontier. On his way back, he is the first to read the inscription on the boulder that serves as a headstone for an outlandish, displaced figment of European history in America. The inscription says that a man admired 'in the tents of savage hunters and the citadels of kings, after so much acquired, accomplished and endured, lies here forgotten'. He passes on, now that the strange spirit is truly dead at last, out of his real and imaginary worlds.

Acknowledgements

═══

This book has had a long gestation, and arises in part from the experience of living in the United States between 1997 and 2001. I am grateful to Pete Hamill, who took me there, and to Harold Evans, Susan Ferraro and all my erstwhile colleagues at the New York *Daily News*, who provided such a congenial context in which to discover the real America. My agent, Derek Johns of A. P. Watt, and my brilliant editors, Neil Belton and Elisabeth Sifton, have helped me patiently through the journey from misconception to forced labour to fraught delivery. Geraldine Kennedy, Gerry Smyth, Paddy Smyth, Deirdre Falvey and my other colleagues at the *Irish Times* have tolerated my absences with grace and, I suspect, some relief.

For invaluable help with research, I would like to thank Liam Connell, Seonaid Valiant at the University of Chicago, Donald Harman Akenson at McGill-Queen's University and the staff of the following institutions: the National Library of Ireland, the library of Trinity College Dublin, the New York State Archives in Albany, the New York Public Library and the Public Record Office in London. For peace and quiet, my thanks to everyone in Ballyvaughan.

For everything else in life, I must thank Clare Connell and, for merely rolling their eyes and sighing gently every time I mentioned William Johnson, my sons Samuel and Fionn.

Illustration Credits

_____

Illustrations in the plate section are reproduced by kind permission of the following:

(1) John Verelst / National Archives of Canada / C-092414

(2) *Sir William Johnson* (1715–1774) by John Wollaston (1736–1767), c.1750–1952, oil on canvas, Albany Institute of History & Art / Gift of Laura Munsell Tremaine in memory of her father Joel Munsell / 1922.2

(3) Derby Museums and Art Gallery

(4) National Maritime Museum, London / www.nmm.ac.uk

(5) *Colonel Guy Johnson and Karonghyontye (Captain David Hill)* by Benjamin West, Andrew W. Mellon Collection © 2005 Board of Trustees, National Gallery of Art, Washington / 1779 / oil on canvas

(6) Private Collection, Phillips Fine Art Auctioneers, New York / www.bridgeman.co.uk

(7) Johnson Hall (Sir William Johnson Presenting Medals to the Indian Chiefs of the Six Nations at Johnstown, N.Y., 1772) by Edward Lamson Henry (1841–1919), 1903, oil on canvas, Albany Institute of History & Art Purchase / 1993.44

(8) Unknown artist / National Archives of Canada / C-083514

(9) Unknown artist / National Archives of Canada / C-083498

(10) Toronto Public Library

(11) Johnson Hall State Historic Site

(12) New York State Office of Parks, Recreation, and Historic Preservation

(13) The National Archives, Kew

Notes

═══

The primary sources for the life and career of William Johnson are the collections of letters and other documents assembled at different times in the nineteenth and twentieth centuries by the New York State Library and Archives. The first Johnson manuscripts were acquired by New York State as early as 1801, and the process of bringing together all extant material continued into the late 1950s. Publication of transcriptions began in 1849–50 and ended in 1965. In the meantime, many of the originals were destroyed by a fire in the New York State Archives in 1911. Some rough idea of the contents of burned letters can be gained from the catalogue published in 1909 (Richard E. Day (ed.), *Calendar of the Sir William Johnson Manuscripts in the New York State Library*, University of the State of New York, Albany, 1909). The collections in which transcriptions of the Johnson documents appear are referred to here by the following abbreviations:

SWJP
James Sullivan, Alexander C. Flick, Milton W. Hamilton, Albert Corey (eds.), *The Papers of Sir William Johnson*, in fourteen volumes, University of the State of New York, Albany, 1921–65

Doc. Col. Hist.
E. B. O'Callaghan (ed.), *Documents Relative to the Colonial History of the State of New York*, in fifteen volumes, Albany, 1853–87; reprinted in facsimile by AMS Press, New York, 1969

Doc. Hist. NY
E. B. O'Callaghan (ed.), *Documentary History of the State of New York*, in four volumes, Weed, Parsons, Albany, 1850–51

Chapter 1, Tears, Throat, Heart

1 In a draft inscription for a family monument (SWJP, 4, p. 898) Christopher Johnson is said to have reached 'the Advanced Age of 84' when he died. However, his son Warren, who was closer to his father and lived much longer in Ireland, noted in a private journal that he died 'at Smithstown on Saturday January 29 1763, in the 80 year of his age', putting his birth around 1684. Warren Johnson, 'Extracts from a Diary of a Tour of Europe', National Library of Ireland, F. S. Bourke Collection, MS 9836.
2 SWJP, 10, p. 721.
3 Dean R. Snow, *The Iroquois*, Blackwell Publishing, Oxford, 1994, p. 59.
4 SWJP, 10, pp.674-5.
5 SWJP, 11, p.103.
6 Edna Kenton (ed.), *The Jesuit Relations and Allied Documents*, Albert and Charles Boni, New York, 1925, p. 195.
7 Johnson's account of this condolence conference is in Doc. Col. Hist., 7, pp. 130ff. The text of the songs is from William M. Fenton, *The Great Law and the Longhouse*, University of Oklahoma Press, 1998, pp. 733-7.
8 Dean R. Snow, *The Iroquois*, op. cit., p. 66.
9 Doc. Col. Hist., 7, p. 150.
10 Arthur C. Parker, 'The Code of Handsome Lake', in William N. Fenton (ed.), *Parker on the Iroquois*, Syracuse University Press, 1975, p. 126.
11 Winifred McGoona, 'Funeral Caoine in Meath', *Riocht na Midhe* (Journal of the Meath Archaeological and Historical Association), vol. 3, no. 2, 1964, p. 131.

Chapter 2, Spectres and Apparitions

1 Richmond P. Bond, *Queen Anne's American Kings*, Clarendon Press, Oxford, 1952, pp. 32-3.
2 William N. Fenton, *The Great Law and the Longhouse*, University of Oklahoma Press, 1998, p. 369.
3 Quoted in Bond, *Queen Anne's American Kings*, op. cit., pp. 2-3.
4 Thomas Arnold (ed.), *Selections from Addison's Papers Contributed to The Spectator*, Clarendon Press, Oxford, 1900, pp. 427-30.
5 Quoted in Joseph Addison, Richard Steele et al., *The Spectator*, vol. 3, Everyman's Library, London and New York, 1907, p.287.
6 *The Spectator*, vol. 5, no. 347, 8 April 1712.
7 SWJP, 9, pp. 53-4.
8 SWJP, 13, p. 19.
9 See Timothy J. Shannon, 'Dressing for Success on the Mohawk Frontier: Hendrick, William Johnson and Indian Fashion', in Peter C. Mancall and James H. Merrell, *American Encounters*, Routledge, New York and London, 2000, p. 353.

Chapter 3, Amphibians

1 Roy Foster, *Modern Ireland 1600–1972*, Penguin Books, London and New York, 1989, pp. 154–5.

2 See Kerby A. Miller, Arnold Schrier, Bruce D. Boling and David N. Doyle (eds.), *Irish Immigrants in the Land of Canaan*, Oxford University Press, 2003, p. 468.

3 SWJP, 1, pp. 242–5.

4 In May 1726 Peter Warren recorded a visit from his sister Anne and her son William 'aged eleven'. This gives a birth date of 1714 or 1715.

5 The 'town' in place names like Warrenstown and Smithstown does not imply an urban settlement or even a village. It reflects the Irish notion of a 'town-land', a loosely bounded area of dispersed houses and farms.

6 Reverend Thomas Warren, *A History and Genealogy of the Warren Family*, Gresham Books, Henley-on-Thames, 1982 (originally published 1902), p. 187.

7 Mary Warren, sister of Johnson's mother Anne Warren, was married to James Tyrrell.

8 Patrick Fagan, *The Diocese of Meath in the Eighteenth Century*, Four Courts Press, Dublin, 2001, p. 11.

9 See the genealogical patent drawn up for William Johnson's brother Peter Warren Johnson, 'Genealogia Petri Warreni Johnson de Damastown in Comitata Midensi Armigeri, Dublin, octavo die February AD Millesimo Septingentisimo Septuagesimo Quatr', New York State Archives, Albany, folder 14767.

10 See the manuscript 'Antient Anglo-Irish Families', by Sir William Betham, National Library of Ireland, MS 219, vol. 1, p. 209.

11 Darach McDonald, *The Chosen Fews*, Mercier Press, Cork, 2000, pp. 80–81 and pp. 239–41; Marianne Elliott, *The Catholics of Ulster*, Penguin Press, London and New York, 2000, pp. 36–188, *passim*.

12 See chapter 1, note 1. This means that the claim recounted by Augustus C. Buell and repeated by other nineteenth-century biographers that Christopher Johnson was a cavalry officer from 1692 to 1708 and had previously been a schoolteacher is ludicrous.

13 J. G. Simms, 'Irish Jacobite Lists', *Analecta Hibernica*, vol. 22, pp. 22ff.

14 Quoted in Kevin Whelan, *An Underground Gentry? Catholic Middlemen in Eighteenth Century Ireland*, Eighteenth Century Ireland, Volume 10, 1995, p. 11.

15 Julian Gwyn, *The Enterprising Admiral: The Personal Fortune of Admiral Sir Peter Warren*, McGill-Queen's University Press, Montreal and London, 1974, pp. 130–31.

16 Registry of Deeds, Dublin, 85/56/59024.

17 Gwyn, *The Enterprising Admiral*, op. cit., p. 135.

18 John Healy, *History of the Diocese of Meath*, Association for Promoting Christian Knowledge, Dublin, 1908, vol. 2, p. 79.

19 Eileen O'Byrne (ed.), *The Convert Rolls*, Irish Manuscripts Commission, Dublin, 1981.

20 Brian F. Gurrin, 'The Union of Navan in 1766', *Riocht na Midhe* (Journal of the Meath Archaeological and Historical Association), vol. XIV, 2003, p. 144.

21 John Healy, *History of the Diocese of Meath*, op. cit., vol. 2, p. 40.

22 Reverend A. Cogan, *The Diocese of Meath, Ancient and Modern*, Joseph Dollard, Dublin, 1867, vol. 2, p. 356.

23 See 'Abstract of the Prerogative Will of Michael Warren', in the Lyman Horace Weeks Papers, New York Public Library.

24 Patrick Fagan, *The Diocese of Meath in the Eighteenth Century*, op. cit., p. 195.

25 For Reverend Peter Warren see Fagan, op. cit., p. 194; Reverend Thomas Warren, *A History and Genealogy of the Warren Family*, op. cit., p. 188; and Brendan Jennings (ed.), 'Louvain Papers 1606–1827', Irish Manuscripts Commission, Dublin, 1968, documents 416, 417, 428 and 461.

26 Reverend Thomas Warren, op. cit., p. 188.

27 Julian Gwyn, *The Enterprising Admiral: The Personal Fortune of Admiral Sir Peter Warren*, op. cit., pp. 129–30.

28 Tom Harris, 'Fairs and Markets in the Environment of County Meath', *Riocht na Midhe* (Journal of the Meath Archaeological and Historical Association), vol. IX, no. 4, 1998, pp. 149ff.

29 SWJP, 13, p.21.

Chapter 4, 'Most Onruly and Streperous'

1 Dieskau, who was a German fighting in the French army, was also known as Jean-Armand.

2 SWJP, 2, pp. 44–6.

3 Dieskau to the Count d'Argenson, Doc. Col. Hist., 10, pp. 316ff.

4 SWJP, 2, p. 185.

5 SWJP, 2, p. 422.

6 Reverend Thomas Warren, 'Baron de Warren of Corduff', *Journal of the Royal Society of Antiquaries of Ireland*, series 5, vol. VI, 1896, pp. 246–52.

7 Quoted in Kevin Whelan, 'An Underground Gentry? Catholic Middlemen in Eighteenth Century Ireland', in *Eighteenth Century Ireland*, vol. 10, 1995, p. 19.

8 'Caoineadh Airt Ui Laoghaire', in Sean O Tuama and Thomas Kinsella, *An Duanaire: Poems of the Dispossessed 1600–1900*, Dolmen Press, Dublin, 1981, pp. 200–219.

9 Laurence Whyte, *Original Poems on Various Subjects*, Dublin, 1740, p. 72.

10 Patrick Fagan, *The Diocese of Meath in the Eighteenth Century*, op. cit., pp. 19–21.

11 Mid-eighteenth-century New Yorkers used two forms of currency: pounds sterling, as coined by the Royal Mint of Great Britain, and New York pounds, issued by the New York legislature, which were exchanged in the decades leading up to the Revolution at about 170 New York pounds for £100 Sterling, i.e. with the local currency discounted about 40 per cent in exchanges for pounds sterling.

12 Julian Gwyn, *The Enterprising Admiral*, op. cit., p. 20.

13 The possibility that he may have studied law is suggested by his borrowing of *Nelson's Justice* shortly after his arrival in America and his ordering of '7 Sets of the Laws' in 1772; SWJP, 1, p. 27 and SWJP 8, p. 465.

14 Gwyn, *The Enterprising Admiral*, op. cit., p. 25, n. 28.

15 SWJP, 9, p. 1.

16 Doc. Hist. NY, 2, p. 825.

17 Registry of Deeds, Dublin, 85/56/59024. The deed was signed on 22 January and registered on 15 July 1736.

18 SWJP, 1, p. 257.

19 SWJP, 13, p. 723.

20 SWJP, 8, pp. 958–9.

21 This letter is, unfortunately, missing. It is described in a letter of 16 March 1925 to Lyman Horace Weeks from the Reverend Hamlet McCleneghan of Batterstown, County Meath, who had 'five or six' letters by Peter Warren to John Johnson. See Lyman Horace Weeks Papers, New York Public Library.

22 SWJP, 1, p. 258.

Chapter 5, An Outlandish Man

1 SWJP, 13, p. 192ff. These observations were made by William Johnson's younger brother Warren when he first visited the Mohawk valley in 1760, and they give a good idea of the things that would have struck William in 1738.

2 SWJP, 13, p. 198.

3 SWJP, 13, p. 723.

4 SWJP, 13, p. 185.

5 Quoted in Barbara J. Sivertsen, *Turtles, Wolves and Bears: A Mohawk Family History*, Heritage Books, Bowie, Maryland, 1996, p. 126.

6 SWJP, 9, p. 1.

7 Doc. Hist. NY, 4, p. 349.

8 SWJP, 1, p. 5; SWJP, 13, p. 1.

9 SWJP, 13, p. 5.

10 SWJP, 13, p. 35.

11 Doc. Hist. NY, 2, p. 935.

12 SWJP, 13, pp. 723–4.

13 SWJP, 1, p. 7.

14 SWJP, 13, pp. 199–201.

15 SWJP, 9, p. 87.

16 SWJP, 1, p. 19.

17 SWJP, 1, p. 6.

18 SWJP, 12, p. 1063.

19 This ad, which rather ironically gives more information about Catharine Weisenberg's personality than any other surviving document, was unearthed by Milton Hamilton and is reprinted in Milton W. Hamilton, *Sir William Johnson, Colonial American 1715–1763*, Kennikat Press, Port Washington (NY) and London, 1976, p. 33.

20 SWJP, 12, p. 114.

21 Jeptha R. Simms, *The Frontiersmen of New York*, Albany, 1883, vol. 1, pp. 203 ff. Simms drew on interviews with the children of contemporary witnesses, which does not make his account obviously reliable but at least makes it broadly credible.

22 Barbara J. Sivertsen, *Turtles, Wolves and Bears*, op. cit., p. 127.

23 Milton W. Hamilton, *Sir William Johnson, Colonial American 1715–1763*, op. cit., p. 34.

Chapter 6, How the White Man Came to America

1 Dean R. Snow, *The Iroquois*, op. cit., p. 158–9.

2 Arthur Parker, 'The Code of Handsome Lake', 'The Seneca Prophet', in William N. Fenton (ed.), *Parker on the Iroquois*, op. cit., pp. 16–19.

3 See James Axtell, 'The First Consumer Revolution', in *Natives and Newcomers: The Cultural Origins of North America*, Oxford University Press, 2001, p. 117.

4 Adolph B. Benson (ed.), *Peter Kalm's Travels in North America: The English Version of 1770*, New York, 1966, pp. 190–91.

5 SWJP, 2, pp. 576, 587 and 618.

6 Doc. Hist. NY, 4, p. 312.

7 Cadwallader Colden, *History of the Five Indian Nations Depending on the Province of New York in America*, Cornell University Press, Ithaca, p. 49 and p. xx.

8 Quoted in James Axtell, 'The First Consumer Revolution', op. cit., p. 107.

9 Ibid., p. 106.

10 Ibid., p. 108.

11 SWJP, 2, pp. 898–900.

12 Quoted in Timothy J. Shannon, 'Dressing for Success on the Mohawk Frontier', in Peter C. Mancall and James H. Merrill (eds.), *American Encounters*, Routledge, New York and London, 2000, p. 353.

13 Charles T. Gehrig and William A. Starna (eds.), *A Journey into Mohawk and Oneida Country 1634–5*, Syracuse University Press, New York, 1991, p. 4.

14 John Lawson, quoted in Peter C. Mancall and James H. Merrill (eds.), *American Encounters*, op. cit., p. 34.

15 The full letter is published in Edna Kenton (ed.), *The Jesuit Relations and Allied Documents*, Albert & Charles Boni, New York, 1925, p. 185.

16 SWJP, 12, p.952.

17 Adolph B. Benson (ed.), *Peter Kalm's Travels in North America: The English version of 1770*, op. cit., pp. 520–21.

18 SWJP, 12, p. 976.

19 SWJP, 2, p. 900.

20 SWJP, 1, p. 110.

21 SWJP, 2, pp .899–90.

22 SWJP, 10, p. 390.

23 SWJP, 13, p. 194.

24 Doc. Col. Hist., 7, p. 665.

25 Lawson, quoted in Peter C. Mancall and James H. Merrill (eds.), *American Encounters*, op. cit., p. 35.

Chapter 7, The Holy Well

1 Johnson described this ceremony in his long letter on Iroquois culture to Arthur Lee of the Philosophical Society on 28 February 1771, reprinted as an appendix in William L. Stone, *The Life and Times of Sir William Johnson, Bart.*, J. Munsell, Albany, 1865, vol. 2, pp. 481ff.

2 Arthur Parker, 'The Constitution of the Five Nations', in William N. Fenton (ed.), *Parker on the Iroquois*, Syracuse University Press, 1975, p. 155.

3 Reverend Anthony Cogan, *The Diocese of Meath, Ancient and Modern*, Joseph Dollard, Dublin, 1867, vol. 2, pp. 351–2; Patrick Logan, *The Holy Wells of Ireland*, Colin Smythe, Gerrard's Cross, 1980, pp. 33–4.

4 See Daithi O hOgain, *The Sacred Isle: Belief and Religion in Pre-Christian Ireland*, Collins Press, Cork, 1999, pp. 165–6.

5 Ibid., p. 158.

6 Philip Dixon Hardy, *The Holy Wells of Ireland*, Dublin, 1840, pp. 98–9.

7 The Journals of the House of Commons of the Kingdom of Ireland, vol. II, Dublin, 1796, p. 669.

8 Cogan, op. cit., p. 351.

9 Quoted in Alfred W. Crosby, 'Ecological Imperialism', in Peter C. Mancall and James H. Merrell, *American Encounters*, op. cit., p. 62.

10 SWJP, 9, p. 117.

11 Dean R. Snow, *The Iroquois*, op. cit., p. 110; Doc. Col. Hist., 6, p. 497.

12 Doc. Col. Hist., 6, p. 294.

13 Ibid., p. 741.

14 Doc. Col. Hist., 8, p. 419.

15 SWJP, 1, p. 931.

16 Pomeroy's journal note of 7 July 1755, printed in 'Colonel Seth Pomeroy', the *American Whig Review*, vol. 7, issue 5, New York, May 1848, p. 465.

17 Mrs Anne Grant, *Memoirs of an American Lady*, London, 1808, vol. 2, p. 57.

18 The *Gentleman's Magazine*, XXV, September 1755, p. 426.

19 Edna Kenton (ed.), *The Jesuit Relations*, Albert & Charles Boni, New York, 1925, p. 287.

20 SWJP, 13, pp. 192 and 724.

21 SWJP, 2, p. 342.

Chapter 8, Raw Head and Bloody Bones

1 Doc. Col. Hist., 6, pp. 422–4 and SWJP, 1, pp. 146–9.

2 SWJP, 1, pp. 41, 52–3, 58–9, 62–3, 66–7, and 74–5.

3 Eileen O'Byrne (ed.), *The Convert Rolls*, Irish Manuscripts Commission, Dublin, 1981. His conversion is recorded on 2 August 1749.

4 Doc. Col. Hist., 6, p. 201. The last phrase is given here as 'I wish Papists', which is obviously a mistaken transcription.

5 Doc. Col. Hist., 10, p. 62.

6 SWJP, 1, pp. 62–3, p. 89.

7 Doc. Col. Hist., 6, p. 739.

8 Ibid., p. 541.

9 SWJP, 13, p. 188.

10 Quoted in Richard Aquila, *The Iroquois Restoration*, University of Nebraska Press, 1997, p. 87.

11 Doc. Col. Hist., 6, pp. 264–6.

12 Richard White, *The Middle Ground*, Cambridge University Press, 1991, p. 125.

13 W. J. Eccles, 'The Fur Trade and Eighteenth-Century Imperialism', in Alan L. Karras and J. R. McNeill (eds.), *Atlantic American Societies*, Routledge, London and New York, 1992, pp. 223–6.

14 Doc. Col. Hist., 6, p. 286.

15 Barbara J. Sivertsen, *Turtles, Wolves and Bears: A Mohawk Family History*, op. cit., pp. 137–8.

16 Doc. Col. Hist., 6, p. 293.

17 Ibid., p. 300.

18 Ibid., p. 384.

19 Ibid., p. 379.

20 Cadwallader Colden, *History of the Five Indian Nations of Canada*, London, 1747, part 3, p. 164.

21 Doc. Col. Hist., 6, p. 739.

22 SWJP, 9, pp. 15ff.

23 SWJP, 1, p. 60–61.

24 Ibid., p. 81.

25 Reverend John Heckewelder, quoted in James Axtell, *Natives And Newcomers: The Cultural Origins of North America*, Oxford University Press, 2001, p. 262.

26 SWJP, 9, pp. 15–30; entries for 10 March 1747, 13 December 1746 and 23 June 1747.

27 SWJP, 1, p. 772.

28 SWJP, 1, p. 87.

29 SWJP, 1, p. 53.

30 SWJP, 9, pp. 8, 25.

31 Doc. Col. Hist., 6, p. 499.

32 Doc. Col. Hist., 10, p. 205.

33 SWJP, 9, p. 16.

34 Doc. Col. Hist., 6, p. 488.

35 Ian K. Steele, *Betrayals: Fort William Henry and the 'Massacre'*, Oxford University Press, 1990, p. 8, and SWJP, 1, p. 43.

36 Doc. Col. Hist., 6, pp. 343–4.

37 SWJP, 1, p. 107.

38 SWJP, 9, p. 29; Doc. Col. Hist, 6, pp. 389–90.

39 SWJP, 1, p. 113n.

40 Doc. Col. Hist., 6, p. 499.

41 Ibid., p. 383.

42 Ibid., p. 387.

43 Doc. Col. Hist., 10, p. 191.
44 SWJP, 1, pp. 42–3.
45 Doc. Col. Hist., 6, p. 314.
46 Ibid., p. 493.
47 SWJP, 1, pp. 53, 240.
48 Ibid., p. 240; SWJP, 9, p. 36.
49 SWJP, 1, pp. 93, 98.
50 Doc. Hist. NY, 2, p. 619.
51 SWJP, 1, pp. 94, 109, 105 and 143.
52 Doc. Col. Hist., 6, p. 686.
53 Ibid., p. 679; SWJP, 9, p. 13.
54 SWJP, 9, p. 903.
55 Doc. Col. Hist., 6, p. 360; SWJP, 1, p. 106.

Chapter 9, The Power of Absence

1 SWJP, 9, p. 63; Doc. Col. Hist., 6, p. 589.
2 Doc. Col. Hist., 6, p. 592.
3 Ibid., p. 638.
4 Ibid., pp. 739–40.
5 Ibid., pp. 464–5.
6 Ibid., pp. 471, 531.
7 Ibid., p. 619.
8 Ibid., pp. 660ff.
9 Ibid., pp. 540–41.
10 Ibid., p. 669.
11 Ibid., p.523; SWJP, 9, p. 59.
12 Ibid., pp. 688, 691, 695 and 701.
13 Ibid., p. 740.
14 Ibid., p. 638.
15 Ibid., p. 534; SWJP, 9, p. 38.
16 Doc. Col. Hist., 6, p. 429.
17 Ibid., p. 712.
18 SWJP, 9, p. 44.
19 Doc. Col. Hist., 6, p. 417.
20 Ibid., pp. 416, 430.
21 Ibid., p. 420.
22 Ibid., p. 739.
23 Ibid., p. 741.
24 Ibid., pp. 784–8.

Chapter 10, Force, Motion and Equilibrium

1 Benjamin Franklin, *Experiments and Observations on Electricity Made at Philadelphia in America*, London, 1769, pp. 29–31.
2 SWJP, 1, p. 265.

3 Ibid., p. 612.

4 SWJP, 8, p. 341.

5 SWJP, 1, p. 380.

6 Ibid., p. 265.

7 See Richard E. Day (ed.), *Calendar of the Sir William Johnson manuscripts in the New York State Library*, University of the State of New York, Albany, 1909, pp. 272, 294 and 295.

8 SWJP, 5, p. 402.

9 Jeptha R. Simms, *Trappers of New York*, Munsell, Albany, 1850, pp. 22–3.

10 Quoted in Colleen Terell, 'An Experimental Philosophy in Early America', *The Center & Clark Newsletter*, UCLA Center for 17th- & 18th-Century Studies and the Williams Andrews Clark Memorial Library, no. 41 (Spring 2003), pp. 5–6.

11 Jean-Théophile Desaguliers, *A Course of Experimental Philosophy*, London, 1744, vol. 2, plate XX.

Chapter 11, The Late Emperor of Morocco

1 An Adept (Charles Johnstone), *Chrysal: or, the Adventures of a Guinea*, 3rd edition, John Hill, London, 1767, vol. 3, pp. 103–7.

2 SWJP, 9, p. 386.

3 Doc. Hist. NY, 4, pp. 487ff.

4 Patrick Fagan, *The Diocese of Meath in the Eighteenth Century*, op. cit., p. 28.

5 SWJP, 13, p. 277.

6 Barclay's register is reproduced in Barbara J. Sivertsen's *Turtles, Wolves and Bears: A Mohawk Family History*, op. cit., pp. 233ff. Sivertsen's patient disentangling of Mohawk family lineages from baptismal records is enormously useful in the avoidance of confusion between individuals with the same names.

7 SWJP, 9, p. 17.

8 SWJP, 12, p. 1065.

9 SWJP, 1, p. 270.

10 SWJP, 6, p. 771.

11 SWJP, 12, pp.1064–5 and SWJP, 8, p. 1190.

12 SWJP, 1, p. 205.

13 SWJP, 1, pp. 70, 129; SWJP 2, p. 576; SWJP, 3, p. 150; SWJP, 13, pp. 577, 584.

14 SWJP, 8, p. 636.

15 Jeptha R. Simms, *Trappers of New York, or A Biography of Nicholas Stoner and Nathaniel Foster Together With Anecdotes of Other Celebrated Hunters, and Some Account of Sir William Johnson, and His Style of Living*, J. Munsell, Albany, 1850, pp. 44–5.

16 Simms, op. cit., pp. 45–6.

17 SWJP, 1, p. 214.

18 Ibid., p. 67; Doc. Col. Hist., 6, p. 590.

19 SWJP, 1, p. 206.

20 SWJP, 12, p. 1071.

Chapter 12, Master of Ceremonies

1 SWJP, 1, p. 571.
2 Doc. Col. Hist., 6, p. 604.
3 Ibid., pp. 610–11.
4 SWJP, 1, p. 198.
5 Ibid., p. 202.
6 Doc. Col. Hist., 10, pp. 524ff.
7 SWJP, 10, p. 77.
8 Braddock's initial instructions are in Doc. Col. Hist., 6, pp. 920–22.
9 Fred Anderson, *Crucible of War*, Alfred A. Knopf, New York, 2000, pp. 69–70.
10 Doc. Col. Hist, 6, p. 961.
11 Doc. Hist. NY, 2, p. 651.
12 SWJP, 1, p. 468.
13 Doc. Col. Hist., 6, pp. 941–7.
14 See, for example, Doc. Col. Hist., 6, pp. 379, 396 and 416.
15 SWJP, 2, p. 164.
16 SWJP, 1, pp. 514–15.
17 Ibid., p. 539.
18 Francis Parkman, *Montcalm and Wolfe*, The Modern Library, New York, 1999, p. 149.
19 SWJP, 13, p. 197.
20 Quoted in William L. Stone, *The Life and Times of Sir William Johnson, Bart., Volume 1*, J. Munsell, Albany, 1865, p. 140n.
21 See Johnson's account book at SWJP, 2, pp. 570–77.
22 Quoted in Natalie Zemon Davis, 'Iroquois Women, European Women', in Peter C. Mancall and James H. Merrell, *American Encounters*, op. cit., p. 105.
23 SWJP, 1, p. 663.
24 Doc. Hist. NY, 2, p. 941.
25 See SWJP, 1, p. 365.
26 Ibid., p. 925.
27 See SWJP, 2, pp. 575, 578 and 579. Some of these presents are specifically listed as being for Red Head, others for 'the chief Onondaga sachem'. Given the fact that Red Head undoubtedly had this status at the conference, I am assuming that these presents were also for him. Later gifts of cash and clothing for Red Head and his family are recorded at SWJP, 3, pp. 161, 166 and 177.
28 Doc. Col. Hist., 6, pp. 964–6.
29 Ibid., pp. 972–3.
30 SWJP, 2, p. 577.

Chapter 13, An Upstart of Yesterday

1 SWJP, 1, p. 319.
2 Ibid., p. 786.
3 Doc. Col. Hist., 6, p. 959n.

4 SWJP, 1, p. 449.

5 Doc. Hist. NY, 2, pp. 826–7.

6 Ibid., p. 828.

7 Fred Anderson, *Crucible of War*, op. cit., p. 91.

8 Doc. Col. Hist., 6, p. 984.

9 Ibid., p. 385.

10 Ibid., p. 994.

11 See Barbara J. Sivertsen, *Turtles, Wolves and Bears: A Mohawk Family History*, op. cit., p. 140, and Milton W. Hamilton, *Sir William Johnson, Colonial American*, op. cit., pp. 63, 80.

12 Doc. Col. Hist., 6, p. 984.

13 SWJP, 1, p. 615.

14 Doc. Col. Hist., 6, p. 987, and SWJP, 1, p. 733. Because the first of these documents is a sanitised version sent to London, it must be read in conjunction with the second.

15 Doc. Col. Hist., 6, p. 987 and SWJP, 1, pp. 645, 722.

16 SWJP, 1, p. 734.

17 SWJP, 1, p. 735.

18 Ibid., p. 814.

19 SWJP, 9, p. 218.

20 SWJP, 1, p. 841.

21 Ibid., p. 786.

22 Ibid., p. 841.

23 Doc. Col. Hist., 6, p. 998.

24 Ibid., p. 994.

25 SWJP, 9, p. 219.

26 Doc. Col. Hist., 6, p. 995.

27 SWJP, 2, pp. 10–11.

28 Doc. Col. Hist., 6, p. 387.

29 Ibid., p. 963.

30 SWJP, 1, pp. 553, 577.

31 Ibid., p. 832.

Chapter 14, The Precarious Salvo of Applause

1 Quoted in Francis Parkman, *Montcalm and Wolfe*, op. cit., p. 150.

2 Mary Pomeroy to Seth Pomeroy, 9 August 1755, printed in 'Colonel Seth Pomeroy', *American Whig Review*, vol. 7, issue 5, New York, May 1848, p. 465.

3 Seth Pomeroy's journal note of 7 July 1755, printed in 'Colonel Seth Pomeroy', *American Whig Review*, vol. 7, issue 5, New York, May 1848, p. 465.

4 Parkman, *Montcalm and Wolfe*, op, cit., p. 149.

5 SWJP, 9, p. 210.

6 SWJP, 1, p. 540.

7 Ibid., p. 783.

8 Ibid., p. 861.

9 Ibid., p. 732.

10 Journal of James Gilbert of Morton, Massachusetts, *Magazine of New England History*, vol. 3, 1893, p. 189.

11 Thomas Williams, 8 October 1755, published in the *Historical Magazine*, April 1870, p. 212.

12 Seth Pomeroy to Mary Pomeroy, 15 July 1755, printed in 'Colonel Seth Pomeroy', *American Whig Review*, vol. 7, issue 5, New York, May 1848, p. 465.

13 SWJP, 2, p. 164.

14 SWJP, 1, pp. 867–8, 870.

15 SWJP, 9, p. 201.

16 Pomeroy, op. cit., p. 466.

17 SWJP, 9, p. 208.

18 Fred Anderson, *Crucible of War*, op. cit., pp. 94–107.

19 Fred Anderson, *Crucible of War*, op. cit., p. 110.

20 SWJP, 2, p. 66.

21 Quoted in Francis Parkman, *Montcalm and Wolfe*, op. cit., p.150.

22 SWJP, 2, p. 9.

23 SWJP, 9, p. 292.

24 Anderson, *Crucible of War*, op. cit., p.118, and Ian K. Steele, *Betrayals*, op. cit., p. 45.

25 Doc. Col. Hist., 10, pp. 341–3.

26 Doc. Col. Hist., 6, p. 1005.

27 SWJP, 2, p. 17.

28 Doc. Col. Hist., 6, p. 1014.

29 Doc. Col. Hist., 10, p. 343.

30 Doc. Col. Hist., 6, p. 1013.

31 *Daniel Claus's Narrative of his Relations with Sir William Johnson and Experiences in the Lake George Fight*, Society of the Colonial Wars, New York, 1904, pp. 13–14.

32 Doc. Col. Hist., 10, p. 342.

33 *Daniel Claus's Narrative*, op. cit., p. 14.

34 Doc. Col. Hist., 6, p. 1013.

35 Pomeroy, op. cit., p. 466.

36 Doc. Col. Hist., 6, p. 1005.

37 SWJP, 2, p. 420.

38 Doc. Col. Hist., 6, p. 1003.

39 SWJP, 13, p. 197.

40 Pomeroy, op. cit, p. 467.

41 Doc. Col. Hist., 6, p. 1004.

42 Ibid., p. 1005.

43 The *New York Mercury*, 18 September 1755.

44 Letter of 8 October 1755, published in the *Historical Magazine*, April 1870, p. 212.

45 Doc. Col. Hist., 6, p. 1005.

Chapter 15, Unspeakable Perplexity

1 SWJP, 9, p. 231.
2 'Dialogue between Marshal Saxe and Baron de Dieskau in the Elysian Fields', Doc. Col. Hist., 10, pp. 340ff.
3 SWJP, 2, p. 185.
4 Ibid., p.184.
5 Ibid, p. 268.
6 SWJP, 9, p. 300.
7 Ibid., pp. 356–7.
8 Ian K. Steele, *Betrayals*, op. cit., p. 53.
9 Doc. Col. Hist., 10, p. 344.
10 SWJP, 2, p. 173.
11 Doc. Col. Hist., 10, p. 322.
12 SWJP, 2, p. 441.
13 Ibid., p. 153.
14 Ibid., p. 11.
15 SWJP, 9, p. 239.
16 SWJP, 2, p. 100.
17 Ibid., pp. 171–2.
18 Ibid., p. 165.
19 Ibid., p. 173.
20 SWJP, 7, p. 268.
21 The *New York Mercury*, 17 November 1755.
22 *Daniel Claus's Narrative*, op. cit , p. 19.
23 Charles Henry Lincoln (ed.), *Correspondence of William Shirley*, Macmillan, New York, 1912, vol. 2, p. 359.
24 Ibid., p. 362.
25 'Journal of Captain Nathaniel Dwight of Belchertown', New York Genealogical & Biographical Record, January and April 1902, pp. 3–10 and 65–70.
26 SWJP, 2, p. 217.
27 Ibid., p. 219.
28 Ibid., p. 279.
29 'Journal of Captain Nathaniel Dwight of Belchertown', op. cit, p. 8.
30 SWJP, 2, p. 364.
31 Doc. Col. Hist., 6, p. 1020.
32 Ibid., p. 1022.
33 *New York Mercury*, 5 January 1756.
34 SWJP, 2, p. 367, and Milton W. Hamilton, *Sir William Johnson, Colonial American 1715–1763*, Kennikat Press, Port Washington (NY) and London, 1976, p. 192.
35 Doc. Col. Hist., 6, p. 996.
36 SWJP, 13, pp. 91–4.
37 SWJP, 2, p. 435.
38 Ibid., p. 425.

39 Fred Anderson, *Crucible of War*, op. cit., pp. 130–31.

40 SWJP, 2, pp. 293, 384.

Chapter 16, The Largest Pipe in America

1 'Father James McDonnell to Father James Naghten', 4 March 1756, in Brendan Jennings (ed.), *Louvain Papers 1606–1827*, Irish Manuscripts Commission, 1968, document 600.

2 There were two different portages called the Great Carrying Place, and to make confusion more likely, each related to a different Wood Creek. The Great Carrying Place mentioned in previous chapters, where Johnson's forces built Fort Edward, was near the Hudson and Lake George. The one referred to here was far to the west, connecting the Mohawk River to the Wood Creek that flows into Lake Oneida.

3 SWJP, 9, pp. 414–15.

4 Doc. Col. Hist., 8, p. 366.

5 Richard Aquila, *The Iroquois Restoration*, op. cit., p. 199; Richard White, *The Middle Ground*, op. cit., p. 186ff.

6 Richard Aquila, *The Iroquois Restoration*, op. cit., p. 239.

7 SWJP, 2, p. 439.

8 Ibid., p. 418.

9 SWJP, 1, p. 629.

10 SWJP, 9, pp. 361–77.

11 See Chapter 1, p. 5.

12 SWJP, 9, p. 467.

13 Doc. Col. Hist., 7, pp. 133–4.

14 William M. Fenton, *The Great Law and the Longhouse*, University of Oklahoma Press, 1998, p. 439.

15 SWJP, 1, p. 155.

16 William M. Fenton, *The Great Law and the Longhouse*, op. cit., p. 741.

17 Doc, Col. Hist, 10, pp. 448–9.

18 Doc. Col. Hist., 7, p. 151.

19 Arthur C. Parker, 'The Constitution of the Five Nations', in William N. Fenton (ed.), *Parker on the Iroquois*, Syracuse University Press, 1975, p. 41.

20 SWJP, 9, p. 629.

21 SWJP, 2, p. 487.

22 Anthony F. Wallace, *King of the Delawares: Teedyuscung 1700–1763*, University of Pennsylvania Press, 1949, p. 113.

23 SWJP, 2, p. 369.

24 Doc. Col. Hist., 7, p. 119.

25 SWJP, 2, p. 657.

Chapter 17, Miss Molly

1 William Stone, *The Life and Times of Sir William Johnson Bart.*, op. cit., vol. 1, pp. 327–8.

2 Isabel Thompson Kelsay, *Joseph Brant 1743–1807*, Syracuse University Press, 1986, pp. 40–42.

3 See Richard White, *The Middle Ground*, op. cit., pp.186–8.

4 Claus Papers, Public Archives of Canada, MG 19, Ser. F1, vol. 23:20.

5 Gretchen Green, 'Molly Brant, Catherine Brant, and Their Daughters: A Study in Colonial Acculturation', *Ontario History*, vol. LXXXI, 1989, no. 3, p. 237.

6 SWJP, 3, p. 393.

7 Doc. Hist. NY, 2, p. 785.

8 Simms, in *The Frontiersmen of New York*, op. cit., attributes this information to Isaac De Graaf of Schenectady, who told him that 'he had seen the family Bible of Sir William Johnson, and in it the record of his marriage by Rev. John Ogilview [Ogilvie] to Catherine Weisenfelts [sic], ten days before her death'. This Bible was in the possession of Sir John Johnson at one stage, but subsequently disappeared. Sir John would have had a good reason to destroy it if it did indeed contain this evidence that he was born out of wedlock.

9 SWJP, 13, p. 125.

10 SWJP, 12, p. 1063.

11 SWJP, 13, p. 192.

12 See Nathalie Zemon Davis, 'Iroquois Women, European Women', in Peter C. Mancall and James H. Merrell (eds.), *American Encounters*, op. cit., p. 103.

13 SWJP, 1, pp. 539, 384–5, 650–51 and 657.

14 James Axtell refers to what he calls 'Johnson's subtle usurpation of the clan matron's role in instigating wars of revenge'. See *Natives and Newcomers*, Oxford University Press, 2001, p. 264.

15 Doc. Col. Hist., 8, p. 725.

16 See Gail D. Danvers, 'Gendered Encounters: Warriors, Women and Sir William Johnson', *Journal of American Studies*, 2001, no. 35, vol. 2, pp. 187–202.

17 SWJP, 7, p. 865.

18 Ibid., p. 379, SWJP, 6, p. 461.

19 SWJP, 8, pp. 16, 469, 1103 and 1108.

20 See Lyman C. Draper Manuscripts, State Historical Society of Wisconsin, vol. 18, series F, reel 18, pp.63–5.

21 SWJP, 12, pp. 1068–70.

22 SWJP, 8, p. 1179.

23 SWJP, 12, p. 1043.

24 'Journal of General Lincoln,' quoted in Mrs John Rose Holden, *The Brant Family*, Wentworth Historical Society, 1904, p. 17.

25 SWJP, 13, p. 271.

26 The inventory drawn up after Johnson's death notes that 'The Things in Mary Brant's Rooms are not in this List.' SWJP, 13, p. 647.

27 Mrs Anne Grant, *Memoirs of an American Lady*, op. cit., vol. 2, p. 60.

28 SWJP, 13, p. 376.

29 This quotation and the description of the items excavated from Molly Brant's former house are from the text of a presentation to the Kingston Historical Society on 17 April 1996 by Susan M. Bazely of the Cataraqui Archaelogical Research Foundation.

30 Doc. Hist. NY, 4, p. 330.

31 Isabel Thompson Kelsay, *Joseph Brant 1743–1807*, op. cit., pp. 89, 272–3.

32 Public Record Office, London, PC 1/3147.

Chapter 18, Rowing Against the Current

1 SWJP, 2, p. 542.

2 Doc. Hist. NY, 1, pp. 504–14; Doc. Col. Hist., 10, p. 122.

3 SWJP, 2, p. 549.

4 SWJP, 9, p. 620.

5 Ibid., p. 617.

6 Ibid., p. 623.

7 Ibid., pp. 903, 558.

8 Doc. Col. Hist., 7, pp. 988–90.

9 Ian K. Steele, *Betrayals*, op. cit., pp. 71–2.

10 SWJP, 12, p. 9.

11 SWJP, 9, p. 542.

12 Ibid., pp. 547, 600, 591.

13 Ibid., p. 599.

14 Ibid., p. 559.

15 Ibid., pp. 567–8.

16 Ibid., pp. 586–7.

17 Ibid., p. 540; SWJP, 2, p. 715.

18 Doc. Col. Hist., 10, pp. 587–8.

19 SWJP, 9, p. 603.

20 Ibid., pp. 605–6, 637.

21 Ibid., pp. 613, 665.

22 Ibid., pp. 655, 641.

23 Ibid., pp. 639–42.

24 Ibid., pp. 667–8, and Ian K. Steele, *Betrayals*, op. cit., pp. 75–7.

25 SWJP, 9, p. 668.

26 Ibid., p. 679.

27 Ibid., p. 681.

28 Fred Anderson, *Crucible of War*, op. cit., pp. 185–7.

29 SWJP, 9, pp. 794–9.

30 Ibid., pp. 809–10.

31 Ian K. Steele, *Betrayals*, op. cit., p. 104.

32 Doc. Col. Hist, 10, p. 665.

33 SWJP, 9, pp. 819–20.

34 Ian K. Steele, *Betrayals*, op. cit., pp. 168–9, 173.

35 Quoted in Milton W. Hamilton, *Sir William Johnson, Colonial American 1715–1763*, op. cit., pp. 226–7.

Chapter 19, Sir William and His Myrmidons

1 Quoted in Ian K. Steele, *Betrayals*, op. cit., p. 165. Steele provides a brilliant analysis of the role of the myth of Fort William Henry in the emergence of American identity.
2 Fred Anderson, *The Crucible of War*, op. cit., p. 236.
3 SWJP, 9, pp. 812, 816.
4 Richard White, *The Middle Ground*, op. cit., p. 245.
5 SWJP, 9, pp. 888, 907.
6 Doc. Col. Hist., 10, pp. 700–701.
7 White, *The Middle Ground*, op. cit., p. 247.
8 SWJP, 9, p. 855.
9 Ibid., p. 905.
10 Ibid., p. 928.
11 Ibid., pp. 926–9.
12 Ibid., pp. 934–9.
13 Ibid., pp. 944–5.
14 Fred Anderson, *The Crucible of War*, op. cit., p. 248.
15 Ibid., p. 284.
16 SWJP, 2, p. 820.
17 Ibid., p. 825.
18 Ibid., pp. 828–9.
19 Ibid., p. 877.
20 Ibid., p. 879.

Chapter 20, Niagara Falls

1 SWJP, 1, p. 459.
2 SWJP, 3, p. 19.
3 Ibid., pp. 39–43.
4 Ibid., p. 271.
5 Doc. Col. Hist., 10, p. 982.
6 Fred Anderson, *Crucible of War*, op. cit., pp. 335–6.
7 SWJP, 3, pp. 77–8.
8 For both quotations, see Milton W. Hamilton, *Sir William Johnson, Colonial American 1715–1763*, op. cit., pp. 252–3.
9 Quoted in Fred Anderson, *Crucible of War*, op. cit., p. 337.
10 SWJP, 3, pp. 108–10.
11 See Johnson's Niagara diary, published as an appendix in William L. Stone, *The Life and Times of Sir William Johnson, Bart.*, op. cit., vol. 2, p. 394; SWJP, 13, p. 194.
12 SWJP, 10, p. 123.
13 Stone, op cit., pp. 395–6.
14 Ibid., p. 397–8.
15 SWJP, 1, p. 523.
16 Ibid., p. 396.
17 SWJP, 3, pp. 81, 100.

Chapter 21, Barbarians

1 'Journal de Levis', quoted in Fred Anderson, *The Crucible of War*, op. cit., p. 404.

2 SWJP, 3, pp. 189–90.

3 Ibid., pp. 241, 250, 263.

4 Ibid., p. 272.

5 Ibid., p. 273.

6 SWJP, 10, p. 175; SWJP, 13, pp. 202, 187; SWJP, 3, p. 267.

7 SWJP, 13, p. 190.

8 SWJP, 10, pp. 180–85; SWJP, 13, p. 190.

9 Gertrude Stein Kimball (ed.), *The Correspondence of William Pitt when Secretary of State with Colonial Governors and Military and Naval Commissioners in America*, New York, 1906, vol. 2, p. 332.

10 Quoted in Ian K. Steele, *Betrayals*, op. cit., p. 147.

11 Quoted in Fred Anderson, *The Crucible of War*, op. cit., p. 408.

12 Ibid., p. 95.

13 For Mercer and Gage quotations, see Richard White, *The Middle Ground*, op. cit., pp. 256–7.

14 SWJP, 10, pp. 132–4.

15 SWJP, 13, pp. 186–7.

16 SWJP, 3, pp. 269–75.

Chapter 22, Seeds Worth Sowing

1 SWJP, 3, p. 509.

2 Ibid., p. 305.

3 Ibid., p. 566.

4 Ibid., p. 355; SWJP, 13, p. 262.

5 Doc. Hist. NY, 2, p. 664.

6 SWJP, 3, p. 315.

7 SWJP, 13, pp. 215–16.

8 Ibid., pp. 217–18.

9 Ibid., pp. 222–3.

10 SWJP, 13, p. 233.

11 Ibid., pp. 223, 238.

12 Ibid., pp. 243–4.

13 Ibid., pp. 244–9.

14 SWJP, 13, p. 251; James Thomas Flexner, *Mohawk Baronet*, Syracuse University Press, 1979, pp. 242–5; SWJP, 13, p. 257.

15 SWJP, 13, pp. 270–71.

16 SWJP, 3, pp. 475–80.

17 John W. Jordan (ed.), 'Journal of James Kenny', *Pennsylvania Magazine of History and Biography*, vol. 37, 1913, pp. 1–47.

18 SWJP, 3, pp. 484–91.

19 Ibid., p. 494.

Chapter 23, 'Intoxicated with Providential Success'

1 Francis Parkman, *Montcalm and Wolfe*, op. cit., p. 292n, p. 444.
2 SWJP, 10, p. 314; SWJP, 13, p. 258.
3 See J. C. Long, *Lord Jeffery Amherst: A Soldier of the King*, Macmillan, New York, 1933, p. 129, and *The Journal of Jeffery Amherst*, University of Chicago Press, 1931, pp. 216–17.
4 SWJP, 3, pp. 149–81.
5 Ibid., p. 277.
6 Fred Anderson, *The Crucible of War*, op. cit., p. 797, n. 7.
7 Doc. Col. Hist., 8, p. 813.
8 *Daniel Claus's Narrative*, op. cit., pp. 5–7.
9 Doc. Hist. NY, 4, p. 415.
10 Richard White, *The Middle Ground*, op. cit., pp. 264–5.
11 SWJP, 3, p. 515.
12 Ibid., pp. 571, 593, 599 and 600.
13 Ibid., p. 345.
14 SWJP, 10, pp. 286–7, 291.
15 SWJP, 13, pp. 206, 219 and 270; SWJP, 3, p. 603.
16 SWJP, 10, p. 305; SWJP, 3, p. 575.
17 SWJP, 3, p. 565.
18 Ibid., p. 698.
19 Ibid., p. 514.
20 Ibid., pp. 514, 517 and 520.

Chapter 24, A Stop to Their Very Being

1 See Simon Schama, 'The Many Deaths of General Wolfe', *Granta* 32, Summer 1990, pp. 25–37.
2 See Helmut von Erffa and Allen Staley, *The Paintings of Benjamin West*, Yale University Press, 1986, pp. 57–8, 210–12, 523–4. The third of these paintings is in the National Gallery in Washington, where it is identified, wrongly, as a portrait of Guy Johnson. Everything – the strong visual links to the other paintings of William Johnson, the visual reference to Niagara, and the fact that the painting bears no resemblance whatsoever to descriptions of Guy – points to it as a portrait of William Johnson.
3 SWJP, 5, p. 853.
4 Ibid., pp. 653, 670–73; Richard White, *The Middle Ground*, op. cit., p. 299.
5 SWJP, 3, p. 759; SWJP, 4, p. 82.
6 SWJP, 11, p. 697; SWJP, 13, pp. 317–19.
7 SWJP, 13, pp. 320–21; Armstrong Starkey, *European and Native American Warfare 1675–1815*, University of Oklahoma Press, 1998, p. 105.
8 SWJP, 3, pp. 964–5.
9 Ibid., pp. 978–9, 825.
10 Ibid., p. 763.
11 Ibid., pp. 760–91, 822.
12 SWJP, 4, p. 62.

13 Ibid., pp. 98–9.

14 Quoted in Fred Anderson, *The Crucible of War*, op. cit, p. 542.

15 Doc. Col. Hist., 7, pp. 568–9.

16 Colonel Henry Bouquet to General Amherst, 13 July 1763; British Manuscript Project, Library of Congress microfilm reel 34/40, item 305; Amherst to Bouquet, 16 July 1763; microfilm reel 34/41, item 114.

17 Ibid., Bouquet to Amherst, 25 June 1763; microfilm reel 34/40, item 289.

18 SWJP, 4, pp. 166–7; Doc. Col. Hist., 7, p. 545–6.

19 Francis Parkman, *The Conspiracy of Pontiac*, Dent and Dutton, London and New York, 1908, vol. 1, pp. 174–6, pp. 214–16.

20 SWJP, 11, p. 228.

21 SWJP, 10, p. 653.

22 Fred Anderson, *The Crucible of War*, op. cit., p. 552.

23 SWJP, 10, p. 776.

24 Ibid., pp. 749, 856.

25 Ibid., p. 857.

26 Ibid., pp. 878–80, 883.

27 Doc. Col. Hist., 7, p. 567.

28 SWJP, 4, pp. 248–51; Doc. Col. Hist., 7, pp. 559–62, 567, 572–81; J. C. Long, *Lord Jeffery Amherst, a Soldier of the King*, op. cit., pp. 189–92; SWJP, 4, p. 612.

Chapter 25, What the Great Turtle Said

1 Alexander Henry, *Travels and Adventures in Canada and the Indian Territories*, I. Riley, New York, 1809, pp. 165–181.

2 SWJP, 11, p. 12.

3 SWJP, 4, p. 291.

4 SWJP, 11, p. 13.

5 Ibid., p. 27.

6 Ibid., pp. 253, 228.

7 SWJP, 4, pp. 511–12, 295, 299.

8 See *Mémoires, correspondances et ouvrages inédits de Diderot, Précédé de Mémoires pour servir à l'histoire de la vie et des ouvrages de Diderot, par Madame de Vandeul, sa fille*, Paulin, Paris, 1830, vol. 1, p. 402.

9 SWJP, 11, p. 919.

10 Ibid., p. 276.

11 Ibid., pp. 289, 273, 282, 280.

12 Ibid., p. 317.

13 Ibid., p. 895.

14 Ibid., pp. 11, 164, 152, 173, 208, 337; SWJP, 9, p. 795.

15 SWJP, 11, pp. 231–2.

16 Ibid., pp. 173, 326, 340.

17 SWJP, 4, p. 601; SWJP, 11, pp. 515, 832.

18 SWJP, 4, pp. 626, 599–604.

19 SWJP, 11, pp. 250, 839; Richard White, *The Middle Ground*, op. cit., p. 296.

20 SWJP, 4, p. 527.

21 SWJP, 11, p. 284; Richard White, *The Middle Ground*, op. cit., p. 294.

Chapter 26, Many Civil Things

1 SWJP, 11, pp. 836–8, 841, 853, 855; Richard White, *The Middle Ground*, op. cit., pp. 302–4; Fred Anderson, *Crucible of War*, op. cit., pp. 628–32.

2 SWJP, 11, pp. 743, 839; Doc. Col. Hist., 7, pp. 851–67.

3 SWJP, 5, pp. 224–5, 287, 336.

4 Ibid., pp. 288–9, 279.

5 Ibid., p. 333; SWJP, 12, p. 79.

6 SWJP, 12, p. 152.

7 Doc. Col. Hist., 7, p. 858.

8 SWJP, 12, p. 150.

9 SWJP, 5, p. 477.

10 Ibid., pp. 637, 644.

11 Doc. Hist. NY, 2, p. 882.

12 SWJP, 5, pp. 475, 107, 25, 98, 130, 55–6, 61–2.

13 Ibid., p. 3.

Chapter 27, An Imaginary Line

1 SWJP, 13, p. 198.

2 Doc. Hist. NY, 2, p. 848.

3 SWJP, 12, pp. 52–3, 116, 130.

4 Ibid., pp. 74, 53, 115.

5 Ibid., pp. 74–5, 130; SWJP, 5, p. 216; SWJP, 4, p. 771; Doc. Hist. NY, 2, p. 886; Doc. Col. Hist., 7, pp. 953ff.

6 Doc. Col. Hist., 7, pp. 953ff.

7 SWJP, 12, p. 53, p. 92.

8 SWJP, 5, p. 201.

9 SWJP, 12, p. 106; SWJP, 11, p. 879.

10 SWJP, 12, pp. 105–6, 162–3.

11 Doc. Col. Hist., 8, pp. 24–5.

12 SWJP, 2, p. 879.

13 Doc. Col. Hist., 7, pp. 578, 603; Annual Register, London, 1763, pp. 208–13.

14 Doc. Col. Hist., 8, pp. 20, 22.

15 Doc. Col. Hist., 7, p. 733, and 8, p. 22.

16 Doc. Col. Hist, 8, pp. 111–34.

17 SWJP, 12, p. 636; SWJP, 6, p. 472.

18 Doc. Col. Hist., 8, p. 180.

19 SWJP, 6, pp. 472, 609; SWJP, 12, pp. 598, 657, 748, 919.

20 Doc. Col. Hist, 8, p. 316.

21 SWJP, 8, p. 751.

22 Doc. Col. Hist, 8, p. 159.

23 SWJP, 7, p. 215; SWJP, 12, pp. 767–8; Doc. Col. Hist., 8, p. 182.

24 SWJP, 8, pp. 93–4, 112, 503, 565.
25 Doc. Col. Hist., 8, p. 145.
26 SWJP, 7, pp. 17–19.
27 SWJP, 12, p. 376.

Chapter 28, The Patriarch

1 Lois M. Fester, 'Archaelogical Excavations Conducted Between 1991 and 1993 at Johnson Hall State Historic Site', New York State Office of Parks, Recreation and Historic Preservation, Archeology Unit, Waterford (NY), July 1996.
2 SWJP, 5, p. 288.
3 John Long, *Voyages and Travels of an Indian Interpreter and Trader (1791)*, reprinted in Rueben Gold Thwaites (ed.), *Early Western Travels, 1748–1846*, vol. 2, Cleveland, Ohio, 1904, pp. 125–6.
4 SWJP, 1, p. 352.
5 SWJP, 8, p. 823.
6 Ibid., pp. 500, 625, 797.
7 SWJP, 12, pp. 1072, 1073, 773, 1014.
8 SWJP, 7, pp. 1888, 609.
9 SWJP, 7, p. 693.
10 Unless otherwise stated, quotes on life in Johnstown are from the work of Jeptha R. Simms: *Trappers of New York*, op. cit., chapter 1; *Frontiersmen of New York*, op. cit, vol. 1, pp. 260ff; *History of Schoharie County, and Border Wars of New York*, Munsell & Tanner, Albany, 1845, pp. 105–55.
11 SWJP, 7, p. 330.
12 SWJP, 1, pp. 379–80; SWJP, 4, pp. 845, 877.
13 Ibid., p. 265.
14 SWJP, 6, p. 733.
15 SWJP, 1, p. 264; SWJP 4, pp. 86, 359.
16 Mrs Anne Grant, *Memoirs of an American Lady*, op. cit.,vol. 2, pp. 62–3.
17 SWJP, 8, p. 855.
18 SWJP, 12, pp. 773–4.
19 SWJP, 6, p. 167; Richard E. Day (ed.), *Calendar of the Sir William Johnson Manuscripts*, New York State Education Department, Albany, 1909, p. 383; SWJP, 6, p. 106; SWJP, 6, p. 111.
20 SWJP, 6, p. 187.
21 Ibid., p. 166.
22 Ibid., p. 112. This letter was badly burned and parts of it are illegible, so some of the gaps have to be filled in by guesswork.
23 SWJP, 12, p. 479.
24 SWJP, 3, pp. 371, 382.
25 Quoted in Susan M. Bazely, 'Who Was Molly Brant?' Text of a presentation to the Kingston Historical Society, 17 April 1996, by the Cataraqui Archaeological Research Foundation.
26 SWJP, 13, p. 207.
27 Ibid., p. 635.

Chapter 29, Negroes' Handcuffs

1 SWJP, 13, p. 32.
2 SWJP, 13, p. 3; SWJP, 1, p. 8.
3 SWJP, 13, p. 201; SWJP, 8, p. 353.
4 SWJP, 1, p. 43.
5 SWJP, 13, pp. 29–30.
6 SWJP, 9, p. 121.
7 SWJP, 13, pp. 9, 201.
8 SWJP, 13, p. 371; SWJP, 7, p. 231-2; SWJP, 6, p. 691; SWJP, 7, p. 562.
9 SWJP, 7, p. 563.
10 SWJP, 9, p. 3.
11 SWJP, 5, p. 138.
12 Jenny was specifically left to Molly in Johnson's will, SWJP, 12, p. 1070.
13 SWJP, 13, pp. 4, 6.
14 Ibid., p. 208.
15 SWJP, 9, p. 104.
16 SWJP, 1, p. 66.
17 SWJP, 7, p. 326.
18 Jeptha R. Simms, *Trappers of New York*, op. cit., pp. 20–21.
19 SWJP, 8, p. 845.
20 SWJP, 13, pp. 651-2.
21 SWJP, 3, p. 266.
22 SWJP, 3, p. 573; SWJP, 4, pp. 811, 858; SWJP, 8, pp. 918, 968, 1001.
23 SWJP, 1, pp. 34-5.
24 Kerby A. Miller, Arnold Schrier, Bruce D. Boling, and David N. Doyle (eds.), *Irish Immigrants in the Land of Canaan*, Oxford University Press, 2003, pp. 253–4.
25 SWJP, 1, pp. 229–30.
26 SWJP, 4, p. 811 and SWJP, 5, p. 73.
27 SWJP, 12, pp. 1065, 1073.
28 SWJP, 10, p. 248.
29 SWJP, 2, p. 388.
30 SWJP, 10, pp. 411, 521.
31 SWJP, 4, p. 95.
32 SWJP, 3, p. 361 and SWJP, 10, pp. 243, 269.
33 SWJP, 4, p. 495.
34 Ibid., p. 500.
35 SWJP, 5, p. 795.
36 SWJP, 12, pp. 386-9.
37 SWJP, 4, p. 387.
38 Ibid., p. 413.
39 Ibid., p. 485.
40 SWJP, 5, pp. 587, 841; SWJP, 6, p. 164.
41 SWJP, 12, p. 174; SWJP, 11, p. 165.
42 SWJP, 11, p. 201 and SWJP, 4, p. 425.

43 SWJP, 9, p. 37.
44 SWJP, 5, p. 161.
45 SWJP, 12, p. 308.
46 SWJP, 5, p. 152.
47 SWJP, 13, p. 684.

Chapter 30, Irish Dreamtime

1 John W. Jordan (ed.), 'The Journal of James Kenny', *Pennsylvania Magazine of History and Biography*, vol. XXXVII, 1913, no. 1, pp. 191–2.
2 SWJP, 11, p. 343.
3 SWJP, 4, pp. 532–3.
4 SWJP, 11, pp. 394–6; Doc. Col. Hist., 7, p. 674.
5 SWJP, 4, p. 639.
6 SWJP, 13, p. 657.
7 Homer, the *Iliad*, book 6, lines 460–573.
8 SWJP, 8, p. 824.
9 SWJP, 13, p. 203.
10 SWJP, 4, pp. 638, 840, 877, and SWJP, 11, p. 973.
11 SWJP, 5, pp. 382, 733.
12 SWJP, 8, pp. 41, 91.
13 Marianne Elliott, *The Catholics of Ulster*, op. cit., pp. 136–141; Sean O Tuama and Thomas Kinsella, *An Duanaire*, Dolmen Press, Mountrath (Ireland), 1981, pp. 176–82.
14 SWJP, 7, p. 31; SWJP, 8, pp. 41–2, 91–2.
15 SWJP, 4, p. 885; SWJP, 10, pp. 41, 77.
16 James Hunter, *A Dance Called America*, Mainstream Publishing, Edinburgh and London, 1994, pp. 50–56.
17 SWJP, 4, pp. 526, 824.
18 SWJP, 5, p. 19 and SWJP, 12, pp. 224, 1041–2.
19 James Hunter, *A Dance Called America*, op. cit., pp. 75–6.
20 SWJP, 8, p. 915.
21 The letter was destroyed by fire. The summary is in Richard E. Day (ed.) *Calendar of the Sir William Johnson Manuscripts in the New York State Library*, University of the State of New York, Albany, 1909, p.181.
22 SWJP, 8, p. 654.
23 See SWJP, 7, pp. 962–3n.
24 SWJP, 11, p. 925.
25 SWJP, 7, p. 876.
26 SWJP, 10, p. 281.
27 Ibid., p. 392.
28 Ibid., p. 415.
29 SWJP, 8, p. 1195.
30 Kerby A. Miller, Arnold Schrier, Bruce D. Boling and David Doyle (eds.), *Irish Immigrants in the Land of Canaan*, op. cit., p. 470.
31 SWJP, 7, p. 738.

32 SWJP, 13, pp. 634–5.
33 Sean Murphy, *Irish Jacobitism and Freemasonry, Eighteenth Century Ireland, Volume* 9, 1994, pp. 75ff; Larry Conlon, 'The Influence of Freemasonry in Meath and Westmeath in the Eighteenth Century', *Riocht na Midhe*, IX, 3, 1997, pp. 128ff.
34 SWJP, 6, p. 1.
35 SWJP, 7, pp. 6, 14.
36 William L. Stone, *The Life and Times of Sir William Johnson, Bart.*, op. cit., vol. 2, pp. 290–91; Eli Perkins (Melville De Lancey), *Saratoga in 1901*, Sheldon & Company, New York, 1872, pp. 21–2.

Chapter 31, A Death Foretold

1 Francis Parkman, *The Conspiracy of Pontiac*, E. P. Dutton & Co., London and New York, 1908, vol. 1, p. 66.
2 Francis Parkman, Letter of 4 October 1851 to an unnamed correspondent, New York State Archives, 12168.
3 Jeptha R. Simms, *History of Schoharie County, and Border Wars of New York*, Munsell & Tanner, Albany, 1845, pp. 105–55; William L. Stone, *The Life and Times of Sir William Johnson, Bart.*, op. cit., vol. 2, p. 377. Stone describes the rumours but refutes them. Simms, in later works, retracted his suggestions of suicide.
4 Doc. Hist. NY, 2, p. 957.
5 SWJP, 7, p. 171.
6 Doc. Hist. NY, 2, p. 823.
7 SWJP, 11, p. 931; SWJP, 6, pp. 434, 468; Doc. Hist. NY, 2, p. 973.
8 SWJP, 11, p. 931.
9 SWJP, 7, p. 162.
10 SWJP, 7, pp. 161–2, 271, 480, 494, 706–77, 755.
11 SWJP, 11, p. 945.
12 Doc. Col. Hist., 8, p. 302.
13 SWJP, 7, p. 151.
14 Richard White, *The Middle Ground*, op. cit., p. 355.
15 Doc. Col. Hist., 8, p. 303.
16 Ibid., p. 263.
17 Ibid., pp. 301, 341.
18 Ibid., pp. 348–9.
19 SWJP, 8, pp. 587, 615.
20 Ibid., pp. 1128–9, 1198.
21 SWJP, 12, p. 1075.
22 SWJP, 13, pp. 725ff.
23 Doc. Col. Hist., 8, p. 418.
24 SWJP, 8, p. 1198; Doc. Col. Hist., 8, p. 460.
25 Doc. Col. Hist., 8, pp. 479, 471.
26 Ibid., p. 480.
27 Ibid., pp. 480–82.

Chapter 32, The End of the World

1 Letter from John Adams to Abigail Adams, 19 August 1777, Adams Family Papers: An Electronic Archive. Massachusetts Historical Society. http://www.masshist.org/digitaladams/

2 Richard M. Ketchum, *Divided Loyalties*, Henry Holt, New York, 2002, p. 366.

3 William L. Stone, *Life of Joseph Brant-Thayendanegea*, Phinney & Co., Buffalo, 1851, chapter 3, *passim*.

4 Anthony F. C. Wallace, *The Death and Rebirth of the Seneca*, Vintage Books, New York, 1972, pp. 145–6.

5 Ibid., p. 140.

6 Doc. Col. Hist., 8, p. 622–3.

7 George Washington papers at the Library of Congress, 1741–1799: Series 2 Letterbooks. George Washington to Philip J. Schuyler, May 22, 1776.

8 Ibid., p. 663.

9 Isabel Thompson Kelsay, *Joseph Brant 1743–1807*, Syracuse University Press, 1984, pp. 149, 153.

10 Doc. Col. Hist., 8, p. 664; Kelsay, *Joseph Brant*, op. cit., p. 157.

11 James Boswell, 'An Account of the Chief of the Mohock Indians', the *London Magazine*, July 1776, p. 339.

12 Doc. Col. Hist., 8, p. 725.

13 Dean R. Snow, *The Iroquois*, op. cit., pp. 152–3.

14 Wallace, *The Death and Rebirth of the Seneca*, op. cit., p. 184.

15 Gregory Dalmer, *Biographical Sketches of Loyalists of the American Revolution*, Meckler Publishing, Westport and London, 1984, p. 438.

16 Wallace, *The Death and Rebirth of the Seneca*, op. cit., p. 203.

17 Jeptha R. Simms, *The Frontiersmen of New York*, op. cit., vol. I, pp. 256ff.

18 Mrs John Rose Holden, *The Brant Family*, op. cit., pp. 23–4.

19 William Leggo, *The History of the Administration of the Right Honourable Frederick Temple, Earl of Dufferin*, Lovell Publishing, Montreal and Toronto, 1878, pp. 255–7.

20 Katherine Livingston Macpherson, *Pictures from Canadian History for Boys and Girls*, Renouf Publishing, Montreal, 1899, p. 124.

21 William N. Fenton, *The Great Law and the Longhouse*, op. cit., p. 82.

22 Doc. Col. Hist., 8, p. 366.

23 Horatio Hale, *The Iroquois Book of Rites*, D. G. Brinton, Philadelphia, 1883, pp. 39–44.

Chapter 33, The Afterlife

1 James Kirke Paulding, *The Dutchman's Fireside*, College and University Press, New Haven, 1966, p. 102.

2 SWJP, 4, p. 86.

3 An Adept (Charles Johnstone), *Chrysal: or, The Adventures of a Guinea*, 3rd edition, John Hill, London, 1767, book 2, pp. 88–9.

4 James Fenimore Cooper, *The Last of the Mohicans*, Penguin Classics, New York and London, 1986, pp. 97–8.

5 James Fenimore Cooper, *The Pioneers: or, The Sources of the Susquehanna*, Charles Wiley, New York, 1823, volume 1, pp. 1–16.

6 Ibid., p. 276.

7 James Fenimore Cooper, *The Prairie*, Carey, Lea and Carey, Philadelphia, 1827, p. 233.

8 Cooper, *The Last of the Mohicans*, op. cit, pp. 134–6.

9 Quoted in Thomas F. O'Donnell, introduction to James Kirke Paulding, *The Dutchman's Fireside*, op. cit., p. 11.

10 *The Dutchman's Fireside*, op. cit., p. 125.

11 Ibid., p. 94.

12 Ibid., p. 95.

13 Ibid., p. 97.

14 Ibid., pp. 97, 98–100, 103, 108.

15 Ibid., p. 101.

16 Ibid., pp. 102, 222.

17 Ibid., pp. 222, 286.

18 Ibid., pp. 110, 228, 108.

19 Ibid., pp. 115–16.

20 Ibid., pp. 103, 115.

21 See R. L. Stevenson, 'The Genesis of *The Master of Ballantrae*', in *Essays and Poems*, Everyman, London, 1992.

22 *The Dutchman's Fireside*, op. cit., pp. 104, 180.

23 Ibid., pp. 247–8.

24 Robert Louis Stevenson, *The Master of Ballantrae*, Everyman, London, 1992, p. 208.

25 Ibid., pp. 209–10.

26 Ibid., pp. 225–6.

27 Ibid., pp. 228–9, 236.

Index